LEVELS OF
PERSONALITY

LEVELS OF PERSONALITY

Second edition

MARK COOK

CASSELL

Cassell Educational Limited
Villiers House, 41/47 Strand, London WC2N 5JE

387 Park Avenue South, New York, NY 10016–8810

© Cassell Publishers Ltd 1984, 1993

First published by Holt, Rinehart and Winston 1984
Reprinted 1990, 1991

British Library Cataloguing-in-Publication Data
A catalogue record for this book is available from the British Library.

Library of Congress Cataloging-in-Publication Data
Available from the Library of Congress.

ISBN 0–304–32425–6 (hardback)
0–304–32438–8 (paperback)

Typeset by Colset Private Ltd, Singapore
Printed and bound in Great Britain by
Dotesios Ltd, Trowbridge, Wilts.

Contents

Preface to First Edition

I HAVE been intending to write this book for as long as I have been teaching Individual Psychology. I have never really been satisfied with any of the texts I have used, so the logical thing is to write my own. The sources of my dissatisfaction with the texts I have used are various, but the two main shortcomings are: adherence to the 'theory of the month' approach, and being transatlantic. Some texts are also low level and condescending to the reader.

The 'theory of the month' approach – or week, if the lecturer likes to move fast – is probably inspired by Hall and Lindzey's (1957) *Theories of Personality*. This is an excellent and useful work, but as a reference book, not a text. Too many subsequent textbooks have followed its format: a chapter on Freud, a chapter on Jung, a chapter on Sheldon, a chapter on Dollard and Miller, a chapter on Rogers, a chapter on Skinner (who may be an anti-personality theorist, but generates some superbly memorable jargon), a chapter on Allport, perhaps a chapter on Cattell, rarely or never a mention of Eysenck. There are several things wrong with this. Some theorists cover several aspects of personality; Allport discusses traits, habits, motives and the self, while Cattell's account covers all these, and psychodynamics, biological aspects and factor analysis as well. A 'mixed' account is surely better discussed in sections – traits, motives, the self – rather than presented in a great wodge just because one man wrote it all. Some theories are obsolete, long abandoned as dead ends, such as Sheldon's theory of physique and personality. Some theories included in many texts are not scientific theories it all, it is difficult enough extracting testable propositions from Freudian theory, 'but not worth even trying with some of his followers. But the major limitation of the 'theory of the month' approach is its failure to integrate, to say what type of account each theory is trying to give, and how it relates to the others. Chapter 1 tries to present a structure, around which seven types of personality theory can be organized, and uses the analogy of three railway lines, running underground from the surface of behaviour to three termini.

Most personality texts come from across the Atlantic. There is of course nothing wrong with transatlantic origin *per se*; the vastly greater number of psychology students in North America means economics of scale, which means large, well-produced books at very reasonable prices. However, North American authors often seem oblivious of non-American theorists and researchers. The most glaring example of this is Hans Eysenck, whose existence is entirely ignored by some texts (e.g. Wiggins *et al.* (1971), which claims to emphasize biological aspects of personality), and whose contribution is not really done justice even by Mischel's otherwise excellent *Introduction to Personality* (1981). Other British researchers and theorists are similarly 'unpersons' in North American texts. I don't, however, intend this as a flag-waving 'Buy British' book; I've mentioned British theory and research where it's relevant, not for the sake of it. But in doing so, I seem to have mentioned it rather more than transatlantic texts usually do.

When I started writing this book, I was an 'academic' psychologist, engaged in teaching and research. Hence I was critical of most theory and research, for personality is one of the 'soft' areas of psychology, itself a science not noted for rigour and precision. Since then, however, I have become, at least partly, an 'applied psychologist', engaged in counselling, selection and assessment work, actually using the concepts and measures of personality that I'd previously only found fault with. Academic psychologists will probably think the effect is to have made me uncritical of woolly thinking and poor measures. It may have, but there's something to be said for actually having used some of the measures one writes about, in the real world.

I'd like to thank Holt-Saunders for giving me the chance to publish this book; David Oborne for his invaluable assistance with word-processing programs; the Inter Library Loan service and UC Swansea Library; Paul Wood for the illustrations; and my wife for her usual patience while I have been occupied writing this book.

Preface to Second Edition

The ten years since I started writing the first edition of this book have seen a great increase in interest in psychological testing in Britain. At the beginning of the 1980s only a few employers in Britain used personality tests; since then their use has spread from the private sector into the National Health Service and local government. Only the education sector still selects, or tries to select, its staff by inefficient, unscientific methods. Since 1987 I have been a Director of Oxford Psychologists Press Ltd, who distribute and publish tests of personality and intelligence, including the California Psychological Inventory, which readers will find mentioned in Chapters 2, 3, 10 and 12.

This second edition incorporates two new chapters (Chapters 12 and 13), the first on alcoholism and the other on psychological resilience. All the other chapters have been updated and rewritten. The amount of updating needed for each chapter gives an interesting commentary on developments on personality research since 1982. The chapter on psychoanalysis needed the least updating, because research on empirical verification of Freudian theories of personality has largely dried up. The chapter on learning-based approaches (Chapter 4) didn't need much change either. Chapter 5 on biological approaches, by contrast, needed quite a lot of revision. So did the chapters on aggression and sexual variation (Chapters 10 and 11); views on sexual variation have taken a sharply biological turn in the last ten years. The chapters on traits and factors (Chapters 2 and 3) have been extensively altered, partly because criticisms and reformulations of the trait approach continue to pour forth from personality theorists, partly because personnel psychologists have made some real advances. Research on numerous, very various approaches to the self (Chapter 7) has also proliferated. Personal construct theory, by contrast (Chapter 6), seems to be going out of fashion.

I'd like to thank Cassell for giving me the chance to publish a second edition of this book, and my wife, once more, for her patience while I have been occupied writing it.

Centre for Occupational Research Ltd
Swansea
1993

CHAPTER 1

Gideon's Army

The Study of Individual Differences

IN Old Testament times the Israelites were preparing for a war with the Midianites. Gideon was general of the Israelite army, and he had an unusual problem – too many volunteers. He needed to reduce their numbers, but not at random; he wanted to keep experienced and courageous soldiers. Gideon used two rough-and-ready tests. He first reminded his volunteers how great was the risk of death and injury: 'Whosoever is fearful and afraid, let him return and depart early'. About two-thirds of the volunteers changed their minds and went home. But 'the Lord said unto Gideon, The People are yet too many'. Gideon told the remaining volunteers to drink from the nearest stream. Those that lapped the water like a dog 'putting their hand to their mouth' passed the test, but 'all the rest of the people bowed down upon their knees to drink water' – and failed, because experienced soldiers keep watch for enemies at all times, even when slaking their thirst.

Gideon used first a personality test, then an aptitude test. Neither was very good by modern standards. Both are single-item tests, so unlikely to give very reliable results – one question ('Are you afraid of fighting a battle?') and one observation of field-craft (keeping watch while drinking). Gideon's personality test is the first recorded measure of what psychologists now call neuroticism or trait anxiety. The military have remained intermittently aware of individual differences and the need to assess them ever since. (Only intermittently: Cattell (1937) complained that the Army in 1914–1918 'used some of the best brains from civilian life to stop bullets in front-line trenches'.) Modern methods of military selection are much more sophisticated than Gideon's two tests, but preserve the same distinction between *personality* (fearfulness) and *ability* (field-craft). This book deals only with personality; for a good review of ability, see Kline (1991), and for one of psychological testing, see Cronbach (1990).

DEFINITIONS OF PERSONALITY

What personality is NOT
In the scientific sense of the word, everyone has a personality, and all personalities are equal. No personality is better or worse than any other. The lay person talks of John 'having no personality' and Jill 'having a very bad personality'; the lay person means that John has little or no social presence, and that the way Jill behaves will make her and/or those around her unhappy.

What personality IS
Cattell (1965) defines personality very simply as 'that which permits a prediction of what a person will do in a given situation'. Definitions of personality conventionally exclude purely physical differences, such as height or strength, although these obviously affect personality. Most definitions (but not Cattell's) exclude mental abilities. Differences in intelligence may interact with personality; the aggressive and intelligent person can destroy enemies subtly and legally, whereas the aggressive but unintelligent person can think of nothing better than hitting them, so gets put in prison.

Stagner (1961) distinguishes *stimulus, response* and *intervening variable* definitions of personality. Stimulus definitions focus on the impression the person creates on others. However, people create different impressions on different others at different times, so a stimulus definition implies people have multiple personalities. A typical response definition (Guthrie, 1944) says personality is 'those habits and habit systems of social importance that are stable and resistant to change'. Guthrie sees personality as true patterns of consistency in the individual's behaviour across a range of situations, but Chapter 3 shows that attempts to find such consistencies have proved only partially successful. Guthrie's definition slips in an element of circularity with the words 'of social importance', and begs a question by restricting it to 'habits and habit systems'. Intervening variable definitions try to get below the surface and away from the detail of what someone does, or how they appear to others; that of Allport (1937) is typical: 'the dynamic organisation within the individual of those psychosocial systems that determine his unique adjustments to his environment'. The key words are 'organisation', 'systems' and 'within'. The important question – central to any account of personality – is what form do these organized systems take? Are they traits, or habits, or motives, or complexes, or personal constructs, or self-concepts?

TESTS, TESTING AND DISCRIMINATION

The first modern personality measure was the Woodworth Personal Data Sheet of 1917, intended, like Gideon's test before it, to weed out recruits who wouldn't stand the stress of battle. Woodworth's test was released for civilian use after 1918 and, with the Army Alpha test of intelligence, was widely used in America in the 1920s. Psychological tests of all types have always been more popular in North America, whereas a combination of managerial conservatism, union hostility and a shortage of applied psychologists limited their use in Britain until the 1980s.

Paradoxically, just as psychological assessment is beginning to improve personnel selection and career development in Britain, another transatlantic import threatens to limit its use: fair employment legislation. A personality test discriminates between people; if it doesn't, there's no point using it. Individual psychology is founded on the assumption that all men are *not* equal, which makes it politically unpopular. But some dimensions of inequality are more equal than others; some are more or less tolerable to egalitarian thought, some are suspect, and a few are anathema. George Bernard Shaw remarked that the fact that one horse can run faster than another is a source of endless wonder to many and a great source of profit to a few – but it offends hardly any one. A belief in individual differences in mental ability is, by contrast, about as acceptable to most liberal opinion as a commitment to apartheid. Most personality measures occupy the middle ground – regarded with suspicion, but tolerated, at least until a biological basis is postulated.

REASONS FOR STUDYING PERSONALITY

Psychologists have three reasons for being interested in personality:

1. to gain scientific understanding;
2. to assess people;
3. to change people.

The first is theoretical, while the second and third are applied. There is often a gap, in sympathy and understanding, between theoretical and applied psychologists. The former see the latter as technically incompetent, overconfident, either financially motivated or woolly idealists; the latter see the former as ivory tower academics, afraid of the real world, forever finding reasons never to put their ideas into practice, preferring to spend their time picking holes in the efforts of others.

Changing people

The clinical psychologist has a succession of patients coming through his or her door, needing help. The clinician must achieve sufficient understanding of each patient to predict future progress, and choose a form of treatment. The clinical approach tends to emphasize motivation, to see the patient as a meaningful whole, and to be vague. It tends to the *idiographic* approach, which seeks to understand the individual as an individual, not as a point on a dimension. Clinicians rely heavily on experience, and often claim to have developed special powers of assessing people (Cook, 1982).

Assessing people

Everyone who selects staff for employment, or students for university, or anyone for anything, is an assessment psychologist; the vast majority are amateurs but some are trained. The assessment psychologist needs no formal theory of personality, just a measure that predicts. Constructing and testing new measures is a highly technical business, even though the theoretical complexities of selecting managers or police officers may be minimal.

Gaining a scientific understanding

Eysenck (1966) cites a study testing the hypothesis that *massed practice* (numerous tests at very short intervals) would increase the strength of the Muller–Lyer illusion. The results were highly variable, so the small difference averaged across 50 subjects wasn't statistically significant. Only 1 per cent of the variance was accounted for by massed or spaced practice, leaving 99 per cent unaccounted for. (This is a technical way of saying that only 1 per cent of the variation in people's susceptibility to the illusion resulted from the use of massed as opposed to spaced practice, or in other words that massing or spacing made virtually no difference.) It's a poor theory of visual illusions that accounts for only 1 per cent of the variance, but Eysenck argues that any theory that ignores individual differences necessarily cripples itself. A later study compared two rates of presentation in a serial learning task (Jensen, 1962). Again subjects varied enormously; some did better when the interval between items was 2 seconds, some when it was 4 seconds, and some did equally well on either. But this time subjects had completed the Maudsley Personality Inventory, which showed that extraverts and stable subjects were equally proficient at either speed, whereas introverts and anxious subjects made nearly twice as many errors when they had to work fast.

Error variance is a nuisance to the experimental psychologist; it means testing 10 or 20 or 50 people instead of one. If every human being behaved the same way, the experimental psychologist's task would be much easier. As Eysenck notes, most experimental psychologists treat individual variations as unsystematic, as error. A lot are random, but Eysenck argues that some can be accounted for by personality, especially by extraversion and anxiety. The experimental psychologist's nuisance is the individual psychologist's *raison d'être*. Eysenck proposes that general experimental psychology and individual psychology should integrate, and suggests analysis of variance designs can achieve this integration. Not all personality theorists have such a specific ambition (or as critics would say, such a narrow ambition). But most personality theorists are interested in developing general models of personality, rather than finding a tool for curing phobias, or selecting sales staff. In practice the three themes of assessment, therapy, and theory become interwoven. Approaches that start out as theoretical become applied; Cattell (Chapter 2) originally devised the 16PF personality questionnaire to determine the structure of human personality, but it's now widely used in personnel selection. By contrast, the California Psychological Inventory was written for use in selection and counselling, but has been used to develop theories of aggression (Chapter 10). Several theories started life as forms of therapy, but later blossomed into comprehensive theories of personality (Rogers, Chapter 7), or the whole of psychology (Freud, Chapter 9).

But while there is overlap and cross-fertilization, there is also confusion. Most theorists aren't interested in predicting how one individual will behave; they want to demonstrate differences between groups, or correlations between variables. Some start from first principles, and irritate the non-psychologist by experimenting on rats instead of looking at people (because the basic principles of learning are easier to discover in rats). Others study seemingly obscure laboratory phenomena, such as absolute auditory threshhold (AAT), the faintest sound a person can hear, because it's a measure of basic differences in temperament. The rat's maze learning and the human's AAT build a theory of personality, while being a long way removed from anything the lay person considers 'personality'. Eysenck's account, like Skinner's, doesn't account for individual differences, except in the most general way. Differences in temperament don't predict anything specific, such as suitability for a particular occupation; they tend to set the person on a particular course, leaving his or her precise fate largely to chance. Skinner's model of personality doesn't include even basic differences in temperament; any particular individual's personality is a mass of habits created by upbringing, experience and chance. Deciding if someone would make a good police offer or manager is a job for the applied psychologist, not the personality theorist. But paradoxically both Skinner and Eysenck, when not proposing austere theories of individual differences based on operant conditioning or the properties of the nervous system, have a lot to say about complex issues like religion, politics, crime or sexuality.

LEVELS OF PERSONALITY

Students often find personality a confusing topic. One reason is the profusion of different personality theories. A second is that different theories have different aims: assessment, therapy, or theory building. Further confusion arises because some theories emphasize personality *development* – how people become what they are—while others emphasize *structure*—how best to describe adult personality.

   But the worst confusion arises from the 'theory of the week' approach. During the 8 or 10 or 20 lectures of the typical personality course, the lecturer covers a theory each week, and presents each theory in the words used by the originating theorist. At worst this achieves no more than teaching the student 8, 10 or 20 sets of jargon, each with little relation to the next, and often seeming to have precious little relation to human personality. What the student misses is any attempt to explain why theories differ, and how they relate. Theories differ because they focus on either development or structure; they differ because they have different emphases—assessment, therapy, theory construction; they differ because they work at different levels of description. The three causes—aspects, purpose and level—are loosely linked.

   This book tries to relate various approaches to a common structure, so that the relation between, for example, Rogers's self-theory and Eysenck's temperament theory will become apparent. At first sight these theories are so different in every respect that they have virtually nothing in common; the same seems true, incidentally, for their adherents. Rogers's and Eysenck's theories have one basic thing in common—the search for a way of understanding and predicting individual differences. Both seek explanatory constructs that will bring together a lot of diverse phemonena, relate them to a few central explanatory mechanisms, and allow further predictions about future behaviour to be made. That probably is about all their two approaches do have in common. There are similarities between Eysenck's account and parts of Cattell's account, but the parts of Cattell that bear a resemblance to Rogers aren't the same parts that bear any resemblance to Eysenck.

   The structure of the book is illustrated in Figure 1.1. It starts at the surface of personality, then follows three lines below the surface. Each line has stations, which lie different distances down a common route to an ultimate terminus, beyond which that type of explanation can't be extended further without ceasing to be psychology and turning into something else: physiology, biochemistry, neuro-anatomy, metaphysics or demonology. Critics of the various termini often argue that what arrives there has already ceased to be psychology.

The surface of behaviour
Lay people describe what they see: they see other people doing things, saying things, feeling things. People then name what they see, both to remember it and to communicate it to others; they use fairly general names rather than detailed, 'blow-by-blow' descriptions. Lay people typically describe others by using *traits*, broad dispositions that summarize past behaviour and predict future behaviour. The trait approach had worked well for lay people over thousands of years, so it was reasonable for the first scientific accounts of personality to adopt it. Trait approaches (Chapter 2) use lay people's categories as the basis of personality theory and measures. *Factor* theories follow the same general principles, and use

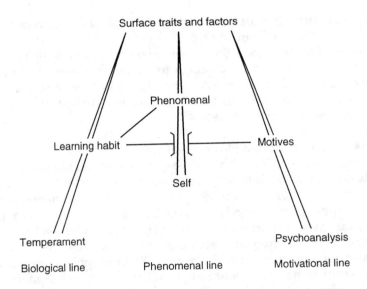

Figure 1.1 *The surface of personality and three lines travelling beneath it.*

the same measures, but forsake the human observer for computation when it comes to analysing the data. Trait and factor approaches work moderately well at the applied level. Trait and factor measures of personality have moderately good predictive power in personnel selection and clinical diagnosis. 'Moderate' shouldn't be taken as a criticism; few assessment methods achieve better than moderate predictive power; many, including most of those that claim excellent or infallible predictive power, prove to have no predictive validity at all. Any experts who claim to have an infallible way of selecting good staff, diagnosing illness or matching marriage partners are deluding their clientele – not necessarily deliberately: they may be deluding themselves as well.

Doubts have been voiced about trait and factor approaches, critics claiming they don't really work even at the surface level. Psychologists clung to trait and factor accounts, say the critics, for the same reasons that lay people originally developed them: traits impose sense on a complex area, by oversimplifying and distorting it, not by accurately reflecting it (Chapter 3). Not even trait theory's keenest supporters could claim it describes much more than the surface of personality; it may list the main dimensions of individual difference in adults, but doesn't explain how they develop, nor what underlies them.

Routes below the surface 1: the biological line

Some early critics of surface accounts of personality were impressed by Pavlov's work on conditioned reflexes in dogs, and by American research on maze learning in rats, so they developed a model of human personality as sets of learned habits. *Learning* or *habit* approaches concentrate more on development of personality than on its structure, because habit models imply no common structure in personality, and some imply little or no individual structure either (Chapter 4).

The terminus of the biological line is *temperament* theory, which proposes that readiness to learn certain sorts of things may have a biological basis, possibly also an inherited basis. Temperament theory's principal contemporary exponent, Hans Eysenck, postulates three broad underlying dimensions: extraversion, neuroticism and psychoticism (Chapter 5).

Routes below the surface 2: the phenomenal line

Phenomenal theories – such as those of Lewin, Snygg and Combs – propose that what people see shapes their behaviour at any given moment, so understanding the *field* is critical for an understanding of the person. The phenomenal field is constantly changing, and largely shaped by factors outside the person, so phenomenal theories emphasize neither development of personality nor its structure; consequently they often have little concrete to say about personality. Many phenomenal theories have an origin in therapy. Phenomenal theories have enjoyed a revival in recent years, in personal construct theory, which is more structured than field theories, and includes a way of measuring how people see the world (Chapter 6).

The most important thing any person sees is him or herself. The terminus of the phenomenal line is *self*-theory, which argues that the way to understand a person is to discover his or her self-concept. Understand how people see themselves, and their behaviour becomes meaningful, and even predictable (Chapter 7).

Routes below the surface 3: the motivational line

Early theorists explained behaviour, human and animal, as deriving from *motives*. Every organism contains a set of forces that drive it towards certain goals. Some motives ensure the organism's survival: hunger, thirst, sex. Others do not have an obvious physical basis: sociability, aggression, acquisitiveness. Motive or instinct theories of personality became unpopular because they seemed too speculative to the hard-nosed empiricists of the 1930s. They have since enjoyed a minor revival, as Cattell has developed some useful new measures and collected an impressive mass of empirical confirmation (Chapter 8).

The terminus of the motivational line is *psychoanalysis* and theories deriving from it. Psychoanalysis sets out to explain all human behaviour from the cradle to the grave (all behaviour, not just personality) by the interplay of a few very powerful forces, very far below the surface of behaviour – so far below that only psychoanalysts can hope to detect them. Much psychoanalysis undoubtedly travels well past the point where it can be called psychology, and arrives at numerous other destinations: literary criticism, social philosophy and metaphysics (Chapter 9).

Branch lines
Figure 1.1 shows the three main lines: biological, phenomenal and motivational. There are also two branch lines, both starting at the learning/habit station; one goes to the phenomenal station of the phenomenal line, and the other to the motives station of the motivational line. Of late, social learning theories of personality have incorporated more phenomenal elements, defining the stimulus in stimulus-response links as the stimulus the person perceives, not the stimulus experimenters think they have provided. This allows social learning accounts to incorporate values, expectancies, insight and long-range plans. The second branch line from learning/habit has been open longer. Some, but not all, learning theories accounts argue that people or rats will only learn if motivated.

Illustrative examples
The final section of the book applies the various levels of explanation to four particular issues. Three of these somehow suggested themselves automatically: sex, drink and violence. Aggression, violence and social disorder (Chapter 10) increase year by year; the general public look to experts for an explanation. Sexual deviation, especially sexual interest in children (Chapter 11), may or may not be increasing, but public awareness of the problem certainly is. Alcohol problems are estimated to cost vast amounts every year, but the reasons why some people drink too much remain unclear (Chapter 12).

The fourth example is intended to strike a more positive note. Psychologists inevitably spend a lot of time with life's casualties; they get called on less often to examine resilient, hardy people, who cope with life's problems easily. Yet it's surely just as important to know how to identify such persons, and to understand what moulds them, as it is to study criminals, alcoholics and sexual deviants. Hence the fourth example (Chapter 13) summarizes what is known about a set of personality factors, variously referred to as hardiness, resilience or ego strength.

SECTION I

The Surface

CHAPTER 2

A Rather Dull Person

Personality as Traits and Factors

'A bit thick. He was a bit slow and not very alert. He seemed quite shy and not very confident.'
'Inferior intelligence level. Lazy. Easily dominated. Apathetic.'
'Pleasant though careless. Untidy. Little personal pride. Tendency towards under-achievement. Dull voice, dull personality.'

These comments were made by university students after they'd all watched the same film of an unemployed teenager, and been asked to say what they thought of him. The great majority, over 9 in 10, used words like 'dull', 'pleasant' or 'weak-willed' to describe him, often qualified by 'fairly', 'rather', 'not very' etc. A few restricted themselves to superficial comments like 'untidy', 'good looking' or 'interested in fishing', while a few tried to draw together different aspects: 'A lost person, with no ambition, because he has never been directed' or 'fairly cheerful, but hides an underlying nervousness'.

PERSONALITY TRAITS

Words that attribute dispositions to people are *trait names*, and have been used to describe personality for as long as people have had the gift of language. Many derive from Greek – 'athletic', 'barbarous' – or Latin – 'cautious', 'devious' – even though their meanings have often changed over time. For example 'effete' originally meant 'having just borne young', then 'worn out by bearing young', and now simply means 'lacking in vigour and energy'. Many traits reflect former ages' ways of seeing personality; some refer to heavenly bodies supposed to direct behaviour – 'saturnine', 'jovial' or 'lunatic' – while others reflect Galen's theory of the four humours – 'sanguine', 'choleric', 'melancholy' and 'phlegmatic', as well as 'hearty', 'heartless', 'good-humoured' etc. A surprising number immortalize individuals whose behaviour was particularly striking – 'napoleonic', 'sadistic', 'masochistic', 'quixotic' or 'chauvinist'. Sommer (1988) notes that fruit and vegetable metaphors, by contrast, are not widely used to talk about personality; only one was recognized by all his subjects – 'nut'.

Allport's trait theory of personality

Allport and Odbert (1936) went through *Webster's New International Dictionary* and listed every trait name they found; the list ran to 17,953 items, which is twice the size of the average person's entire vocabulary. Many of their words were rare, archaic or of doubtful relevance – 'amurcous', 'astonying' or 'amphibious' – but even their first list of definite trait names ran to 4504 entries. And the list is still growing fast. Slang adds new words constantly; Allport and Odbert listed 'hoodlum', 'yes-man', 'Babbitt', 'flapper', 'crabber' and 'rooter'. Psychologists are adding to the list as well: 'introvert', 'neurotic', 'oedipal' and 'schizoid', not to mention 'idiot', 'imbecile' and 'moron', words which once signified specific degrees of mental retardation but have now degenerated into insults.

Allport (1937, 1961) draws a number of useful distinctions between types of traits. Some are *motivational*, whereas others are *stylistic*; an ambitious person goes out looking for things to achieve, but a polite person doesn't go round looking for opportunities to be polite. Some traits are *secondary*; others are *central* – the ones, according to Allport, 'usually mentioned in careful letters of recommendation' or 'brief verbal descriptions of the person'. Allport thought most people have between five and ten central traits, which implies it's easy to give a brief but comprehensive description of what someone is really like. Occasional individuals have a *cardinal* trait – or 'ruling passion' – which so dominates their personality that 'few activities . . . cannot be traced directly or indirectly to its influence'. Molière's famous Miser is a good example – a man who couldn't see anything or anybody or any occasion except in terms of how not to spend money. Allport also distinguished *individual* and *common* traits. He defines a trait as 'a neuropsychic structure having the capacity to render many stimuli functionally equivalent, and to initiate and guide equivalent (meaningfully consistent) forms of adaptive and expressive behaviour', a definition which clearly locates the trait inside its owner, actually in the brain. Figure 2.1 (Allport, 1961) illustrates Mr A's individual trait of 'communist phobia'. Whenever Mr A sees or hears any of the people, things or events listed on the stimulus side of the trait (the left), the perception is routed to the 'neuropsychic structure', where one of the class of functionally equivalent responses (on the right-hand side) is evoked.

Mr A has a neighbour, Mr B, who has a similar trait, so he sees the same things as examples of the same threat, except that trade unions and nationalization

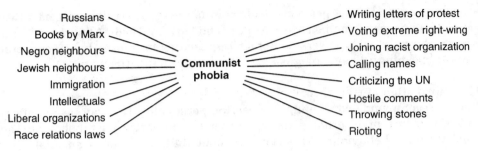

Figure 2.1 *Mr A's trait of 'communist phobia' (after Allport, 1961).*

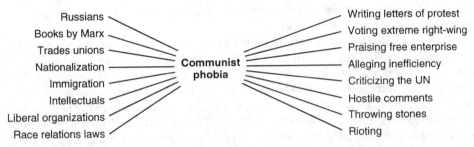

Figure 2.2 *Mr B's trait of 'communist phobia' (after Allport, 1961).*

replace Negro and Jewish neighbours as objects of suspicion (Figure 2.2). Mr B has a different individual trait, but it's a similar common trait; he too has a 'communist phobia', but his 'anti-communism' is less racial and more economic. Allport (1937) thinks 'the original endowment of most human beings, their stages of growth and the demands of their particular society, are sufficiently standard and comparable to lead to some basic modes of adjustment from individual to individual that are approximately the same'. There are enough common traits for people to be able to describe each other's personalities, and convey some useful information to each other. All trait names necessarily refer to common traits, and apply only inexactly to individual traits. Allport can distinguish individual and common traits, because his definition of traits locates them inside the individual, so one could conceivably locate a trait at the neurophysiological level, and even alter it surgically. Allport's definition makes it possible to ask questions like 'How many traits has the average person got?' (Allport suggests between five and ten), 'How many traits has a particular individual got?' and 'What are the (dis)advantages of having more or fewer traits than average?'

In short, traits for Allport are real. Furthermore, personality theorists aren't vitally needed to describe traits, because the accumulated wisdom of past generations, codified by *Webster's New International Dictionary*, has done the job already. 'Linguistic symbols have demonstrated utility; they have been tested throughout the ages for their power of representing stable facts of experience. If many human beings were not in fact egotistic, aggressive, or timid, the epithets would not have found a permanent place in language. If traits exist at all it is natural and proper to name them' (Allport and Odbert, 1936). Allport credits the human observer with powers to detect regularities in human behaviour, trace them to meaningful psychological structures, and name them.

The contribution of trait theory

Allport recommends continuing to describe personality the way people always have – in terms of internal dispositions that summarize past behaviour and predict future behaviour. Allport's own contribution includes an analysis of different types of trait, an impressive list of all the traits known to the year 1936, and some paper-and-pencil measures of ascendance–submission and types of value. Allport's books also have a lot more to say about many other aspects of personality and social behaviour.

Allport's invitation to continue using trait concepts has been taken up most enthusiastically by the inventors of scales for measuring them. Innumerable tests have been written since Woodworth's Personal Data Sheet of 1917, and some of the survivors are described in textbooks of psychological testing (Cronbach, 1990). Two of the best-known trait-based measures are the Minnesota Multiphasic Personality Inventory (MMPI) and the California Personality Inventory (CPI). The MMPI was written by Hathaway and McKinley in the late 1930s to measure nine psychiatric syndromes – hypochondriasis, depression, hysteria, psychopathic deviance, masculinity-feminity, paranoia, psychasthenia, schizophrenia and mania – and was the first major personality questionnaire to be *empirically keyed*. Empirical keying was a first step away from Allport's faith in the powers of the human observer. Earlier questionnaires relied on common sense to select items, a method known technically as *face validity*. A face-valid scale of dominance like Allport's Ascendance – Submission Scale includes items about rebuking queue-jumpers and readiness to criticize inefficiency, because these are self-evidently relevant to dominance. When the authors of the empirically keyed MMPI wanted a depression scale they didn't rely solely on common sense, but checked their choice of item by testing 50 depressed patients and some controls, and included only those items that distinguished depressed from non-depressed people, regardless of the item's apparent connection with depression. Their criterion of depression was psychiatric diagnosis, so the MMPI measures, more quickly and with greater precision, an existing trait-like concept. An empirically keyed inventory cannot introduce a new account of personality, since it has to start from an existing concept.

The CPI is sometimes known as 'the sane person's MMPI'; it starts with common-sense folk concepts, like dominance or sociability, and assembles scales intended to distinguish people seen by others as sociable or dominant from people seen as submissive or unsociable. The dominance scale was written by asking a sample of 100 students to nominate the 10 most dominant and 10 most submissive individuals, picking the 16 with the most dominant reputations and the 16 with the most submissive reputations, and selecting the items that distinguished the two groups most clearly (Megargee, 1972). The delinquency (later socialization) scale assesses social maturity and integrity, and was written from the answers of several hundred delinquents and non-delinquents. The current form of the CPI has 22 main scales, ranging from dominance through to work orientation. Hough (1988) recently compared 37 different personality questionnaires across a very large sample, and concluded the CPI was the 'best all round personality inventory'. The socialization scale in turn got the best results within the CPI, achieving a correlation of 0.64 with 'non-delinquency' in 15,851 subjects.

PERSONALITY FACTORS

Allport's critics didn't share his faith in the human observer's ability to describe the structure of personality. Some critics argue that trait names were just that – names, 'along with all other names as hollow and insubstantial' (Allport, 1937). It makes people happy to describe someone's behaviour as egocentric' or 'inner-directed' or 'cowardly', but there isn't really anything there, certainly not the 'neuropsychic structure' Allport postulated. Furthermore, naming traits leads to the logical fallacy of reification. 'Our initial observation of behavior is only in terms of adverbs of action; John behaves aggressively. Then an adjective creeps in; John has an aggressive disposition. Soon a heavy substantive (noun) arrives, like William James' cow on the doormat; John has a trait of aggressiveness. The result is the fallacy of misplaced concreteness' (Allport, 1966). This line of argument, developed in Chapter 3, ultimately concludes there's no such thing as traits; they are convenient but misleading fictions in the eye of the observer. The lay person's trait-based view of human personality is oversimplified and inaccurate, just like pre-scientific ideas about anatomy or physiology.

Factor theorists offer more constructive criticism. They agree there are regularities in human behaviour, but argue it's wrong to rely on the human observer to detect them, and equally unwise to rely on *Webster's New International Dictionary*. The trait of 'communist phobia' includes eight items of behaviour, but real traits cover many more, and a cardinal trait directs a person's every action, thought and feeling. Furthermore, the eight stimulus items in Figures 2.1 and 2.2 are abstractions; the item 'intellectuals' summarizes a large set of separate encounters with different individuals. Allport thought the human observer good at detecting order in the chaos of behaviour; modern research proves Allport wrong. Even restricted sets of data, like the nine scores of the MMPI, or six facts about a patient's fitness to go home for the weekend, are used very inefficiently (Cook, 1979), so little reliance can be placed on a naive observer's summary of personality derived from the complex stream of human behaviour. Factor theorists prefer to replace the fallible and inefficient human observer by mathematical methods – correlation and factor analysis. Table 2.1 illustrates the principle.

Each of a large number of persons is studied on each of a number of occasions, and their behaviour converted into a score. Then correlations are calculated

Table 2.1   *Fictitious data showing response of* n *subjects in six tests of behaviour*

	Subjects 1	2	3	4	5	6	... n
Refuses to donate to charity (times per term)	1	5	0	6	0	4	... 4
Avoids buying friends a drink (times per term)	0	2	0	3	1	2	... 1
Sits in cold to save putting 50p in meter (times per week)	0	4	1	7	0	7	... 2
Steals neighbour's milk (times per year)	4	3	1	0	1	4	... 4
Doesn't buy TV licence (either-or)	1	1	0	0	1	1	... 1
Doesn't buy car tax disc (either-or)	1	1	0	1	0		... 1

Table 2.2   *Fictitious correlation matrix calculated from fictitious data of Table 2.1, showing inter-correlations of six measures of behaviour across* n *persons*

	1	2	3	4	5	6
1. Doesn't donate		0.75	0.61	0.15	0.09	0.00
2. Doesn't buy drink			0.81	0.07	0.20	0.17
3. Sits in cold				0.01	−0.10	0.21
4. Steals milk					0.45	0.60
5. No TV licence						0.65
6. No car tax						

between every pair of measures, to show how well a person's behaviour on one occasion predicts their behaviour on another. Table 2.2 is a fictitious correlation matrix that might result from this imaginary research. It shows there's a high correlation between avoiding donating to charity and sitting in the cold to save putting 50p in the gas meter, but a zero correlation between these two behaviours and stealing the neighbours milk. Table 2.2 also shows that stealing next door's milk does correlate highly with not buying a TV licence or car tax disc. Table 2.2 suggests clearly the six behaviours studied form two groups; the person who doesn't donate prefers to sit in the cold and avoids buying a drink when it's their turn, while the milk stealer is also the tax and TV licence dodger. Having discovered these two sets of correlations empirically, it's easy enough to name the first one 'meanness' and the second 'petty dishonesty'. These two traits have been defined empirically, by the observed co-occurrence of the six behaviours studied, not by common sense or recourse to a dictionary. Traits defined by correlating across subjects are necessarily common traits.

Table 2.3 *Correlations between seven sets of tests of honesty in children, obtained by Hartshorne and May (1928), from Burton (1963)*

	A	B	C	D	F	H	I
A. Copying (3 tests)		0.45	0.40	0.40	0.29	0.14	0.35
B. Speed (6 tests)			0.37	0.43	0.35	0.17	0.25
C. Peeping (3 tests)				0.30	0.23	0.20	0.11
D. Faking (3 tests)					0.30	0.35	0.26
F. Athletic (4 tests)						0.28	0.23
H. Stealing (1 tests)							0.13
I. Lying (1 test)							

The correlation coefficient was invented by Charles Spearman in 1907, to determine whether intellectual ability was one single thing or many, and factor analyses of tests of ability commonly give results almost as clear as the fictitious data of Table 2.2. Analyses of personality data, by contrast, don't generally give such neat results, which is why Table 2.2 uses fictitious data. Table 2.3 gives the results of a real survey of honesty; Hartshorne and May (1928) used seven sets of honesty tests with primary school children, from which Burton later (1963) calculated intercorrelations. The correlations were all positive but also all fairly low, and no tidy pattern immediately appears, unlike the fictitious data of Table 2.2. Perhaps copying, speed, peeping and faking form a separate group – or perhaps they don't.

Factor theorists don't rely on inspection to find order in tables of correlations; they use a further set of calculations – *factor analysis*. Factor analysis extracts from a correlation matrix a number of statistical abstractions, or factors, that account for the observed correlations. In Table 2.2 the correlations clearly fall into two groups, suggesting there two underlying factors. For the subjectively identified trait, factor analysis substitutes the objectively defined factor. Factor analysis soon settled disputes about the structure of intellectual ability, and gave rise to early hopes it might do the same for personality. Cattell (1965) wrote: 'The problem which baffled psychologists for many years was to find a method which would tease out these functionally unitary influences in the chaotic jungle of human behaviour. But let us ask how, in the literal tropical jungle, the hunter decides whether the dark blobs which he sees are two or three rotting logs or a single alligator? He watches for movement. If they move together – come and go together – he infers a single structure'.

Cattell's 16 personality factors
Cattell, like Allport, is a trait theorist; he sees traits as 'in' the individual's personality, as mental structures. Cattell draws similar distinctions to Allport. Traits may be *unique* or *common*; they may be *dynamic*, *temperamental* (corresponding roughly to Allport's motivational/stylistic distinction) or of *ability*; they

may be *constitutional*, or *environmentally determined*. Finally, they may be *surface* traits or *source* traits. Source traits can only be found by factor analysis.

Cattell (1946) embarked over 45 years ago on the ambitious task of studying the whole *personality sphere* to find the source traits, or factors, underlying it. But his starting point wasn't a survey of actual behaviour like Hartshorne and May's honesty study. Instead Cattell used Allport and Odbert's list of traits, reducing it stage by stage to a set of 12 personality factors. He used only the first of Allport and Odbert's four lists, numbering 4504, which he reduced to 160 by excluding obvious synonyms, but then increased back up to 171 by adding some technical psychological terms (such as 'frustration tolerance'). The list was further reduced to 50, then 35, *nuclear clusters* (Table 2.4) by paired comparisons for apparent similarity. A recent critical review of Cattell's work (John *et al.*, 1988) suggests he overemphasized emotional stability, and underemphasized intelligence and conscientiousness. These 35 or 50 clusters are surface traits, patterns of behaviour that go together superficially, but have more than one underlying cause. The surface trait 'emotionally mature – character neurosis', which includes dishonesty, results from two source traits or personality factors: factor C – emotionally mature stable character, and factor G – positive character integration. People can be dishonest because they are emotionally immature and unstable, or because they lack positive character integration, or both.

In the final stage of Cattell's research 208 men rated each other on the 35 surface traits; the ratings were factor-analysed to yield 12 source traits or personality factors (Table 2.5). A person's profile across these personality factors summarizes him or her as completely as Allport's list of 5–10 central traits. Cattell's 12 personality factors increased to 16 when he used questionnaires as well as ratings. Even 16 isn't Cattell's last word; Cattell and Kline (1977) list 22 personality factors. Cattell originally identified his factors by letters and invented words (e.g. 'parmia' for 'parasympathetic immunity to tension'), to drive home his point that his factors provide an entirely new account of personality. He later had to compromise and use plain English names, so parmia translated as 'shy–venturesome'.

The personality questionnaire as short-cut

Cattell took a short-cut by factor-analysing trait-ratings, ones already heavily preprocessed by comparisons of similarity, instead of analysing real behaviour like Hartshorne and May. Critics argue that Cattell isn't showing what pieces of behaviour actually go together to define a true trait or factor of honesty, but rather which trait words have meaning in common. Cattell (1979) suggests a new base for a factor analysis of personality should an 'actual sampling of what people in our culture are doing over a typical 24-hour period' using a stratified sample of 1000 subjects. To date no comprehensive factor analysis of personality has been calculated from measures of actual behaviour in real life. Most other personality researchers take a different short cut – the personality questionnaire. Following someone around to see if they cheat on arithmetic tests, or pocket 10p

Table 2.4 *Seven nuclear clusters of traits from Cattell (1946). These clusters defined factor C – emotionally mature stable character.*

(10) − 0.42 Realistic, facing life (Realistic, practical) (Persevering) (Facing life)	− v. − Demoralized autistic (Unrealistic) (Quitting) (Subjective, evasive)
(28) − 0.38 Stable, integrated character (Stable emotionally) (Self-respecting) (Self-controlled)	− v. − Changeable, characterless, unrealistic (Changeable) (Un-self-controlled)
(26) − 0.38 Calm, self-effacing, patient (Unemotional) (Phlegmatic) (Patient)	− v. − Restless, sthenic, hypomanic (Emotional) (Excitable) (Impatient) (Sthenically emotional − Burt)
(17) − 0.38 Emotionally mature (Balanced) (Loyal) (Honest)	− v. − Character neurosis, psychopathic (Neurotic, irritable, uncontrolled) (Fickle) (Dishonest)
(27) − 0.37 Emotionally mature adjusting to frustration (Mature emotionally) (Self-effacing)	− v. − Infantile, demanding, self-centred (Infantile) (Self-pitying) (Exhibitionist)
(4) − 0.36 Thoughtful, stoic, reserved (Thoughtful) (Deliberate) (Austere)	− v. − Changeable, frivolous (Unreflective) (Impulsive) (Profligate)
(20) − 0.36 Unemotional (Unemotional) (Content) (Phlegmatic)	− v. − General emotionality with maladjustment (Emotional (in all ways)) (Dissatisfied) (Excitable)

Table 2.5 *The 12 personality factors derived by Cattell (1946) from trait ratings, with later different names in parentheses. In later work, D, J, and K were dropped, and seven new ones added.*

Factor	Personality
A.	Cyclothymia–schizothymia (sociability)
B.	Intelligence
C.	Emotionally mature stable character (ego strength)
D.	Hypersensitive infantile emotionality (excitability)
E.	Dominance–submission
F.	Surgency–desurgency
G.	Positive character integration (superego strength)
H.	Adventurousness ('parmia')
I.	Sensitiveness ('premsia')
J.	Neurasthenia
K.	Trained cultural mind–boorishness
L.	Surgent cyclothymia–paranoia

coins they think no one else has seen, is very time consuming, and frequently impossible. Why not ask them instead? The personality questionnaire or inventory offers great economy of time and effort. In the time it takes to determine whether one person contributes 5p to charity, the researcher can learn 50 facts about each of 100 persons, by distributing copies of the Cook Meanness Inventory (fictitious again) to a captive lecture audience. Furthermore, as Cronbach (1970) points out, the questionnaire can get at thoughts and feelings as well as behaviour, and ask whether people like giving to charity or just do it because it's expected. In fact, more questionnaire items ask about thoughts and feelings than about behaviour, because the questionnaire didn't start life as a labour-saving substitute for observing behaviour; its true parent was the medical interview. Questions like 'Do you worry a lot?' or 'Do you have have trouble getting to sleep at nights?' which made up the Woodworth Personal Data Sheet of 1917, and appear in its many descendants, originally came from psychiatric texts.

Cattell followed his factor analysis of trait ratings by a factor analysis of questionnaire items, which yielded 16 factors. (To be precise, Cattell (1973) favours factor-analysing scores from small sets of items, called *parcels*, because individual questionnaire items have low reliability, and do not cross cultural boundaries well; other researchers, e.g. Heath *et al.* (1988), do factor-analyse data from individual items.) Of these factors, Cattell thought 12 were the same as his 12 rating factors; the other four were new. If the same factor can be found in both rating and questionnaire data, one has more faith in its existence as a real entity – a point Cattell emphasizes heavily. His critics, however (Becker, 1960), dispute his claim to measure the same factors by rating and questionnaire, and point out that the correlations between different measures of the same factor

Table 2.6 *Four of Cattell's personality factors, measured by ratings and by questionnaire (Becker, 1960). The coefficients in parentheses are those for the same measured by different methods.*

	Rating measures				Questionnaire measures		
	A	F	H	L	A	F	H
Rating measures							
Factor F. Surgency	0.44						
Factor H. Adventurousness	0.43	0.78					
Factor L. Surgent cyclothymia–paranoia	0.40	0.79	0.71				
Questionnaire measures							
Factor A. Cyclothymia–schizothymia	(0.11)	0.26	0.28	0.29			
Factor F. Surgency	0.18	(0.49)	0.53	0.29	0.14		
Factor H. Adventurousness	0.16	0.60	(0.59)	0.52	0.40	0.49	
Factor L. Surgent cyclothymia–paranoia	0.27	0.30	0.19	(0.25)	0.25	0.03	0.29

are often no greater than the correlations between different factors measured by the same method (Table 2.6). Cattell also uses an impressive collection of 400 objective tests, variously measures of aesthetic preference, tests of motor co-ordination and performance, perceptual tests, physiological responses such as heart rate, and projective tests like the Rorschach inkblot (but not observations of real-life behaviour). Cattell has factor-analysed these to find a set of *T-factors*, which he claims further confirm the 16 personality factors. Again, his critics are sceptical.

Eysenck's factor model
Cattell's 16 factors aren't independent of each other; they correlate. In technical terms, they are *oblique*, not *orthogonal*. A sociable person also tends to be dominant, surgent and adventurous, but not self-sufficient. Cattell's 16 personality factors can be correlated and factor-analysed just like any other set of data; this is called *second-order* factor analysis, and finds eight second-order factors (Figure 2.3). The largest second-order factor is *exvia–invia*, which characterizes the sociable, dominant, surgent, adventurous, un-self-sufficient person. Cattell's factor model of personality shows it as hierarchically organized, much like factorial models of intellectual abilities. All measures correlate, but some intercorrelations are higher than others. Depending on one's purpose, one might prefer an account featuring a dozen or so correlated factors, or one with only two or three higher order factors. Several authors (Barrick and Mount, 1991) have argued for a compromise between 2 and 16 – the so-called *big five* model of personality: extraversion, autonomy, neuroticism, conscientiousness and tender-mindedness, also

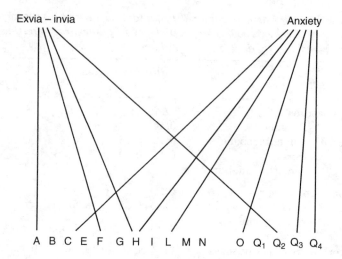

Figure 2.3   *Higher-order factors,* exvia–invia *and anxiety in Cattell's 16 personality factors.*

known as power, love, work, affect and intellect (John *et al.*, 1988) or friendly compliance, extraversion–introversion, ego strength, will to achieve and intellect (Digman and Takemoto-Chock, 1981).

American accounts of personality, as of intelligence, generally prefer a larger number of correlated factors to a smaller number of uncorrelated factors, possibly because a 12- or 16-point profile is more useful for selection, guidance or assessment. A recent analysis of 16PF data (Mershon and Gorsuch, 1988) shows this preference is well founded. Using all 16 factors accounted for twice as much of the variance of real-life outcomes, such as success at work, as did a simplified *big six* model. The simplified model would lose a lot of useful information about individual differences. Some personality measures offer both levels. The latest form of the CPI has 22 scales, but it also has three *vectors* – internality, norm-favouring tendency and competence – corresponding to three large uncorrelated factors underlying the CPI.

H. J. Eysenck, the leading British personality theorist, prefers two or three uncorrelated factors. He initially identified two fundamental dimensions of personality – extraversion and *neuroticism*. (Neuroticism means literally proneness to neurotic breakdown, and more broadly a tendency to worry.) Eysenck's two factors correspond roughly to the two largest factors in Cattell's second-order analysis, *exvia–invia* and anxiety-adjustment. Eysenck later (Eysenck and Eysenck, 1976) added a third factor, *psychoticism*, meaning antisocial, hostile and disturbed. Eysenck's work has much in common with Cattell's: both start with a trait model of personality; both collect large amounts of data from large samples, and factor-analyse it; both favour objective tests of personality, Unlike

Cattell, Eysenck isn't primarily interested in giving a comprehensive account of personality structure, nor in writing comprehensive personality inventories. Eysenck's two or three dimensions give a somewhat limited account of individual personality, and aren't meant to be very useful for assessing individuals. Eysenck's main interest lies in theory, and his questionnaires are used mainly in research (Chapter 5).

Contribution of the factor approach

There are three reasons for calculating a factor analysis. Two are straight-forward – eliminating unnecessary measures, and testing the purity of measures. Factor analysis distinguishes redundant variables, which correlate highly with something already used, from those which add fresh information. Psychologists 40–50 years ago constructed long, elaborate rating scales for education or industry, to find they had only succeeded in measuring a few factors, the largest usually being evaluative; the good, punctual, well-adjusted, likely-to-succeed pupil/employee also proving to be the one the teacher/supervisor liked. Factor analysis tests the purity of a measure too. If several different factors emerge from tests of rigidity (Forester *et al.*, 1955), then either there's no such thing, or the researcher hasn't used the right tests for it. Ideally 10 tests of X will find a single X factor (although strictly speaking the single factor emerging fron ten tests of X might not be 'X'; factor analysis doesn't name factors).

Cattell thinks factor analysis serves a third, much more important, function, and it's here his critics, like Allport (1937) and Lykken (1971), disagree. Cattell uses factor analysis to uncover the true structure of personality. The critics argue that factor analysis is simply a mathematical procedure for summarizing sources of variability in a set of scores, so that finding a weak set of correlations across 500 subjects completing a questionnaire doesn't imply each and every one of them has the same set of internal dispositions or mental structures.

Factor analytic *solutions* (the number of factors, and measures they *load* on) aren't always very reliable. Table 2.7 shows the loadings of Cattell's assertiveness factor on 15 objective tests in seven successive analyses. Cattell considers these data prove the existence of an assertiveness factor; his critics (Sells, 1959) say the results of the various analyses bear little resemblance to each other, that Cattell has really found seven quite different factors, and is committing the fallacy of reification by naming all seven 'assertiveness'. Factor solutions vary because samples aren't large or representative enough. Comrey (1978) suggests 2000 subjects are needed to find a truly reliable solution; factor analytic studies of personality rarely achieve this target. Critics of Cattell (e.g. G. Matthews, 1989) often complain they can't reproduce Cattell's 16 factors from their 16PF data, and usually argue that Cattell has over-factored his data, meaning that he has extracted too many factors from a relatively short inventory.

But even the same set of data can yield different factor solutions. Different techniques of factor analysis produce different results; the classic example is Thurstone's use of *group* factor analysis to obtain six factors from intelligence

Table 2.7   *T-factors of assertiveness derived in seven successive factor analyses, showing low and fluctuating factor loading (Sells, 1959)*

	Successive factor analyses						
	1	2	3	4	5	6	7
Paper-and-pencil maze measures							
Long exploratory distance in maze					38	39	46
High total score in 'cursive miniature situation'			46	03	40		01
Excessive use of circles in 'cursive miniature situation'	−03		04	18	28	38	15
Motor tests							
Fast tempo in arm–shoulder swing		14			52	24	06
Fast tempo in tapping					38		76
Low motor rigidity	−06	−02	−01	10	−21	−13	−10
Reading tests							
Big reduction in reading time by frustration			53				−03
Fast tempo in reading	53				64		
Attitude measures							
Highbrow social tastes			26	48	47	12	
No questionable reading preferences	26	57	31	22	18		15
Maturity of opinion	12	−21	07	−14	−11		10
Low authority suggestibility	−16	−48	−26	−04	−08	07	09
Miscellaneous							
Many objects perceived in unstructured picture						35	34
Care in following instructions		05					22
Fast speed in letter comparison						17	56

test data, which Eysenck (1939) then reanalysed to find one general factor running through all the tests. Burton (1963) factor-analysed Hartshorne and May's honesty data (Table 2.3) using several different factor analytic methods. *Principal components* analysis found a general factor underlying all the tests, and several smaller factors loading on one or two tests only (Table 2.8). *Orthogonal rotation*, however, produced a factor loading only on copying, speed, peeking, faking and two minor factors. The factor solutions differ because different methods of calculation are designed to produce different answers.

Some early studies factor-analysed measurements of simple things like boxes, and found factors – length, breadth and depth – that seemed to reveal their structure. Lykken (1971) factor-analysed data from something more complicated – the motor car. He used road test reports in a US motoring magazine that reported

Table 2.8   *The data of Hartshorne and May's study of honesty, factor-analysed by Burton (1963) using principal components and orthogonal rotation methods. (NB The two smallest factors of the principal components analysis have been omitted.)*

	Principal components analysis					Orthogonal rotation analysis		
	Factor					Factor		
	I	II	III	IV		I	II	III
A. Copying	76	09	21	−17	A. Copying	63	22	43
B. Speed	75	11	−21	−05	B. Speed	61	48	12
C. Peeping	58	66	08	−23	C. Peeping	88	−09	−04
D. Faking	70	02	−14	68	D. Faking	52	46	19
F. Athletic	56	−50	−54	−29	F. Athletic	03	92	10
I. Lying	53	−50	64	−03	I. Lying	08	11	96

several dozen measures: acceleration, braking distance, top speed, fuel consumption, weight, length, cost, number of seats, etc. Would the factors obtained, asked Lykken, help an engineer, or a visiting Martian, understand what went on inside the car's metal skin? His results suggest they would not. Two factors – II, brake size and price, and IV, uphill speed, driver comfort, price and engine oil capacity – make little or no sense, and certainly reveal nothing about the way cars work. A third factor violated both common sense and the laws of mechanics, by apparently showing that the heavier the car, the faster its acceleration and top speed. As Lykken says, 'Other things being equal large massive objects accelerate more slowly than small ones; things aren't equal in the car market.' The larger the car, the even larger its engine. Lykken's data suggest factor analysis might not be very useful for revealing the inner structure of complex things, like motor cars or personality.

Critics of factor analysis often complain 'You only get out what you put in', a criticism Cattell dismisses with scorn: 'No form of science . . . can claim the conjuring trick of proving relations to exist among variables it has not used.' The critics have a point nevertheless. 'What you put in' may not always be quite what it seems. Trouton and Maxwell (1956) factor-analysed psychiatric case histories, and concluded that neurosis and psychosis were separate dimensions of mental illness. However, examination of the data Maxwell and Trouton 'put in' suggests they hadn't really proved neurosis and psychosis are different things, only that the psychiatrists writing the case histories thought they were. Their neurosis factor includes at least six direct references to neurotic symptoms, e.g. 'neurotic traits in childhood'. One doesn't need factor analysis to prove that 1950s diagnostic practice drew a clear distinction between neurosis and psychosis. On the analogy of *Webster's New International Dictionary*, any 1950s psychiatry text shows that. Some critics see a more general case of the 'get out what you put in' fallacy running through all factor analyses of trait ratings; Cattell thinks they reveal the true structure of human personality, while the critics argue they reveal only the structure of meaning of trait words. This point is pursued in Chapter 3.

There is no doubt that factor analysis has proved very useful in the study of intellectual abilities, and has provided a definitive account of how it's structured. At the same time it's generally agreed, except of course by factor theorists, that it hasn't been quite so useful in the study of personality. Perhaps the answer to this paradox lies in the contrast between personality research and research on ability. The latter usually finds uniformly positive and fairly high correlations, from which a clear set of factors emerges. The former more often finds a set of low to zero correlations that yield a confused and unreliable set of factors. As Lykken points out, factor analysis can confirm a hypothesis that a set of tests are all measuring the same thing, but it's not so good at discovering possible structure underlying sets of low correlations.

Conclusion

CHAPTER 3

The Prisoner of Spandau

Criticisms of Traits and Factors

ON 10 May 1941 Hitler's deputy Rudolf Hess flew to Scotland to negotiate an armistice between Germany and Britain. He was held as a prisoner of war and later sentenced to spend the rest of his life in prison. In 1979 Hugh Thomas, a military surgeon who'd examined Hess in Spandau prison, made the startling claim that the prisoner wasn't Hess, and never had been. The real Hess, according to Thomas, was murdered in 1941, and a double flew to Scotland instead. Thomas's starting point, and best single piece of evidence, was his discovery that the prisoner bore no sign of the serious bullet wound the real Hess had suffered in 1916.

Thomas also claimed that the prisoner didn't *behave* like Hess. Hess was a vegetarian and a fastidious eater; the prisoner wolfed down everything in sight, including meat. Hess played tennis well and with enthusiasm, while the prisoner said he'd never played and didn't know the rules. Hess had two irritating habits – whistling and playing with the chair he was sitting on; the prisoner was never seen to do either. Hess used homoeopathic medicine, which the prisoner brought with him, but never used or asked for. Finally the real Hess was 'a man of wide political experience, of natural good manners, and of proven skill in handling negotiations'; the prisoner cut a poor figure intellectually in the eyes of his captors, spoke 'with almost complete vacuity', displayed a childish simplicity, and was afraid to meet British government representatives. He became suspicious his food was being poisoned, and complained that his sleep was being deliberately interrupted. His behaviour throughout his time in Britain was so odd that he was thought to be insane.

Are these changes sufficient to prove the prisoner wasn't Hess? Thomas assumes that behaviour like whistling and fidgeting is characteristic of people, produced from inside them, and carried around with them, wherever they may be. Thomas sees Hess's habits and traits as being as much part of him as his bullet scar of 1916; their absence after May 1941, like the absence of the scar, proves the prisoner wasn't Hess. Is Thomas's model of personality correct? Is behaviour, like fidgeting or interest in sport or ability to negotiate, consistent over time? If Hess played tennis in Egypt in the 1900s, should he want to play in Aldershot in 1941? And is it consistent across different settings? If Hess fidgets with his chair in the Landsberg jail, shouldn't he fidget with the one in Spandau prison too? But if behaviour lacks internal consistency, what does account for the way people behave? The first two questions are crucial, for trait theory obviously implies that behaviour will be consistent over time, and across different settings. The third question – if not traits, then what else? – has been one centre of interest in personality research for the last 20 years.

THE CONSISTENCY OF BEHAVIOUR

Stability over time

Any good personality test has been completed by the same people twice, and a *re-test reliability coefficient* calculated. Questionnaires like the CPI and MMPI usually achieve reliabilities around 0.80 over short periods, declining steadily as the interval between tests increases. For some reason the reliability of extraversion scales is consistently slightly higher than that of scales reflecting anxiety or poor adjustment (Schuerger *et al.*, 1989). Projective tests like the Rorschach inkblots achieve much lower reliabilities. Other research reports data on the stability of questionnaire scores over longer periods. Helson and Moane (1987) tested the same group of American college women with the California Psychological Inventory at ages 21, 28 and 43. In the shorter term – 21 to 28, or 28 to 43 – scores were reasonably stable, but across the whole span from 21 to 43, stability was lower: $r = 0.21$ to 0.50. Kelly (1955) reports self-descriptions of interests and values on the Strong Vocational Interest Blank and the Allport–Vernon Study of Values remained fairly similar between 1935/8 and 1954 ($r = 0.45$ to 0.60). Even across a 45-year time span Conley (1984) reports that neuroticism and extraversion scores show some consistency ($r = 0.31$ and 0.27).

The Berkeley Growth Study (Block, 1971) assessed its cohort in early and late adolescence, and then again in their thirties, using the California Q Sort, in which expert raters assign 100 statements to each of nine categories, according to how well they describe the individual. Block finds that people typically create very similar impressions on others over the shorter time span of early to late adolescence. Over the longer span from adolescence to mid-thirties a more varied picture emerged, but many people still create much the same impression after 15 to 20 years. Block divided his sample into people who changed a lot, and those who changed little, and found (Table 3.1) people who changed a lot generally had poorer personalities in adolescence. Lives do not always show continuity, however. Men who joined the army in 1941–2 (Elder, 1988) found their lives changed drastically in the short term, by what one person called the 'knifing off' of previous experience, and in the longer term by getting a far better education, through veterans' (ex-servicemen's) entitlements. In *retrospective studies*, data collected earlier for another purpose are related to present personality; Roff (1963) examined school records of people who subsequently developed criminal, homosexual or schizophrenic behaviour, and found many clear patterns of difference in childhood. For example, future schizophrenics, as children, were often described by teachers as lacking friends, acting oddly, and being very inattentive.

Consistency across different settings

Obviously the trait model doesn't deny the possibility that people might change a lot over time; consistency across place is more crucial. An honest person should behave honestly in the supermarket on Monday, when completing a tax return on Tuesday, and by returning a lost wallet to its owner on Wednesday – even if ten years later hard times have turned him or her into a criminal. But trait theory's critics argue that behaviour lacks precisely this short-term, cross-situational consistency.

Three large studies, all carried out 50 to 60 years ago, are the principal evidence. Dudycha (1936) collected data on students' punctuality for: eight o'clock lectures, breakfast in college dining hall, appointments with tutors, college choir and band practice, evening service, and college athletic meetings and entertainments. Dudycha didn't rely on paper-and-pencil measures, as most modern psychologists would; he stood and watched the students arriving, and collected a minimum of 20 observations per student for lectures, breakfast and tutorials (for the other occasions he could only manage three observations). It's a very solid piece of research; no one could criticize Dudycha for not collecting enough hard data. Dudycha quoted remarks like 'You can depend on him; he's always early' or 'We had better call the meeting at 7.45, then Mr Martin will be sure to arrive by eight o'clock' to show how people assume punctuality is a reliable personality trait. Dudycha's data, however (Table 3.2), give a completely different picture. Correlations between punctuality for the six events are significantly greater than zero, but nevertheless generally low. Students' ratings of each other's punctuality correlated with observed behaviour equally poorly. Questionnaire responses proved unrelated to behaviour, partly because the majority of students claimed to be more than averagely punctual. Hartshorne and May's research on honesty in school children produced similar results (Table 2.3); Newcomb's (1929) observations of children at summer camp failed to find evidence of consistent patterns of extraversion.

Dudycha's results imply it's uninformative, or positively misleading, to say 'Smith is punctual' since there's little or no transfer from one occasion to another; the student who is late for lectures isn't necessarily late for breakfast, or choir

Table 3.1 *Q-sort data, collected in late adolescence, describing men and women who changed a lot, or not much, by the time they were 30 to 38 (Block, 1971)*

Q-sort items 'relatively characteristic' of MEN who CHANGED a lot from late adolescence to early adulthood.

—brittle, uncomfortable with uncertainty, self-defensive, extrapunitive, withdraws when frustrated, self-defeating, self-pitying, other-directed, rebellious, pushes limits, negativistic, bothered by demands, expresses hostile feelings directly, communicates through non-verbal behaviour; claims the privileges and excuses afforded the adolescent, covertly hostile to adults, rebellious with adults.

Q-sort items 'relatively characteristic' of MEN who did NOT CHANGE much from late adolescence to early adulthood.

—wide interests, prides self on objectivity, values intellectual matters, philosophically concerned, has high aspiration level, views self as causative, insightful, aesthetically reactive, interesting, verbally fluent, productive, dependable, protective, satisfied with self, comfortable with past decisions; views his family as interested, perceives parents as equitable, protective of friends, selective in choice of friends.

Q-sort items 'relatively characteristic' of WOMEN who CHANGED a lot from late adolescence to early adulthood.

—brittle, self-defensive, withdraws when frustrated, undercontrolled, unpredictable, rebellious, pushes limits, self-indulgent, affected, communicates through non-verbal behaviour, negativistic, basic hostility, deceitful, distrustful, feels a lack of meaning in life, extrapunitive, self-dramatizing; covertly hostile to adults, attention-getting behaviour with peers, assertive with peers, condescending with peers.

Q-sort items 'relatively characteristic' of WOMEN who did NOT CHANGE much from late adolescence to early adulthood.

—dependable, straightforward, clear-cut and consistent personality, overcontrolled, productive, high aspiration level, giving, sympathetic, arouses liking, aware of impression created, insightful, submissive, arouses nurturant feeling, wide interests, protective, prides self on objectivity, warm, values intellectual matters, aesthetically reactive, satisfied with self, favours status quo; closer to mother than father, respecting of parents, perceives parents as fair and consistent, sees parents as singling her out for special evaluation, able to have appropriate relationships with adults, protected by peers.

Table 3.2   *Correlations between punctuality at six types of event (Dudycha, 1936)*

	8 a.m. lectures	Breakfast	Tutorials	Choir and band practice	Evening service
8 a.m. lectures					
Breakfast in hall	0.36				
Tutorials	0.28	0.16			
Choir and band practice	0.30	–	–		
Evening service	0.16	0.10	0.24	−0.19	
College entertainments	0.08	0.44	0.11	0.20	0.25

practice, or tutorials. Dudycha's results imply one must always ask 'Punctual for what?' The Hartshorne and Newcomb studies similarly imply 'Jones is honest' and 'Robinson is sociable' need qualification. People do qualify statements about others' personality; asked to 'Tell me everything you know about (X) so I will know him as well as you do', adults added 'ifs' and 'whens' to some statements: aggressive, if frustrated, or when threatened by peers (Wright and Mischel, 1988). People only qualified 1 in 10 statements, but Wright and Mischel argue qualifications are implicit in many more.

The early researches of Dudycha and others remained largely forgotten for many years. Vernon (1964) and Hunt (1965) mentioned the poor predictive validity of trait concepts and measures, but no one took much notice until Mischel's (1968) critique. Mischel reviewed the early research, then listed further examples of traits lacking strong proof of consistent behaviour: dependency, masculinity, conformity, rigidity, intolerance of ambiguity, attitude to authority, and aggression. Following Mischel, similar results have been published for assertiveness (Bouchard *et al.*, 1988), curiosity (Coie, 1974), flexibility (Paulhus and Martin, 1988), and social skill and social anxiety (Curran *et al.*, 1980).

The 0.30 barrier

Mischel also argued that traits generally fail to predict behaviour in real life. He cites the classic early study of LaPiere (1934), who found questionnaire measures of racial prejudice completely failed to predict restaurant owners' actual behaviour towards non-white customers. Mann (1959) catalogued consistently low correlations between leadership and tests of adjustment ($r = 0.14$), dominance ($r = 0.10$), extraversion ($r = 0.10$), etc. Reviews of the predictive value of personality tests for personnel selection came to similar pessimistic conclusions: correlations that fluctuate wildly about a very low average (Ghiselli, 1966). Critics of the trait approach argue that correlations between personality measures and outcomes rarely exceed 0.30, and postulated the '0.30 barrier'. A correlation of 0.30 explains 9 per cent of the variance, leaving 91 per cent to be explained by other

Table 3.3 *Data on attitudes to father, boss and peer, on three measures (Burwen and Campbell, 1957). The correlations in parentheses are those obtained by the same measure.*

	Father			Boss			Peer		
	I	DSO	AI	I	DSO	AI	I	DSO	AI
Attitude to FATHER, measured by									
Interview (I)		40	09	(64)	19	−06	(65)	27	08
Description of Self and Others (DSO)			40	08	(23)	−14	09	(21)	00
Autobiographical Inventory (AI)				15	09	(−08)	24	03	(15)
Attitude to BOSS, measured by									
Interview (I)					−10	−17	(76)	11	09
Description of Self and Others (DSO)						09	−03	(45)	04
Autobiographical Inventory (AI)							20	03	(15)
Attitude to PEER, measured by									
Interview (I)								23	−04
Description of Self and Others (DSO)									20
Autobiographical Inventory (AI)									

factors. But if the trait model, or tests based on it, only explains one tenth of the variation in leadership or proficiency at work, can either model or test be worth using?

THE CONSTRUCTION OF CONSISTENCY

Mischel goes on to argue that even the limited consistency that researchers have found is 'constructed' by the measurement methods they used, and doesn't really exist. *Method variance* means positive correlations result because the same type of measure is used, not because the traits are 'really' correlated. Interview measures of attitude to father, boss and symbolic authority correlate quite well, and so do questionnaire measures of attitudes to the same three authority figures (Burwen and Campbell, 1957); what's lacking is sizeable correlations between questionnaire and interview measures of the same attitude (Table 3.3). The largest correlation is 0.35, and the average a negligible 0.08. Campbell later advocated multi-trait, multi-method (MTMM) assessment, where each trait is measured by more than one method (Campbell and Fiske, 1959); different measures of the same trait should correlate more highly than the same measure of different traits. Table 2.6 showed this doesn't always happen; questionnaire measures of different factors of Cattell's 16 sometimes correlate better than questionnaire, rating and objective measures of the same factor.

Mischel lists a number of ways questionnaires can 'construct' correlations between different traits.

1. *Qualifiers*   Questionnaires use a lot of vague qualifiers ('often', 'sometimes', 'rarely'), which different people interpret as widely differing real frequencies. A constant *response set* could inflate correlations between traits.

2. *Overlap between scales*   In some questionnaires scales overlap; items are scored for more than one scale, which creates correlations between scales. Even within scales items often seem to repeat themselves (possibly because scales have to be long enough to achieve acceptable split-half reliability, so a meanness inventory asks 35 questions about meanness and generosity, even if there aren't 35 separate, sensible questions to ask).

3. *Social desirability set*   Some people give socially desirable answers to questionnaires, trying to present themselves in a consistently favourable light, which tends to create a positive correlation between any pair of desirable traits.

4. *Acquiescence set*   Some subjects answer 'yes' rather than 'no', whatever the question. If the number of yes- and no-keyed questions aren't exactly equal, which they aren't in most questionnaires, answering 'yes' consistently throughout the test tends to create positive correlations between scores.

5. *Instructions*   The instructions in many questionnaires tell people to complete them quickly and without thinking too hard, which may increase the risk of points 1–4 creating spurious correlations.

6. *Assuming consistency*   Most questionnaire items assume behaviour is consistent across different occasions. 'Are you usually cheerful?' must be answered 'yes' or 'no'; subjects aren't allowed to say it all depends where they are, who they're with, what time of the day/week/month/ year it is, etc.

Ratings can also construct consistency.

1. *Social desirability*   Ratings often create strong pressure to give socially desirable answers, which in turn creates positive correlations.

2. *Position preferences*   People sometimes show position preferences for

parts of the scale, often the middle which avoids committing them to extreme judgements.

3. *Halo effect*   Ratings are notoriously liable to the halo effect, in which the rater's like or dislike of the person rated exerts a pervasive influence on a wide range of unrelated traits: the person who is rated 'polite' is also rated 'well-adjusted', 'intelligent', etc. The halo effect clearly has great power to create a lot of positive correlations.

4. *Assuming consistency*   Ratings usually assume behaviour is consistent across situations, by including only trait words: sociable, agreeable, questioning, etc.

Some of Mischel's criticisms of questionnaires and ratings are not a lot newer than the early researches on honesty or punctuality; social desirability, halo and acquiescence have been discussed endlessly since the 1950s. His analysis of the way measures beg the question by assuming consistency breaks newer ground.

The search for simple meaning

Finally, Mischel argues that people find traits because they need or want to find them. People like to oversimplify the complexities of each other's behaviour into a handful of broad categories. Unfortunately personality theorists fall into the same trap, and are too ready to accord fallible lay theories of personality the status of objective, scientific data.

Reanalysis of five major trait rating studies, including Cattell's original (1946) data, found the same five factors in all five studies, although raters and rated were fairly diverse: teachers rating children, college students rating each other, officer candidates rating each other, psychologists rating trainees (Digman and Takemoto-Chock, 1981). Other research shows that ratings of real people and of stereotypes ('suburban housewife', 'air force general') produce similar factors (Mulaik, 1964). Ratings based solely on appearance after 15 minutes' acquaintance produce the same five factors as ratings of people one has spent three months in the Peace Corps with (Norman and Goldberg, 1966). Ratings of total strangers one hasn't spoken with can only be superficial stereotypes – yet these superficial stereotypes analyse into the same five factors as ratings based on long, close acquaintance in fairly testing conditions. Furthermore, ratings of trait words themselves produce the same set of factors, which implies the factors may derive from the conceptual similarity of the words themselves (D'Andrade, 1965). The results are consistent with the hypothesis of five 'robust' personality factors – but also with the argument that rating-based factors exist only in the eye of the beholder, because the same factors emerge regardless of who or what is being rated.

Perhaps questionnaire measures of personality can help. Lay and Jackson (1969) collected data on the perceived similarity of pairs of questionnaire items, and found it predicted quite well how people actually complete the inventory. Lay and Jackson thought this proved people are accurate judges of a real structure of personality, but this assumes the inventory is an accurate measure of personality. Suppose that when people complete inventories, their answers don't report real consistencies in their behaviour, but reflect consistencies in the way they interpret the questionnaire items (Shweder and D'Andrade, 1979). Questionnaire items, and the answers people give to them, are still only words. Suppose one measured real behaviour, and compared its structure with the structure of people's impressions. For example, the contributions people make to group discussions were sorted into 16 types: makes a joke, gives information etc. Observations of successive 15-second slices of the discussion defined the true structure of the 16 behaviours (Borkenau and Ostendorf, 1987). This was compared with global estimates of their correlation, made after seeing all 50 minutes of the discussion, and with estimates of the likelihood of their correlating, made by people who hadn't seen the discussion at all. The three sets of data agreed fairly well, suggesting that people observe and remember behaviour fairly accurately, and that their implicit personality theories about the likely relationship between characteristics have some basis in reality, whereas the thrust of Mischel's critique was that people allow their implicit personality theories to distort, or even wholly construct, the way they remember and observe others' behaviour.

IN DEFENCE OF TRAIT THEORY

Trait theorists were not slow to reply to Mischel's critique. Low correlations, they pointed out, do not necessarily prove the non-existence of traits; low correlations can arise for many other reasons.

1. Poor methodology Mischel's critics claim it's very easy to prove a negative, to find no correlation between measures, or no differences between groups; all you have to do is carry out sloppy, careless research. Block (1977) argues some of the studies Mischel cites were so badly done it wasn't in the least surprising no significant results emerged.

2. Poor measures A badly written questionnaire that doesn't measure what it claims to, and may not measure anything at all, is likely to result in low or zero correlations. Block argues that Burwen and Campbell's measures of attitude to authority (Table 3.3) had never been used before and had no proven validity.

3. Trivial measures It's rarely possible to study people in extreme situations; threatening people with imminent death might reveal very significant individual differences, but ethics, conscience and practicalities limit researchers to studying trivial behaviour in whatever captive population of students or school-children they can find.

4. Unsuitable subjects Burwen and Campbell's subjects were USAAF personnel; the report suggests some weren't taking the study seriously, while others

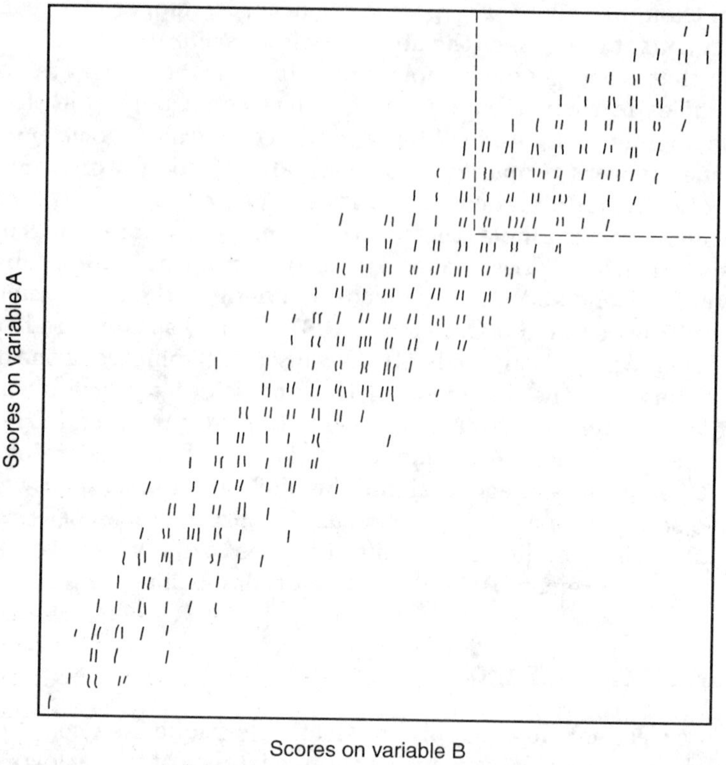

Figure 3.1 *The effect of restricted range of a correlation coefficient.*

adopted a 'guarded differential attitude that was difficult to overcome'. Other studies used children as subjects; children may not display the same consistency as adults. Specifically, research on moral development implies the children in Hartshorne and May's survey of honesty were probably too young to have developed generalized moral standards, and so exhibit consistently honest or dishonest behaviour.

5.   *Homogeneous subjects* Other critics (Carlson, 1971) complain that too much personality research is done on college students, who are all fairly much alike. Homogeneity of subjects restricts range, and restricted range means low correlations (Figure 3.1).

6.   *Not enough subjects* The correlation coefficient is notoriously unstable when calculated from small samples. Figure 3.2 shows how a 'true' correlation of 0.22 varies between 0.03 and 0.48 when calculated from small sub-sets of the data; two-thirds of the correlations aren't statistically significant. How small is small? Schmidt *et al.* (1988) had divided a large sample of 1455 US postal workers into

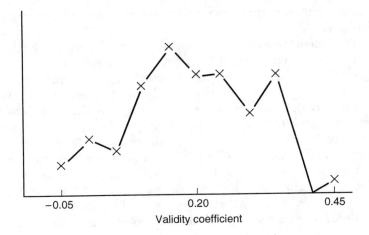

Validity coefficient

Figure 3.2 *Distribution of validity coefficients for 63 'pseudo-samples', each of 68, drawn randomly from a larger sample of 1455. Data from Schmidt et al. (1985)*

63 pseudo-samples of 68 each. They chose 68 because it was the median sample size in personnel selection research. Their message doesn't seem to have reached personality researchers, who still regularly test hypotheses about the consistency of personality or the validity of personality measures with samples smaller than 68, thereby running the risk of missing correlations by sampling error.

Breaking the 0.30 barrier

Trait theory's critics answer complaints about poor methodology with a simple challenge: break the 0.30 barrier, prove that traits can predict behaviour. If the problem is poor research, then conduct better research. 'And if these [methods] predict behavior across situations better than +0.30, Mischel will fold up his tent and steal away' (Bem, 1972a). Some researchers have accepted the challenge, and developed new ways of getting better results.

1. Collect enough data It's a basic principle of measurement in psychology that many observations of behaviour are needed to give a reliable score. ('Many' here implies as many as will produce an acceptable split-half reliability, meaning one half of the scores has the same mean and standard deviation as the other half.) No experimental psychologist would dream of recording only one reaction time in each condition of an experiment; hundreds are collected and averaged to iron out random variations. This is called *aggregation*. Similarly a single-item personality questionnaire wouldn't have much predictive validity; 20 items is one rule of thumb for the minimum needed. But many of the tests criticized for failing to correlate with each other, or anything else, were single-item tests, and hence highly unreliable. Specifically, most of Hartshorne and May's tests of honesty, while very ingenious and plausible, produced only one observation: cheated/didn't, stole/didn't.

Epstein (1979) collected a range of measures every day for 14 days: self-ratings of pleasant and unpleasant experiences, observed frequency of social approach to others, frequency of being late, forgetting pencils, and mistakes and erasures in completing a form. Figure 3.3 shows one day's observation correlated fairly poorly, about 0.30 or 0.40, with the next day's, whereas six days' data correlated with the next six days 0.60 to 0.90. Six observations are enough to generate a reliable score, and break the 0.30 barrier. Epstein extracts the same conclusion from reanalysis of Hartshorne and May's honesty data; while any one test didn't predict any one other, a score from 10 tests predicted well ($r = 0.73$) a score from a second set of 10. However, Epstein overlooks Dudycha's study, where an average of 20 arrivals at breakfast correlated only 0.36 and 0.28 with similar averages for lectures and tutorials, and barely broke the 0.30 barrier.

2.   *Analyse the data properly* Most psychologists believe leadership isn't a trait, so that it can't be measured or fostered, despite the insistence of industry and the military on trying to do both. Leadership, argue most psychologists, is a *role* that emerges in every group, to be filled by whoever fits it best. Research on leadership uses the *rotation* paradigm, in which groups are reshuffled to determine whether the same persons take the lead, or whether – as the 'role anyone can fill' hypothesis predicts – different persons take the lead in different groups. More recent reanalysis of rotation research finds that individuality accounts for between 40 per cent and 80 per cent of the variance in leadership (Kenny and Zaccaro, 1983), which means that leadership is a substantial individual difference, and not just a role.

3.   *Analyse the data properly – 2: meta-analysis* The traditional way of making sense of research is the *narrative review*, as published by the *Psychological Bulletin*. The reviewer seeks out every study of, for example, extraversion and classical conditioning, notes that some find a relationship while some do not, and looks for features that distinguish the 'successful' studies from the 'unsuccessful'. Narrative reviews emphasize inconsistent results, and allow both 'sides' in any debate to claim they are right, by focusing on studies that support their 'side', and picking holes in the others that don't.

Meta-analysis pools the results of all relevant research to yield a single estimate of the size and direction of any relationship. Most research using psychological tests reports correlations; meta-analysis averages the correlations, weighting them by sample size. Ghiselli (1966) assembled 111 studies of mechanical comprehension and trainability as a repairman, in which the correlation varied from −0.25 to +0.75, and calculated a median of 0.39. Meta-analysis takes this median as an estimate of the true relationship between mechanical comprehension and repair work, which ignores irrelevant chance variations arising from different tests of mechanical comprehension, different measures of trainability in repair work, different locations, different age groups etc. (Meta-analysis can

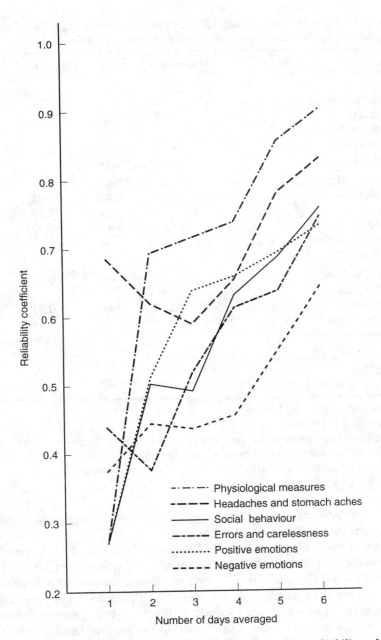

Figure 3.3 *Data from Epstein (1979), showing increasing reliability of six measures when averaged over a larger number of days.*

Table 3.4   *Meta-analysis of the validity of scales of the California Psychological Inventory, against six criteria (Hough, 1988)*

Criterion	Train[a]	Profy[b]	Commend[c]	Non-del[d]	Non-abuse[e]	Educ[f]
Dominance			0.30	0.38		
Capacity for status				0.39		
Sociability				0.25		
Social presence				0.29		
Self-acceptance				0.20		
Well-being				0.35		
Responsibility			0.44	0.56	0.32	0.57
Socialization			0.32	0.64	0.41	
Self-control				0.20	0.24	
Tolerance				0.48		
Good impression						
Communality						
Achievement via conformance				0.43	0.26	0.25
Achievement via independence	0.21		0.33	0.42	−0.27	
Intellectual efficiency				0.46	−0.23	0.29
Psychological-mindedness						
Flexibility						
Femininity/masculinity						

[a]   Training grades and ratings.
[b]   Overall job proficiency; technical proficiency, advancement.
[c]   Commendable behaviours: reprimands, disciplinary, dismissals, demotions.
[d]   Non-delinquency: theft, offences, imprisonment.
[e]   Non-substance abuse: drugs, alcohol consumed, addiction.
[f]   School and college marks/completion.

identify age or other effects, if they are really there, meaning they appear consistently in different studies.)

Table 3.4 summarizes Hough's (1988) meta-analysis of California Psychological Inventory predictions of six outcomes, based on between 2 and 31 samples totalling between 1000 and 16,000 persons. Some correlations broke the 0.30 barrier by a generous margin; in particular, the CPI predicts very accurately who won't fit into an organization or conform to its rules and systems. Hough subsequently devised a new measure, Assessment of Background and Life Experiences (ABLE), based on the 12 most widely used inventories, and validated ABLE scores against five criteria of proficiency in the US armed services, in 7000 to 8000 service personnel (Hough *et al.*, 1990). ABLE scores didn't predict technical proficiency or general soldiering proficiency but did achieve modest correlations with effort and leadership, personal discipline, and physical fitness and military bearing. The results of Hough's two meta-analyses suggests inventory scores can't predict how well someone does their job, but might be able to predict how hard the person will try.

4.   Analyse the data properly – 3: validity generalization analysis Personnel psychologists were also concerned about the 0.30 barrier, and devised *validity generalization analysis* (VGA), which extracts more positive conclusions from test X outcome data (Schmidt *et al.*, 1985). Correlations between tests and outcomes tend to be low and unstable, because range is restricted (Figure 3.1), because the sample is too small (Figure 3.2), and because the outcome isn't measured reliably (*criterion reliability*). For example, ratings of people, widely used in research on both personality and personnel, typically achieve a re-test reliability around $r = 0.60$. Criterion reliability imposes an upper limit on the possible correlation between test and outcome. Nothing can correlate with the outcome measure better than it correlates with itself. Correlations can be recalculated to correct for criterion reliability, and to indicate how much predictable variance they account for. This is routinely done in personnel research, but not in personality research.

Validity generalization analysis corrects for sampling error, restricted range and criterion reliability to estimate the *true validity* of measures of individual differences. Reanalysis of Ghiselli's (1966) data on mental ability tests found their true validity typically about twice as great as their observed or uncorrected validity (Cook, 1988; Schmidt and Hunter, 1977). Ghiselli's observed uncorrected average validities hovered below the 0.30 barrier, whereas estimated true validities often exceeded 0.60. Reanalysis of Mann's (1959) review of leadership (Lord *et al.*, 1986) finds a substantial true correlation between leadership and intelligence ($r = 0.52$), but poorer results, still falling short of the 0.30 barrier, for adjustment ($r = 0.24$), dominance ($r = 0.21$), extraversion ($r = 0.15$). Barrick and Mount (1991) combined the data of 117 researches on personality and job performance, and found that the broad class of traits they grouped as conscientiousness predicts performance in every type of work: professionals, police, managers, sales and skilled/semi-skilled. The broad class of extraversion predicts for managers and sales. The broad classes of emotional stability, agreeableness and openness to experience aren't related to proficiency in any area of work. The size of the correlations, even after correcting for every limitation of the data, including the reliability of the tests themselves, is disappointing – 0.23 at most. Perhaps the analysis allowed research using bad personality tests, of which there are many, to swamp a minority of studies using better tests, of which there are relatively few. It may be better to follow Hough's approach, and analyse each personality test separately.

THEORETICAL DEFENCES OF TRAIT THEORY

Some personality theorists accuse Mischel of attacking a 'straw man' trait theory, and argue it's absurd to expect a single trait to predict the same behaviour across a large number of people with near-perfect accuracy (Alker, 1972). A subtler approach is needed – one approaching the subtlety of human personality.

Multiple regression

If a single trait doesn't predict behaviour well enough, perhaps a combination of traits will. Assessment psychologists rarely restrict themselves to one single trait, but usually make their predictions from a combination of scores. Individual scales of the California Psychological Inventory predict creativity in architects to a fairly modest extent, from $R = 0.19$ to 0.31. However, a combination of the best three scales did considerably better – $R = 0.47$ (Hall and MacKinnon, 1969). There are regressions based on combinations of five or six CPI scores, for predicting whether someone will finish school or college, whether someone is a good risk for parole, whether they have a *Type A personality* that increases their risk of heart attack, or whether they would make a good doctor, scientist or policeman (Gough, 1987). Multiple regressions can easily capitalize on chance, so they 'shrink' when calculated again on a second set of data; hence they should always be *cross-validated*. (The value of $R = 0.47$ for creative architects was cross-validated, and did shrink considerably, from an original $R = 0.57$.)

Moderator variables

Willingness to take risks was very extensively researched in the 1960s. One finding soon emerged with depressing predictability: different risk-taking measures correlated very poorly (Kogan and Wallach, 1964), casting doubt on the very existence of the trait. However, more careful analysis showed risk-taking measures correlated very well for highly anxious and highly defensive individuals, but not at all for low-anxiety, low-defensiveness subjects. Anxiety and defensiveness are a *moderator variable* for risk-taking. Gender sometimes works as a moderator variable. The dominance scale of the California Psychological Inventory has modest success in predicting who will assume control in a discussion between two persons (Megargee, 1972) – unless one is male and the other female, in which case the male tends to exert more influence than his dominance score predicts, and the female less (Davis and Gilbert, 1989). A series of studies have sought moderator variables in the correlation between self-ratings and peer-ratings; under what special circumstances will someone's peers describe them as they describe themselves? Analysis of eight studies (Zuckerman *et al.*, 1988) finds agreement is greater when subjects describe their own behaviour as consistent, when they describe the trait as having relevance for them, and when behaviour is observable. The three moderator variables in turn moderate each other; self-peer agreement is far greater when all three moderators are present, while the absence of any one greatly reduces agreement.

Person × situation

A moderator variable means one trait interacts with another. 'Person × situation' means personality interacts with time and place. Moos (1969) studied eight simple pieces of behaviour in six settings; his results are shown in Table 3.5.

Table 3.5 *Proportion of variance in observed behaviour accounted for by person, 'situation', 'person × situation', and error (Moos, 1969)*

Action	Person	Situation	Person × situation	Error
Hand and arm movement	16.8	11.9	31.9	39.4
Foot and leg movement	27.4	10.0	26.7	35.9
Scratch	30.7	13.1	24.5	31.6
General movement and shifting	17.3	1.4	47.1	34.1
Nod yes	4.2	42.9	33.5	19.4
Smile	35.3	3.6	35.4	25.6
Talk	10.5	68.3	13.9	7.4
Smoke	41.9	7.1	20.7	30.9

- there were individual differences in every behaviour studied, but,

- individuals accounted for more variability of some behaviours than others – over 40 per cent for smoking but only 4 per cent for nodding yes.

- the time and place also determined how people behaved, and,

- the influence of time and place varied for different pieces of behaviour, accounting for 68 per cent of the variance in talking but only 7 per cent in smoking.

- there was an interaction between people, and time and place, such that, for example, subject number 10 scratched a lot during group therapy, whereas subject number 3 did his scratching during his 'intake assessment', and finally,

- this interaction was larger for some sorts of behaviour than for others, being greatest for 'general movement and shifting' and least for talking.

This not entirely surprising set of findings set the pattern of much personality research during the 1970s and early 1980s. Two related issues were researched: the influence of the time and place (situation); and the interaction of situation with individual differences – interactionism or person × situation.

Traits as genotypes

Traits express themselves complexly, interacting both with other traits and internal factors such as moods, and with the constraints of the outside world. A very crude trait model (Figure 3.4) – cruder than any ever seriously proposed – requires an aggressive person to perform every aggressive act listed, from punching their neighbour to kicking the office cat. Yet, runs the genotype argument, that isn't what an aggressive person is like; in reality the expression (or *phenotype*) of the aggressive disposition (or *genotype*) depends on a variety of

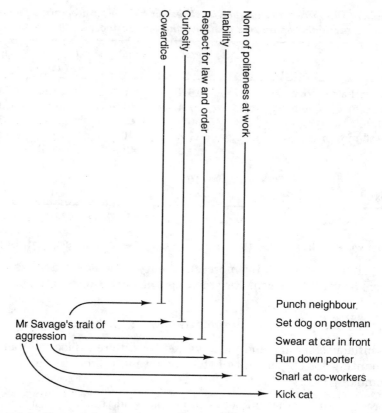

Figure 3.4   *Supposed genotypic trait of aggression.*

internal and external factors. Mr Savage's urge to punch his neighbour is inhibited by the realization that his neighbour is bigger than him (cowardice/realistic self-preservation). His urge to set the dog on the postman conflicts with his need to get his post (curiosity/greed). Mr Savage doesn't swear at the car ahead in the queue of traffic because it's a police car (respect for law and order). Mr Savage would like to run down the porters at the factory car park, but they're out of reach (lack of opportunity). He'd like to growl and snap at his colleagues but everyone is always sickeningly nice to each other at work (rule and custom). So far Mr Savage's trait of aggressiveness hasn't had a chance to show itself and a simple-minded investigator might have concluded it didn't exist. Then in comes the office cat, and there's nothing to stop Mr Savage showing his true nature, so the cat gets kicked.

  Research on aggression gives the best confirmation of the genotype argument. Fantasy aggression correlates 0.43 with overt agression in boys whose mothers encouraged aggression, but −0.41 in boys whose mothers discouraged it (Lesser, 1957), the implication being that fantasy aggression serves as a substitute for the boys who couldn't express open aggression. Other research finds high positive correlations between overt and fantasy aggression for boys with no inhibitions about anxiety, but fairly high negative correlations for boys with strong inhibitions on aggression (Olweus, 1974). Unfortunately the genotype argument doesn't work as well for other traits. It's difficult to find examples of complex relations between traits and behaviours, and it's very difficult to find ones that will replicate. The model in Figure 3.4 has other problems; it recklessly multiplies entities: cowardice, curiosity, respect for authority, all of which have to be measured reliably before the model can be tested. And it's too easy to generate different sets of traits: cowardice or self-preservation? curiosity or greed?

Individual structure

Allport died the year before Mischel's critique, but his answers can all be found in his 1937 and 1961 books. For example, concerning the Hartshorne and May study: 'Child A steals pennies because he has a consistent trait of bravado based upon his admiration for . . . gangsters; child B steals because he has a persistent interest in tools and mechanics that drives him to buy more equipment than he can honestly afford. Child E lies (about his cheating) because he is afraid of hurting the feelings of the teacher whom he adores; child F lies because he is greedy for praise'. (Allport, 1937). The children behaved consistently – by their standards but not by Hartshorne and May's. The child sees cheating and doing well at maths as 'pleasing the teacher', whereas Hartshorne and May see lying and cheating as equivalent, and the child as inconsistent.

Even behaviours that are manifestations of the same trait can appear inconsistent through *individual structure*. Bem and Allen (1974) give the example of two lecturers, who both have a trait of friendliness, which shapes behaviour towards students in lectures, seminars and social gatherings. Lecturer A is friendly on social occasions, formal and distant at lectures, and in between during seminars; lecturer B, by contrast, is at his friendliest during lectures, and at his most distant and formal at social gatherings. Measure friendliness at each occasion, correlate across subjects, and a zero correlation results: 'the traditional trait-based research study , will yield evidence of cross-situational consistency only if the individuals in the researcher's sample agree with the investigator's *a priori* claim that the sampled behaviours and situations belong in a common equivalence class and only if the individuals agree among themselves on how to scale those behaviours and situations'. (Bem and Allen, 1974) Lanning (1988) introduces the notions of *evocativeness* and *scalability*, through which Bem and Allen's example might be reduced to an orderly and measurable state. Particular occasions evoke a certain level of friendliness, defined by how people in general react; a library doesn't evoke very much, whereas a party evokes a lot. If someone's friendliness conforms to this average pattern – more friendly at parties than in libraries – it is scalable. So long as traits are scalable, a friendliness score, plus information about the evocativeness of occasions, will give a fairly accurate prediction of behaviour.

Metatraits

Allport (1937) reanalysed Dudycha's punctuality data, and found some students were consistently punctual, or unpunctual, while others weren't. Allport argued that punctuality was a genuine trait for some students, the ones whose behaviour was consistently punctual or unpunctual, but wasn't a genuine trait for others; they arrived on time, or not, depending on chance, luck or outside circumstance, but not because they had a trait. Allport's reanalysis was revived many years later as the *metatrait hypothesis*. A metatrait is the 'trait of having a particular trait'. The consistently punctual student in Dudycha's research has the metatrait of punctuality, and is 'traited'; the inconsistently punctual student hasn't the metatrait, and is 'untraited'. Metatraits should be better predictors of behaviour, because the picture isn't being confused by people who don't really have the trait. Baumeister and Tice (1988) report correlations of around 0.50 for traited subjects, but zero correlations for untraited subjects.

Most metatrait measures are based on consistency in answering questionnaires. Consistent responding can't be used in conventional endorsement format 'true/false' questionnaires, because responding consistently necessarily means having an extreme score; subjects get average scores on questionnaires by answering 'inconsistently'. Metatrait questionnaires use 9- or 10-point rating scales to allow subjects both to answer consistently – e.g. four or five throughout – and to get average scores. Bem and Allen (1974), however, use *ipsatized variance ratios*, meaning that consistency is estimated for one trait, relative to three others, within each subject. But subject A's most consistent trait could be less consistent than subject B's least consistent. Bem and Allen also used a simple self-rating of the type 'How consistently irritable are you?'; this is likely to be unreliable, because it's a single-item test, as well as presupposing subjects possess insight into their consistency or lack of it. A genuinely punctual person does more than arrive everywhere on time; he or she judges people in terms of actual and expected arrival times. Figures 2.1 and 2.2 show that Allport's trait model includes readiness to perceive things in certain ways. This part of the trait can be measured too, giving another set of metatrait measures that aren't based on consistency of behaviour. Chapter 6 describes Repertory Grid and other perceptual measures of personality.

Conclusion

Replies to Mischel's critique all argue that traits determine behaviour in a complex way that takes account of other traits, external constraints and individual structure of traits. To predict someone's behaviour, one must construct an individual model of their traits and their social world. Clinical psychologists and psychiatrists try to achieve an understanding of the person as an individual, but there's no proof individual accounts are more successful than ones based on common traits and factors (Meehl, 1954); clinical accounts of personality are no better at predicting specific outcomes than combinations of personality scores or biographical details. This implies descriptions of personality in terms of individual traits prove no more useful than descriptions using common traits.

ALTERNATIVES TO TRAIT THEORY

Situationism
Sociologists and social psychologists argue that behaviour is shaped from without by social forces, not from within by traits. Behaviourists think in much the same way, seeing the stimulus rather than social forces as what causes behaviour. These alternative approaches are called *situationism* and *interactionism*. The changes Hugh Thomas detected in Rudolf Hess's behaviour wouldn't surprise either school of thought. Hess's circumstances had changed drastically, so naturally his behaviour would too. On 9 May 1941 he was deputy leader of victorious Germany; on 11 May he was a helpless prisoner in the hands of his enemies. Lectures on homoeopathic medicine that attracted sycophantic interest in Berlin entirely failed to impress his captors. Changes in what he ate and how he ate it could reflect a first encounter with real hunger. His apparent intellectual deterioration is harder to explain, unless one argues his first contact with professional politicians showed him up for the intellectual lightweight he'd always been. A disappearing knowledge of tennis and the extinction of irritating mannerisms are odd, but hardly sufficient to prove Thomas's case.

'Situationists' believe that there's no such thing as personality; people are all puppets dancing on strings variously pulled by other people, social forces, past experience or the whims of fate. Barker and Wright (1954) give a very detailed account of the times and places people find themselves in; they catalogued 2030 separate *behaviour settings* in a small town in Kansas. (This meant there were nearly three times as many 'situations' as persons, the town's population numbering 707; 'situational' explanations aren't going to be any shorter than ones centred on people.) But describing how time and place affect behaviour doesn't entail denying individual differences. As Endler and Magnusson (1976) note in their review, no one actually takes such a radically 'situationist' view, which is just as well, since it's patently untenable. People do differ in all sorts of ways, mental as well as physical.

Person × situation
More moderate critics argue that individual differences are much less important than 'situational' factors. Behaviour depends on both individual and 'situation', but 'situation' accounts for much more variance. Interactionism – as this is called – sounds profound, but really says very little; behaviour can't be a function of much else besides person and situation. The proposition that situation accounts for more variance in behaviour than person has been the focus of a lot of research since Mischel argued for the poor predictive power of trait measures. Person × situation analyses of the type pioneered by Moos (1969) have

proliferated. Most, like Moos, partition variance between persons, situations and their interaction. Most, unlike Moos, use questionnaires or self-ratings, not observations of actual behaviour. Person × situation analyses have been reported for aggression, anxiety, hostility, temptation and interpersonal behaviour (Bowers, 1974). Endler and Hunt (1966) add a third factor to the person × situation design, namely *mode*; their subjects reported anxiety experienced in 11 situations, then distinguish 14 modes of experiencing it – perspiration, nausea, accelerated heart rate etc. Mode accounts for some variance, as does person, situation, person × situation, person × mode, etc.

Critics fail to understand what person × situation studies prove, still less which particular model of personality they cause one to reject. Situation and person × situation usually account for more variance than person, which implies that knowing where someone is might often be more useful than knowing who they are, especially when predicting relatively trivial pieces of behaviour like standing or sitting, or talking as opposed to being silent. Such estimates of variance are always local, and apply only to the range of situations sampled, and the detail with which they are specified. So listing 12 different charities, as opposed to 'gives to charity', increases the proportion of variance accounted for by situation and person × situation, by allowing subjects to express their preferences for different charities. Adding a third factor to the analysis, such as mode, allows the investigator to partition up the variance still further. Research could continue splitting off sections of personality in this fashion, until 'person' was effectively eliminated as a source of variance. 'Situation', by contrast, is left unanalysed, as little more than all reliable variance unaccounted for by persons, which is possibly why it often appears to account for so much. So long as 'situation' is left as a ragbag factor that covers everything that isn't an individual difference, it's arguable that neither understanding of behaviour nor ability to predict it are going to improve much.

One could argue that person × situation studies prove little except that analysis of variance is very useful for analysing variance; such studies certainly don't contradict any genuine theory of personality. No one has ever argued that people behave with complete disregard for where they are or who they're with. Wind up the clockwork Mr Savage, and he'll hit and kick everything, or nothing, that happens to be within range at the time. No sane person acts with complete disregard for where they are, or who they're with: 'A soldier, for example, ordinarily expresses his aggressiveness towards the enemy differently than he would be aggressive with his wife. Only a probably deranged individual in such circumstances would booby trap his wife's hair brush' (Alker, 1972). Person × situation studies usually find the largest slice of the variance pie is error (Sarason *et al.*, 1975); the person slice, by contrast, is usually fairly small (just as the variance accounted for by the 'typical 0.30 correlation' is 10 per cent or less). This is somehow felt to reflect doubt on the notion of personality. But what other result could one reasonably expect? Suppose a test of aggressiveness did predict 75 per cent of the variance in aggressive behaviour: wouldn't it have to be very short-term, and very trivial – at the level of asking 'Will you punch that person if he or she spits in your eye?'

Habits in place of traits?

Alker (1972) argues traits are just bundles of person × situation interactions. Aggression means a soldier blowing up the enemy, and shouting at a spouse, and kicking the cat. But what holds the bundle together? Allport thought it was a common 'neuropsychic mechanism'. But this common element is elusive; it can't be proved to exist by simple correlational methods, and ascribing it a complex existence, as in the genotype argument, means postulating an uncomfortably large number of unobservable entities.

Perhaps the solution lies in reversing perspective; instead of assuming behaviour is consistent across many occasions, assume that it's specific until it's proved to have greater generality (Bem, 1972a). The 0.30 correlation should be viewed against a baseline of an expected 0.00, not an expected 1.00. Personality then becomes a large set of person × situation interactions, or as Allport more elegantly put it, a bundle of habits.

THE prisoner of Spandau died in 1988, aged 93. Soon after, Hugh Thomas published a new edition of his book, arguing that Hess's double had in his turn been murdered, to prevent him revealing damaging secrets when Mikhail Gorbachev reversed the Soviet Union's long-standing refusal to consider releasing Hess.

Detailed examination of Thomas's evidence unearthed some awkward facts. The original hospital records of the real Hess's rifle bullet wound described the scar as 'pea-sized' – small enough to be hard to find 50 years later. Voiceprints of the prisoner, recorded at his trial in Nuremburg in 1947, and of the indisputably real Hess, recorded at a rally in Nuremburg in 1936, both showed the same, very distinctive, high-pitched voice.

Thomas's best bit of evidence – the missing scar – suddenly looked much less convincing, while another precisely measurable individual difference – voice – seemed to prove the prisoner was Hess.

Below the Surface 1

The Biological Line

TRAIT and factor approaches have proved moderately successful. Their predictive powers are limited, but real — which is more than can be said for many other techniques of psychological assessment. Their contribution to therapy is also modest but real; the MMPI and measures derived from it have been in daily use for nearly 60 years. The trait approach succeeds in quantifying the lay person's or clinician's concepts, but could be criticized for failing to make much contribution to understanding personality. Trait theory's defenders argue that even capturing how the lay person or the clinician assesses is a significant advance.

The factor approach, as exemplified by Cattell, but not forgetting Eysenck, Guilford and others, improves on the lay person's view of personality by devising standard statistical methods of determining how many major sources of individual differences there are. When applied to personality, the factor approach gives disappointingly inconsistent results, compared with its outstanding success in making sense of intellectual abilities.

Hence the need for a route below the surface, to a source of order and consistency. The first such route runs through learning approaches, to biological differences in temperament. Historically, the trait approach came under attack from learning theorists almost as soon as it was first stated, and certainly before its best measures had been devised. Watson was convinced over 60 years ago that personality existed only as learned habits and learned fears; his views have since been developed by Dollard, Miller, Skinner and Bandura.

The learning model does not in itself reveal any hidden sources of consistency; in fact it minimizes consistency, and regards personality as no more than a bundle of habits. Its only source of consistency lies in a few simple mechanisms of learning and conditioning, not intrinsically different from ones that can be studied in animals.

The terminus of the biological line gives hope of a very simple and very definite account of human personality, not in terms of what people learn, or of the mechanisms by which they learn it, but in terms of their readiness to learn. Eysenck's theory develops beyond that, and argues for temperamental differences based on the nervous system, and affecting learning, perception, attention and personality. Eysenck's theory, if correct, suggests human personality has three main dimensions of difference, each of which can be measured biologically.

CHAPTER 4

Brave New World?

Learning and Habit Models

IN Aldous Huxley's fictional twenty-second-century Britain, children of the Delta caste are presented with books and flowers, but when they touch either, alarm bells sound and the floor delivers painful electric shocks. Unsurprisingly they soon become frightened of both books and flowers. Why, asks one of a class of visiting Alphas, make it impossible for them to like flowers? 'He could see quite well why you couldn't have lower-caste people wasting the Community's time over books, and that there was always the risk of them reading something which might undesirably decondition one of their reflexes', but why flowers? On grounds of high economic policy, comes the answer. Once upon a time, Deltas, Gammas and even Epsilons had been conditioned to like flowers and nature, so they travelled to the countryside at every opportunity and consumed a lot of transport. 'And didn't they consume transport?' asks the student. 'Quite a lot' replies the director, 'but nothing else'.

Huxley's psychology is all wrong, for he proposes 200 pairings of flowers, books and shock to establish the aversion; modern research on traumatic avoidance learning suggests one might be quite sufficient. But what of the basic idea – is it feasible? Some psychologists at the time certainly thought so, and others since have devised techniques for controlling behaviour and shaping personality. Huxley had heard of Pavlov, for the scene is set in the 'neo-Pavlovian Conditioning Rooms'. Pavlov's conditioning research had inspired some of his followers to propose general models for explaining and controlling human behaviour. Behaviourism's founder, John B. Watson, who saw the newborn child as a blank slate on which only learning could write, had issued his famous challenge: 'Give me a dozen healthy infants, well-formed, and my own specified world to bring them up in and I'll guarantee to take any one at random and train him to become any type of specialist I might select – doctor, lawyer, artist, merchant, chief, and, yes, even into beggarman and thief' (J.B. Watson, 1925).

Theories of personality that emphasize learning are variously called *stimulus-response* theories, *habit* theories or *social behaviourism*, and have been proposed by Miller and Dollard (1941), Skinner (1953) and his followers, Bandura and Walters (1963), and more recently Mischel (1968, 1973). Their accounts differ in detail, but have five linked common features:

1. they see personality as 'bundles of habits', and do not expect to find generalized dispositions at the level of traits and factors, so,

2. they are unconcerned with the structure of adult personality, because every personality will be a unique configuration of habits, and

3. hence they rarely seek to develop personality tests.

4. they concentrate on the development of personality, and on upbringing and childhood.

5. they emphasize that behaviour can be changed.

Learning theory accounts differ on some points of principle. Miller and Dollard admit the existence of *drives*, both *primary* (hunger) and *secondary* (desire for money), whereas Skinner austerely avoids postulating any intervening variables. Bandura moves away from models based on rats, and emphasizes human ability to learn by watching others. Mischel goes one stage further to argue that people respond to what they see, not what's there, developing a cognitive learning theory.

HABITS AND HOW TO ACQUIRE THEM

One of my cats has learned a very good way of causing me or my wife to get up and let him out; he starts tearing pieces off the wallpaper just by the door – an illustration of Thorndike's Law of Effect. Thorndike (1898) shut a cat in a cage whose door would open when the cat pushed a concealed latch; the cat roamed about the cage pawing things until by chance it pushed the latch and got out. With practice the cat got quicker and quicker at pushing the latch, allowing Thorndike to state his Law of Effect: responses which are rewarded are learned while ones which are punished are abandoned. Rewards or *reinforcements* form habits; punishments or *negative reinforcements* eliminate them. If I threw something at my cat instead of opening the door, he'd probably stop tearing the wallpaper.

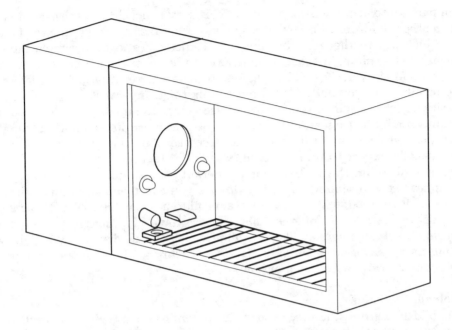

Figure 4.1 *A Skinner box, showing the lever the rat presses, lights for discrimination learning, and the tube for delivering the food pellet.*

Most research on animal learning uses rats or pigeons instead of cats, and has often used the *Skinner box* (Figure 4.1). When the animal presses or pecks a bar, the apparatus delivers a pellet of food; the animal soon learns to press the lever repeatedly. This is called *operant conditioning*. Skinner saw his box as a model of human behaviour and personality. The animal rewarded for pressing the bar learns to keep on pressing; the child rewarded – by sweet or word of praise – for saying 'please' learns to say 'please'. The parent moulds the child's behaviour by creating habits. The pre-school child is almost entirely dependent on its parents, so perhaps they have the power to realize at least some of John B. Watson's ambitions.

Generalization and discrimination
A rat that has learned to press the lever when it hears C sharp will also press when it hears C or C flat. The child rewarded for talking to mother and father may *generalize* the habit to other adults. If the child's readiness to talk generalizes widely, it becomes almost a trait of talkativeness. But learning theorists don't expect unlimited generalization, and argue that behaviour in one setting often won't predict behaviour in another. Generalization gradients on simple stimulus dimensions, like the pitch of a tone, are fairly predictable in rats; human generalization gradients are more idiosyncratic. A child's talkativeness may generalize

from parents to other adults, or may not. It may generalize to other adults, but not to other children. In humans, responses generalize along gradients of meaning, which are further-reaching and more idiosyncratic than simple physical dimensions like pitch. Mischel's cognitive learning theory of personality develops this point. Moreover, the child's readiness to generalize is often checked. The child who readily talks to adults is told not to talk to strangers. The boy encouraged to 'stick up for himself' at school isn't praised for bullying his younger sister, and certainly not for hitting out at his parents. But the more discriminations the child learns, the less consistent its behaviour becomes. This is why learning theorists don't usually expect to find personality traits or factors.

As stated so far, the contribution of operant conditioning to personality may not appear very profound. Everyone knows you can teach an animal tricks by giving it bits of food, just as you can train children to say 'please' and 'thank you' by praise and rebuke. Skinner and his followers have a lot more to say about how to form and change personality, not all of which can be dismissed so lightly as 'telling us what we knew already'. Besides, Skinner (1951) thinks most people don't even know how to teach animals tricks.

Unintended learning
The child is learning habits, even when parents aren't trying to teach them. Parents who like their children to talk a lot and run about a lot may rear talkative, active children; parents who prefer them to sit quietly and read a book may rear quiet passive ones — not on purpose, but as a by-product of their quest for a quiet life. Skinnerians also argue that deliberate efforts to mould a child's behaviour often don't work, because the parents go about it the wrong way. Often parents of 'difficult' children despair of persuading them to keep quiet or stop biting themselves; no matter how many times they tell the child not to, it keeps on doing it. Skinnerians define reinforcement as anything that increases the frequency of a response; if telling a child not to do something, or even punishing the child, results in the child continuing the unwanted action, it follows that reprimands or punishment are somehow rewarding. But why should punishment encourage the behaviour it's intended to eliminate?

When he extended his model to human behaviour, Skinner found he had to list a set of *generalized reinforcers*, including approval, affection and attention. Any attention from the parent, even criticism or blows, may be better than none. But if behaviour is reinforced by attention, it can be extinguished by inattention. Therefore the parent should ignore the child when it misbehaves, or even send it to an empty room to emphasize the withdrawal of attention. Parents should also reward the child with attention when it's not misbehaving. Too often parents ignore the child as long it behaves itself, so misbehaviour becomes the child's only way of attracting attention. This line of reasoning has inspired several case studies of difficult children (Williams, 1959) and has even found its way into 'parenting manuals'. Many parents are suspicious of Skinnerian advice, and claim that they don't want to bring up their children the way Skinner trains his rats.

Skinner argues that parents are necessarily continuously shaping their child's personality, so they might as well do it consciously and efficiently.

Superstitious behaviour

Sometimes habits are formed entirely by accident. In one of Skinner's experiments he rewarded the pigeon with a food pellet every 30 seconds whether it pressed the lever or not; the birds learned whatever movement they happened to be making when the pellet came, and so developed strange postures and bizarre dance routines. Skinnerians call this *superstitious behaviour*, and detect a human analogy in lucky mascots, good luck rituals, or idiosyncratic unnecessary movements at times of stress. Herrnstein (1966) suggests that some neurotic symptoms – tics, obsessions and compulsions – have the same origin.

Intervals and schedules

Common sense may already know that rewarded acts are repeated, and punished acts abandoned, but common sense knows less about the most effective forms of reward and punishment. The reward should follow the action, not precede it, and should follow soon after. If the time between bar-press and reward in the Skinner box exceeds 1 second, no learning takes place. Very short intervals are usually needed for rats or dogs to learn anything, except in certain special cases. Animals learn to avoid food that makes them sick, even though ill-effects may take hours to become apparent (Rozin and Kalat, 1971). If an action is rewarded every time, the habit is acquired faster, but lost equally fast when unrewarded. A habit rewarded sometimes but not always – *partial reinforcement* – takes longer to acquire, but lasts longer. In the real world most habits are formed this way; the parent cannot always be on hand to reward or punish the child's behaviour. Skinner (B.F. Skinner and Ferster, 1957) developed this point at some length, distinguishing various *schedules of reinforcement*. In a *fixed-ratio* schedule the rat is rewarded every 5th or 100th bar press, a form of control Skinnerians see as analogous to piecework in industry; it establishes high rates of responding. In a *variable-ratio* schedule, the rat gets rewarded every 10th bar press on average, so the reward is unpredictable. Skinnerians see this as analogous to door-to-door selling, or gambling; the more you try, the more rewards you get, but you never know when the next is coming. Habits created by variable-ratio schedule are very durable; parents who want their children always to say 'please' and 'thank you' should reward occasionally and unpredictably.

Shaping

In his own childhood Skinner saw a circus act in which pigeons performed remarkable tricks; he later learned how to teach birds to play table-tennis or ten-pin bowling. Playing bowls required the pigeon to make a sidewards jerk of the beak, a movement pigeons rarely, if ever, make spontaneously. Skinner started rewarding responses that resembled however slightly what was required; he then restricted reward to responses closer and closer to what he wanted. 'In a few minutes' the bird was bouncing the ball off the sides of the box like a champion squash player. Shaping can be very successful with mute psychiatric patients, who haven't spoken to anyone for years. At first the patient is rewarded – with chewing gum – just for looking at the experimenter; next the patient has moved his or her lips, then grunted, and finally said 'gum please' (Isaacs *et al.*, 1960).

LEARNING EMOTIONS

In Pavlov's experiments on *classical conditioning*, dogs learned to respond to a bell as if it were food; after a number of pairings of bell with food (bell first – half-second wait – then food), the bell alone would cause the dog to salivate. Classical conditioning is passive; the conditioned response is involuntary. Classical conditioning in humans uses *eye-blink* or *GSR* methods. In eye-blink conditioning, a puff of air at the eyeball causes the unconditioned response of blinking. In GSR conditioning, an electric shock or a loud noise is used to frighten or startle the subject, its effect measured by changes in heart rate, blood pressure, respiration, or electrical activity of the skin. Watson (J. B. Watson and Rayner, 1921) created a conditioned fear in a 1-year-old boy – little Albert. While Albert was playing with a white rat, Watson struck an iron bar with a hammer, making a very loud noise that frightened Albert. Albert became afraid of rats, and his fear generalized to a rabbit, a dog, a Santa Claus mask and Watson's hair. Conditioned fears generalize readily, last a long time, sometimes indefinitely, and can be created by a single event. Scoline is a drug that's used, with anaesthetics and tranquillizers, to cause complete paralysis during electroconvulsive therapy and prevent the patient breaking any bones. Campbell *et al.* (1964) used it without anaesthetics or tranquillizers, but paired with a tone, on conscious volunteers, who found themselves unable to move or breathe for 90 seconds, and thought they were dying; the volunteers said they found it more frightening than anything in their World War II combat experience. The tone continued to cause fear for 100 further presentations; the fear did not extinguish.

Little Albert left hospital before Watson could try to cure his fear of rats, so presumably remained afraid of rats, rabbits and Santa Claus masks for some time after, perhaps indefinitely. (Watson certainly thought he'd created a lasting fear, and speculated how Freudians might explain it 20 years on.) Albert's fear could have had all sorts of consequences, far outlasting the fear itself. A child afraid of rats, dogs and rabbits might be teased and bullied at school, which might in turn create a school phobia. Or the child might devise elaborate ways of avoiding dogs to conceal his or her fear. (Watson's experiment was very unethical; psychologists today observe much stricter standards for research on human subjects.)

Preparedness?
Eye-blink conditioning is a notoriously difficult phenomenon to demonstrate; the room must be quiet, the interval between tone and air-puff exactly right, and even

then many subjects fail to condition. Conditioned fears, by contrast, are very easy to establish if the right *unconditioned stimulus* is used. People frequently develop fears of cats, dogs, spiders, snakes or the dark, but hardly ever of motor cars, which cause far more death, pain and injury. Seligman (1971) reintroduced the concept of instinct, discarded by Watson, but called it *preparedness*. Insects, snakes, the dark, and the wide open spaces were dangerous to our remote ancestors, so individuals who were prepared to learn rapidly to fear them survived. Evolution hasn't had time to prepare humans for the motor car.

Punishment

In the 1950s a survey of American child-rearing practices found only 1 per cent of parents never used physical punishment. About one in five used 'spanking' as their main technique of discipline; the rest used it occasionally. The working class tended to use physical punishment more (Sears *et al.*, 1957). Informed opinion can't decide whether punishment is a good way of moulding children.

Thorndike's Law of Effect states that punishment stamps out responses, as rewards stamp them in. Skinner, however, considered punishment ineffective; at best it merely suppresses the behaviour punished, by causing emotional upset. The results of Sears *et al.*'s survey were widely taken as support for Skinner's view: children whose parents used physical punishment tended to be less well-behaved, and more aggressive. In fact the correlation was fairly small, and the direction of cause unclear; commentators assumed punishment caused bad behaviour, but it's equally possible badly behaved children attract more physical punishment.

Solomon (1964) argued that psychologists were letting their biases about punishment blind them to the facts, and reminded them of an early study showing that rats learned discriminations faster and more thoroughly if the wrong response was punished, as well as the right one being rewarded. Lovaas and Simmons (1969) describe curing a child of self-mutilation in a few minutes, after nurses had spent years trying and failing. Lovaas used an electric cattle prod every time the child started biting or tearing itself, and reports that a few shocks sufficed. The nurses' well-meant efforts were actually rewarding the self-mutilation by showing concern and rushing up whenever the child started. Psychologists remain wary of recommending punishment in rearing children, arguing that it can cause anxiety or passivity and depression. Animals given powerful electric shocks which they can't escape develop *learned helplessness*; in a later phase of the experiment, when they could escape the shock by jumping out of the box, they don't (Seligman, 1975). Punishment should only be used when the child understands clearly what to do to escape or avoid it. Another study by Lovaas illustrates *escape learning*. He taught schizophrenic twins to stop temper tantrums and public masturbation, and respond to his voice, by giving them an electric shock which continued until they stopped misbehaving and answered his call (Lovaas *et al.*, 1965). Other dangers of punishment, according to its critics, are that it can be reinforcing if it's the only attention the child gets, and that it can easily serve as a model to the child.

DEVELOPMENTAL HURDLES

Skinner's account of personality development is ahistorical; personality is the present sum total of a person's habits. Habits come and go as the pattern of rewards changes. Hence Skinnerians attribute less significance to childhood than the most personality theorists. What happens in the first five years of life is important at the time but not necessarily later on. In contrast, Dollard and Miller's (1950) learning/habit approach organizes itself around a common set of developmental hurdles: feeding, toilet training, sexuality, aggression and sex-role learning. The child has to learn to:

- eat what he or she is given, when he or she is given it (including stopping breast-feeding when the mother decides to);

- urinate and defecate at the appointed time and place;

- follow the parents' requirements for control of sexual expression (which may mean suppressing all expression);

- control his or her temper, and show aggression only when, and to whom, the parents approve;

- adopt the behaviour, values, outlook, attitudes of the same sex parent.

Observant readers may detect some similarity between these five hurdles and Freud's psychosexual stages (Chapter 9); Dollard and Miller's learning theory account was written as a 'tidied-up' and testable version of Freud's theory of development. Dollard and Miller broaden Freud's interpretations of childhood events, besides adding aggression to the list of hurdles. Thus breast-feeding and weaning include food and feeding in general, which can be a problem long after weaning. The Oedipus conflict is broadened, and split into two: the control of sexuality in general, and masturbation in particular, and the child's need to learn the right sex role. (This is a bigger problem for boys, who usually have to transfer identification from mother to father, whereas girls can usually identify with the mother uninterruptedly.)

Dollard and Miller argue that the way the parents deal with these hurdles has a lasting effect on the child. At the time they wrote their account (1950), feeding to schedule was a common practice; the child was fed every so many hours, on the dot, whether hungry or not, and not fed before then even if crying for food. Hence, Dollard and Miller argue, the child that cried for food, but was left waiting until the exact hour appointed, learned it had no control over food in particular or things in general. Such children tended to grow up with a passive and pessimistic outlook on life. By contrast, the child whose parents fed 'on demand' grew up confident in its ability to get what it wanted, and control its environment, and so became an active, optimistic person. On the same analogy, the child whose parents controlled very strictly any sexual expression tended to grow up anxious about sexual expression, and liable to develop sexual dysfunctions and neuroses. The child allowed reasonably free expression of sexual curiosity grew up without these worries, and enjoyed a normal, healthy sex life.

Two features of this account merit comment. First, adult personality isn't the shifting, formless mass of individual habits that Skinner proposes, but derives some structure from the five developmental hurdles. It might be possible to characterize adults according to how they learned to cope with sexual expression, aggression, getting food, sex-role learning and toilet training. Hence Dollard and Miller's account is historical, and does attribute structure to personality. Secondly, their account has fairly clear implications about the way children ought to be brought up; feeding to schedule is obviously 'a bad thing', as is overstrict control of sexual expression or aggression, and overstrict or premature toilet training. During this period, psychologists' ideas about child-rearing began to permeate the public consciousness and cause fads and phobias, especially in American parents. Psychology ought to influence child-rearing—but preferably after the theory has been proved, not before.

LEARNING BY OBSERVING

Skinner based his model of human personality on operant conditioning of rats and pigeons; critics argue the analogy is false. Suppose, asks Bandura (1962), people learned to drive by pure Skinnerian methods:

> As a first step our trainer, who has been carefully programmed to produce head nods, resonant hm-hms, and other verbal reinforcers, loads up with an ample supply of candy, chewing gum, and filter tip cigarettes.... Our trainer might have to wait quite a long time before the subject emits an orienting response toward the vehicle. At the moment the subject does look even in the general direction of the car, this response is immediately reinforced and gradually he begins to gaze longingly at the stationary automobile ... Eventually, through the skilful use of differential reinforcement, the trainer will teach the subject to open and close the car door. With perseverance he will move the subject from the back seat or any other inappropriate location ... until at length the subject is shaped up behind the steering wheel.

And there, as Bandura says, the trainer's problems really start. Can he shape up steering-wheel turning behaviour before they reach the first corner? Of course people don't learn to drive this way; the instructor shows them what to do, and tells them what to do. People, unlike rats and pigeons, can learn simply by watching, listening, or reading. Bandura (Bandura and Walters, 1963) emphasizes the importance of learning by observation. Cognitive learning theorists (Rotter *et al.*, 1972; Mischel, 1973) recognize that people talk and think about what they do, and about what the result will be.

The Bobo Doll experiment

A Bobo Doll is a rubber inflatable about one metre high, with a face painted on the top, and a weight in the base so it swings to and fro if struck. Bandura and Walters (1963) prepared a videotape of a woman attacking a Bobo Doll in various unusual ways; after seeing the film, children were left with the doll, and in turn filmed. Bandura showed that all children could imitate the model, but that they only did so spontaneously if the model had been rewarded for her behaviour; all had *learned* her responses from watching the film, but not all chose to *perform* them. Bandura has used the Bobo Doll method to show that children imitate the adult with power, not the one with status (Bandura *et al.*, 1963), that children don't imitate aggressive models in order to appease them (Walters and Thomas, 1963), and that children who describe the model's behaviour imitate more. Fear as well as aggression can be learned by observation. Adults watched someone who showed signs of fears after hearing a buzzer; the fear was feigned, but seeing it was enough to produce a conditioned fear in the observers (Bandura and Rosenthal, 1966). This implies children could acquire fear of thunder, or snakes, or spiders from watching their parents. Perhaps children can learn general fearfulness (or fearlessness) from observing their parents (not by inheriting the same type of nervous system – Chapter 5).

What is learned can be unlearned – a discovery that also dates back to Watson's little Albert. Watson's associate Mary Cover Jones (1924) cured a fear of furry objects – a natural fear, not one created by Watson – in a 3-year-old boy by showing him other children playing happily with furry animals. The dominating influence of psychoanalysis prevented Jones's lead being followed for many years; unlearning fears by modelling or *vicarious deconditioning* didn't come into general use until the 1960s. Bandura successfully eliminated fear of dogs in children (Bandura *et al.*, 1967), and cured snake phobia in adults (Bandura *et al.*, 1969), by showing films of models gradually approaching feared objects and eventually touching and playing with them. Psychoanalysis dismisses this as treating symptoms not the illness, and predicts *symptom substitution*; an equivalent phobia will rapidly replace the one desensitization has 'cured'.

Bandura (1977) outlines a four-stage model of learning by observation: *attention, retention, reproduction* and *motivation*. If the child doesn't notice the behaviour (attention), he or she obviously can't imitate it; if the child forgets what he or she has seen (retention), he or she can't imitate it either. Even if the child remembers the behaviour, he or she may not be able to reproduce it; most skills require practice and can't be perfected by observation alone. Finally, the child needs motivation to reproduce the behaviour; Bandura and Walter's original Bobo Doll study showed children don't imitate acts they see punished.

COGNITIVE LEARNING THEORY

With rats, the experimenter can keep very tight control of everything, and can be fairly certain what stimulus the rat is responding to. In real life, and when the subjects are people, this certainty is reduced. A real life event is complex and multi-faceted, so one may not know what aspects influence the person. People see events and other people in idiosyncratic ways, so the most thorough 'objective' description may still miss the point. Meehl (1978) offers a good example of an event that is hard to observe but very significant: 'the precise tone of voice and facial expression that a patient's father had when he was reacting to an off-colour joke that the patient innocently told at the dinner table at age 7'. An army of psychologists recording the meal in full colour could still fail to realize anything significant had happened.

Cognitive learning theory modifies the Skinnerian model to take account of language and thought, and lists five *cognitive social learning person variables*:

1. *competencies* – what you know you can do;

2. *personal constructs* – how you see things;

3. *expectancies* – what you expect to happen;

4. *subjective values* – what the outcome is worth to you;

5. *systems and plans* – how you will achieve your goal.

The Skinnerian analogy of 'man the rat' is retained, but with far greater emphasis on how the individual sees events. 'Man the cognitive rat' will press the bar, if he can; if he expects it to produce food; and if he wants food; so long as it doesn't conflict with any long-term plan, for example to persuade the experimenter he's a poor subject and terminate the experiment; and, to complete the analogy, if he sees the room as a Skinner box. If he sees it as a car-crushing plant, he'll probably leave the lever alone. Within these limits, Skinnerian principles continue to apply. Cognitive social learning theory (Mischel, 1973) allows for the differences between rats, cats, pigeons, dogs and humans, but has the major disadvantage of making itself virtually untestable. If a person fails to learn something, one concludes simply that he or she couldn't make the response, or didn't want the reward, or didn't expect a reward, or had some other plan, or saw events differently.

UPBRINGING AND PERSONALITY

Learning theory implies that the way people are brought up largely determines their personality. Every example given describes parents behaving in ways predicted to create enduring effects on the child. Common sense also assumes personality is largely shaped by the way parents treat their children. Yet convincing scientific proof is largely lacking, partly because the research is very difficult to do properly. There is a lot of research on the way parents bring up children. Becker (1964) describes two dimensions underlying the way parents treat their children: permissiveness–strictness and warmth–coldness. Later, Baumrind

(1971) distinguished authoritarian, permissive and authoritative 'parenting styles'. Authoritative parents set clear standards, expect mature behaviour, enforce rules firmly, but encourage independence and maturity in the child, communicate freely with the child, and respect the child's rights. Children of authoritative parents do better at school (Dornbusch *et al.*, 1987).

Some studies relate parents' behaviour to children's behaviour at the time (Sears *et al.*, 1957), but this isn't really relevant to adult personality. That only emerges 15 to 20 years later, which is longer than most researchers can afford to wait. Researchers have tried ingenious short-cuts, like asking college-age subjects to describe key aspects of their upbringing 15 to 20 years ago, or asking their subjects' parents. People can't remember, or don't want to, or they read their own ideas about upbringing into what they think they remember. For whatever reason, recollections of upbringing prove very inaccurate when they can be checked (Yarrow *et al.*, 1970) against contemporary records. Relatively few researches have done it the hard way by collecting data on upbringing during childhood, then following their cohort into adult life. One programme, the Cambridge Somerville follow-up, is described extensively in Chapters 10, 11 and 12.

No effect of upbringing?
Most personality theorists assume they could show a strong link between personality and upbringing, if only they could collect the right data. However, research on the heritability of personality differerences, reviewed in Chapter 5, casts some doubt on this. Quite a few studies find that shared family environment doesn't contribute anything to personality (Plomin and Daniels, 1987). Being brought up in the same home, by the same parents, apparently doesn't make people resemble each other. This excludes all the factors that generations of sociologists and educationalists have thought so vital to development: income, cultural level, neighbourhood, parental occupation, social class. It also excludes most factors that psychologist and lay person assume matter: permissiveness, warmth and discipline. Research reviewed in Chapter 5 concludes that personality is shaped by heredity, and by non-shared family environment, meaning factors that make children in the same family differ from each each other. These include:

- pregnancy and birth problems;
- accidents and illness;
- birth order and family size;
- differences in how parents treat different children;
- relations between brothers and sisters;
- different schools, teachers, sets of friends, etc.

BIRTH ORDER. Alfred Adler (1931), a follower of Freud, developed a whole series of hypotheses about birth order. The first-born is confident and secure, but only until the arrival of the second child, after which the first-born must compete for a share of parental attention and affection; this often creates insecurity, and may lead to drink problems, criminal behaviour, sexual problems. The youngest of the family is likely to be spoiled as a child, and to have problems as an adult. The second-born is always trying to out-do the first-born, so tends to be pushy and ambitious. However, a large literature on birth-order effects, reviewed by Schooler (1972), finds small, inconsistent effects, or none at all.

PARENTS. Several lines of research confirm that parents generally treat their children alike. Videotapes of mothers with successive 1-year-old children show they express the same affection, control and attention to each (Dunn *et al.*, 1985). Parents treat different siblings almost as consistently the same as they treat the same child. This isn't terribly surprising, for most parents have clear, well-worked-out ideas about how to bring up children, often tied in with their whole outlook on life. Most parents think it important to treat all their children as similarly as possible. Perhaps what look like very small differences to outsiders look very large to the children. Plomin and Daniels (1987) use a questionnaire (Sibling Inventory of Differential Experience) that asks children whether mother and father show more control or affection towards other siblings. Only 9 per cent reported 'much difference'.

SIBLINGS. Brothers and sisters see more differences in the way they treat each other; about one in five see substantial differences in closeness, jealousy, antagonism and taking care of each other. Some researchers have suggested siblings may react against each other, a process inelegantly called *de-identification*. If two sibs try to be as unlike each other as possible, they would get unusually large differences in scores on a personality test; a large survey of over 900 twin pairs, who had completed the CPI, found no such differences (Loehlin and Nichols, 1976), failing to confirm the de-identification hypothesis.

CONCLUSION. The absence of between-family effects in research on heredity implies parents can't shape their children's personality by the home they provide for them, nor by following a carefully thought-out programme of example, discipline and moulding. Personality is shaped by heredity, and by within-family effects. But within-family effects are mostly outside parents' control – pregnancy and birth problems, accident, illness – or very hard to control – sibling rivalry, friends, school, subtle differences in parental behaviour. How can these conclusions be reconciled with other research, mentioned in other chapters, that describes how upbringing or family life are linked to ambition, aggression, homosexuality, sexual deviation, alcoholism, criminality or resilience?

- Perhaps some traits can be shaped by upbringing, and others can't. However, research on aggression (Chapter 10) both describes how upbringing shapes aggression (Olweus, 1980) and reports no shared family effects in questionnaire measures of aggression (Rushton *et al.*, 1986).

- Perhaps temperament is inherited, while attitudes, values, standards, ambitions, etc. are shaped by upbringing.

- Perhaps parents can only create problems in their children, such as criminality or alcoholism.

- Perhaps research only appears to show that upbringing shapes personality. Eysenck (Rushton *et al.*, 1986) argues that most research on upbringing entirely ignores heredity and simply assumes any link between parents' behaviour and child's behaviour demonstrates parental influence at work. Suppose aggressive parents give birth to aggressive children, and bring them up aggressively, but the child's aggression is shaped by heredity, not upbringing. This is not entirely fanciful; twins brought up apart resemble each other on many traits as much as twins brought up together, which clearly implies that who brings them up, and how, makes no difference.

LIMITATIONS OF THE LEARNING/HABIT MODEL

Learning/habit explanations of personality originally looked very promising. They had a firm base in animal experimentation, which can control variables precisely and produce replicable results. However, the analogy of 'man the rat' has come to look increasingly inappropriate and unhelpful, as critics of learning/habit approaches have listed problems.

FUZZY CONCEPTS.   Learning/habit accounts lose much of their precision when translated from animals to humans. Rewards are no longer tangible and measurable – water or food pellets – but intangible and unquantifiable – approval, need to demonstrate one's competence to oneself, etc. Arguably all such *generalized reinforcers* or *higher-order drives* lead to circularity, because one has no independent proof of their existence. Notcutt (1953) equates the choice of learning theory with a preference for mechanistic and materialistic explanations; 'Materialist psychology never became more than a program. In principle, everything can be explained along these lines; but in practice the detail was so complicated that nothing was explained at all'.

HEREDITY.   Watson claimed he could mould any child into any profession, but heredity would impose limits on his efforts. Doctors and artists require abilities not everyone possesses or can acquire. Merchants and 'chiefs' (senior managers, presumably) tend to need traits, like extraversion, that are partly inherited, (Chapter 5). Learning/habit accounts of personality needn't exclude inherited factors, and some don't. Eysenck's account is partly a learning/habit one, but Eysenck emphasizes broad, inherited differences in readiness to learn, rather than the detail of what is learned and how (Chapter 5).

PASSIVE CHILDREN. Learning/habit accounts tend to assume the child is the passive recipient of the parents' attempts to shape its behaviour. As every parent knows, children are anything but passive.

AWARENESS AND REACTANCE. The rat in the Skinner box lacks any insight into events there; the human doesn't necessarily, and, having realized what is happening, can choose whether to co-operate with or react against the experimenter. (Much ingenious effort has been put into describing such choices in stimulus-response terms, but it's doubtful whether they amount to much more than verbal contortions.)

LANGUAGE AND THOUGHT. Earlier versions of the learning/habit approach ignore or underestimate the role of language and thought, based as they are on animal evidence.

LOSS OF PREDICTIVE POWER. Learning/habit accounts can be elaborated to include language and thought, and awareness, becoming cognitive social learning theory; in the process, however, they lose more of their already depleted predictive power, as apparent exceptions can be even more readily explained away.

CONDITIONING THE ONLY MECHANISM? Operant and classical conditioning can shape personality, but do they in practice, and do they alone shape it? Is little Albert the model of all human fears? Or is he a rare example of how psychologists can create an artificial fear – a fear as atypical as a wooden leg? Proving that operant and classical conditioning do shape personality, as opposed to being possibly able to, would be very difficult. Animal data don't prove the case; nor even do laboratory studies of humans; nor even demonstrations of behaviour change. A truly convincing proof would need to show that a particular person's every habit, feeling, attitude and skill had been acquired by operant learning or classical conditioning; which in turn would require more minutely detailed information than even the most comprehensive biography could provide.

OTHER TYPES OF LEARNING. Classical and operant conditioning may not be only types of learning; Kohler (1925) described *insight learning*. An ape is faced with a problem – how to reach a banana with two sticks, one too short and one out of reach – and suddenly achieves a solution – use the shorter stick to get the one which is out of reach but long enough. There is no learning curve nor any trial and error. If apes can sometimes 'see' the answer to a problem, humans certainly can. Cognitive social learning theories allow for insight learning.

Other psychologists have proposed less rational forms of complex learning. Research on *authoritarian personality* concluded that anti-semitism, dislike of blacks and political-economic conservatism are learned, but not by simple conditioning or Bandura-type modelling. Rather, the parent forces the child to suppress all feelings of aggression or sexuality, which then get displaced onto socially defined targets such as Jews or blacks (Adorno *et al.*, 1950). Argyle (1964) proposed *introjection* as a mechanism underlying the conscience, which grows out of a desire to please the parents by adopting their outlook, and isn't simply a set of conditioned reflexes, as Eysenck (1964) argues. Argyle points to the lastingness of the conscience, and its generalized standards, as distinguishing it from other sorts of learning. Critics point out it's just these characteristics of never extinguishing and generalizing very widely that Campbell *et al.* (1964) observed in conditioned fears.

CONDITIONING AS EXPLANATION OF ALL INDIVIDUAL DIFFERENCES? Operant conditioning may account for simple habits, and classical conditioning may account for fears and other emotions, but can they account for our finer feelings and higher mental processes? The lay person, as well as learning theory's critics, argues that learning theory can't explain self-concepts, ideologies or religious beliefs. People are not Catholics (or communists, or vegetarians) simply as the end-product of a conditioning process. Nevertheless, Skinner (1953) seeks to explain religion solely in terms of habits created by reinforcement. At a mundane level, the child brought up as a Roman Catholic will acquire a lot of relevant habits – saying prayers, wearing a cross, going to church. Religion is also superstitious behaviour; the priests persuade the faithful they must make a human sacrifice the third Sunday of every other month or the world will come to end. They do; it doesn't; no one sees the logical fallacy, or no one risks trying to explain it. Religion and ideology are reinforced by attention; new beliefs gain for those who propound them an interested audience. Religion may be part of a general system for controlling society, and may dispense powerful rewards and punishments. A stable social order, which religion helps support, is in itself reinforcing for many. Religions also create their own reinforcers; '[a religious] agency punishes sinful behaviour in such a way that its authority generates an aversive condition which the individual describes as a sense of sin', whereupon 'the agency then provides escape from the aversive condition through . . . absolution' (Skinner, 1953).

Skinner's analysis of religion is very dismissive. On the one hand, religion boosts the ego of the leaders; on the other hand it's a cynical exploitation of the simple-minded believers. Skinner equates the sense of guilt and sin with a rat's fear of a place where it gets electric shocks. But Skinner sees fear and escape from fear as the reality; 'sin' and 'absolution' are just rationalizations. What set of observations – to repeat the positivist challenge – could prove, or disprove, Skinner's statements about religion?

EXPLAINING ITS OWN EXISTENCE.   If religion is a set of beliefs shaped by learning, so is behaviourism. Behaviourists must logically agree that their own view of psychology is shaped by past experience. The beliefs may appear quite rational, but the behaviourists' reasons for coming to hold them could include all sorts of chance, comic or unmentionable factors: getting a place on a solidly Skinnerian psychology course, meeting their first love during a Skinner box practical, reading Freud's *Three Essays on Sexuality* in bed. Or suppose the behaviourists' beliefs were shaped by a well-designed course, using the teaching machines Skinner himself invented – then who shaped the teachers, and the people who programmed the learning machines? Skinner's theory of personality is not alone in having considerable difficulty in accounting for its own existence.

CHAPTER 5

Eysenck's Demon

A Biological Account of Personality

SUPPOSE, says Eysenck, there were a demon 'sitting near the point where the long pathways of the central nervous system enter into the lower pathways of the brain'. The demon has two levers, one marked 'excitation', the other marked 'inhibition'. 'Whenever sensory stimuli are coming in through these pathways, he presses sometimes one lever, sometimes the other, sometimes both. Stimuli produced by the levers are then sent on to the brain, where they either facilitate the passage and the interplay of the incoming neural stimuli, or suppress and inhibit them. In part, therefore, the demon acts as a kind of amplifying valve, and part as a suppressor' (Eysenck, 1965a). And suppose that some demons are right-handed and use the inhibition lever more, while others are left-handed and use the excitation lever more, while the rest use both levers equally frequently.

Eysenck offers a model of human *temperament*. His demon's preference for excitation or inhibition lever can:

- help determine how sociable and impulsive a person is;

- shape a person's political opinion;

- turn him or her into a criminal or a good radar operator;

- make his or her sex life more active and varied.

Temperament theories postulate a bodily base to personality. They are very ancient; the Greek physician Galen, writing in the second century AD,

Table 5.1   *Stages of personality description and interpretation*

1	2	3	4	5
Inherited differences in anatomical and physiological structures:	Psycho-physiological differences:	Observed differences: Experimental studies:	Personality:	Special phenomena:
	EEG	Conditioning	Extraversion/ introversion	Neurosis
Visceral brain	EMG	Learning		Crime
Reticular formation → Neocortex	GSR →	Sensory thresholds →	Neuroticism/ stability →	Accident-proneness
	Uric acid	Perception		Sexual behaviour
	Catecholamines	Motivation		

distinguished melancholic, choleric, sanguine and phlegmatic temperaments, which depend on the balance of four humours or bodily fluids. More recently, Sheldon (1942) argued that physique shapes personality; he distinguished three body types, fat, tall and thin, and muscular, which tended to go with jolly, miserable and aggressive personalities respectively. Allport (1961) defined temperament as 'susceptibility to emotional stimulation, . . . customary strength and speed of response, the quality of . . . prevailing mood.' Most modern tempera-ment theories, including Eysenck's, look to the brain and nervous system for a physical basis for personality.

Temperament models identify underlying sources of individual differences, and make very general statements about potential for aggression, or anxiety, or sociability. Once a bodily basis is identified personality can, at least in theory, be measured in the laboratory, from brain-wave patterns, response to drugs, hormone levels, eye-blink conditioning or reaction time. Some lab measures need no co-operation from the subject, and most would be hard to fake. A bodily basis is enduring and probably inherited, so estimates of adult personality can be made in early childhood, or even before the child is conceived. The suggestion that tests of brain or nervous system could identify potential criminals before they ever committed a crime strikes many as sinister, and explains why temperament theories are unpopular with many social scientists.

Eysenck thinks human personality works at a number of levels of description. He starts, at his fourth level (Table 5.1), with a conventional trait/factor approach, essentially similar to those of Allport or Cattell (Chapter 2). He is

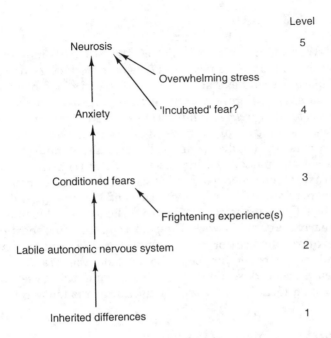

Figure 5.1   *Eysenck's five levels of description as applied to anxiety and neurosis.*

also a learning/habit theorist, but isn't so much interested in how or what people learn, as in differences in readiness to learn. Differences in readiness to learn reflect differences in psychophysiology (level 2) and ultimately in the brain and nervous system (level 1). Tracing the five levels in reverse order, someone born with a particular type of brain (level 1) will show particular patterns of brain and nervous system activity (level 2), which may predispose him or her to form conditioned fears more readily (level 3), which tends to make him or her generally more anxious (level 4), which will, other things being equal, make him or her more liable to suffer a neurotic breakdown (level 5) (Figure 5.1). But there isn't a one to one correspondence at each transition from one level to another. Some neuroses occur in people who normally experience little anxiety, but who have been subjected to overwhelming stress. People with overactive autonomic nervous systems may learn ways of controlling them, or live in a society where the pace of life is so slow that anxiety never turns into neurosis.

Unlike Allport or Cattell, Eysenck thinks personality can be described in as few as two dimensions – extraversion/introversion, and neuroticism/stability. (He later adds psychoticism, and also thinks intelligence an important dimension.) Roughly speaking, Eysenck's progress from level 4 (traits and factors) to level 1 (inherited differences) parallels the historical development of his ideas, so a short account of his work since 1940 helps illustrate the descent from the surface of personality to its biological basis.

DIMENSIONS OF PERSONALITY

During World War II, Eysenck worked at the Mill Hill military psychiatric hospital in North London (Eysenck, 1947), where he factor-analysed 39 items from 700 case histories, and extracted four factors, of which he interpreted two. One, the vertical axis in Figure 5.2, he identified as *neuroticism*; the other he initially called *hysteria–dysthymia* but later renamed *extraversion–introversion*. His 39 items were a mixture of diagnostic categories, symptoms, rather vague psychiatric observations ('badly organized personality'), and biographical facts ('married'). He set the pattern of his later work by (1) selecting small groups of extreme extraverts, introverts or neurotics and comparing them on laboratory tests such as leg persistence, manual dexterity and body sway, and (2) writing the Maudsley Medical Questionnaire (MMQ) from the items of his main neuroticism factor. At this early stage in his work, Eysenck took the same short-cut as Cattell, substituting a questionnaire for more cumbersome laboratory measures. (The MMQ acquired an extraversion scale to become the Maudsley Personality Inventory, then a social desirability scale to become the Eysenck Personality Inventory, in which form it's very widely used in personality research.)

CONDITIONABILITY AND EXTRAVERSION

So far Eysenck's theory of personality is a fairly conventional one, which uses broad descriptive categories – extraversion and neuroticism – derived from factor analysis and measured primarily by questionnaire. Eysenck's approach resembles Cattell's factor model in using factor analysis, in using questionnaire and rating measures, and in extensive use of 'objective' tests. The obvious difference is the number of factors; while Cattell extracts 16, Eysenck finds initially only two. But the difference is more apparent than real, for Cattell's factors are correlated while Eysenck's aren't; when Cattell's 16 factors are themselves factor-analysed (Cattell, 1973), two higher-order factors emerge – exvia–invia and anxiety – that resemble Eysenck's extraversion and neuroticism (Figure 2.4).

What really distinguishes Eysenck's work is the search for a physical basis to the factors. (Not that Cattell denies a physical basis to personality, rather that the main thrust of his work hasn't been towards uncovering one.) Eysenck first saw *conditionability* as the best candidate for the psychological mechanism underlying personality differences. He proposed (Eysenck, 1957) that introverts acquire eye-blink and GSR conditioning more readily, and argued that these apparently unimportant laboratory measures were fundamental to personality development. Being brought up consists largely of learning not to do things your parents have forbidden; real or threatened or symbolic punishment creates a multitude of conditioned fears. The introvert learns more quickly and certainly than the extravert, so, other things being equal, the introvert will learn society's

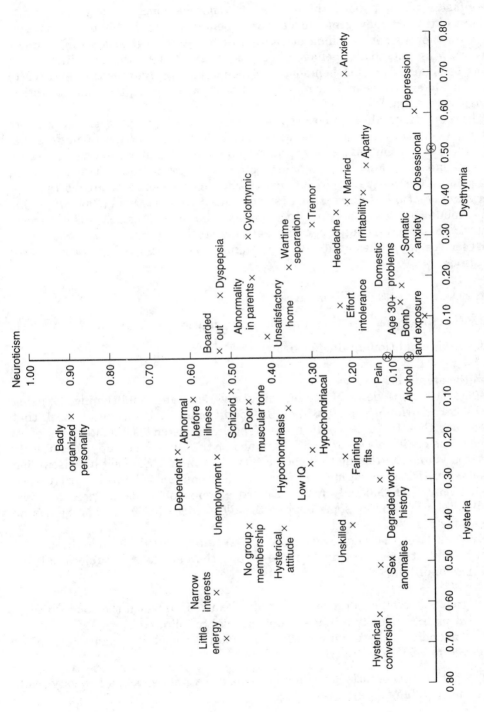

Figure 5.2 *Data from Eysenck's original factor analysis of the histories of 700 military psychiatric casualties, showing two dimensions of hysteria–dysthymia, later renamed extraversion–introversion, and neuroticism.*

rules faster. (One of many things that may not be equal is parental training. A born extravert may grow up very well behaved because his or her parents are very thorough in teaching standards of behaviour, while a born introvert may grow up very badly behaved because his or her parents make little or no effort to shape his or her behaviour.) Eysenck (1964) proposes that extraverts are more likely to become criminals, but with many exceptions, where 'other things' aren't equal.

The conditionability hypothesis also explains why extraverts are more outgoing, adventurous and talkative. Assuming a proportion of one's social initiatives are rebuffed, and a proportion of one's adventurous acts cause disaster, and assuming the punishing effects are greater for introverts, then, other things being equal again, introverts will learn sooner not to greet strangers, start conversations, jump on the first bus that comes etc. Reid (1960) dubs this the 'Freud–Eysenck theory of socialization', because Eysenck has reconceptualized the Freudian super-ego as a set of conditioned anxieties.

Eysenck's hypothesis about conditioning and personality poses three questions:

1. Do introverts condition more readily?

2. Can one generalize from one form of conditioning to another?

3. Does conditioning predict behaviour?

Conditionability differences

Eysenck (1965c) reviews 21 studies of introversion and conditioning, 12 using eye-blink conditioning and 9 using GSR conditioning, and satisfies himself that researches that failed to confirm the hypothesis weren't adequate tests of it. Some of his criticisms seem a trifle strained or trivial; in one study the subjects were too young, and in another they are racially mixed. Some of his discussion was later criticized as highly selective; McPherson (1965) claimed that Eysenck failed to mention that only males showed a conditionability difference in one study, while in another some introverts failed to condition at all, whereas no extraverts did.

Eysenck later (Eysenck and Levey, 1972) reformulated his hypothesis, and argued that introverts condition more readily than extraverts, subject to three limiting conditions:

1. that a partial reinforcement schedule is used, in which the conditioned stimulus – usually a tone – is not invariably followed by the unconditioned stimulus – puff of air, loud noise, electric shock (*partial reinforcement*);

2. that the unconditioned stimulus is weak – a mild shock, a not very loud noise, a faint puff (*weak UCS*);

3. that the interval between conditioned and unconditioned stimulus is shorter than the optimal half second (*short ISI*).

Eysenck and Levey (1972) reported a large-scale study of conditioning and extraversion, using 144 subjects selected as very extravert, very introvert, or in between. Their results confirmed the new hypothesis and found large personality differences where conditioning used the favourable conditions; whereas under unfavourable conditions–continuous reinforcement, strong UCS and long ISI – extraverts actually conditioned more readily than introverts. The theoretical justification for the three limiting conditions depends on the next stage of development of Eysenck's theory, and is discussed in the next section.

Extraversion or impulsivity?
Eysenck divides extraversion into two sub-factors: sociability and impulsivity. Eysenck and Levey (1972) found impulsivity, not sociability, correlated with eye-blink conditioning. Later research (Frcka and Martin, 1987) confirmed this, and showed that only *narrow* impulsivity – acting quickly without thinking – correlates with conditioning. *Broad* impulsivity, defined as sensation-seeking or low threshold for boredom, isn't related to conditionability.

General conditionability
Different measures of conditioning don't correlate all that well. Readiness to form conditioned GSRs doesn't predict readiness to form conditioned changes in heart rate, blood pressure or other autonomic nervous system reactions (Cadoret, 1966). Readiness to form conditioned GSRs doesn't predict readiness to form conditioned eye-blink responses (Davidson *et al.*, 1964). One study (Barr and McConaghy, 1972) did find some correlation between conditioned sexual arousal and GSR conditioning, but the correlations were far from perfect. The evidence for a general trait of conditionability is poor.

Conditioning and personality
Eysenck faces the same problem as learning and habit theorists; he explains how personality *might* be formed by conditioning, but has no positive proof that it *is*. He hasn't proved directly the central proposition of his account: that a given number of parental rebukes or punishments have more effect on the introvert child, and render him or her quieter and less adventurous. Mangan (1982) argues that conditionability can't explain enough; he concludes that personality differences in conditionability do exist, but are subject to so many limiting factors – short interval, weak UCS, etc. – that the difference is unlikely to have much impact on upbringing. Reid (1960), by contrast, thinks conditionability explains too much; he asks why Eysenck restricts differences in learning readiness to anxiety: '[introverts] should be better at all learned activities. They should talk earlier; they should perform better at school subjects;

Table 5.2   *Eysenck's (1957) typological postulate, in tabular form. (Note that Eysenck does not say there are personality differences in the rate at which 'excitation' dissipates.)*

Stimulus	Extraverts	Introverts
'Excitation'	Generated slowly Relatively weak	Generated fast Relatively strong
'Inhibition'	Generated quickly Relatively strong Dissipates slowly	Generated slowly Relatively weak Dissipates quickly

they should learn faster to swim, skate, speak French, and play the violin . . . The theory seems to account for more than has been observed.'

EXCITATION AND INHIBITION

By the time the limits of the conditionability hypothesis were becoming apparent, Eysenck was already moving on to another level of explanation, which by-passed conditioning altogether. He introduced the Pavlovian concepts of *excitation* and *inhibition*, which explain differences in conditionability (and the three limiting conditions), but also generate further predictions about personality differences, independent of conditionability. Pavlov is best known for his work on classical conditioning but in fact most of his *Conditioned Reflexes* (1927) is devoted to developing a typology of temperament. Pavlov noticed differences in the way his dogs behaved during conditioning, which he explained by postulating excitation and inhibition in the cerebral cortex. Excitation refers to the response of the nervous system, in particular the cerebral cortex, to a stimulus; inhibition is activity in the cortex that counteracted excitation. (In general, inhibition means the stopping or slowing down of one process by another.)

In 1957 Eysenck adopted a modified form of Pavlov's ideas, which he called his *typological postulate*. Eysenck hypothesized that, in introverts, a given stumulus generates *stronger* excitation in the cortex more quickly; the introvert's brain reacts faster, and reacts more strongly, to an outside stimulus. In introverts inhibition is generated mare slowly, is weaker and lasts a shorter time. These five predictions are summarized in Table 5.2. The terms 'excitation' and 'inhibition' are a potent source of confusion. If one – wrongly – equates excitation with excitement, one reaches the paradoxical conclusion that extraverts are less excited or excitable, and if one equates inhibition – equally wrongly – with being inhibited, one reaches the equally paradoxical conclusion that introverts are less inhibited.

Reactive inhibition

Eysenck adds another meaning to inhibition, derived from Hull's learning theory. Hull (1951) argued that every repetition of an action creates *reactive inhibition* – 'a negative drive akin to tissue injury, fatigue or pain'. Reactive inhibition dissipates at a constant rate. when an act is repeated many times at rapid intervals (*massed practice*), reactive inhibition builds up and can eventually prevent the act being repeated, so an *involuntary rest pause* occurs. After a break from massed practice, performance typically shows a spontaneous improvement – *reminiscence*. Equating reactive inhibition with Pavlovian inhibition, Eysenck predicts that extraverts generate greater inhibition, so their performance on repetitive tasks will be poorer.

Conditioning

Eysenck could now explain why introverts condition more readily than extraverts, and also why there are three limiting conditions. Strong excitation favours the formation of classical conditioning, while strong inhibition hinders it. Hence the introvert, whose excitation is strong, conditions readily, whereas the extravert, whose inhibition is strong, conditions poorly. This sounds at first dangerously like a circular argument, without some further proof that excitation and inhibition exist. In fact, excitation and inhibition explain some puzzling phenomena in classical conditioning. After a conditioned response has been extinguished by presenting the conditioned stimulus (bell) without the unconditioned stimulus (food), it may *recover* the next day so that the bell once again makes the dog salivate. Extinction is a positive process of learning to inhibit response to the bell when it's no longer rewarded; assume that inhibition dissipates over time, and recovery is explained. Inhibition can also be dissipated by an intense stimulus, which accounts for *disinhibition*, when a loud noise or a flash of light causes a previously extinguished conditioned response to reappear undiminished.

Differences in excitation/inhibition can also account for Eysenck and Levey's three limiting conditions:

1. In partial reinforcement, the unreinforced presentations of the conditioned stimulus create inhibition, which is stronger in extraverts.

2. A weak UCS creates more excitation in an introvert, which causes better conditioning. But shouldn't a strong UCS create proportionately greater excitation in the introvert, and hence even faster learning? Eysenck now uses inhibition in a third sense, this time Pavlovian again. Pavlov and his followers postulate *transmarginal* or *protective* inhibition. Once excitation reaches a certain level, protective inhibition damps it down. Since excitation is stronger in introverts, they reach this *threshold of transmarginal inhibition* sooner; hence a strong UCS may have less effect on introverts, not more (Figure 5.3).

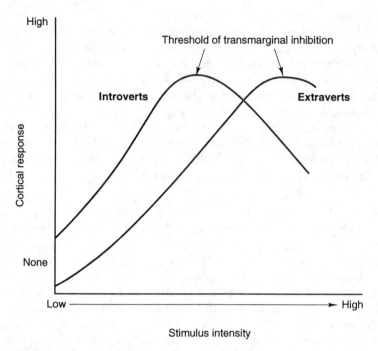

Figure 5.3 *Transmarginal inhibition of cortical response to increasing stimulation in extraverts and introverts.*

3. A short ISI favours the introvert, because his or her strong excitation means he or she can react quickly. When a short (400 ms) interval is used, the extravert may still be responding – cortically, with a wave of excitation – to the conditioned stimulus, when the unconditioned stimulus is presented, which interferes with learning.

Vigilance, reminiscence and involuntary rest pauses
The excitation/inhibition hypothesis generates a wide range of further predic-tions, independent of conditionability (too wide a range, perhaps, suggesting a certain fuzziness in the concepts 'excitation' and 'inhibition'?). Three predictions derive from reactive inhibition, which builds up during repetitive tasks, and does so more rapidly in extraverts. Hence extraverts take more frequent involuntary rest pauses during a continuous tapping task (Spielman, unpublished: see Eysenck, 1967). In 1947 Eysenck had found extraverts poorer in a tweezers test – picking up tiny screws and inserting them in holes – because they couldn't develop the same tempo as introverts. In *vigilance* tasks, like watching a radar screen, involuntary rest pauses may cause targets to be missed, hence Eysenck predicts that extraverts will be poorer at vigilance tasks. Davies and

Parasuraman (1982) review 13 studies of vigilance and extraversion, and found only one failed to find introverts superior at detecting signals, or avoiding false alarms, or maintaining vigilance. (One example of a specific practical implication in Eysenck's theory is that introverts will make better radar operators.) If extraverts generate more inhibition, they will show greater reminiscence, following massed practice. Studies using a pursuit rotor, in which the subject tracks a continuously revolving target, show greater reminiscence in extraverts.

Sensory thresholds and stimulus hunger

Two predictions derived from excitation trace a very direct route from psychophysiology to social behaviour. If a given stimulus creates more excitation in introverts, it follows introverts can perceive fainter stimuli — ones so faint they wouldn't create enough excitation in the extravert to be perceived at all. *Absolute thresholds* for hearing sound (Smith, 1968) and feeling pain (Haslam, unpublished: see Eysenck, 1967) are lower in introverts. These results give direct proof that excitation is greater in introverts. If outside stimulation creates more excitation in introverts, it may be predicted that they will reach sooner the point where they seek a reduction. Similarly if stimulation creates less excitation in extraverts, they may show *stimulus hunger*. Weisen (see Eysenck, 1967) found that introverts pressed a lever, in a Skinnerian operant conditioning task, to obtain a three-second period of silence, whereas extraverts pressed a lever to obtain three seconds of loud music and flashing lights (Figure 5.4). Gale (1969) obtained similar results; extraverts pressed four buttons that made four different noises more often, and varied their choices more. Eysenck has now by-passed his earlier problematic over-/undersocialization hypothesis, and generated a more direct and powerful stimulus-hunger hypothesis of extraversion–introversion.

Other predictions

Eysenck (1967) predicts brain damage will tend to have an extraverting effect, because it reduces the strength of inhibition; the effect of brain damage, especially in the frontal cortex, could roughly be described as extraverting. A lot of research has studied drug effects. Claridge (1967) used sedation threshold, in which the sedative barbiturate is gradually injected into the bloodstream until the subject's speech begins to slur. Introverts absorb more barbiturate before slurring, consistent with Eysenck's hypothesis that they have stronger excitation. Recent research takes fewer risks with its subjects, and uses small doses of the stimulant caffeine. Caffeine improved extraverts' performance on a difficult intelligence test, but made introverts' performance worse (Revelle *et al.*, 1976). Caffeine increases excitation, which in extraverts may be too low for efficient performance, so a stimulant raises it to an optimal level, whereas the introvert's excitation is already at the optimal point, so increasing excitation makes performance worse.

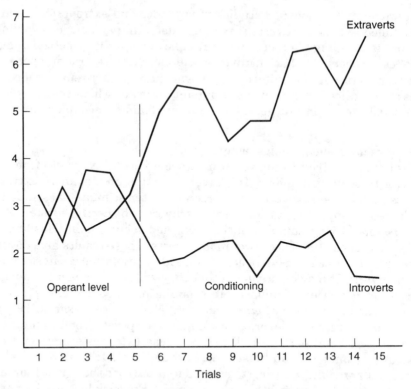

Figure 5.4　*Operant conditioning reinforced by lights and music, in extraverts and introverts (Weisen, unpublished, cited by Eysenck 1967).*

BRAIN AND PERSONALITY

Eysenck finally finds an anatomical home for excitation and inhibition in the *ascending reticular activating system* (ARAS) of the brain stem (Figure 5.5). The ARAS regulates wakefulness, alertness, vigilance and response to sensory input. The upwards pathways cause generalized activity of the cerebral cortex; a stimulus that doesn't produce this change via the ARAS is in effect not perceived. A cat whose reticular system has been severed from the cortex doesn't respond to outside stimulation and cannot be wakened for more than a few seconds. The descending pathways counteract the ascending excitation. The ARAS – which is much more complicated than this brief account suggests – plays an important part in controlling motivation, emotion and learning. Eysenck locates excitation in the upward arousing paths from the reticular system to the cortex; he locates inhibition in the downward inhibiting paths from cortex to reticular system.

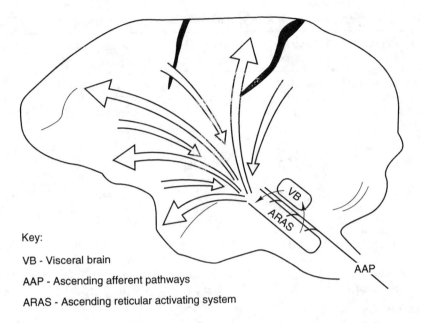

Key:

VB - Visceral brain

AAP - Ascending afferent pathways

ARAS - Ascending reticular activating system

Figure 5.5 *Schematic diagram of the brain, showing visceral brain, and reticular system, in relation to sensory pathways and cerebral cortex.*

Proving hypotheses about the reticular system in humans is difficult, because researchers can neither cut the pathways at selected points, nor insert electrodes into them. One can only employ the electro-encephalograph (EEG), which records general activity over wide areas of the cortex (and has been likened to trying to guess what a factory is making by listening to the machinery through the wall). Nevertheless, excitation and inhibition are, according to Pavlov, general cortical processes, so it's not unreasonable to expect some confirmation from EEG studies. Research on extraversion and EEG, reviewed by Gale (1973), is confusing, but overall tends to confirm Eysenck's prediction that introverts will show higher levels of cortical arousal, defined as low-amplitude, high-frequency alpha activity.

HERITABILITY

Research on heritability of personality relies on twin and adoption studies. Earlier reseach used the less powerful comparison of fraternal and identical twins. Identical twins are genetically identical, whereas fraternal twins are merely genetically similar. Identical twins' scores on extraversion and neuroticism questionnaires are more similar than fraternal twins' scores (Rose *et al.*, 1988), which is consistent with heritability. However, Rose *et al.* also confirm

Table 5.3   *Separated twin study data from London, Sweden, and Minnesota*

Twin type: Reared:	Identical Apart	Identical Together	Fraternal Apart	Fraternal Together
Sample size (twin pairs)				
London	42	43	21	11
Sweden	95	150	220	204
Minnesota	44	217	27	114
Extraversion				
London	0.51	0.42	−0.17	(all fraternal)
Sweden	0.30	0.54	0.04	0.06
Minnesota	0.34	0.63	−0.07	0.18
Neuroticism				
London	0.53	0.38	0.11	(all fraternal)
Sweden	0.25	0.41	0.28	0.24
Minnesota	0.61	0.54	0.29	0.41
Impulsivity				
London	–	–	–	–
Sweden	0.40	0.45	0.15	0.09
Minnesota	–	–	–	–

Sources: London data from Shields (1962); Swedish data from Pedersen *et al.*
(1988); Minnesota data from Tellegen *et al.* (1988), using Multidimensional
Personality Questionnaire.

what critics had long suspected – that identical twins are closer to each other
and spend more time together, which could account for their greater similarity
of personality.

The separated identical twin method is more powerful, because similarity
between separated identical twins can only be explained by inherited differences
(so long as the researchers can exclude the possibility of selective placement,
meaning the twins were separated into similar homes). Shields (1962) had studied
42 pairs of separated identical twins in London, and found strong similarity in
extraversion and neuroticism. Recently two more studies in Minnesota (Tellegen
et al., 1988) and Sweden (Pedersen *et al.*, 1988) confirm that identical twins
reared in different homes resemble each other in extraversion, neuroticism and
impulsivity (Table 5.3). The larger samples used in recent separated twin studies
allow heritability to be calculated item by item, which poses the intriguing
possibility of two neuroticism scales, one of highly heritable items, implying
aspects of behaviour that are difficult to change, the other containing less
heritable items where modification of personality would be, if not actually easy,
at least feasible (Eysenck, 1989).

Table 5.4 *Data for 503 fraternal and 692 identical twins completing the California Psychological Inventory (Carey* et al., *1978)*

	Identical	Fraternal	Heritability
Dominance	0.59	0.31	0.56
Capacity for status	0.61	0.46	0.30
Sociability	0.54	0.21	0.66
Social presence	0.54	0.28	0.52
Self-acceptance	0.51	0.23	0.56
Well-being	0.46	0.31	0.30
Responsibility	0.49	0.33	0.32
Socialization	0.47	0.25	0.44
Self-control	0.52	0.30	0.44
Tolerance	0.52	0.35	0.40
Good impression	0.48	0.23	0.50
Communality	0.30	0.12	0.36
Achievement via conformance	0.40	0.25	0.30
Achievement via independence	0.53	0.37	0.32
Intellectual efficiency	0.54	0.38	0.32
Psychological-mindedness	0.43	0.21	0.44
Flexibility	0.50	0.30	0.40
Femininity/masculinity	0.42	0.25	0.34

The same research also calculates the influence of shared family environment on inventory scores, from comparisons of twins reared apart and together, and comes up with the very surprising conclusion that being brought up together, by the same parents, in the same home, doesn't make twins any more alike in personality. The same conclusion emerges from several studies of adopted children (Goldsmith, 1983); being brought together up in the same home doesn't make unrelated children resemble each other in personality. Personality is affected by non-shared family effects, such as illness or sibling rivalry (Chapter 4). These results are so surprising that one immediately suspects an artefact: that for some reason personality questionnaire answering, rather than personality itself, is strongly influenced by heredity, but not by shared family environment. Yet the effect can't be an artefact of the questionnaire method, because the same result also emerges in parents' ratings of emotionality, activity, sociability and impulsivity in identical and fraternal twins (Buss, *et al.*, 1973). On the other hand, research with the California Psychological Inventory, which covers a wider range of personality than just extraversion and anxiety, finds some scores less heritable than others (Table 5.4), suggesting there may be some aspects of personality shaped by environment and upbringing (Carey *et al.*, 1978).

NEUROTICISM

The second dimension of Eysenck's system is neuroticism, or proneness to anxiety. High N scorers like worrying, and find lots of things to worry about. A high N score doesn't mean the person is neurotic, merely at greater risk. If he or she avoids stress, he or she may escape neurotic breakdown. By the same token, enough stress will cause even the most stable individuals to break down. This is called the *diathesis–stress* model. Neuroticism also interacts with extraversion; an anxious introvert develops phobias, anxiety neuroses and obsessions, whereas an anxious extravert develops hysterical illness or psychopathy, or becomes a criminal. (The extravert is poorly socialized; the neurotic extravert's high anxiety levels energize antisocial impulses.)

Eysenck had little trouble finding an anatomical base for neuroticism; the obvious candidate is the *autonomic nervous system* (ANS), which underlies emotions, especially fear. Eysenck predicts the high N scorer will respond more strongly on measures of heart rate, respiration, skin conductance, muscle tension, blood pressure, pupil dilation and even digestion, and cites evidence confirming this (Eysenck, 1967). Critics argue that ANS measures are notorious for their failure to correlate, so Eysenck has no grounds for assuming a general trait of ANS responsiveness. More recently, Eysenck has shifted the location of neuroticism to the *visceral brain*, or *limbic system*, which co-ordinates ANS activity and is closely linked to the ARAS, the physical basis of extraversion.

Neurosis

Eysenck originally adopted the Watson–Mowrer conditioned fear model of neurosis. Watson saw phobias as classically conditioned fears; the child frightened by a loud noise when looking at a rabbit becomes afraid of rabbits. But phobias can be very persistent; a person continues to be frightened of quite harmless objects, sometimes for many years. Shouldn't the fear rapidly extinguish when the person finds that rabbits aren't accompanied by loud noises or electric shocks? Mowrer (1950) proposed a two-stage model. The first stage is the conditioned fear described by Watson; the second is *instrumental avoidance*. If little Albert sees more rabbits and they prove to be harmless, the fear will extinguish. But if Albert avoids rabbits, the fear will persist. Thinking about entering a room where there's a rabbit makes Albert anxious. Not entering the room reduces the anxiety, and reinforces the avoidance; phobia sufferers in effect train themselves to be afraid.

Eysenck accepted the two-stage theory for many years, but eventually (1979) concluded it didn't fit the facts. Some neurotics do 'run away from their fears', as Mowrer argued, but quite a few repeatedly encounter the harmless object of their fears without losing their phobia. In fact, the phobia may get stronger. Conditioning can't explain this; Eysenck proposes *incubation*. After the loud noise frightened little Albert, and made him afraid of rabbits, rabbits were no longer neutral stimuli. They too made him afraid. He was at the start of a potential vicious circle of 'see a rabbit – feel afraid – strengthen learned fear of rabbits'. In humans this vicious circle can keep turning, regardless of what's happening in the real world, because the sufferer can think of a rabbit, and so feed his or her own fear. Eysenck cites a study by Napalkov (1963), using a gunshot as unconditioned stimulus, a touch with a feather as conditioned stimulus, and a dog as experimental subject. If the gun was fired once, preceded by the touch of the feather, then repeated touches of the feather subsequently caused increasingly stronger reactions in the dog – incubation – instead of extinction, as common sense and conditioning theory would predict. Critics argue that Napalkov's study was poorly controlled, was based on only one dog, and hasn't been convincingly replicated (Bersh, 1980; Davey, 1989); unreinforced presentation of the conditioned stimulus results in extinction, they argue, not incubation.

PSYCHOTICISM

Psychoticism is the third dimension of personality in Eysenck's system, and a relatively new arrival. Eysenck had factor-analysed laboratory tests of personality in psychotic patients (Eysenck, 1952), but didn't publish anything substantial (by his standards) on psychoticism until 1975. Eysenck concluded from his work that psychosis and neurosis are different illnesses, not different degrees of the same illness, and that the psychotic patient is at the far end of a dimension on which everyone can be placed, not in a separate category altogether. Hence the need for a third dimension, and the assumption it could be measured in everyone, not just psychotics. The P(sychoticism) scale was added to E(xtra-version) and N(euroticism) to produce the Eysenck Personality Questionnaire. The high P scorer is: 'solitary, not caring for people . . . often troublesome, not fitting in anywhere . . . may be cruel and inhumane, lacking in feeling and empathy, and altogether insensitive . . . hostile to others, even his own kith and kin, and aggressive, even to loved ones . . . has a liking for odd and unusual things, and a disregard for danger . . . likes to make fools of other people and upset them' (Eysenck and Eysenck, 1975). On the model of neuroticism and neurosis, a high P score doesn't mean the person is psychotic, just more likely to become schizophrenic, manic or depressed.

However, the P scale measures more than proneness to psychosis. Psychopaths, criminals, alcoholics, drug addicts and VD patients (female but not male) all have high P scores (Claridge, 1981); in fact, they have higher P scores than psychotic patients, who often have quite low scores. This implies the P scale is measuring something broader than proneness to psychosis, something more akin to social deviance in general. The many sociologists who make their living by telling the world that all forms of deviance are socially defined would probably attack the suggestion that social deviants have a common personality profile that sets them apart from normal people, if they hadn't long since despaired of Eysenck altogether.

There's some evidence that psychosis and criminality have an underlying common factor. Research in Denmark (Kierkegaard-Sorenson and Mednick, 1975) and the USA (Heston and Denney, 1968) has found children of schizophrenics more than likely than average become criminals. Heston found criminal tendencies in the children of schizophrenic mothers, adopted and brought up by normal parents, which suggests a heritable disposition to schizophrenia and/or criminality. P scores have been shown to be heritable (Zuckerman *et al.*, 1989). Claridge (1981) adds a further component to psychoticism, namely genius; high P scorers do well on tests of divergent thinking. Gotz and Gotz (1979) found very high P scores in commercially successful artists, which they interpreted as evidence of a combination of originality in the art itself and a ruthless drive to sell it. Eysenck's research hasn't yet found an anatomical location for psychoticism, although its heritability implies it has one. He tentatively (1976) suggested sex hormone imbalance, since women get lower P scores. Gray (1973) suggests the fight/flight circuit of the limbic system. Zuckerman (1989) reviews a growing literature on hormonal and physiological correlates.

LEVEL 5

Eysenck traces human personality down through eye-blink conditioning and absolute thresholds to obscure parts of the nervous system and brain stem. These parts of his theory are heavy going and academic; there's a wealth of often conflicting data, none of which has much immediately apparent relevance to everyday aspects of human behaviour. Eysenck, however, doesn't just work down to the physical basis of personality; he works upwards to the effects of differences in temperament. At Level 5 (in Table 5.1), Eysenck applies his theory to a range of social problems, never failing to generate intense controversy. Some examples follow.

CRIME. Criminals are extravert (= undersocialized), are neurotic (anxiety energizes behaviour) and have very high psychoticism scores (= hostile, thought-disordered). Eysenck's prediction hasn't been confirmed by subsequent research (Passingham, 1972; Burgess, 1972). Zuckerman *et al.* (1989) argue that psychoticism alone is a better candidate for the personality trait that predisposes to criminality.

SEX. Extraverts have more active and varied sex lives, because they constantly seek new stimulation. A survey of German students (Giese and Schmidt, 1968) found extraverts more likely to have had sexual intercourse, to have had it at an earlier age, to have had more partners, to have intercourse more often, in a greater variety of coital positions, and to be more likely to have tried oral sex. Eysenck (1971) found that *hysterical personalities* (= high extraversion and high neuroticism) had more active and varied sex lives, but worried about them instead of enjoying them.

POLITICS. Extraverts hold tough-minded attitudes, while introverts have tender-minded attitudes (Eysenck, 1952). Tough-minded people favour authoritarian extremes, so that communists and fascists are equally tough-minded, while Labour and Conservative supporters are equally fairly tender-minded. Eysenck tested the attitudes of the four parties and confirmed his prediction – a difficult piece of research because card-carrying fascists were thin on the ground in London in the 1950s.

SMOKING. Most people believe smoking causes lung cancer; Eysenck, however, has reservations. He accepts that people who smoke also develop lung cancer, but suggests the former may not cause the latter. Extraverts smoke more, being both more sociable and under-aroused; suppose, asks Eysenck (1965b), the extravert temperament also predisposes one to cancer? Then extraverts who give up smoking will not improve their life expectancy.

LIMITATIONS OF EYSENCK'S ACCOUNT

Oversimplifies Pavlov?
Table 5.2 lists three aspects – speed, strength and duration – of two processes – excitation and inhibition; Eysenck argues all are closely related. The extravert has weak excitation, slow to develop; the extravert also has a strong inhibition, quick to develop, and slow to dissipate. Why should strong excitation develop quickly? And why should strong excitation imply weak inhibition? Pavlov's original typology did link the two, but later Russian theorists propose more complex models. In Nebylitsyn's (1972) model, individuals can have both strong excitation and strong inhibition. Nebylitsyn distinguishes *strength of the nervous system* from *dynamism*; he found that sensitivity to stimulation (strength) is independent of speed of forming conditioning reflexes (dynamism). Eysenck's model, by contrast, implies that the same person – the introvert with strong excitation – will have a lower absolute threshold, and will condition more readily. Rusalov (1989) proposes eight dimensions of temperament (Table 5.5), and has written a questionnaire to measure them.

Oversimplifies the brain?
The brain is an immensely complex structure; the reticular system contains nearly 100 separate nuclei, complexly interconnected. Is it likely that something so intricate will operate as simply as Eysenck's demon model implies, having effectively only a volume control?

Circularity
Weisen (cited in Eysenck, 1967) reported personality differences in operant conditioning reinforced by lights or music, or by silence and darkness, which Eysenck interprets as stimulus hunger in extraverts. Weisen defined extravert and introvert groups by questionnaire (MMPI, not EPI), so a less-interesting

Table 5.5 *Eight dimensions of temperment (Rusalov, 1989)*

Dimension	Description
Object-related ergonicity	Need to master the material world, striving for mental and physical activity, involvement in labour activity
Social ergonicity	Need for social contacts, striving for leadership, involvement in social activity
Plasticity	Ease of switching from one object-related activity to another, striving for a diversity of forms of object-related activity
Social plasticity	Ease of entering into social contacts, ease of switching from one type of communication to another
Tempo	Speed of mental operations and motor activity
Social tempo	Speed of speech
Emotionality	Sensitivity to discrepancy between what one expects and what one achieves, e.g. reaction to failure in work
Social emotionality	Sensitivity to failures in communication or in expectations of other people

explanation of the results cannot be excluded. Some questionnaire items reflect liking for lights, music or company, while others ask about solitude, quiet or reading books. Perhaps Weisen's study shows simply that people tell the truth when completing questionnaires; those who say they like noise and excitement choose it when offered, while those who say they like quiet choose quiet. Similar circularity arises with Eysenck's research on criminality. Eysenck (1964) found low extraversion scores in long-stay convicts, where his theory predicts high scores; he explains the discrepancy by arguing that prison doesn't offer much scope for lively parties, meeting lots of new people or travel. Circularity is a risk whenever questionnaires include items that bear directly on differences between groups. Laboratory tests can avoid circularity. Sales *et al.* (1974) measured absolute auditory threshhold, and found that subjects with high thresholds (= weak excitation = extravert) drank more coffee; caffeine is a stimulant which increases excitation, and might ease extraverts' stimulus hunger. Subjects with high thresholds also arrived early for the experiment, demonstrating their desire for novel experience.

Overall research strategy

Eysenck and the Russians are working in opposite directions, hoping to meet in the middle. Eysenck started with an account of personality at his level 4, and pursued it downwards towards level 1. The Russians started at level 2 or 3, trying to develop a typology based on conditioning and sensory threshholds, before moving upwards towards levels 4 and 5. The Russian strategy has the advantage that a physical basis, at level 1 or 2, is real, while accounts at level 4 are more in the nature of statistical abstractions, and have attracted a lot of criticism (Chapters 2 and 3).

Empirical confirmation

Eysenck makes an impressive number of predictions, and in his *The Biological Basis of Personality* (1967) cites an impressive number of confirmations. How has his theory fared since then? The heroic task of reviewing every test of Eysenck's biological theory of temperament was undertaken by Mangan (1982); space here permits examination of only one small area, which compares laboratory measures with questionnaire data, is unfakeable, contains no circularity of argument, and derives directly from excitation/inhibition balance and stimulus hunger: absolute threshold – the prediction that introverts can see, hear and feel things the extravert cannot.

Smith (1968) found absolute auditory threshhold (AAT) higher in extraverts, using a test in which subjects reported which ear the sound was heard in. Stelmack and Campbell (1974) confirmed this, but for low-frequency sounds only. Elliott (1971) found a striking difference in tolerance for noise in 5- and 10-year-old children; the extraverts tolerated 30 dB more than the introverts. Siddle *et al.* (1969) found absolute visual threshold higher in extraverts. Starrett (1982) failed to find a correlation between AAT and extraversion, but included extraversion in a battery of tests, which implies the range of extraversion might not been great. (Research in this area generally compares selected groups of extreme introverts and extraverts.) Subsequently Stelmack (Stelmack and Campbell, 1974; Stelmack and Wilson, 1982) has found personality differences in the brain's response to sound; a given tone produces a stronger response in the introvert's brain, consistent with the hypothesis of greater excitation. Unless the journal editor's maxim 'No news is not news' has suppressed a large number of negative results, this part of Eysenck's theory stands up well.

Below the Surface 2

The Phenomenal Line

LEARNING approaches have proved very popular, although their critics accuse them of offering a model of how personality could work, not an account of how it does work. This criticism may be a little unfair. Watson felt free to experiment on children, and create possibly lasting fears in them, but modern psychologists have much stricter ethical standards. To the extent that learning-theory-based advice on how to bring up children is successful, the approach may be considered vindicated. Similarly the success of behaviour therapy – what has been learned can be unlearned – confirms learning/habit approaches.

Biological accounts of personality, like Eysenck's, have been extensively researched. They are based on the assumption of broad individual differences in brain and nervous system functioning, which dispose the person to behave in certain ways rather than others. Extraverts, with their chronically under-aroused brains, are always looking for excitement; highly anxious people, with their overactive autonomic nervous systems, are more likely to worry, and even to form neuroses. It is still difficult to give more than a provisional verdict on Eysenck's account. As a general approach, it appears to many psychologists to have great promise; while to many other psychologists, it seems at best fundamentally misguided, at worst highly sinister. Some people see it as having great promise because it offers the possibility of demonstrating a few dimensions which can be proved to exist on several levels at once: overt behaviour, learning and perception, and psychophysiology. Others see it as fundamentally misguided because it is reductionist, and will ultimately take psychology back to where it was with Pavlov, as a branch of physiology. Some see it as highly sinister, because it could eventually go a long way towards predicting what some people will do, long before they do it, and because many psychologists automatically distrust biologically or hereditarian explanations. Eysenck's three-dimensional account will probably prove oversimplified, given not only the complexity of the brain and the nervous system but also the number of potential dimensions of individual differences this complexity could generate.

The next line below the surface has one thing in common with the biological line; it starts with relatively superficial aspects, and then tries to go deeper. The first station on the phenomenal line stops at theories that concentrate on what people see, rather than what they feel or do. The second station on the line, which is also its terminus, goes a little below the surface to focus on one aspect of what people see, namely themselves. The self-concept is thought by some to be the single most important influence on a person's behaviour; know the self-concept, and you know the person.

CHAPTER 6

Tumbleweed or Boulder?

The Phenomenal Approach to Personality

SEVERAL years ago one of the authors was driving a car at dusk along a western road. A globular mass about two feet in diameter suddenly appeared directly in the path of the car. A passenger in the front seat screamed and grasped the wheel, attempting to steer the car round the object. The driver tightened his grip and drove directly into it.

In each case the behaviour of the individual was determined by his own phenomenal field. The passenger, an Easterner, saw the object in the highway as a boulder and fought desperately to steer the car around it. The driver, a native of the vicinity, saw it as a tumbleweed and directed his efforts to keeping his passenger from overturning the car. (Snygg and Combs, 1949)

People respond to the world they see, not the world that's really there. The outside observer doesn't know how people interpret the world, so cannot understand or predict their behaviour. The trait theorist fails to find consistency of behaviour, because the theorist's way of seeing things and judging consistency isn't the subject's way of seeing things; people are consistent by their standards, but not by the psychologist's. The learning theorist's extrapolation from Thorndike's cats or Pavlov's dogs to humans fails, because people respond to the stimulus they see, not the one the psychologist has provided. Perceptual and phenomenological accounts of personality argue that understanding how people see and interpret the world and the people in it gives the key to understanding personality.

Perceptual approaches vary in the extent of their ambition. Some simply try to include perceptual factors in a more general model. Thus Mischel's cognitive

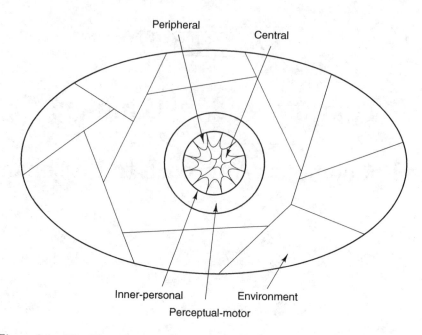

Figure 6.1 *The life space according to Lewin (1935).*

social learning theory takes account of how people see the world, and how they value what they see. At this level, any adequate theory of human personality should include perceptual factors, as indeed Allport's trait theory does. Other perceptual approaches go far beyond this, and assert that how people perceive things is the sum total of personality, or even of all psychology. The *Oxford English Dictionary* defines phenomenalism as 'the metaphysical dogma that phenomena are the only objects of knowledge or the only realities'.

FIELD THEORY

Kurt Lewin was a German psychologist who settled in the USA after the Nazis came to power, and who proposed an early phenomenal account of personality, called *field theory*. Lewin's (1935) basic postulate states that behaviour is a function of the *life space*. The life space (L) sub-divides into the *person* (P) and the *environment* (E); the person in turn sub-divides into *perceptual-motor* and *inner-personal* regions; inner-personal in turn sub-divides into *peripheral* and *central*. Environment also has sub-divisions. Lewin provides maps of the life space (Figure 6.1), so his model is topographical, like Freud's account of the divisions of the mind (Figure 7.1). Each region of the life space corresponds to a fact in the mind of the individual. The number of regions, and hence of facts, varies from time to time. Normally differentiated into a number of regions, the life space may contract into one region only under intense pressure. A person overcome with terror, like Snygg or Combs's passenger, sees only one fact – the boulder – until his field differentiates itself into two regions – danger and escape – and he acts on the second fact by grabbing for the steering-wheel.

Boundaries between regions of the life space also vary in *permeability*. Where a boundary is permeable, events in one region can affect those in the other. Lewin's research on permeability mostly used an unfinished task paradigm. A child started Task A, was interrupted and given Task B, then – when Task B was finished – offered the chance of resuming Task A. If the child didn't resume Task A, in the condition where it resembled Task B closely, Lewin said the boundary between A and B was permeable. But if completing Task B didn't satisfy the desire to complete Task A, because the subject didn't see the tasks as interchangeable, the TaskA/Task B boundary was impermeable. Although the boundaries of the life space are fluid, there are some stable individual differences. The mentally retarded child has a less differentiated life space, with less permeable boundaries. In the unfinished task experiment, the retarded child tends always to want to go back to finish Task A, even when it's very similar to Task B. Lewin's account implies that the retarded child draws few distinctions between people and situations, but sticks to them rigidly.

Lewin also borrowed from general science the concepts of *valence* and *vector*, which he thought gave his theory scientific precision and predictive power; his critics disagreed. A region in a child's life space may have a positive valence if it contains something desirable like a chocolate bar, or a negative valence if it contains something unpleasant like a savage dog. A valence creates a vector, a force having both strength and direction. A child wants (= positive valence) a chocolate bar, but can't get it for lack of money (= barrier). The region 'mother' acquires positive valence if the child thinks mother will produce money; the resulting vector towards mother causes the child to seek her out. If the child knows mother won't give any money, the region 'friend' may acquire positive valence instead, causing a vector round mother to friend.

Lewin (1935) offers further examples, which anticipate later ideas of *approach – avoidance conflict* and *displacement activity*. A child wants a chocolate bar badly (= strong positive valence, and vector towards chocolate) but can't get it (= barrier); the vector is so strong and points so directly at the chocolate that the child can't pull itself far enough back from the obstacle to see the way round it. Or the child wants to sit down, but the resulting 'vector' towards the chair is so strong the child can't turn its back on the chair, so can't sit but circles the chair instead (Figure 6.2). Lewin's third example anticipates the ethologists' concept of displacement activity. A 3-year-old is deprived of drawing paper, when very keen to start drawing; the child watches others drawing, starts other games but immediately abandons them, and caresses pencils longingly. The vector to drawing is so strong it leads to meaningless activity and substitute actions.

The limitations of Lewin's theory are simply stated; it only works backwards. It can explain behaviour after the event, but neither the topographical analogy

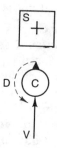

Figure 6.2   *Representation of a child (C) drawn to chair (S), but unable to turn round to sit on it (Lewin,1935).*

nor the mathematical formulation can predict anything. The mathematical expression of the theory has been especially severely criticized, as based on a false analogy (topography of physical space = topography of mental space) and as trivial (certainly equations on the lines of B = f (P,E) – behaviour is a function of the person and his or her environment – don't add much to the sum of human understanding). Field theory lacks predictive power because it provides no methods for measuring valences, vectors and barriers. Forces in the field can only be inferred when they cause an action, which renders the theory entirely circular.

SNYGG AND COMBS'S PHENOMENAL THEORY

Snygg and Combs's phenomenal account of personality is less elaborate than Lewin's; it neither draws maps of the life space, nor includes equations for predicting behaviour. It reflects the authors' clinical background, and their feeling that trying to understand delinquents by trait or habit models was unsuccessful. They state a basic postulate: 'All behaviour, without exception, is completely determined by and pertinent to the phenomenal field of the behaving organism.' In the near-accident example, the driver's *phenomenal field* contained a tumbleweed, while the passenger's contained a boulder. A person's phenomenal field may be full of error and illusion, but to that person, it is reality. Reality is the lowest common denominator of everyone's phenomenal fields. To understand why someone does something, one must understand their phenomenal field; similarly to predict what someone will do, one must know how they see things. The phenomenal field is fluid and organized. People seeing the same event attend to different aspects of it, remember it differently, act differently, according to their varying perceptions. The phenomenal self includes 'all parts of the field the individual experiences as part or characteristic of the self'. The 'preservation and enhancement' of the phenomenal self is the basic human motive.

Snygg and Combs develop their theme by case study and anecdote. They describe an Australian aborigine visiting a big city for the first time, and calling cars and buses 'houses that run around'; the aborigine saw windows, and people looking out of them (= house), but did not see wheels. They mention Whorf's (1952) hypothesis, that language shapes what people can see; the Eskimo have four words for four different types of snow which they can tell apart at a glance, whereas Europeans have only one word so can only see one type of snow. Quite recently Winter *et al.* (1985) devised a very ingenious demonstration of the way people automatically categorize what they perceive. In the first part of the experiment subjects memorized lists of random numbers. Between hearing the numbers and trying to recall them, they read descriptions of people's behaviour, e.g. 'The businessman steps on his girlfriend's feet'. At the end of the experiment subjects were asked what they could remember of the sentences, and given one of several types of prompt. If the prompt was a trait name, e.g. 'clumsy', their recall was excellent, regardless of how difficult the digit-learning task was. This implies people code information about others' behaviour in trait terms so quickly and automatically that it doesn't interfere with anything else they are doing.

PROBLEMS OF THE PHENOMENAL APPROACH

Methodological difficulties

The phenomenal approach has methodological problems. In theory, knowing how the world looks to someone at a particular instant allows the psychologist to predict that person's reaction — but in practice, how can one achieve this insight? Snygg and Combs mention drawings as an insight into the way children see things, and inferring a rat's sensory mechanisms from the discriminations it can learn, but go no further. Measuring a person's phenomenal field creates problems on several levels.

SPEED. The phenomenal field is 'fluid', continuously changing, so any measure must allow information to be collected very quickly.

SOURCE. The phenomenal personality theorist can ask people to describe their fields, or can infer people's fields by introspection and analogy, or can try to measure aspects of the field. Ideally the process of measurement shouldn't affect what it's measuring, but most measures of the phenomenal fields cannot avoid changing them.

Self-description. This assumes people can talk or write fast enough to describe the world as they see it, and assumes they are aware of all salient aspects of it. (And suffers from the fatal flaw that a person cannot simultaneously behave *and* continuously describe their behaviour; self-description inevitably disrupts the flow of behaviour, thereby altering what it seeks to measure.)

Psychologist's description. Most field theorists are clinicians, trying to understand their clients' problems by seeing those problems as the client sees them. The clinician/field theorist uses a combination of introspection into his or her own field, and inference by analogy. 'Client sees a big dog; I'd be frightened of that dog; client is probably frightened too'. A large body of research on accuracy of person perception has shown conclusively how fallible such inferences are; lay person and clinician are equally bad at inferring other people's thoughts, motives and feelings (Cook, 1979).

Objective measurement.   Questions like 'Can Eskimos distinguish more types of snow than English people?' or 'Do dogs see colours?' can be answered by testing the powers of discrimination of Eskimos, English people and dogs. But objective measures, besides being cumbersome, deny the basic premise of phenomenalism. The dog is presented with objectively defined stimuli – lights of precise wavelengths – and makes an objectively defined response – salivation or bar-pressing. The question 'But what does it look like to the dog?' is dismissed as anthropomorphic, and unanswerable.

'REALITY'.   At the third level of difficulty, the phenomenal approach runs into deep philosophical questions. Take the case of a person introspecting on the world as he or she sees it, and his or her reasons for doing things. How can the psychologist disagree with that account, to attribute some half-realized motive, or Freudian interpretation? (A Freudian sees introspective accounts as transparent rationalizations, merely the starting point of understanding a person.) The psychologist can compare the client's account with the psychologist's own – but if they disagree, as the phenomenal approach implies they often will, how can one determine who is right? By comparing each account with 'reality'? But there is no 'reality' outside the phenomenal field. Therefore everyone's view of the world is as good as everyone else's, an argument freely, if unevenly, aired by sociologists, educationalists and the like (unevenly, because the urge to see things as the delinquent or deviant sees them rarely extends to a desire to empathize with Conservative politicians or hereditarian psychologists). Thorough-going phenomenalism conflicts with the way ordinary people see things – for they draw a very clear distinction between the world as it is, and the world as some people see it. Thorough-going phenomenalism makes it difficult to distinguish between 'true' perceptions, and delusions and hallucinations, or even to talk about someone's judgement being clouded by hunger, alcohol or fatigue.

Ambiguity of phenomenalism

A young man is approached by an aggressive drunk in the street, asked for money, and hands over 20p. Five onlookers variously describe his behaviour as 'generous', 'cowardly', 'mean', 'tactful' and 'polite'. This is apparently a clear proof that 'reality' is defined in the eye of the observer – but it is actually profoundly ambiguous.

- Do the observers attribute different motives, perceiving the same act but interpreting it differently (generous v. cowardly)?

- Do they differ in what they predict will happen next (generous v. mean)?

- Do they differ only in their choice of a word to describe what they see (tactful v. polite)?

- Do they actually see (or hear, touch, smell) different things? Such is the implication of Snygg and Combs's anecdote about the aborigine who called cars and buses 'houses that move' and didn't notice they had wheels.

But even Snygg and Combs's example is ambiguous. They presumably don't mean that the aborigine couldn't see the wheels, or couldn't have described them — however incompletely — if asked to. The bus example illustrates perceptual learning; anyone with an interest in something learns to see differences others miss. The aborigine had never seen wheels before and didn't know what they were for; the average city dweller can tell car wheels from bus wheels; the motoring enthusiast can distinguish at a glance many different sorts of wheel — standard, wide, low-profile, alloy, etc. Culture determines what distinctions people learn to make, but within a culture perceptual learning depends on occupation, hobbies, interests — and personality.

Not a personality theory?

Vernon (1964) points out that field theory emphasizes the transient, at the expense of the enduring; people are controlled by their fields, and their fields are dominated by extraneous factors that hardly concern personality at all. This makes field theories a variation on the 'situational' theme, emphasizing that behaviour is controlled by external factors, such as role, custom and chance. But one can also look for dispositions within phenomenal accounts, on at least two levels. Vernon points out that phenomenal fields are effects, as well as causes. A man who sees all women as a threat avoids them or treats them with suspicion — but why does he see women as a threat? Because he had unfortunate experiences with women; in other words, because he *learned* suspicion.

Perceptual styles

These are dispositions to perceive things in particular ways, regardless of what is being perceived. *Levelling-sharpening* is measured by the Squares test, in which the subject estimates the absolute size of a set of squares, unaware that as the test proceeds the experimenter is removing the smallest square and adding larger ones. Some subjects — *levellers* — completely fail to realize that the squares have increased in size from 15 cm to over 30 cm. Stagner (1961) sees this as a greater willingness to generalize across different stimuli, and gives the example of someone who sees other adults as they saw their mother and father. On this argument, levellers will show much greater consistency in their behaviour, possibly at the expense of being able to adapt quickly to changing circumstances.

Another perceptual style is *field dependence*, measured by two perceptual

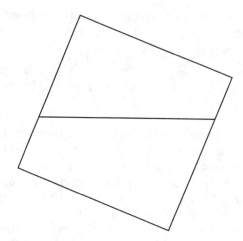

Figure 6.3   *The Rod and Frame test. The subject has to set the 'rod' to true vertical ignoring the misleading 'frame' (enclosing square) of reference.*

tests – Embedded Figures and Rod and Frame (Figure 6.3). In the Embedded Figures test the subject finds a small geometrical design embedded in a larger and more complex one; the simple and complex design are not presented simultaneously. In the Rod and Frame test the subject adjusts to true vertical a rod enclosed in a tilted frame. In some versions the subject is bodily tilted to one side as well. Both tests measure ability to select certain cues from the perceptual field, and ignore others; in the Rod and Frame test the subject must ignore the misleading tilted frame, as well as the effect of being tilted him or herself, and try to concentrate on kinesthetic cues of true vertical. Witkin *et al.* (1954) found field-dependent persons to be passive, helpless, un-self-assertive and afraid of their own sexual and aggressive impulses. Large sex differences are typically found, women being more field dependent than men. This may well be learned as part of their sex role, but could possibly reflect a biological basis.

PERSONAL CONSTRUCT THEORY

Of the various phenomenal approaches, Kelly's Personal Construct Theory (PCT) has shown the most promise. It has been used to study a number of issues – such as stuttering, schizophrenia and neurosis – and has produced a useful personality measure – the Role Repertory Grid test. PCT is a theory; it's stated formally in Kelly's (1955) book, and doesn't have to be quarried out of his Collected Works. Moreover, according to Bannister and Fransella (1971), Kelly's British disciples, it's a proper theory, not a mere 'notion', 'simple and vague', 'stuck to other notions by the glue of common sense, ad hoc argument and arbitrarily selected concepts' (Bannister and Fransella's examples of 'mere notions' include cognitive dissonance, need for achievement, and arousal). It's a very economically stated theory, consisting of one basic postulate, and 11 corollaries. The basic postulate states: 'a person's processes are psychologically channelized by the ways in which he or she anticipates events'. This states phenomenalism's argument that people respond to what they see, not what's there, and illustrates Kelly's belief that people do more than just react. PCT differs from earlier field theories in emphasizing the control people have over their perceptual processes, rather than the control perceptual processes have over people. People are positive, constructive agents, not the passive victims of Skinner's learning theory or Freudian psychodynamics.

Kelly also calls his theory *constructive alternativism*, because 'even the most obvious occurrences of everyday life might appear utterly transformed if we were inventive enough to construe them differently'. Kelly says 'construe' rather than 'perceive', because 'perceive' implies passive recording like photography, whereas 'construe' emphasizes the interpretation of events, the search for meaning, and the construction of hypotheses about people, events and relationships. 'Alternativism' points to PCT's emphasis on an active search for meaning, which manifests itself – or should do – in willingness to change *constructs* when they are proved wrong or unhelpful. PC theorists criticize those who cling to unhelpful and outmoded ways of thought – such as other personality theorists? – and Kelly talks of people suffering from 'hardening of the constructs'.

Humans as scientists

Kelly argues a theory of personality should account for every human activity – including writing personality theories. The psychologist cannot play God and analyse other people from a lofty position of superiority. If the average person is a mass of unconscious desires to commit obscene acts, so too is the psychologist, and his or her personality theory is just as much a feeble attempt to divert or transform unacceptable impulses as the hysteria patient's medically impossible paralysis. Similarly, if the average person is a puppet dancing on the strings of operant and classical conditioning, then so too is the psychologist, which poses the question: Who taught the psychologist to write personality theories and why? Kelly's theory of personality has no problem at all accounting for its own existence, because Kelly sees the constructing and testing of theories as the basic human activity. Every human is an amateur scientist – observing the world, devising hypotheses, testing hypotheses (by acting on them), revising hypotheses when they don't work. On this analogy, personality theorists are very ordinary, typical humans, except for their regrettable reluctance to revise their theories when evidence proves them wrong. Kelly was especially scathing about Freud – see pp. 154–5 for his comments.

The Rep Grid test

PCT has enjoyed considerable popularity, especially in Britain since the late 1960s, partly because it's vaguely humanistic; it offers an optimistic and constructive account of personality, compared with the mechanistic views of Skinner, and the frankly pessimistic opinions of Freud. PCT also provides what phenomenal theories tend to lack – a method.

Kelly's method of measuring how people construe the world is the *Role Repertory Grid test*, shortened to Rep Grid (Fransella and Bannister, 1978). The Rep Grid illustrates a number of important aspects of Kelly's thinking. The Grid method proceeds in six stages:

1.   The subject enters at the top of the grid (Figure 6.4) the initials of 22 actual people corresponding to the 22 roles listed.

2.   The subject considers three such role figures, designated by the experimenter and indicated to the subject by circles.

3.   The subject decides *which two* of the three (self, father, mother) differ from the third,

4.   and *how*, writing the name of the distinction in the column of constructs on the right of the grid. In Figure 6.4, the person and his or her mother are 'nice'; his or her father is 'nasty'.

5.   The subject now applies the same distinction to the other 19 role figures, by ticking the appropriate cells in the grid; as well as self and mother, brother, sister, male and female friends, and boy/girlfriend are nice, whereas father, teacher and neighbour are nasty.

The Grid imposes dichotomous – either/or – thinking three times. The first is when deciding which one role differs from the other two; the subject can't say they're all the same, nor that all three differ. And the second is when applying the distinction to the other 19 roles; each one must either be 'good' or 'bad' etc. Kelly's Dichotomy Corollary states: 'a person's construction system is composed of a finite number of dichotomous constructs'. And the third is when naming the distinction; the name must be bipolar – good/bad, nice/nasty, etc. Bannister and Fransella (1971) explain: 'even where there is no label readily available for the contrast, we do not affirm without implicitly negating within a context.' Therefore apparently non-dichotomous names such as 'bully' are dichotomized by adding the implicit opposite pole – '*not* a bully'.

6.   The subject repeats steps 2–5 another 21 times, to give 22 *sorts* in all. Each time the subject considers a different set of three role figures, selected to cover family, friends, work and casual acquaintances. Each time the subject must generate a fresh construct, and may not use the same label twice.

The Grid is now complete, and two sets of information can be extracted: the names given to the constructs, and the structure of the grid itself. The construct

Elements			Constructs							
#	Roles	Initials	nice / nasty	good / bad	like me / not like me	mean / generous	tidy / untidy	punctual / late	polite / rude	stubborn / lax
1	Self	MC	⊘	⊘	⊘	○	✓	✓	✓	✓
2	Father	SC	○		○	✓		✓		
3	Mother	BC	⊘	✓	✓					
4	Brother	JC	✓	○	○	○	⊘	✓		
5	Sister	FC	✓	⊘	✓		⊘	✓	✓	
6	Male friend	RW	✓	✓	✓	○	⊘	⊘	⊘	✓
7	Female friend	RS	✓	✓	✓			○		
8	Teacher	WM			✓	✓	✓	○	⊘	⊘
9	Neighbour	PP				✓	✓	✓	✓	⊘
10	Boy/girlfriend	Jh	✓	✓				○		○
. . . 22										

Sorts: 1 2 3 4 5 6 7 8 . . . 20

Figure 6.4 *Part of a completed Role Repertory Grid.*

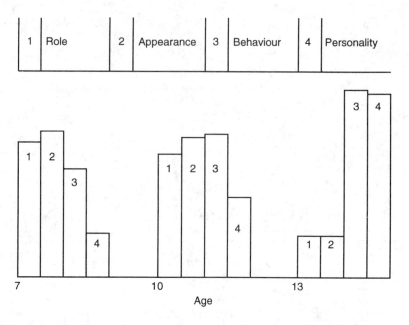

Figure 6.5   *Change in frequency of use of four types of construct between age 7 and age 13 (Brierley, unpublished, cited by Bannister and Fransella, 1971).*

names reveal how the person construes his or her social world, which makes construct names the primary means of understanding that world, and predicting the subject's behaviour. The way constructs are applied to people helps both the psychologist and the author of the grid understand how and why the author responds to the important people in his or her life. Constructs can be also be categorized. Brierley (unpublished: see Bannister and Fransella, 1971) distinguished six types (Figure 6.5) and found significant changes in their use as children grow into adolescence; an increasing number of psychological (personality and behaviour) constructs are used, and fewer referring to appearance ('spotty') or role ('teacher').

The analysis of structure is more complex. Kelly used a form of non-parametric factor analysis; most modern PC theorists use computer programs (Shaw, 1980). The fictitious data of Figure 6.4 illustrate the principle. Comparing rows 1 and 2 ('nice/nasty' and 'good/bad') shows that, with one exception, everyone seen as good is also seen as nice. Looking now at row 3 ('like me/not like me'), the pattern is preserved, with two exceptions. The grid's author sees people like him or her as good and nice, and people unlike him or her as bad and nasty. Proceeding on to row 4 ('mean/generous'), the pattern reverses, with ticks (for 'mean') appearing where blanks appeared in row 1, 2 and 3. Row 4 is a perfect mirror image of row 1. Everyone who is nice is not mean, so the construct expands to 'like me = nice = good = not mean'. Row 5 breaks the pattern, and is quite unlike rows 1–4; inspection reveals, however, a detectable resemblance to rows 6–8.

Completing a grid takes two or three hours, and the results often surprise people, who'd never realized how limited their categories are, or that they like only people who closely resemble them, or dislike anyone taller or stronger. It's sometimes recommended that everyone professionally engaged in passing opinions on others should complete and analyse their own Grid, to gain some insight into the way they think. The Grid isn't a fixed method, unlike the MMPI or 16PF, no word of which may be changed without permission, nor without incurring the need to restandardize. The Grid is a class of methods, adaptable to any purpose; Vernon (1964) described it as 'so flexible as to be almost unmanageable'. The elements can be varied to cover different types of employee, different types of psychiatric problem, different political parties, etc. The method of completion can vary too. Kelly used dichotomous yes/no checkings of each element, but most subsequent researchers use five-point ratings or rankings, in the ratio 70 per cent rating/30 per cent ranking (Shaw, 1980).

Constructs are hierarchical. 'Kind/unkind' subsumes the more specific 'polite/impolite', which in turn subsumes 'spits in the spittoon/spits on the floor' (Bannister and Fransella's example). Constructs have a *range of convenience* according to the Range Corollary: 'a construct is convenient for the anticipation of a finite range of events only'. The subordinate construct 'spits on the floor' only deals with people who spit, whereas 'kind/unkind' can apply to any one. The Range Corollary also implies behaviour isn't necessarily consistent across time or place. Someone with different constructs for home and work will behave differently in the two places. However, the time it takes to complete a Grid necessarily means it measures relatively lasting features of the person; the Grid method can't deal with events on the minute-to-minute or second-to-second time scale of Lewin's examples.

Kelly draws a distinction between *pre-emptive, constellatory* and *propositional* constructs. A constellatory construct implies others; categorizing someone as 'an academic' automatically attributes a constellation of other constructs— intellectual, dreamy, ineffective. Constellatory constructs are stereotyped thinking, under a new name. A pre-emptive construct blocks other constructs, and pre-empts further thought. Back in 1966, Bannister and Fransella gave an example of the pre-emptive construct: 'a homosexual' who could only be seen as a homosexual and could not be thought of as a friend, or a competent manager, or a good chess-player. Propositional constructs are neither constellatory nor pre-emptive.

Since 1955, Grid technique has developed in two opposite directions— simplification and sophistication. Simplifications include supplying the constructs, by telling subjects what labels to use, and supplying the elements, by giving subjects a fixed set of people to be construed. Supplying constructs and elements saves time, but violates PCT's basic assumptions. Kelly devised the Grid to reveal how the subject's thoughts are channellized; supplied elements and constructs reveal how the researcher's thoughts work. One extreme of simplification is Bannister's Grid Test of Thought Disorder (Bannister and Fransella, 1966), in which the elements are a set of eight photographs, the constructs a list of eight adjectives, and the task is to rank order the eight photographs on each adjective – a Grid so simplified that it bears little resemblance to Kelly's original. A sophistication of grid technique, the Imp Grid (Hinkle; see Fransella and Bannister, 1977), builds hierarchies of constructs. Once the person has generated a first construct, e.g. 'verbally fluent', they are asked which pole they'd like to be at and why, thereby generating a higher-order construct, such as 'able to get ideas across'. The person would like to be verbally fluent in order to get ideas across. But why does the person want to get ideas across? He or she may reply 'in order to be admired'. So now there are three levels – to be fluent, to get ideas across, to be admired. Research by Hampson *et al.* (1986) confirms the hierarchical nature of constructs; 'extravert' subsumes 'sociable' which subsumes 'talkative'.

Research in the 1980s agrees with Kelly that personal constructs, renamed *social concepts*, have 'central status as structures of personality' (Cantor and Kihlstrom, 1987) and are 'organised bundles of knowledge about kinds of people . . . situations . . . social episodes'. A few interesting new ideas emerge.

Fuzziness and prototypicality
Social concepts tend to be *fuzzy sets* around central *prototypes* (Cantor and Mischel, 1979), e.g. the fuzzy set of Tory politicians – John Major, Lord Carrington, Jeffrey Archer – around the prototype of Margaret Thatcher. Tory politicians form a fuzzy set because it's difficult to say precisely what they all have in common. Fuzziness means that the list of people (Enoch Powell?) or beliefs (in favour of hanging?) that belong in the Tory party is uncertain at the edges. Margaret Thatcher is prototypical because she is someone most people would not have the least hesitation in identifying as a Tory politician. Social concepts may be defined by lists of abstract features; a 'serial killer' is male, kills strangers, in a ritualized way, often mutilates them, is very hard to catch, etc. or they may be defined by a list of examples: Peter Sutcliffe, the Boston Strangler, Ian Brady, Jack the Ripper. Genero and Cantor (1987) report that students of clinical psychology often use a *mixed exemplar strategy*, a list of abstract symptoms and specific persons.

Social concepts don't just describe people, they also describe social situations (formal garden party) and social *episodes* or *scripts* (saying goodbye to one's host at the end of a party). Forgas (1982) analysed commonplace social episodes, and found three underlying dimensions: intimacy, pleasantness and 'knowing how to behave'. Cantor and Kihlstrom (1987) argue that people who have more elaborated understanding of social events are better able to cope with them. Figure 6.6 contrasts the 'school brain's' representation of taking a test with a novice's. The novice has simplistic, unrealistic ideas about preparation, and no ideas at all about anxiety.

Expert representation: scholarship competition

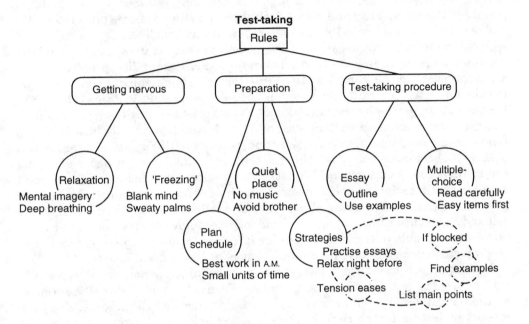

Novice representation: scholarship competition

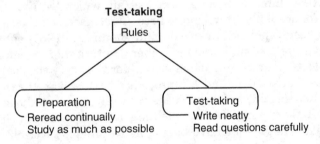

Figure 6.6 *Expert and novice representations of taking a test (Cantor and Kihlstrom, 1987).*

Many social concepts use *procedural short-cuts*, logically very suspect but seeming to serve quite well: 'people of that type' (Fiske, 1982), caricatures (Andersen and Klatzky, 1986) or social analogies like 'another Mike Tyson' (Read, 1984). In *schema-triggered affect* (Fiske and Pavelchak, 1986), if the target person clearly fits a prototype, they may immediately arouse the same emotion. In *prototype matching*, people are immediately judged 'the right type' (or 'not the right type') for a job offer, or a date (Snyder and Simpson, 1984).

The Grid as a personality measure

Critics see the Grid technique as just another paper-and-pencil test, and ask about reliability, validity and social desirability. Kelly dismisses both reliability and validity with a typically cavalier redefinition: 'reliability is the extent to which a measure is insensitive to change, and validity is its capacity to tell us what we already know'. PC theorists argue social desirability problems don't arise, because people complete the Grid for self-enlightenment, and have no reason not to tell the truth. So why don't people completing 16PF feel the same? Perhaps they do; the humanistic side of PC theorists makes them reluctant to share the questionnaire writer's assumption that everyone tells lies. But Rep Grids aren't used for personnel selection, whereas 16PFs are. Bannister and Mair (1968) conclude that the grid is acceptably reliable, in the sense of giving the same account of someone's constructs on successive occasions; they don't address the question of social desirability bias. More searching forms of the grid create some risk of rationalization or crystallization of opinion. Asked why self and sister differ from brother, people may not know, or may not want to say, or may not be able to think of a word for it, or may want a page to explain how, so they compromise by giving a name that is at best approximate.

Validation of the Grid mostly relies on clinical populations, especially schizophrenics, and intensive case studies. Fransella and Adams (1966) report an interesting analysis of an arsonist; six Grids revealed the arsonist liked the instant of setting match to fire, which seemed linked with sexual arousal, but once the fire had started, the man would rush off, horrified at what he had done. He did not see himself as an arsonist at all, which led Fransella and Adams to predict he'd probably start more fires if released. One larger-scale validation study has been reported; Fransella and Bannister (1967) administered Grids to 28 Conservative, 24 Labour and 22 Liberal voters shortly before the 1964 British General Election, and found people voted for the party they construed as 'sincere', 'like me', 'as I'd like to be' and '[un]prejudiced'. However, the three parties' images didn't predict second choices very successfully, i.e. who the subjects would have voted for if their party weren't fielding a candidate – which implies Fransella and Bannister might not have been able to predict tactical voting.

APPLICATIONS OF CONSTRUCT THEORY

Earlier phenomenal theories failed to generate any research, just a few *post hoc* anecdotal explanations. Construct theory, by contrast, explains the causes and cure of stuttering and the nature and origin of schizophrenic thought disorder, and has generated an individual difference measure – *cognitive complexity*.

Stuttering

If asked to nominate a problem where construct theory or method could help, most people probably wouldn't think of stuttering; most people see stuttering as an anatomical defect or neurological abnormality. Fransella argues that stutterers have problems because they've learned to think of themselves as 'stutterers', not as 'fluent people'. Hence stuttering is meaningful to them, whereas fluency is something they don't think about much. Fransella required her stutterers to construe in great detail every episode of fluent speech, and complete a series of Imp Grids for 'me as a stutterer' and 'me as a *non*-stutterer'. Learning to see themselves as non-stutterers gave the subjects much more positive self-images, and caused 13 of the 17 to become more fluent in speech.

Cognitive complexity

In the Grid in Figure 6.4 two sets of rows (1–4 and 6–8) appear internally similar. Cognitive complexity analysis extracts the smallest number of factors needed to account for the information contained in the Grid. Occasionally one single factor accounts for virtually every row, meaning that the Grid's author has only one way of categorizing people (even though he or she has to generate 22 different names for it). Occasionally 22 different factors emerge from 22 sorts. More typically, between six and eight factors emerge, the largest being evaluative; the subject likes people who are kind, helpful, punctual, wise. Cognitively simple people draw few distinctions between other people, in extreme cases perhaps only one. *Cognitive simplicity* correlates with poorer ability to predict others' constructs (Adams-Webber, 1969) and to reconcile conflicting information about others (Nidorf and Crockett, 1965), and a greater tendency to *recency effects*, i.e. basing opinions on the last piece of information received (Mayo and Crockett, 1964). Cognitive simplicity is found in some neurotics (Ryle and Breen, 1972), in obsessionals (Mahklouf-Norris *et al.*, 1970) and in a few schizophrenics.

Serial invalidation

Cognitive complexity is a desirable trait, up to a point. Beyond that point, cognitive complexity turns into cognitive confusion. Some schizophrenic patients suffer *thought disorder*; their thoughts are so confused and so full of private meanings that no one else can understand them. Some schizophrenic patients feel thoughts are being put into their minds by outside agencies, usually hostile, or that their thoughts are being stolen. Bannister (1963) thinks thought disorder develops through *serial invalidation* of the patient's construct system. The schizophrenic-to-be has parents who are so inconsistent and irrational that he or she can never make sense of their behaviour. No sooner has he or she developed a hypothesis about their behaviour or motives than they 'invalidate' it by doing something inconsistent. The schizophrenic-to-be develops a fresh hypothesis, only to have it disproved in turn. Sufficient exposure to serial invalidation, at a formative age, leaves victims so bewildered by their parents that they give up and withdraw into a private world of fantasy. Thought disorder is a disease of the phenomenal field; the schizophrenic lacks an organized apparatus of constructs for making sense of the world and the people in it. Thought disorder is the normally useful trait of cognitive complexity made harmful by excess.

Bannister used Grid methods to detect the effects of serial invalidation, to plan construct-based therapy, and even to demonstrate experimentally the production of thought disorder by serial invalidation. Bannister used a very simplified Grid which people completed twice, and derived two indices of thought disorder—*intensity* and *consistency*. Consistency is the similarity of the first and second Grids, which is normally substantial, because normal people have set ways of seeing the world. (A conventional personality tester would identify consistency as test-retest reliability.) Serially invalidated schizophrenics lack consistency, because they have no lasting framework for making sense of events and people. Intensity is the degree of similarity between rows, and is another name for cognitive simplicity. Too much structure is a 'bad thing', leading to inflexibility and 'cognitive crippling', but equally too little structure is also a bad sign, indicating the person cannot make sense of the social world. The thought-disordered schizophrenic is at the far end of the cognitive complexity dimension, where complexity has degenerated into mere confusion.

Bannister created an analogue of thought disorder in healthy volunteers (Bannister, 1965). Telling them their judgements of people were wrong 'loosened their constructs'; finding their predictions consistently wrong, the subjects began 'going out of the theory holding business' and getting lower intensity scores. In a later study, Bannister *et al.* (1975) tried to reverse the process. They identified 'vague expectations' about other people's behaviour in thought-disordered schizophrenics, and attempted to confirm these by manipulating staff behaviour and ward routine. For example, having found that a particular patient vaguely expected people with loud voices to be mean, to side with the patient's mother, to dislike pop music and to flirt, Bannister *et al.* asked the ward staff to try to be consistently loud-mouthed, cigarette-refusing, pro-patient's mother, anti-pop music and flirtatious. This ambitious attempt at therapy by *serial validation* showed some promise, but wasn't an unqualified success (but given the enormous difficulties of such a project, even partial success is impressive).

LIMITATIONS OF THE PHENOMENAL APPROACH

Emotion and biology
Critics of PCT—and by implication of other wholly phenomenal theories—accuse it of failing to take account of emotion or biology. Kelly's model of humans as scientists is too cold and rational. People can't think rationally when emotion clouds their judgement or biological facts, such as hunger, take over their 'processes'. Kelly provided definitions of anxiety: 'the awareness that the events with which a man is confronted lie mostly outside the range of convenience of his construct systems', as well as of hostility: 'the continued effort to extort validational evidence in favour of a type of social prediction which has already been recognised as a failure', and of guilt, fear, threat and aggression. Kelley's definition of anxiety omits any reference to psychophysiology. Bannister and

Fransella (1971) instance the case of an illiterate person made anxious by a book, presumably because he or she knows that he or she can't read it, or even understand its purpose. But can people only be anxious about things they don't fully understand? If heights make someone nervous because they understand the frailty of the human body and the law of gravity, what lies 'outside the range of convenience of [their] construct systems'? Judging by Fransella's work on stuttering, the answer might be they don't have the construct 'me as person unafraid of heights' – but that is blatantly circular.

Anti-reductionism
Phenomenal approaches tend to ignore human biology; some proponents see this a virtue. Bannister and Fransella (1971) dismiss anatomical and neurological accounts of stuttering; 'let the neurologists look for neurological defects . . . and psychologists construe in psychological terms'. Bannister seems to be arguing that only phenomenal accounts are psychology; anything else is physiology or belongs in another department. It's a mistake to try to reduce everything to physiology, and ultimately to chemistry, but it's equally wrong to stick rigidly to your own terms, especially when they are as narrow as Bannister's.

Unavailable data
A thorough-going phenomenal account limits itself to what people can tell you, which misses out a lot. Even assuming they are telling you the truth, they can't tell you about things that happen very quickly or which are very highly practised, nor can they tell you how their physiology is affecting them. By definition they can't tell you about unconscious motives, if any such exist. A wholly phenomenal account will always be incomplete.

Uninformative
It's a truism that people respond to the world as they see it, not to the world that's really there. (But it's a truism that cannot make any sense to a thorough-going phenomenal theorist, for the 'world as it really is' is unknowable.) The truism implies a profound distinction, but in practice phenomenal accounts of personality seem very often to get stuck at the level of anecdote and invented example. Earlier phenomenal theories – Lewin's and Snygg and Combs's – proved to have no predictive power whatever. Kelly's personal construct theory has had some notable successes, but still tends to fall a bit flat quite often. That people who say they think Conservative voters are sincere, unprejudiced and proud of being British tend to vote Conservative is itself verging on being a truism.

CHAPTER 7

I Didn't Get Where I Am Today by Reading Stuff Like This

Explaining Personality by the Self-concept

'C.J.' KNOWS dozens of ways in which he didn't get where he is today: by having his wife let him down, by not knowing a real winner when he sees one, by waffling, by not knowing how to handle people, by having anonymous letters put through his letter box, by wearing underpants decorated with pictures of Beethoven. C.J. is a fictional character, invented by David Nobbs. He's the stereotypical, over-bearing, pompous Managing Director of Sunshine Desserts, and boss of Reginald Perrin, from the BBC TV comedy series *The Fall and Rise of Reginald Perrin*. C.J. has a very well-defined self-concept, in psycho-logists' jargon; he knows exactly who he is, how he got there, and where he's going.

Humans have two gifts animals lack: one is language, the other is self-awareness. So far as anyone can tell, rats, dogs or even monkeys do not stop to think 'Is this really me?' before running down a maze, barking at an intruder or mating. Humans, after the age of 2 or so, start to have some idea of who they are and how they want others to see them. The *self-concept* affords the personality theorist a possible way of explaining behaviour. Personality isn't an elusive set of traits or factors, nor a vast bundle of habits, nor the ever-shifting phenomenal field; it's how the person sees him or herself. Discover that the meek bank clerk really sees himself as James Bond, and you achieve understanding of his actions. Realize that the aggressive telephonist is trying to project the same image as Bette Midler and you can predict her reactions.

A number of personality theorists have incorporated the self-concept in their

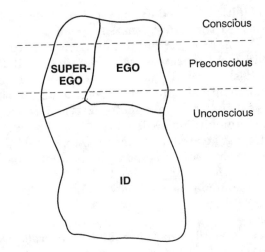

Figure 7.1   *The topography of the human mind, according to Freud.*

theories, and a few have gone the whole hog and produced accounts of personality that say it's nothing but the self-concept. This general line of reasoning leads ultimately to self-theories of personality. How people see things determines how they act, but these perceptions are not unconnected; they have a central theme and organizing force – the self-concept. The way the individual sees him or herself shapes how he or she sees everything else. Therefore, understand the person's self-concept and you understand the person. Most self-theories view the self as developing, not as present from birth; it develops from the infant's and child's struggle to control its urges and please its parents.

THREE SELF-THEORIES

Freud's ego

Sigmund Freud was a self-theorist, as well as an instinct theorist and a psycho-dynamic theorist. He had a topographical model of the human mind as an area divided into regions with boundaries between them (Figure 7.1). The three regions were the *ego* or self, the *super-ego* or, very roughly speaking, conscience, and the *id* or instincts, the 'mental expression' of 'instinctual needs' (Freud, 1933/1966). Of these three, the id is entirely unconscious, the ego and super-ego partly so.

The id is present from birth; the other two areas develop from it. Blind instinc-tive urges can't satisfy themselves; the infant cannot distinguish reality from fantasy, which won't serve it well, as imaginary food doesn't fill the stomach, 'hence a portion of the id has undergone special development' to act 'as an intermediary between the id and the outside world' (Freud, 1940/1966). This is the ego. (Freud actually used the German word 'Ich', meaning 'I', which his translators, in the tradition of medical classicism, replaced by the Latin 'ego', also meaning 'I'.) Later a third part, the super-ego, splits off, as 'part of the inhibiting forces in the outer world becomes internalised' to form the 'representative of the parents (and educators) who superintended the actions of the individual in his earliest years' (Freud, 1939/1966). The human mind consists therefore of two fundamentally opposed forces, the id, the sum of the person's blind instinctual urges, and the super-ego or internalized representation of the family's and society's prohibitions, which largely conflict with the id's impulses, with the ego or self trying, generally unsuccessfully, to hold the balance between the two. Freud's view of human personality is notorious for its pessimism; the ego never achieves more than a limited control of the dark forces of the id. The average member of the human race will always be selfish, nasty and ignorant.

Cattell's self-sentiment

Cattell is even more versatile than Freud; he's a trait and factor theorist (Chapter 2), a motive theorist (Chapter 8), to some extent a temperament theorist, and he's a self-theorist. Cattell first described 16 personality factors (Chapter 2), then at a later stage introduced motives (which he called *ergs*; see Chapter 8), and *sentiments*. A sentiment is 'a set of attitudes the strength of which has become correlated through their being all learnt by contact with a particular social institution' (Cattell, 1965). Common sentiments include home, career and sweetheart. Sentiments, unlike motives, are socially defined. Career is an important sentiment for middle-class people in Western countries, but not for every member of the human race. Cattell adapted the concept, and took the name, from McDougall (1908).

But what is the first 'institution' everyone acquires a set of attitudes about? Cattell argues it's the self. The *self-sentiment* is the most important sentiment and, unlike the others, a universal fact of everyone's experience. Cattell's fifth 'uneasy consensus' proposition (see p. 140) states that 'there emerges by learning an ego, or self-sentiment, which gains control over the simply reactive impulses from the basic drives, and tries to integrate them in legitimate and socially acceptable expressions'. The self-sentiment emerged from Cattell's factor analysis, in the shape of items like: controlling violent impulses, never damaging self-respect, knowing oneself better, being proficient in one's career, having a normal sexual adjustment and never being insane. Cattell and Child (1975) defined the self-sentiment as a 'collection of attitudes all of which have to do with that self-concept which the human level of intelligent abstraction makes possible and which we all possess'.

Cattell's self-sentiment exercises control over the 'impulses of the basic drives'. The basic drives are essentially selfish, so the more control the self-sentiment can exercise, the better behaved the person is. Cattell's account of the self parallels Freud's views on the structure of the mind and the development of moral standards. The impulses of the basic drives correspond to the forces of the id, which the child learns to control by developing an ego or self. Cattell's self-sentiment corresponds to the Freudian ego. (Cattell, in sharp contrast to Eysenck, thinks Freud's ideas on personality valuable and incorporates many into his own account.)

Factor analysis also found a super-ego sentiment 'which directs moral behaviour with a categorical imperative', defined by items like: satisfying a sense of duty, ending all vice, being unselfish and avoiding impropriety. Cattell's sixth 'uneasy consensus' proposition states that conflict occurs between ergs (which Cattell equates with the id) and the self, and between the self and the super-ego; Cattell's seventh 'uneasy consensus' proposition states that these twin conflicts underlie most clinically observed neuroses. The self-sentiment and the super-ego can be measured in adults by the Motivation Analysis Test, and in children by the School Motivation Analysis Test. Cattell shares Freud's pessimism about the ability of the average person's ego to control his or her drives. Over 50 years ago (Cattell, 1937), he predicted the social fabric of Britain would start to break up, as differential fertility produced increasing numbers of people of low intelligence and with poor self-control. The effect would include: 'systematized relaxation of moral standards', a proliferation of worthless unintellectual amusements, more spent on education to less effect, a 'sensitiveness to ordered government', newspapers whose low tone is a national menace, and possibly a puritan backlash.

Carl Rogers's self-theory

Rogers's self-theory of personality has become increasingly popular over the last thirty years. He has been ranked in opinion polls of American psychologists as third most influential, beaten only by Freud and Skinner. (Since his approach to psychology is the antithesis of both Freud's and Skinner's, this may have dented his self-concept slightly.)

Rogers (1951) describes the development of the self in phenomenal terms. He divides the person into *self* and *organism*. The organism is the real world, seen, as everything must be, through the eyes of the individual. For example a student may think him or herself very bright (= self-concept), but in reality be only mediocre (= organism); exams results reveal the discrepancy, and create anxiety. The self develops from the phenomenal field, much as Snygg and Combs proposed. Rogers defines it as: 'the organised, consistent conceptual gestalt composed of perceptions of the characteristics of the "I" or "me" and the perceptions of the relationships of the "I" or "me" to others and to various aspects of life, together with the values attached to these perceptions.' Rogers also proposes that everyone has an *ideal self*, a concept of what they ideally would like to be. Several studies (R.B. Burns, 1979) find little variation in people's ideal selves, which suggests the ideal self is a cultural stereotype.

Rogers emphasizes the development of the self-concept, like Freud and Cattell, but otherwise his point of view differs dramatically. Freud saw the ego fighting a hopeless battle against the much stronger forces of the id; Cattell saw the self developing as society imposes order on the chaos of individual instincts. Rogers sees the self starting with beautiful potential, and being progressively distorted by the demands of society and the parents. In many individuals this distortion eventually gets so bad that the person needs Rogerian therapy. The organism, within the child, seeks to do things, such as hit little sister, or urinate on the carpet, that the child's parents don't allow. When the organism does it anyway, the parents express disapproval, and withdraw affection from the child. The child thereby experiences *conditional positive regard*. Experiences that attract censure are excluded from the self-concept, starting its progressive distortion. The boy who hits his little sister and is rebuked must incorporate in his self-concept one of several propositions: 'I am a bad boy' or 'My parents don't like me' or 'I don't want to hit my little sister'; all, however, are false. The child is forced by *conditions of worth* to do things that aren't organismically satisfying, such as schoolwork instead of play, and is prevented from doing things that are satisfying, such as hitting his little sister. Experiences that aren't consistent with the individual's self-concept are ignored, denied or distorted. Paradoxically, for a phenomenal theorist, Rogers introduces defence mechanisms, which imply an unconscious mind.

So far Rogers's theory runs only to describing how children acquire moral standards. His account is very similar to Cattell's, and even to Freud's, but differs in seeming to imply that learning to behave yourself is bad for you. He speaks of *unconditional positive regard* with approval; the parent should express approval of and love for the child regardless of what it does. Rogers (1959) says 'if an individual should experience only unconditional positive regard, then no conditions of worth would develop, self-regard would be unconditional, the needs for positive regard and self-regard would never be at variance with organismic evaluation, and the individual would continue to be psychologically adjusted, and would be fully functioning.' So how can the parents prevent one child strangling the other, without causing irreparable damage to the personality? The parents must accept that the child likes hurting the other, but also accept the child, and explain nicely that the behaviour cannot be allowed. In this way the undesired behaviour is prevented, but without damage to the developing structure of the self. The older child doesn't need to deny to awareness (repress?) the impulse to strangle little sister, but must refrain from giving it expression. Maladjustment occurs because the self is distorted by the imposition of conditions of worth. It can be cured by a therapist who imposes no such conditions. The Rogerian therapist expresses no value judgements and accepts completely everything the patient says. Under 'complete absence of any threat to the self-structure, experiences which are inconsistent with it may be perceived, and examined, and the structure of the self revised to assimilate and include such experiences' (Rogers, 1951). *Non-directive* or *client-centred* therapy allows individuals to realize their hidden problems and gradually resolve them, and by so doing to gain greater acceptance of other people as well as of themselves.

MEASURES OF SELF-CONCEPT AND SELF-ESTEEM

Allport (1961) thought 'It is much easier to *feel* the self than to *define* the self'; the same is true of measuring self-concepts. Some approaches are open-ended, asking people to complete sentences like: 'When I am with other people I . . .', 'I am always happy when . . . ', 'I cannot . . .', or, most basically, 'I am . . .'. Variations on this theme include asking people to write a page describing where they hope to be in 10 years' time or listing their major achievements, or, macabre but very widely used, to assume they die tomorrow and to write their own obituaries. More structured methods include the Q sort and the Repertory Grid. In the Q sort, the subject sorts a number of statements into piles according to how closely they fit his or her view of him or herself. This method was first devised by Stephenson (1953) and has been used extensively by Rogers (Rogers and Dymond, 1954), Block (1961) and others. The Q sort isn't a fixed measure like the 16PF, but adaptable to a variety of purposes. The self-concept can also be measured by the Repertory Grid, either the basic form, in which the first element is 'me', or adaptations. As Burns (1979) notes, it isn't difficult to discover at least the 'public' part of most people's self-concepts; they're usually quite ready to talk about themselves, sometimes at tedious length.

Actual and ideal self-comparisons are widely used. Subjects first describe themselves as they actually are, by Q sort or rating scale, then describe themselves as they would like to be. Actual self and ideal self are then compared, usually by correlation. The average self–ideal self correlation for normal people is around 0.60. A low correlation means self and ideal are dissimilar, which indicates a low level of self-esteem; Rogers and Dymond (1954) found zero correlations between self and ideal self in neurotic patients, which shifted to a modest 0.34 after non-directive therapy. Byrne (1966) argues that a very high, near-perfect correlation between real and ideal self is also a bad sign, indicating a rigid, over-defensive personality. Block and Thomas (1955) verified this; the MMPI profiles of very high 'self–ideal congruent' persons showed them to be over-controlled and defensive. Variations on the self–ideal theme include the *undesired self* and *possible selves*. Ogilvie (1987) reports that the relation between 'how I hope never to be' – undesired self – with actual self is a better predictor of current satisfaction with life than self–ideal self. Markus and Nurius (1986) find that most people have a wide range of possible selves, which form a sort of private future agenda. Most college students could see themselves as rich, admired, successful, secure, important, a good parent, in good physical shape and travelling the world; few, if any, could conceive of themselves as welfare recipients, child abusers, janitors or prison guards.

There are also numerous questionnaire measures of self-esteem (R.B. Burns, 1979). Some give a single global index; others elaborate. For example, the Tennessee Self Concept Scale emphasizes the 'multidimensionality of self', covering a matrix of five external facets (physical, moral, personal, family and social selves) and three internal frames of reference (identity – 'what I am', satisfaction – 'how I feel about myself', behaviour – 'how I act'). Factor analysis confirms three external selves – family, physical and social – but not the rest (Marsh and Richards, 1988).

DEVELOPMENT OF THE SELF-CONCEPT

The very young child has not yet learned that its body is part of itself, and may bite its own toe and wonder why it hurts. Experiences of this sort, and proprioceptive feedback from movements the infant makes, teach the child a body image. Occasionally adults lose awareness of bodily self. A few schizophrenic patients have the delusion that other people are controlling their movements or thinking their thoughts, and certain sorts of brain lesions render the person unable to make simple movements like a military salute, and unaware that the hand hasn't moved to the right place. The child becomes aware of itself, as a conscious person with continuity of memory and experience, largely through hearing its name applied to itself, its actions and its possessions (Allport, 1961). Children sometimes confuse reality and fantasy, and may expect the adult to see them as the bear they imagine themselves to be. Very occasional cases have been reported of adults who do not have a sense of continuous self-identity, but who exhibit the 'split' or 'multiple' personality of popular fancy, in which separate sets of memories exist with no connection between them. Thigpen and Cleckley's (1954) 'Eve' claimed three separate, unrelated identities.

The child comes to realize that some sorts of behaviour win approval, while others do not. Cooley and Mead argued that the way others react to the child is vitally important to the child's development. Cooley (1902) coined the phrase 'looking-glass self', and said 'we always imagine, and in imagining share, the judgements of the other mind'. Mead (1934) developed this theme, and argued that a person always 'takes the role of the other' when deciding what to do, and so comes to judge self and actions as others – parents, teachers, friends, people in general – have judged him or her. The child chooses one of several courses of action by anticipating how others will react to it. According to Mead, no sense of self could develop in a person who never mixed with others, because such a person could never learn to react to his or her own behaviour as others do.

Physique
Sheldon's work, discussed in Chapter 5, argued there is a link between physique and personality at the physical level. Self-concept theorists agree that there's a close link, but not that it's physical. Children are very conscious of physical differences and physical appearance, and have clear ideas about what's desirable. Brodsky (1954) found that students had very clear ideas about different physiques; a short fat person would make 'the worst soldier . . . can endure pain the least well . . . would make the poorest university president . . . would be least preferred as a personal friend . . . and would probably put his own interests

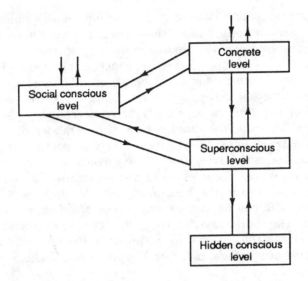

Figure 7.2   *Multi-level model of the self (Parker and Cook, 1991).*

before those of others'. A muscular athletic person, by contrast, would 'assume leadership ... be a nonsmoker ... be self-sufficient, in the sense of needing friends the least ... [but be] most preferred as a friend, and was judged to have many friends ... be least likely to have a nervous breakdown'. A child that's good-looking and has a good physique is popular, and so is likely to develop a favourable self-concept. Concern with appearance is largely a childhood and adolescent preoccupation. Havighurst *et al.* (1946) found that 10–15-year-olds' ideal selves were typically 'glamorous' figures, a phase most grew out of after 15.

There are also gender differences. American college men are happier if their physique is big, whereas females are happier if they are smaller than average (Jourard and Secord, 1955). Being physically handicapped affects self-image; males are concerned about restricted movement and not being being able to defend themselves against aggression, while both sexes feel they have difficulty forming relations with others (Richardson *et al.*, 1964). What's considered an ideal physique depends largely on cultural stereotypes; Ford and Beach's (1952) survey of criteria of female attractiveness in many cultures found an amazing diversity. They, or the anthropologists who collected the original data, don't say much about male appearance. Parker and Cook (1991) report that appearance is more closely linked to self-esteem in women than men, at all ages from 15 to 69.

Parker and Cook go on to propose a four-level model of the self (Figure 7.2). The *concrete level* represents the person's needs, both physical and emotional, and corresponds roughly to the 'organism' in Rogers's account. The *social conscious level* is the 'myself as others expect me to be'. If the person matches up to the self others expect, he or she will be accepted by others, and have his or her needs for regard and esteem and affection, at the concrete level, met. If, however, the person doesn't meet the targets set by others, particularly by being an unattractive person, then his, or more frequently her, needs for warmth and affection from others are less likely to be met. Experiences of being shunned or rejected will come that person's way quite often. The reactions the person gets from others, whether accepting or rejecting, are stored up in the *hidden conscious level* of the self. In an unattractive person, it's likely this hidden conscious level will become the repository of the memories of many rejections, where in a very attractive person it's more likely to contain happier memories of being accepted warmly, having one's faults overlooked, having one's appearance lavishly praised etc. These experiences, especially the negative ones, are hidden, but not repressed in the Freudian sense; the individual can remember them, but is also affected by the general expectation they create about how others will react. The fourth layer of the self is the *superconscious* level, which corresponds in part to the ego or self-sentiment in Freud's and Cattell's models, in part to the level of strategic plans and systems in Mischel's cognitive social learning model.

In attractive or average-looking people, the superconscious level works fairly rationally, trying to maximize the rewards the person gets at the concrete level. In unattractive people – whose lack of charm may be real or imaginary – serious distortions may sometimes be observed. An unattractive person may try to resolve the discrepancy between 'how I should look', at the social conscious level, and 'how others treat me', at the concrete level, by denying the hunger in order to try to satisfy a stronger need for regard and affection from others. In extreme cases, the high level of experiences of rejection stored at the hidden conscious level causes distortions in perception at the social conscious level, resulting in, for example, the person continuing to reject food long past the point where he or she – usually she – has become too thin, possibly even physically ill, but still thinks of him or herself as fat and unattractive.

Family and friends

Cooley's and Mead's account of how the self develops imply that the parents play a large part in shaping it; Freudian theory implies the same, and so for that matter does common sense. Parents are the ones who make the rules and tell the child when its behaviour is acceptable. However, a survey of over 200 pre-school children found they were far more likely to list other children, including their own brothers and sisters, as people who liked them (and whose approval could therefore shape their self-concepts). When parents were listed, mother was mentioned much more often than father (Kirchner and Vondraek, 1975). This would be unsurprising in school-age children or teenagers, but is unexpected for 3–5-year-old children who should be in the throes of the Oedipus or Electra complex.

A large survey of self-esteem in 1200 10–12-year-olds found that children with high self-esteem came from homes where the parents showed warm interest in the child, but also demanded consistent obedience to strict rules (Coopersmith, 1967). Children with low self-esteem, by contrast, came from homes where parents were very permissive, but also very punitive; the children saw them as unfair, and thought their permissiveness reflected lack of interest. (Both patterns of upbringing are classics; the warm but strict parent has children with high need for achievement (Chapter 8), while the permissive and punitive parent has aggressive children (Chapter 10).) Children whose parents are in the armed forces move house frequently; Wooster and Harris (1973) predicted the frequent changes of teachers, neighbours, friends and schoolmates would hinder the development of a clear self-concept. The results show the children are less sure of their parents' affection, doubt their value as friends, and don't think they'll be a success outside school. Guthrie (1938) reports an interesting case; a group of male students played what was meant as a cruel joke on a dull, unattractive female student. They treated her consistently as if she were tremendously attractive and popular. Within a year the woman's behaviour and manner changed radically, and she became self-confident and popular. The change was apparently lasting; once the woman had developed a positive self-concept, her self-confidence was self-sustaining.

Stability of self-image
Some accounts emphasize the stability and durability of the self-image, even citing its resistance to Chinese communist indoctrination techniques in the Korean War (Schein, 1956). Other approaches, however, such as the looking-glass self, argue the self is defined by others' reactions, which implies it's constantly changing. Theories of multiple social selves also imply change and malleability. An ingenious study by Markus and Kunda (1986) partly reconciles the disagreement. People were made to feel different by a set of confederates who consistently disagreed with their colour preferences; they didn't change their self-image, but did hesitate over the 'different' parts of it, showing they were conscious how they appeared to others. Swann and Hill (1982) show that people who see themselves as dominant, and are then told they are judged submissive, subsequently behave more dominantly.

SELF-CONCEPT, SELF-ESTEEM AND BEHAVIOUR

Self-concept and self-esteem can be measured. Their development can be traced. But can the self-concept fulfil its promise as a means of understanding and predicting behaviour? Research on the self-concepts of smoking and non-smoking schoolboys finds the typical smoker sees himself as tough, and the non-smoker as not tough and immature. The smokers also saw themselves as more adult in another direction – being interested in the opposite sex earlier. By contrast they saw themselves as academic failures, and non-smokers as academically successful. The smoker does poorly at school, so tries to present a more adult image in areas outside school, like dating and smoking (McKennell and Bynner, 1969).

Coopersmith's study of self-esteem found children with high esteem were active and successful both at school work and in their social lives. They joined in discussions, weren't put off by criticism, and were generally very self-confident. They weren't troubled by anxiety or psychosomatic problems. The low self-esteem children by contrast, were passive and pessimistic, didn't join in, and were sensitive to criticism and given to dwelling on their own inner problems. They suffered a high incidence of psychosomatic illness. One can never be sure of the direction of cause in survey data – does low self-esteem cause illness or illness cause low self-esteem? – but Coopersmith's findings form an interesting pattern. He found no link between self-esteem and height or attractiveness (unlike other studies), nor between self-esteem and social class or family income. Differences in self-esteem correlated most strongly with upbringing, which suggests that parental attitude and discipline affected self-esteem, which in turn affected behaviour at school.

Rogers predicts that the person who accepts him or herself will also accept others: 'What if it turns out that industrial friction, attitudes towards minority groups, hostilities towards foreign peoples, are based largely on the attitudes one holds towards oneself?'. Early content analyses of client-centred therapy reported positive correlations between respect for others and for oneself (Sheerer, 1949). Later work on a larger scale, using a non-clinical population, found correlations between attitude to oneself and attitudes to specific figures such as father, to specific groups such as people from the West Indies, and to the *generalized other* (R. B. Burns, 1975), confirming that a positive attitude to oneself goes with a positive attitude to others.

Self-monitoring
Some people are at pains to project an image, and try to control their behaviour so as to create the desired impression on others, changing their behaviour to suit the occasion, or the audience. Self-monitoring is measured by an 18- or 25-item 'true/false' questionnaire, containing items like: 'I would probably make a good actor' and 'I am particularly good at making other people like me' (Snyder, 1987). Low self-monitors aren't trying to create an impression on others, so they behave more consistently. Snyder's own research shows high self-monitors date more partners, change partner more readily and are generally less 'committed' to the relationship (Snyder and Simpson, 1984). High self-monitors are more likely to achieve managerial and supervisor jobs in insurance companies and supermarkets (Snyder, 1987). Snyder sees high and low self-monitors as two distinct types of personality, not as ends of a normal distribution; he also produces evidence from a twin study that self-monitoring is heritable (Snyder and Gangestad, 1986). Critics (Furnham, 1989) wonder whether self-monitoring is just another name for extraversion, need for approval, or being devious.

Self-efficacy

The notion of *self-efficacy* grew out of Bandura's work on learning by observation, particularly learning not to be afraid of things. Bandura (1986) concluded 'It is mainly perceived inefficacy to cope with potentially aversive events that makes them anxiety provoking'. If someone's self-image includes the idea that they can't cope with something, e.g. snakes or spiders, then the expectation is likely to be fulfilled. 'Among the type of thoughts that affect human motivation and action, none is more central or pervasive than those concerning personal efficacy' (Bandura, 1986). Bandura *et al.* (1985) measured level of catecholamines in the blood, an index of stress, while snake phobics tried to approach, touch or even pick up snakes. Stress levels were highest if people were asked to do something they knew they couldn't, but much lower if asked to do something the experimenters had previously shown them they could master. *Self-efficacy beliefs* are judgements about one's own ability to carry out actions required to achieve control over a situation. People's beliefs about efficacy are shaped by experience, including vicarious experience, i.e. watching others. Beliefs about efficacy are also shaped by what others say, especially about what one can't do, but can be changed by training. Barling and Beattie (1983) wrote a self-efficacy questionnaire for insurance salespersons, containing items like 'I believe I can listen attentively' and 'I believe I can re-sell the need to the client on delivery of a policy', and showed that high scores predicted number and value of policies sold.

THE SELF AS A SOURCE OF CONCEPTUAL CONFUSION

While the self-concept has some promise as a way of imposing order on personality, 'the self' is also a source of potential confusion. 'The self' can have two quite separate meanings, and can lead the unwary into logical fallacies. The meanings are:

1. *Self as object.* This corresponds to the self-concept or self-sentiment – the ideas every one about has who they are, what they can do, what they are worth, what other people think of them. Rosenberg (1965) says the self-concept is simply an attitude and that 'there is no qualitative difference in the characteristics of attitudes towards the self, and attitudes towards soup, soap, cereal or suburbia'. (Except that most people think themselves more important than soup or soap, and everyone would like to have a good opinion of him or herself.)

2. *Self as agent.* Freud's topography of the mind splits off two levels of the individual – the drives of the id and the constraints of the super-ego – and leaves the main burden of explanation with the ego. Critics see this as a classic case of the *homunculus fallacy*, the introduction into explanations of human behaviour of a 'little man

inside the head'—the ego—who does all the thinking and deciding. Since this thinking and deciding is the very process the theory is trying to explain, postulating a homunculus leads to an infinite regress; to explain the decisions of the little man, one postulates a second even smaller man inside the first little man's head, and to explain the decisions of the second even smaller man, a third yet tinier man . . . and so on *ad infinitum*. All self-theories risk falling into this fallacy, as soon as they delegate functions of the personality to a self or ego.

VERNON'S MODEL OF THE SELF

Vernon (1964) distinguishes a number of levels of the self, in order of depth. The first level is the *social self* or selves: the various fronts or self-presentations (Goffman, 1959) the person has for different occasions. Mischel's fifth cognitive social learning person variable—self-regulatory systems and plans—covers part of what Vernon means by social self. A person who has a limited repertoire of social selves will find many encounters or social occasions difficult. Social skills training schemes exist to help shy or awkward people increase the number of roles they can play. At present there are no very good ways of assessing how extensive and how useful a person's social repertoire is. Paper-and-pencil social intelligence tests tend to be little more than disguised measures of general and verbal intelligence. Moreover, knowing what to do on a social occasion is not the same thing as being able to do it. The conclusion seems unavoidable that social selves can only be measured behaviourally; Arkowitz *et al.* (1975) have made a start by devising behavioural tests of a male's ability to ask for a date.

Vernon's second level is the *conscious private self*. This is generally, but not always, revealed to one's close friends. Vernon suggests that even at this level the person him or herself may not have full insight. Some people see themselves only at the level of the social self, believing that the part they're playing is really them. Personality questionnaires probably only measure the first level, but may some of the time tap the second; when they are used anonymously, for research purposes, subjects may report the conscious private self—assuming they are aware of it. Used for any more public purpose, questionnaires are more likely to describe the social self. Strang (1957) content-analysed adolescents' self-descriptions, and found four selves, including a 'transitory self'. Some aspects of the self are changeable, reflecting moods and immediate experience—presumably the 'social self' and 'conscious private self' of Vernon's model.

Vernon's third level is the *insightful self*—the person as he or she might realize he or she really is, after Rogerian therapy has helped him or her break down defence mechanisms, or friends have pointed out serious inconsistencies in the way the person thinks and acts. By definition, people will not generally see themselves clearly at this level. At this level, too, methodological and conceptual problems arise. Who is to say what the person is 'really' like? And how do they prove their assertions? An expert, perhaps, in the shape of a Rogerian therapist, may make the judgement; but experts, especially experts on psychology, are very fallible. 'Reaching a new understanding of oneself' might be a process of real discovery, akin to finding why one's car won't start, or might prove a process of verbal conditioning in which people learn to say the sorts of thing about themselves that please the therapist. Strang's (1957) analysis also confirmed the existence of the 'ideal self', which in Vernon's model presumably exists at the conscious private and insightful levels (because people don't always understand fully what their 'ideal' is, and may realize, with the aid of therapy, that it's immature or unrealistic).

The fourth level of the self is the *repressed depth self*, unknowable save through psychoanalysis. Freud and his followers argue that most of personality functions at the unconscious level, so people are never fully aware of their drives, nor of the true reasons for what they do. A phenomenal theorist like Snygg or Lewin, or a phenomenal self-theorist like Rogers, cannot consistently admit this level of self. If the world is the phenomenal field, how can there be parts of it the person doesn't know? Snygg and Combs deny the existence of the unconscious self; Rogers, however, does accept that some experiences are denied to awareness (Rogers, 1951).

THE SELF-CONCEPT: AN EVALUATION

Theories that explain personality solely in terms of the self-concept create major problems for themselves. They cannot admit the existence of any unconscious processes, because by definition everything is known to the person. What the person doesn't know does not exist, cannot even be conceived of. Rogers nevertheless wants to keep psychodynamic ideas of defence mechanisms that push unwelcome thoughts out of the mind. Vernon's analysis of levels of self points to a similar paradox. He argues that many people lack insight into themselves, not at the full-blown Freudian level of being unable to gain access to the information, but a more everyday level of simply not fully understanding why they do certain things. They can gain insight relatively easily through a sympathetic, tactful friend; they don't need psychoanalysis. But Vernon's model implies the self-concept cannot be the only way of understanding someone's behaviour, nor even the best, if an outsider can sometimes understand a person better than the person him or herself. On Vernon's analysis the self-concept has several layers, and only at the most superficial level does the person necessarily have complete insight. Hence the self-concept is only one of many ways of understanding and measuring personality.

The more modest class of theory that includes the self-concept alongside other concepts and measures fares rather better, as more modest theories often do. Several lines of research converge to reach the conclusion that the way the parents treat the child affects the child's self-concept, and especially its self-esteem, which in turn affects school work, health, moral standards and popularity. This research, however, tends to concentrate on self-esteem, rather than self-concept, and often measures it by questionnaires, thereby reducing self-esteem to just another trait. Research and theory also face uncertainties over direction of cause. Coopersmith found differences between high and low self-esteem groups, but his data cannot prove that self-esteem creates these differences, and doesn't simply reflect them. One can also question whether an individual's self-concept makes them behave in particular ways, or whether it is shaped by external forces, or forces within the personality, such as habit, motive or complex, that the individual can't control. Social psychological research on *cognitive dissonance* and *self-attribution* (Bem, 1972b) suggests people often rationalize when forced to do or say something they didn't really want to.

Below the Surface 3

The Motivational Line

THE phenomenal line runs through theories that concentrate on what people see, rather than what they feel or do. Self-theories, which form the terminus of the line, do not penetrate very far below the surface, and in practice often achieve little more than adding another trait – self-esteem, self-monitoring, etc. – to an already lengthy list. Measurement tends similarly to rely on paper-and-pencil methods. However, the trait line was examined in Chapters 2 and 3, and its advantages and disadvantages fully reviewed; the aim of a journey down the phenomenal line was to arrive somewhere else. Ironically, the first station on the line, phenomenal accounts, achieves more in the way of a fresh insight than does the terminus, self-theories.

The third route away from the surface of behaviour is the motivational line. Its first station is motives or instincts. If a restricted set of inherited and/or physiological forces shapes behaviour, then variations in the profile of these forces may determine individual differences. A motive can manifest itself in various forms, and a need can be satisfied in many different ways, so an account of personality based on needs, motives, instincts, etc. tends by its nature to dig some way below the surface of behaviour.

The terminus of the motivational line is psychoanalysis, whose constructs explaining individual differences lie at least as far below the surface as the neurophysiological differences postulated by temperament theories, and whose dimensions of individual difference are as few in number. There the resemblance ends, for the constructs postulated by the two approaches are otherwise totally unlike each other. Psychoanalysis emphasizes motivation, in the shape a few, sometimes only one, all-embracing and very powerful drives. Personality is formed by the way the drives are controlled. Psychoanalysis also emphasizes early life, to the extent of claiming that personality is shaped for good by the age of 5, or even earlier. Because the significant aspects of personality lie very far below the surface of behaviour, and because they can't be measured physically, they are very difficult to uncover.

CHAPTER 8

The Ancient Greek Export Drive

Motives and Instincts

BETWEEN 900 BC and 100 BC the inhabitants of classical Greece wrote speeches, verse and books, and travelled about the Mediterranean exporting oil and wine in large earthenware jars. Both activities have been studied in sufficient detail by classicists and archaeologists to enable a psychologist specializing in human motivation to link the rise and fall of Greek fortunes to the ambitions of Greeks of each period, which ambitions in turn were shaped by what they read.

During those eight centuries Ancient Greek civilization developed to a peak in the Golden Age of 475–362 BC, then declined. The area of the Mediterranean to which Greek oil or wine jars were exported, to be discovered and dated by modern archaeologists, similarly grew to a peak in the fifth century BC, then declined, as Roman influence increased.

Themes of winning or doing well, concern for success, or unique achievements (such as inventing the sailing ship) were coded from six selected classes of writing, including funeral orations, war speeches and books on farm management. Such themes were most frequent in the period of growth, and thereafter declined steadily through the Golden Age and the period of decline. Placing the two measures on a common time scale (Figure 8.1), McClelland (1961) concluded that achievement themes in Greek literature preceded and, in part, caused the changes in exports. The emphasis on achievement in the writings of the early period produced generations of Greeks who traded further and further afield. But while the Greeks of the fifth century were selling wine and oil over an area of 3.4 million square miles, Greek youth back home were reading literature with fewer mentions of achievement, which was to cause them and future generations to go into the decline of 362–100 BC.

The lag is significant, for it suggests cause and effect. A simple positive correlation between literary themes and exports wouldn't prove much, for spurious correlations, based on general economic climate, are notoriously easy to demonstrate.

McClelland attributed the rise and fall of the export drive in Ancient Greece to *need for achievement*, a motive or need of individual Greeks, shaped by the way they were brought up. The need for achievement, or n(eed) Ach(ievement), was first described by Murray (1938). Murray defined a need as a 'force which organises perception, intellection, conation, and action in such a way as to transform in a certain direction an existing unsatisfying situation'. A need gives rise to an emotion; a need continues to be felt until it's satisfied. These latter two distinguish a need from a trait, for otherwise Murray's definition looks very similar to Allport's definition of a trait.

From an intensive study of 51 individuals, by interview, questionnaire, projective test and motor and psychophysiological test, Murray and his research team at the Harvard Psychological Clinic arrived at a list of 20 human needs (Table 8.1). The list is only provisional; Murray mentions seven other needs he thought important for some people, but not for the young, male, well-educated subjects he studied. Murray distinguished various sub-types of need: primary or *viscerogenic* needs require physical satisfaction, whereas secondary needs don't. Murray's list consists largely of secondary needs, with the exception of

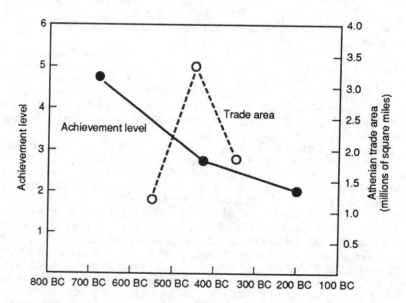

Figure 8.1 *Achievement themes in literature, and extent of Greek exports between 700 BC and 200 BC (McClelland, 1961).*

Table 8.1   *Murray's (1938) list of human needs*

Need	Meaning
n Abasement	To submit passively to external force
n Achievement	To accomplish something difficult
n Affiliation	To draw near and enjoyably co-operate with another
n Aggression	To overcome opposition forcefully
n Autonomy	To get free, shake off restraint
n Counteraction	To make up for a failure
n Defendance	To defend the self against assault, criticism and blame
n Deference	To admire and support a superior
n Dominance	To control one's human environment
n Exhibition	To make an impression
n Harmavoidance	To avoid pain, injury, illness and death
n Infavoidance	To avoid humiliation
n Nurturance	To give sympathy to and gratify the needs of a helpless person
n Order	To put things in order
n Play	To act 'for fun' without further purpose
n Rejection	To separate oneself from a disliked object
n Sentience	To seek and enjoy sensuous impressions
n Sex	To form and further an erotic relationship
n Succorance	To have one's needs gratified by a sympathetic person
n Understanding	To ask or answer general questions

nSex. This illustrates the principle that a human motive or need tends not to shape personality until society frustrates that need. Americans are rarely hungry, so nFood isn't on Murray's list. Needs may be *focal* – closely linked to particular objects – or *diffuse*. Needs may be *process* – the desire to do something – or *modal* – the desire to do something well – or *effect* – satisfied by getting something.

NEED FOR ACHIEVEMENT

Murray's theory of needs was influential in its day. Murray himself was recruited in World War II to attempt one of the most difficult feats of personnel selection ever – choosing secret agents to be parachuted into Nazi-occupied Europe. (Conventional validation of personnel selection first defines a criterion of effective performance, then collects data on each person's success; both would be extraordinarily difficult in Murray's programme.) Murray's needs form the basis of two major personality questionnaires, the Edwards Personal Preference Schedule and Jackson's Personality Research Form. One or two needs have been researched very intensively – nAch most conspicuously, but also nAff(iliation), nAgg(ression) and one not on Murray's list, nPower.

Need for achievement is measured by a version of Murray's Thematic Apperception Test (TAT). The TAT consists of 12 deliberately vague pictures, which the subject looks at, thinks about, then 'projects' his or her thoughts on to, answering questions like: 'What is happening?', 'Who are the persons?' and 'What will happen?'. A typical picture shows a boy sitting looking at a book. High nAch themes include wanting to win a school prize or feeling proud of being able to read grown-up books; low nAch themes include daydreaming or describing homework as irksome. With careful training, researchers can code answers to the TAT with impressive inter-judge agreement, although the measure suffers from the usual low retest reliability of projective tests. McClelland initially validated the TAT by increasing need for achievement by failing people on alleged tests of superior ability, which caused a significant rise in achievement themes (McClelland *et al.*, 1953).

Other measures of need for achievement are almost as ingenious as that of the distribution of oil and wine jars. Folk tales can be coded for achievement themes, making a wide variety of cross-cultural and historical analyses possible. For non-literate cultures, or those whose literature hasn't survived, drawings and decorations on pots can be coded. Even doodles can reveal nAch; Figure 8.2 shows that high achievers favour single discrete lines, diagonals, and S-shaped lines, while low achievers prefer fuzzy, multiple, 'multi-wave' lines (Aronson, 1958). High achievers have different colour preferences, preferring subdued blue tartans whereas low achievers choose bright red ones (Knapp, 1958). Questionnaire measures of nAch include Jackson's Personality Research Form, the EPPS, and two scales on the California Psychological Inventory. Unfortunately these various measures correlate very poorly, in fact not at all according to Fineman (1977); need for achievement looks like a candidate for Mischel's list of personality traits whose very existence is in doubt.

Research on need for achievement has studied both causes and effects. The most interesting effect, for many American psychologists, is the ability to make money by being a successful entrepreneur. People with nAch are more upwardly socially mobile (Duncan *et al.*, 1972) and have a more positive attitude towards work (Veroff, 1982). If they join a large organization like American Telephone and Telegraph, they advance further, without, however, getting all the way to the top (McClelland and Boyatzis, 1982). College graduates with high nAch are more likely to go into business, especially small business (McClelland, 1965). Women with high nAch are more likely to enter the workforce in the first place (Stewart and Chester, 1982). Businesses run by people with high nAch tend to do better, employing more workers, producing more and investing more (Kock; cited McClelland, 1987). Jenkins (1987) reports a long-term follow-up of college women tested for nAch in 1967; high nAch predicted which women went into teaching, provided their ambition back in 1967 also pointed them towards a 'traditional' feminine career, meaning one where women were in the majority.

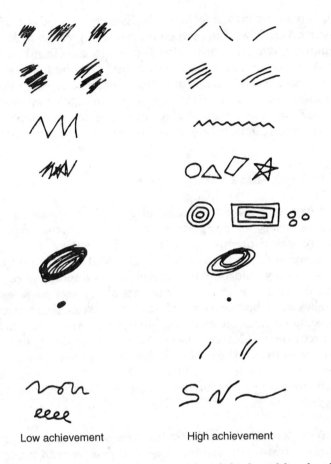

Low achievement   High achievement

Figure 8.2 *Characteristic doodles of people with high and low levels of achievement (Aronson,1958).*

The causes of differences in nAch lie partly in upbringing and partly in culture. Upbringing has been researched by asking children to build a tower of bricks, blindfolded and using only one hand, while their parents watch and comment (Rosen and D'Andrade, 1959). The mothers of high nAch sons are warm, encouraging and affectionate; the fathers of low nAch sons order them about and get cross when they fail. Later McClelland tracked down some of the people whose upbringing, at age 5, had been studied by Sears *et al.* (1957). Their nAch, tested at age 31, correlated surprisingly well with two very early examples of parental insistence on achieving correct standards — severity of toilet training ($r = 0.41$) and feeding to schedule ($r = 0.33$) (McClelland and Pilon, 1983).

McClelland is particularly interested in the way culture shapes nAch. After analysing why some cultures have a higher need for achievement than others, McClelland attempted the more ambitious project of changing a culture. His team offered 52 small businessmen in one Indian city intensive training designed to increase their nAch. The trained men created an average of six or seven new jobs each, compared with one or two each prior to training; however, for some reason the control group in another similar city, who hadn't been trained, also employed more men, although not as many as the trained group (McClelland and Winter, 1969). The experimental city subsequently weathered an economic depression better than the control city, in terms of the numbers of workers employed by businesses employing 10 or more people.

MOTIVES AS PERSONALITY CONSTRUCTS

Notcutt (1953) explains the advantages of motives as personality constructs: 'if the enormous variety of human acts could be reduced to a few universal motives, the way would be open to scientific description of behaviour'. Every person could be summed up by a profile of the relative strengths of their main motives. The account would be truly universal, as applicable to an Australian aborigine as to a British psychology student. Many motive-based accounts of human personality have been offered. Motives are variously referred to as needs, or drives, or instincts; Maslow coins the inelegant term *instinctoid*, Cattell the scarcely less awful *erg*. 'Motive', 'need', 'drive' or 'instinct' are not of course synonyms; choice reflects theorists' differing emphases on physiological or innate aspects.

But motives present problems, some already familiar from the discussion of traits:

- Are motives real forces inside the person, or are they simply attributions, convenient fictions used by observers to make sense of what they see?

- Do motives explain anything, or do they merely create circular arguments? Bernard (1919) says one could argue for a Chinese instinct to eat birds' nests and a French instinct to eat garlic. Why? Because the Chinese do eat birds' nests, and the French do eat garlic. The instinct explains nothing.

- Are motives common or idiosyncratic? Can every human being's behaviour be explained by the same fixed set of motives? The answer 'yes' leads inevitably to the next question.

- How many human motives are there? And what are they?

- What is the difference between a motive and a trait? Unless the two can be clearly distinguished, the concept of motive begins to look redundant.

- What proof is there of the existence of motives?

Single-motive theories

Psychoanalysis errs on the side of extreme simplicity to argue that all human behaviour has basically only one motive. All human behaviour, in Freud's early theory, is motivated by sex – not the simple desire for intercourse or procreation, but a pan-sexual desire finding its way into every human activity. As Freud's theorizing passed into the definitely metaphysical, and unverifiable, phase of his later years, he added a 'death wish'. How Freud's views could be proved, and whether anyone has succeeded in doing so, forms the subject of Chapter 9.

One of Freud's followers, who broke away from orthodox psychoanalysis fairly early on, was Alfred Adler, who coined the immortal phrases *inferiority complex* and *overcompensation*. Adler attributes to humanity the Nietzschean motive of the 'will to power', the 'great upward drive', the 'striving for superiority', which 'lies at the root of all solutions of life's problems'. Phenomenal theorists (Chapter 6) also think humans have only one motive – 'the preservation and enhancement of the phenomenal self' (Snygg and Combs, 1949). Carl Rogers (Chapter 7) proposed a similarly vague and all-embracing single motive – the 'forward thrust of life'. Single motives of the 'forward thrust'/'will to power' type do not explain very much. Any behaviour can be explained by invoking them, but nothing can be predicted. Nor do single-motive theories throw much light on individual differences. Everyone has an *actualizing tendency*, which manifests itself differently in different people; one person actualizes him or herself by painting, another tries to – but fails – by going into business. Maslow (1954) argues people cannot achieve *self-actualization* until their baser needs are satisfied.

Two other single-motive theories deserve a brief mention. Hull's (1951) theory of learning and motivation argues that all needs – hunger, thirst, sex – are effectively interchangeable. A person's – or a rat's – motivation, measured by readiness to learn, is at any given moment a function of all the drives within him, her or it. This isn't in itself a theory of personality, but the basic idea has been incorporated into *arousal* theories of personality such as Eysenck's (Chapter 5). Paul Meehl suggests (1975) that some people have an inborn deficit in pleasure capacity – 'some men are just born three drinks behind'. Meehl tentatively located this deficit in the pleasure centres of the brain demonstrated – in rats – by Olds (1958). Meehl listed *anhedonia* as one of the four cardinal symptoms of schizophrenia; finding every human activity and every human contact unrewarding, the schizophrenic withdraws to a private world of fantasy. Questionnaire measures of anhedonia (Chapman *et al.*, 1976) have proved moderately successful in distinguishing schizophrenics from non-schizophrenics (Cook and Simukonda, 1981) and showing that anhedonic students lack social skill (Haberman *et al.*, 1979). Anhedonia means some people are generally less well motivated to do anything.

PERSONALITY AS A PROFILE OF MOTIVES

In the many editions of his *Social Psychology* (1908 onwards), McDougall proposed instincts as the basis of human social behaviour and personality. He listed six reasons for postulating human instincts:

1. Some behaviours appear spontaneously and don't have to be learned.

2. Some behaviour patterns appear universally, regardless of culture.

3. Some behaviour patterns appear in animals, usually apes and monkeys (the comparative argument).

4. Some behaviours are served by structures, parts of the body adapted to a particular function.

5. Each instinct has an accompanying emotion; the instinct of aggression is accompanied by the emotion of anger.

6. An instinct creates a readiness to perceive things in certain ways.

McDougall's account suffered from major drawbacks, which caused it be discredited by the 1940s. He failed to produce any evidence for his postulated motives, or any measures of them. He failed, like most instinct theorists, to decide how many instincts humans have, listing between 8 and 18 at various times. Other instinct theorists produced their own various lists, which Bernard (1919) collated; he listed in all no less than 14,046 instincts – a figure to rival Allport's 17,953 traits. Bernard's listing includes instinctive mechanisms in animals and even insects, alongside some very improbable human instincts: 'the thoroughly English instinct that what a man can't earn, or get for himself, he does not deserve', the 'old instinct and fear of the connubium of patricians and plebeians', an instinct that 'forbids the Turkish peasant to inhabit a lonely farmhouse', and the German 'instinct for monarchy', which very suddenly evolved out of existence the year before Bernard published his book.

The obvious nonsense written by some instinct theorists doesn't prove McDougall wrong; his criteria for postulating instincts are quite reasonable. If certain behaviours are observed in all humans, and/or appear without being learned, it follows they probably are instinctive – or 'wired-in' as modern psychologists prefer to say. Ekman (1972) has presented reasonably convincing evidence that this is true of facial expressions, just as Darwin argued a century ago.

The comparative argument – if monkeys do it, so must humans – has some force but is very easily misused, as witness the wilder speculations of the 'Naked Ape' variety. It's very easy, and very lucrative, to write books arguing that all animals have territorial instincts – a gross oversimplification – therefore humans have a territorial instinct, therefore people will be subtly discomforted if you sit on their desk . . . therefore war is inevitable . . . therefore people will be

Table 8.2   *Classification of human motives by universality (Klineberg, 1940)*

Class	Motives
Absolutely dependable	Hunger, thirst, rest and sleep, excretion, breathing, activity, aesthetic drive
Physiological basis but not absolutely dependable	Mother caring for the infant, (possibly) self-preservation
Occur with great frequency	Aggression, flight, self-assertiveness
Occur with some frequency	Gregariousness, paternal instinct, pre-maternal instinct (woman's desire to have children), filial motive, acquisitiveness, self-submission

happier living in houses with gardens. More moderate and carefully documented versions of the comparative argument are put forward by sociobiologists, such as E.O. Wilson (1975). All versions of the comparative argument, however plausible to some, however much like fascist propaganda to others, suffer equally from being almost impossible to prove.

The structure argument is less popular these days; one exception is Comfort's (1971) contention that human pheromones (sexual odours) exist, because humans have a 'virtually complete set of organs which are traditionally regarded as non-functional, but which if seen in any other mammal would be regarded as part of a pheromone system', i.e. armpits and pubic hair. Comfort has to postulate very thorough repression of awareness of sexual odours to explain why armpit and groin smells don't appear attractive to most civilized humans.

Psychologists often ignore anthropological data; Klineberg (1940) made a detailed cross-cultural survey, trying to list 'absolutely dependable' human motives, that had a clear physiological basis and were observed in all humans without exception (Table 8.2). Most of his 'absolutely dependable' list – hunger, thirst, rest and sleep, excretion, and breathing – doesn't have much to do with personality. The obvious exception, in Freudian eyes, is excretion, the social control of which Freudians believe shapes personality very significantly. (Klineberg says very little about either activity or aesthetic drive.)

One striking omission from Klineberg's 'absolutely dependable' list is sex. It has a physiological and biochemical basis, but people can manage without, voluntarily or involuntarily. Sexual expression is closely regulated in nearly all human societies, so the principle that a frustrated need contributes more to personality than a satisfied one implies it's important. Virtually all the interesting motives that might shape human personality fall under Klineberg's 'occur with great/some frequency' headings: aggression, flight, self-assertiveness, gregariousness, paternal instinct, pre-maternal instinct (woman's desire to have children), filial motive, acquisitiveness and self-submission. Some of these are much more promising as dimensions of personality, but Klineberg can't list them as dependable, because his review of cross-cultural data finds exceptions to McDougall's criterion of universality. Most humans live in tribes or similar groupings, but quite a few, in various parts of the world, live in small family groups or entirely alone. Most human societies possess private property, but again there are many exceptions where people regard possessions, including land, as communal property.

Hydraulic or *energy* models of sexual motivation are popular with lay person and psychologist alike; such models equate sex with hunger or thirst, arguing that pressure builds the longer the need goes unsatisfied. Ethologists argue the resulting pressure is relieved by *displacement behaviour* or in extreme cases by *vacuum reactions*; the organism first displaces energy to an inappropriate target, then performs the act in a vacuum, without a partner or without any apparent stimulus. Psychoanalysts also see the pressure of a frustrated sex drive forcing its way into other areas of behaviour, to cause dreams, slips of the tongue, perversions or neuroses.

Current opinion among psychologists doesn't regard the concept of instinct as very useful, even though most will happily agree there are innate bases to human and animal behaviour, as well as a physiological substrate. The reason is familiar — specificity. The more carefully one researches into physiological aspects of thirst, or the role of inheritance in aggression, the more it becomes apparent that the broad general categories of the instinct theorists are an oversimplification. Cannon (1932) showed 60 years ago that there were up to 11 homoeostatic mechanisms based in the human bloodstream, disturbance of any one of which would set in train corrective mechanisms: too little or too much water, salt, sugar, protein, fat, calcium, oxygen or hydrogen ion, as well as variations in temperature. Klineberg's plausible listing of hunger and thirst proves an oversimplification. Since Cannon's day, the list has lengthened, diversified and become ever more specific. Similarly, research on instinct in animals has replaced the broad categories beloved of the 'Naked Ape' school by much more specific *innate releasing mechanisms, sign stimuli* and *fixed action patterns*. In animals there is little or no generalization across innate responses and stimuli; the rodent dominant in one test isn't dominant on another (Dimond, 1970).

ERGS—A FORM OF HUMAN INSTINCT?

Cattell is the only major modern personality theorist to include instincts in his account of personality. His thinking follows McDougall's, but is backed up by empirical evidence. In his 1965 book *The Scientific Study of Personality*, Cattell lists seven propositions about human personality, on which he thinks an 'uneasy consensus' exists among personality theorists. The first proposition states that 'man inherits certain drives, akin to those in higher mammals, which provide the original mainspring of his actions'. (The other six propositions are equally unlikely to be accepted by any consensus, uneasy or not, of modern personality theorists.) Cattell calls these instinctive drives ergs: 'innate reactive tendenc[ies] the behaviours of which are directed towards and cease at a particular consummatory goal activity'.

Cattell argues that humans probably have instincts because:

- some behaviours are universal;
- similar behaviour can be observed in animals;
- some behaviours are present from birth, hence not learned;
- some behaviours cannot be eliminated by training;
- some behaviours are accompanied by unlearned facial and visceral responses;
- some behaviours result from 'an impulse to a course of action which has a particular goal at its end', such as hunting, killing and eating prey.

Cattell lists three defining characteristics of an erg:

1. An erg creates a readiness to perceive relevant objects.
2. An unsatisfied erg arouses an emotion.
3. The erg starts a cycle of activity which continues until the goal is achieved. Lack of food causes hunger (tension or emotion) which persists or increases until the person eats, which reduces hunger (satiation).

Like other motive theorists, Cattell must state how many ergs there are, what they are and what his proof is. Characteristically, Cattell relies on measurement and factor analysis, not the light of reason or comparative data. He devises a large and varied set of measures, then applies them to a large population of subjects, then factor-analyses the data. The results suggest 10 ergs exist and can be measured – food-seeking, mating, gregariousness, parental, exploration, escape to security, self-assertion, narcistic (*sic*) sex, pugnacity and acquisitiveness. Another four – appeal, rest-seeking, constructiveness and self-abasement – are of 'uncertain independence', while two – disgust and laughter – exist in Cattell's opinion, although research hasn't succeeded in demonstrating a factor (Cattell, 1957; Cattell and Child, 1975).

Cattell lists no less than 68 possible measures of motivation, but his Motivation Analysis Test (MAT) restricts itself to four types of measure in its group version, expanding to a possible seven if administered individually (Cattell and Kline, 1977):

- *Autism*: questions of the general form 'What percentage of the population think that . . .' measure the tendency of an erg to make people misperceive consensus opinion. An assertive person will predict a high proportion of people want to be head of government.

- *Utilities:* preference between different priorities, e.g. for spending research money.

- *Information:* a multiple-choice general knowledge test; people know more about things that are relevant to their needs, so an aggressive person knows about weapons.

- *Word association:* choosing the association 'lips' to the key word 'hot' scores for the sex erg.

- *Reaction time, GSR* and *blood pressure* measures are only available if the test is administered individually.

Cattell's measures are ingenious, but they lean rather heavily on paper-and-pencil techniques, so the dividing line between erg and trait becomes blurred. Validation of the MAT is partly factorial; when factor-analysed, the scores yield five factors corresponding to five ergs (as well as five more scores for *sentiments*: a sentiment is a generalized attitude such as 'career', 'home', 'self'). Factorial validation proves the MAT measures 10 things, not 1 or 20, but doesn't identify the 10 things; hence it can't prove 5 of them are instincts. Validation of the MAT relies mostly on experimental manipulations designed to change the strength of needs; one study showed that sex erg scores rise after people look at erotic pictures, while hunger erg scores rise after a day's fasting (Cattell *et al.*, 1972). Another study (Kline and Grindley, 1974) measured five ergs every day for 28 days in a single college student, and linked changes in measured ergs to significant events in the subject's life (Figure 8.3). Her fear erg peaked twice: on day 12 when she felt rejected by her colleagues, and on day 16 when she had to drive an unsafe car.

FUNCTIONAL AUTONOMY

Allport (1937, 1961) objects to all theories of motivation that take away 'the right to be believed' by arguing that people 'really' do things because of the way they were brought up, or because of psychodynamic conflicts. He criticized Murray's needs model as 'too abstract, too disembodied and depersonalised to represent the ongoing motivation of actual individuals'. He argued that any one of Murray's needs could be satisfied in an infinite diversity of ways; the need for abasement could be satisfied equally by the rigours of monastic life or sado-masochistic perversions. Allport sees motives as primarily idiosyncratic, but with enough common features within a given culture for some generalization to be possible.

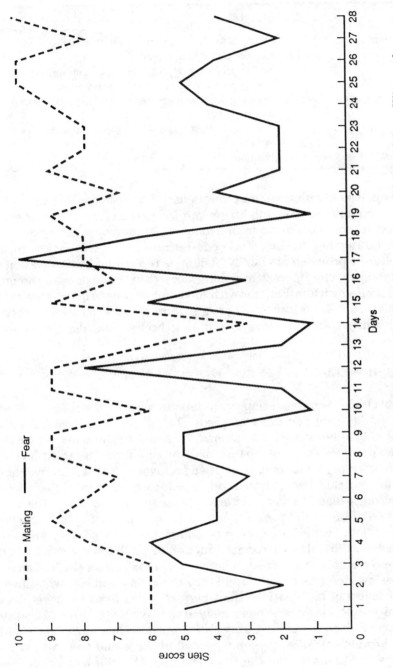

Figure 8.3 *Fear and mating ergs measured daily for 28 days in one person (adapted from Kline and Grindley, 1974).*

Table 8.3 *Maslow's hierarchy of needs*

Need	Meaning
Self-actualization	Doing what you are fitted for: 'what a person *can* be, he or she *must* be'
Esteem	Self-confidence, worth, strength, capability, 'being useful and necessary in the world'
Belongingness and love	From spouse or sweetheart, friends and people in general
Safety needs	To avoid being frightened, ill, in pain, cold, wet etc.
Physiological needs	Hunger, thirst, sleep, sex

Allport dismissed learning/habit accounts based on secondary reinforcement. Thus a learning/habit account might explain (or predict?) an adult interest in fishing by two-stage secondary reinforcement. In childhood, the angler's father used to take him or her fishing. Father is rewarding by association with the food and shelter he provided his family; fishing is rewarding by association with father. Allport asks why interest in fishing doesn't extinguish even though it's no longer associated with father, nor with food and shelter. Allport sees motives as contemporary, not historical; fishing has acquired for the fisherman *functional autonomy* — it's interesting in its own right, not through long-dead associations.

HIERARCHY OF NEEDS

Maslow (1954) thought the most important human motive was *self-actualization*, but added the idea of a hierarchy of needs (Table 8.3). The lowest level is of physiological needs: hunger, thirst, sleep. The second level is of safety needs: avoiding fear, pain, illness, disturbance and uncertainty. The third level is of needs for belongingness and love, from friends, lovers, spouse, family, children and people in general. The fourth level is self-esteem. The highest level is self-actualization, which Maslow said 'may be loosely described as the full use and exploitation of talents, capacities, potentialities etc.'. Self-actualizing people 'seem to be fulfilling themselves and to be doing the best that they are capable of doing' (Maslow, 1954). People cannot function at the higher levels while their lower-level needs remain unsatisfied. A starving person cannot think of anything but food. Maslow describes five individuals, living in a jungle, who illustrate the first four levels of need satisfaction: 'person A has lived for several weeks in a dangerous jungle, in which he has managed to stay alive by finding occasional food and water. Person B not only stays alive but also has a rifle and a hidden cave with a closable entrance. Person C has all of these and has two more men with him as well. Person D has the food, the gun, the allies, the cave, and in addition, has with him his best-loved friend. Finally, person E, in the same jungle, has all of these, and in addition is the well-respected leader of his band.' No one, in Maslow's hypothetical jungle, achieves self-actualization.

Maslow's hierarchy is intuitively plausible, and has some research backing, at least at the lower levels. Extreme hunger has been shown to affect the way people see things (Sanford, 1937). At higher levels, the hierachy hypothesis becomes less easy to prove. It implies that a person whose need for belongingness and love isn't satisfied can't be motivated by self-esteem. This hypothesis could be tested in the short term by depriving people of company. One could test it in the longer term by finding people whom fate or bad luck has deprived of affection – but problems of direction of cause arise. Does a person with no friends lack self-esteem because his or her need to belong isn't satisfied, or does that person lack friends because he or she is an obnoxious person, which also accounts for his or her low self-esteem? In any case Maslow admits levels 3 and 4 may sometimes change place in his hierarchy; for some people self-esteem is more basic than belongingness and love.

At the level of self-actualization, empirical verification becomes very difficult. The concept is somewhat vague – indeed, a carping critic might dismiss Maslow's definitions as circular – and it's difficult to provide a measure of it. Maslow himself used case studies of unusually fulfilled individuals, such as Lincoln, Einstein or Eleanor Roosevelt. This is an interesting starting point but open to obvious objections. Who says Abraham Lincoln was a fulfilled, self-actualized person? Maslow says. Why Lincoln, and not J.F. Kennedy? (One place not to find self-actualized persons, according to Maslow, is the average college campus.)

Shostrom (1965) devised a questionnaire measure of self-actualization, the Personal Orientation Inventory (POI), validated against ratings of personal adjustment, creativity and academic achievement. POI profiles improve in an individual undergoing therapy, including encounter groups, suggesting people are overcoming their problems and achieving greater insight. People who don't conform in laboratory conformity experiments have better POI profiles, suggesting greater self-reliance and independence (Knapp *et al.*, 1978).

MOTIVES AND BEHAVIOUR

Predicting someone's behaviour from their motives isn't straightforward. One must take into account culture, subsidiation and the dynamic lattice, and possibly the unconscious mind.

Culture

Maslow, although a humanistic psychologist, recognizes our simian ancestry, and admits that parts of it occasionally influence behaviour. But he doesn't think these influences are anywhere near as important as the influence of culture. The great range of cultural variation in the expression of sex, aggression, even hunger and thirst, described by Klineberg (1940), tends to prove Maslow's point.

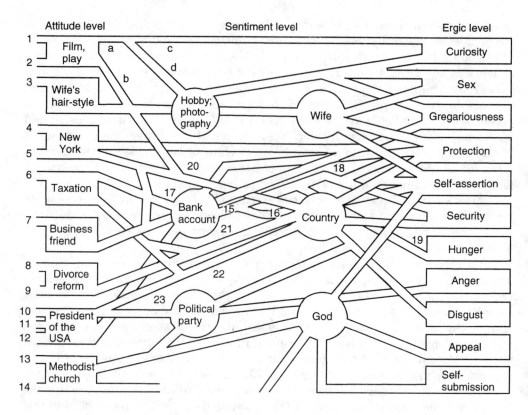

Figure 8.4   *Fragment of a dynamic lattice, showing attitude subsidiation, sentiment structure, and ergic goals (Cattell, 1965).*

Subsidiation

Motives have hierarchies of importance which Murray called *subsidiation*: 'A person may study accountancy in order that he may keep his job in a big business in order that he may earn money in order that he may marry and have a family' (Cattell, 1965). Subsidiation also resolves apparent inconsistencies in behaviour; Mr Savage, in Chapter 3, wants to attack the postman, but wants even more to get the letters he is bringing. Cattell introduces the idea of the *dynamic lattice*, in which specific attitudes – to New York, say, or the Methodist church – can be related to sentiments such as career or home, which in turn are the product of the person's culture, individual circumstances, and ergs (Figure 8.4). If one had a complete map of a person's dynamic lattice, one could in theory predict his or her attitudes, and possibly behaviour.

Unconscious motivation

Subsidiation and the dynamic lattice can be measured by questioning the person about likes, dislikes, reasons and priorities. But some motives may not be open to introspection; the person may not know always know why he or she wants something. Unconscious motives tend to be the preserve of psychoanalysts, but Cattell (1965) lists as the sixth of his seven 'uneasy consensus' propositions 'the notion that a substantial segment of our motivation is unconscious'. Allport and the humanistic psychologists Maslow, Rogers and Kelly are among those who don't belong to the consensus.

CONCLUSION

The concept of motive in personality has gone down two paths, splitting itself effectively into two classes of explanation, each of which eventually turns into something different. The first path is biological. A physiological basis and probably an innate one can be demonstrated in animals and, less certainly, in humans. Unfortunately the biological motives that can be shown to exist in humans turn out to be the ones least interesting to the personality theorist – the need to eat, sleep, breathe, excrete or drink. The potentially more interesting ones – gregariousness, aggression, territoriality – remain only possibilities, whose contribution to human personality cannot be untangled from those of experience and culture. The analogy of animals suggests that innate mechanisms in humans, when precisely documented, will prove very specific – the equivalent of the kitten's readiness to spring on any moving object.

The second path has its origin in Murray's needs and is represented by need for achievement and by Cattell's ergs. The group form of the Motivation Analysis Test measures five ergs by the answers people give to a large number of questions on an inventory. Cattell's written definition distinguishes motives from traits or factors clearly enough, but his operational definition (what he does to measure them) blurs the distinction. Motives become merely a variant of traits, or vice versa. But the merits and demerits of the trait model were discussed in Chapters 2 and 3. This chapter was looking for something new, and doesn't seem to have found it.

CHAPTER 9

The Man Who Collects Bradshaws

Psychodynamic Accounts of Personality

A 'BRADSHAW' is a complete timetable for all the railways in the British Isles. With it the reader can plan long, complicated train journeys. Suppose, for example, one wished to travel the 94 miles from Lampeter to Hay on Wye, an awkward journey by rail, against the grain of the country. Bradshaw reveals that it would take 6 hours, with changes at Carmarthen, Llandeilo, Builth Road and Three Cocks Junction, which contrasts unfavourably with the hour or two a modern car on modern roads would need for the same journey. The Bradshaw used to plan this journey isn't a current one; it was published in 1938. You can't get to Lampeter or Hay by train any more; the lines were all closed 30 years ago. Nevertheless the 1938 Bradshaw is a collector's item, worth between £10 and £20.

Why – the unenlightened generally ask – would anyone pay good money for an out-of-date railway timetable? A learning theory account might say that collecting timetables is a habit, hence that it was learned; reading Bradshaw and planning long journeys from A to B is reinforcing – but why? A trait account will probably subsume the habit under a trait or traits, such as collecting old books and/or an interest in railways, but again fails to answer – or even ask – the question why? One theory of personality specializes in saying why people do things, and just happens to give a very specific answer to this particular question. The man who collects Bradshaws is driven to do so by ancient forces hidden deep in his personality. The urge to possess copies of Bradshaw, and in particularly severe cases to collect a complete set, is the expression of long repressed childhood urges to do something much more basic.

Explanations of this general type – people who collect old railway timetables are symbolically reliving childhood conflicts – are *psychodynamic* explanations. Trait theory (Chapters 2 and 3) views personality as a fairly small number of inner dispositions; genotype trait theory argues that these inner dispositions operate complexly, and that their relation to actual behaviour is influenced by outside events, and by other traits. The hypothetical Mr Savage's aggression couldn't express itself on the first five possible occasions because fear or respect for authority inhibited it, or because social norms or physical barriers blocked it. A casual observer might easily conclude that Mr Savage isn't aggressive at all; only a perceptive student of human behaviour realizes Mr Savage is 'really' a very aggressive person beneath his apparent meekness.

Psychodynamic models of personality take this line of reasoning one stage further. Some take it to, if not well beyond, its limit. They explain behaviour and individual differences by the interplay of a very few, very powerful, very deeply concealed forces. Psychodynamic explanations of behaviour specialize in saying that the person is 'really' insecure, or 'really' immature, or that the 'real' reason for someone's behaviour is an unconscious desire to do something highly improbable and frequently disgusting. Like learning and habit approaches, psychodynamic approaches emphasize the development of personality and often assume everything of any consequence happens in the first five years of life, or even in the first six months. The child shapes the adult, in devious ways that are hard to reverse. Unlike learning and habit approaches, psychodynamic theories rarely attempt to incorporate the results of laboratory research, and never use animal behaviour to explain human behaviour.

Origins of psychodynamic theory

Sigmund Freud specialized in neurology, which in the nineteenth century encompassed psychiatry as well. He started studying cases of *hysteria*, from which he began to develop the theory and method of psychoanalysis (Breuer and Freud, 1895/1955). The hysteria patient suffers a loss of bodily function, such as paralysis, for which no organic cause can be discovered. Freud elicited memories of forgotten events, which, since bringing them to light cured the illness, Freud supposed must have somehow caused it; in every case the patient remembered being seduced by a male relative during childhood. Freud soon reached the conclusion that these childhood seductions had never happened; he argued that the patient 'remembered', it because she unconsciously wished it had happened. (Nineteenth-century medicine thought hysteria a disease of the womb, so the diagnosis could only be made for women.) The hysterical patients, like all women, and all men, had strong sexual desires in childhood, directed towards opposite-sex members of their own family; strong incestuous desires were universal. (Freud's account of the five 'Studies in Hysteria' has been attacked from several directions; critics claim that the women weren't really hysterical, that they weren't really cured and, by implication, that they weren't necessarily imagining the sexual experiences in childhood they described. Chapter 11 shows how sexual abuse in childhood, often by close relatives, happens far oftener than people like to think.)

To uncover these universal, hidden, sexual desires, Freud developed the techniques of psychoanalysis: *free association* and *dream interpretation*. In free association the patient is encouraged to say the first thing to come into his or her mind; with skill and patience the analyst can infer the patient's inner conflicts. In 1900 Freud published his massive work on *The Interpretation of Dreams*, describing how unconscious desires and fears are revealed in dreams, in censored and coded forms. Psychoanalysis began to attract followers, and to expand and diversify until it offered an explanation for practically every aspect of human behaviour. Freud himself wrote on matters as diverse as the psychology of humour and the interpretation of Leonardo da Vinci's personality as revealed in his drawings (unfortunately Freud derived his insights from details included in a bad copy, but absent in Leonardo's original (Farrell, 1963)).

From this vast output one can extract a theory of personality, but nowhere does Freud state his theory in the way that Allport or Cattell or Eysenck does; rather it has to be assembled from scattered hints, many of them elaborated by Freud's followers. Furthermore, Freud's views developed over the years, especially his ideas about motivation, which were changed by the First World War. Freud's critics often say that psychoanalysis is more like a religion than a science; certainly deriving a theory of personality from the 24 volumes of Freud's Collected Works is more akin to biblical criticism than scientific activity.

FREUD'S THEORY OF PERSONALITY

Three areas of Freud's thought are relevant to his account of personality: the divisions of the mind (described in Chapter 7), the psychosexual stages of development, and the defence mechanisms.

The theory of psychosexual stages

The drives of the id consist of very generalized sexual impulses, which centre in turn on different areas of the body, or *erogenous zones*. The theory of *psychosexual development* was first formulated in 1905 in *Three Essays on Sexuality* (Freud, 1905/1966). (It's difficult to get the true flavour of Freud's thought without reading some of the original; the *Three Essays* is probably the best starting point for the student of personality. The flavour is stronger in the original German.) The shell-shock cases of World War I caused Freud to add a death instinct to the life-giving sexual instincts of the id. The death wish can account for suicide and 'life-threatening' behaviours such as alcoholism and drug addiction.

Freud had two very unusual, and very unpopular, ideas about human sexuality. He argued that children have a definite sexuality, and that a wide variety of apparently non-sexual activities have a large sexual component. The two ideas together form the theory of *pan-sexualism*. The ideas that 4-year-old children have sexual impulses, or that breast feeding is a sexual experience, strike many people even today as absurd and revolting, so one can imagine the impact in the 1890s. Freud wrote 'When I later began more and more resolutely to put forward the significance of sexuality in the aetiology of the neuroses, he [Josef Breuer] was the first to show the reaction of distaste and repudiation which was later to become so familar to me, but which at that time I had not yet learnt to recognise as my inevitable fate' (Freud, 1914/1966).

The three events in childhood to which Freud attributed immense sexual significance, and which he thought shaped the individual's personality lastingly, were breast-feeding and weaning, toilet training, and what came to be called the Oedipus complex. Freud saw the forces of the id centring successively on the mouth, the anus and the genitals. Each contains a mucous membrane, so each could be a source of sexual satisfaction. Each, in turn, is a source of sexual satisfaction for the child, at the age of 12–18 months, 2–2.5 years, and 4–5 years. Freud unaccountably overlooked an important set of mucous membranes – in the nose; his followers have, however, hastened to remedy this oversight (Hollender, 1956). The child runs the risk of *fixation* at each of the stages. Fixation can be caused by *excessive gratification*, as when the child is allowed to continue breast-feeding too long, or by *frustration*, as when the child is weaned too early or too abruptly. Fixation causes *regression*; forever after, the fixated person reverts under pressure to that childhood phase's behaviour patterns, but in very indirect or symbolic ways.

THE ORAL PHASE. The excessively gratified breast-feeder tends to be optimistic and dependent, to desire a regular income, to be generous and cheerful, and to like soft foods; the frustrated breast-feeder tends to be pessimistic, clinging, impatient, hostile and cruel. The reasoning here is fairly clear; the gratified breast-feeder expects the good things of life to last, while the frustrated one doesn't. Some psychoanalysts distinguish two phases in breast-feeding, a first, sucking phase, and a later, biting phase, where the child derives satisfaction from biting the breast or nipple. The *oral-sadistic* person is characterized by hostility, and – a typical Freudian metaphor – has a 'biting' or sarcastic manner. When frustrated – presumably the usual fate of the oral-sadistic infant unless born of a masochistic mother – the outcome is envy, hostility, jealousy and malice.

THE ANAL PHASE. This part of the theory usually strikes people as the least probable, and most offensive. Here Freudian theory shows its 'self-sealing' nature to advantage; the more offensive one claims to find the idea of the anal personality, the more clearly one is proving its truth. The critic, so the argument runs, objects so strongly to the anality hypothesis not because it's absurdly wrong but because it's true, and because the critic is anally fixated. Criticism of the theory is motivated by the critic's unconscious fear of his or her unacceptable sexuality. Dealing with criticism by interpreting it as a symptom is an *ad hominem* argument; the personality of the critic cannot detract from the validity of his or her criticisms.

At age 3, the forces of the id centre on the second erogenous zone – the anus – where pan-sexually satisfying sensations can be derived either from excretion or from retaining a full bowel. The child also tends to regard the excrement as its own property and, until checked by parents, to play with it. Parents have definite ideas about the right time and place for excretion, and seek to toilet train or 'pot' the child as early as possible; hence the child's desire to retain his or her excrement is usually frustrated. The result is the *anal triad*: obstinacy (= refusal to excrete to parental order), parsimony (= desire to retain own excrement) and orderliness (= trained to excrete in right place at right time). Freud's followers (E.E. Jones, 1923; Abraham, 1921/1965) elaborate the theme; the anal character may include procrastination, persistence, inability to deputize, minute attention to detail, resentment of advice, urge to clean things, and interest in the backs of things. The anal person often goes on hoarding things, as he or she once tried to hoard excrement. It may be money, which is often brown, and frequently referred to with possibly excrement-inspired metaphors – 'filthy rich', 'rolling in it' – or it may be possessions; 'all collectors are anal erotic' (Abraham, 1921/1965). Abraham adds the insight that people who like statistics and timetables are anal.

Here then – at last – is the explanation of the man who collects Bradshaws; he is doubly anal. Not merely does he have a desire to hoard things, but he is obsessed with timing, just as his parents once were – with the timing of his bowel movements. Anal erotism is particularly significant, precisely because almost none of it can be expressed directly; it must find indirect expression in ways that shape personality. Oral erotism, by contrast, can be expressed directly, through kissing, 'page three girls' etc., so has less need to find indirect expression.

THE OEDIPUS AND ELECTRA COMPLEXES.   By age 5, the child's pan-sexual drive has shifted from the anus to the genitals, and from the child's own body to another person's. The 5-year-old wants to possess physically the opposite-sex parent and to push aside the same-sex parent, who constitutes a rival for the opposite-sex parent's affections. The child experiences the strong incestuous desires that Freud first detected in the false memories of childhood seductions reported by his hysteria patients. Freud called the male version of this the *Oedipus complex*, after the figure of Greek legend who 'accidentally' achieved as a man his childhood desire to kill his father and marry his mother. No single concept of modern psychology has made more impact on the popular imagination than the Oedipus complex. The equivalent female experience – desire to kill mother and possess father – is called the *Electra complex*.

The 5-year-old boy does not, however, achieve his murderous and incestuous ambitions; instead he *represses* his desires because he fears he will be castrated if he doesn't. He fears castration when he sees that his sister has no external genitalia like his, and infers that she once did have but was deprived of them for an offence like the one he is contemplating; he develops a *castration complex*. To avoid castration the boy represses into the unconscious mind his desire for his mother and his hostility to his father. To appease the father, who is the likely castrator, the boy adopts the father's outlook and values – *identification*. The 5-year-old girl, by contrast, does not fear castration, but infers from observation of her brother's external genitalia that she once had a set like it, but lost it as a punishment for misbehaviour. She goes through life mourning the loss of her penis and feeling, as a consequence, inferior to the male – *penis envy*.

LATENT PERIOD. For both sexes the events of the Oedipal/Electral phase are so threatening that they are repressed, along with all interest in sex, and all memory of the first five years of life. Any memories people think they have of this period are likely to be false, and psychodynamically determined. (This is another self-sealing feature – the fact that people can't remember ever having incestuous desires 'proves' the theory.) Sexual impulses remain dormant throughout the *latent period*, and the child busies itself with sports, games, hobbies, etc. until the onset of puberty reawakens the conflicts created in the first five years of life.

The Oedipal/Electral hypothesis generates one highly controversial prediction about sex differences. Because the female believes she has already been punished, by castration, for displeasing her mother, she has less incentive to appease, so adopts less thoroughly the mother's outlook and values. Hence, according to orthodox Freudian theory, women have inferior moral characters. Otherwise, perhaps because the Oedipus/Electra complex is universal, it doesn't create any obvious individual differences. It may be predicted (Kline, 1972), in a rather vague sort of way, that children raised in orphanages or communes or single-parent families will differ, but no particular direction of difference is specified. However, the Oedipus/Electra complex creates a reservoir of psychic energy, the control of which by defence mechanisms shapes many aspects of adult personality.

Defence mechanisms

Everyone experiences conflict between the id wanting to perform actions and the ego which cannot permit them; everyone wants to bite the maternal breast, or smear excrement on the wall, or get into bed with the opposite-sex parent, but daren't, and daren't even think about it. These unacceptable impulses and thoughts are dealt with by defence mechanisms: *sublimation, repression, denial, projection* and *reaction formation*. Like other parts of Freudian theory, their operation has been described in greater detail by Freud's followers. The ones that contribute most to individual differences in adult personality are reaction formation, projection and sublimation.

REACTION FORMATION. Anal fixation normally causes meanness, but sometimes the person reacts against this trait – unconsciously of course – and instead of being psychodynamically mean, becomes psychodynamically over-generous. Critics (Eysenck, 1953) see this as another 'self-sealing' device. If someone whose toilet training was very frustrating turns out not to be mean, one simply invokes reaction formation to explain the discrepancy. Eysenck's criticism is a little unfair, because reaction formation does predict an either/or – either very mean or very generous – and excludes the in-between.

PROJECTION. Paranoia is the expression of repressed homosexuality; 'I love him' becomes 'I hate him' (by reaction formation), which in turn becomes the delusional belief 'He hates me' or 'He is plotting against me'. The unacceptable impulse is first turned upside down, then projected on to the other person. Sears (1936) researched the projection of meanness. Mean people cannot admit they are mean, because the trait is psychodynamically shaped by the anal phase; therefore they project meanness, by misperceiving themselves as generous and other people as mean. This is – apparently – a readily testable prediction: in a group of students, those who are actually the meanest will rate the rest of the class as mean and themselves as generous. The first problem in Sears's study was finding a criterion of actual meanness; Sears used the average rating given each person by the rest of the class, so used as criterion the very ratings whose fallibility he hoped to demonstrate. His second problem was that no one in the class on his criterion, was particularly mean, so there was no reason to suppose anyone needed defences.

SUBLIMATION. This can explain a wide variety of career choices. It differs from the other defence mechanisms because it is usually successful; a sublimated impulse is permanently redirected, and doesn't keep trying to re-express itself. Anal erotism may be sublimated by painting; oil paint is messy stuff that can be legitimately handled. The playing of musical instruments, and by extension interest in music generally, is a sublimation of the urge to masturbate. The surgeon sublimates oral sadism by the legitimate and useful cutting of bodies. Virtually any career or achievement can be interpreted as the sublimation of some unacceptable childhood impulse; as Stafford-Clarke (1965) puts it, 'Freud did believe that the highest excursions of the human spirit, in the worlds of creative art and science, gained their impetus at the human level from the reserves of libidinal energy diverted to their use'. But a theory that explains why artists paint, musicians play and surgeons operate must logically explain why psychoanalysts psychoanalyse. The researcher into the human mind or human behaviour is, 'really', in sublimated form, trying to satisfy his or her sexual curiosity, specifically to find out what his or her parents are doing behind the bedroom door. All psychologists are sublimated voyeurs.

VERIFYING FREUD'S THEORY

When George Kelly, the personal construct theorist, first read Freud, he described his reaction as 'incredulity that anyone could write such nonsense, much less publish it'. Psychoanalytic theory, Kelly complained, 'is shot through with anthropomorphisms, vitalisms and energisms that are only a few short steps removed from primitive notions of demoniacal possession and exorcism' (1955). Freud formed his ideas a century ago, when ideas about scientific proof and evidence weren't as strict as they are today. To the critical modern eye, Freudian personality theory is full of glaring omissions, obvious self-contradictions and fantastic assertions. To mention a few:

- Most adults can, and do, derive sexual pleasure from the mouth and breast; some, rather fewer, from the anus. Can one equate some adults with all children and argue that all children derive sexual pleasure from excretion and/or non-excretion? An ingenious experimenter, armed with modern techniques of measuring sexual arousal, and unencumbered by either ethical standards or any marked concern about an academic future, could probably contrive a direct test of this hypothesis. However, proving some children are sexually excited by excretion would still leave an immense inferential gulf to bridge, from childhood sexual excitement to adult personality.

- The Oedipus/Electra complex raises a number of questions. Will every child see a child of the opposite sex naked, and so make the all-important observation of different genitalia? What about only children? Did parents in nineteenth-century Europe allow their children to see each other naked? Why should boy and girl react to the anatomical sex difference by supposing the girl had once been like the boy?

- The Oedipus hypothesis also offends the scientific principle of parsimony. The boy is supposed to fear castration after seeing a naked female, and drawing the false inference she once had a penis. Yet Freud's own analysis of 'little Hans' recalls much more direct threats to the nineteenth-century child. Little Hans played with his penis, and was told not to by his parents; if he persisted, they threatened, the doctor (their GP, not Freud) would come and cut it off (Freud, 1909/1966). Threats like that were probably fairly common, for the nineteenth-century terror of masturbation was at its height, with blindness, deafness, insanity and general debilitation blamed on it by respectable medical authorities. (A few unfortunate 'persistent masturbators' really were castrated to 'cure' them of the vice.) But if boys were being directly threatened with castration, why postulate that castration anxiety arose from observation of sex differences, with all the implausibilities and unanswered questions involved?

- Freud argues that gender-role learning, which is part of identification, results from the Oedipus/Electra complex. Suppose parent–child conflicts at this age arise through gender-role learning? The 4–5-year-old boy must start modelling himself on his father, whereas girls can continue to model themselves on their mothers. Note that this generates the opposite prediction to Freud's theory. Girls don't have to transfer identification from mother to father, so it isn't weakened, so they adopt mother's moral standards more completely, with the result that female moral standards are superior. (Both theories assume the parental standards being absorbed are moral ones.) The available evidence (Sears *et al.*, 1957) shows a very slight tendency for 5-year-old girls to be better behaved than boys.

Empirical research on Freudian personality theory

Trait theory can be tested by correlating across time and place. Eysenck's psychophysiological theory predicts that extraverts will condition better, or that neurotics will show greater autonomic lability. Learning approaches can be tested in principle; the difficulties are the practical ones of finding a sample of parents willing to act naturally with their children in front of the experimenter, having the good fortune to be on hand when important events happen, and then waiting 10 to 20 years for the resulting adult personality to emerge. Freudian theory has the same problems, of inaccessible events and long time scales, but adds extra difficulties by demanding to be verified on its own terms. For the Freudian, evidence derives from free association, dreams, slips of the tongue, minute gestures, etc. Analysis is a very lengthy, very skilled, one-to-one process, so it's pointless to ask about inter-analyst agreement or replication.

Any apparently relevant information collected by non-analysts is of no interest; Freud wrote in 1905: 'None, however, but physicians who practise psychoanalysis can have any access whatever to this sphere of knowledge' (Freud, 1905/1966). He goes on to say: 'if mankind had been able to learn from a direct observation of children, these three essays [*Three Essays on Sexuality*] could have remained unwritten'. Freud did not form his ideas about childhood by studying children, but by psychoanalysing adults. Freud did say, in his analysis of little Hans (Freud, 1909/1966), that analytic theory could be confirmed by studying children. However, the evidence from little Hans is more of the same: interpretations of Hans's fantasies, dreams and fears, the truth of which are supposedly demonstrated by Hans's often far-from-whole-hearted acceptance of them.

The 'analysts only' argument may be countered in three ways. First, the onus of proof lies with those who make improbable assertions, not with those who doubt them. Secondly, it's fundamentally unscientific to claim that only a special class of person can gain insight into personality formation. Thirdly, Farrell (1963) argues that psychoanalysis 'is not so much a tool of observation and discovery as a technique of human transformation, with obvious resemblance to the techniques of religious conversion and brainwashing.' The analyst offers interpretations to the analysee, and puts considerable pressure on him or her to accept them; reluctance to accept them is seen as *resistance*, as proof that the interpretations are correct. Eysenck and Wilson (1973) go one stage further and argue that analysts, because they have all been analysed as part of their training, are actually unsuited to collect scientific data, because they are necessarily biased.

If data provided by analysis – collected 'on the couch' – are not scientific data, it falls to non-analysts to test predictions derived from Freudian theory. A necessary starting point is a list of predictions that are testable and genuinely psychoanalytic. Rapaport and Gill (1959) draw a useful distinction between four levels of psychoanalytic proposition:

1. *Empirical propositions*. Around age 4 to 5, boys regard their fathers as rivals.

2. *Specific psychoanalytic propositions.* The solution of the Oedipus conflict is a decisive determinant of character formation and pathology.

3. *General psychoanalytic propositions.* 'Structure formation by means of identifications and anticathexes explains theoretically the consequence of the "decline of the Oedipus complex"'.

4. *Metapsychological propositions.* 'The propositions of the general psychoanalytic theory which explain the Oedipal situation and the decline of the Oedipus complex involve dynamic, economic, structural, genetic, and adaptive assumptions'. Farrell (1963) notes dryly 'This is, of course, the most general statement of all'.

Of these four levels of proposition, only the first is empirically verifiable. The second might be confirmed by demonstrating that all empirical propositions contained in the theory of the Oedipus complex were true. No observations of any sort could verify the third- and fourth-level propositions. However, the first level, that of empirical proposition, isn't specifically psychoanalytic; hence, strictly speaking, psychoanalytic theory isn't verifiable.

Research testing propositions derived from Freudian theory has been reviewed several times (Sears, 1940; Kline, 1972, 1982). There are six types of evidence:

1. studies of adult personality;

2. studies of child-rearing and child behaviour;

3. projective and percept-genetic techniques;

4. retrospective studies;

5. longitudinal or follow-up studies;

6. cross-cultural research.

Studies of adult personality seek evidence of psychosexual traits in adults. Studies of child-rearing and behaviour look for evidence that parents do the sort of things Freud describes, and that they have the effects he predicts. Neither in itself can prove Freudian hypotheses, but both can throw doubt on them. Thus finding evidence of anal personality syndromes in adults doesn't prove they developed from toilet training, but finding no proof of the existence of the anal personality in adults casts doubt on the whole theory of anality. Similarly, evidence of boy–father hostility doesn't in itself prove the theory of the Oedipus complex, but absence of hostility tends to disprove it. Neither type of data can positively prove Freudian theory, for both fail to make the vital link between child-rearing and adult personality. *Projective* and *percept-genetic* techniques look for Freudian themes in the way adults or children interpret ambiguous pictures.

The 10-year gap between early child-rearing and adult personality can be bridged by the fourth and fifth types of data—restrospective and longitudinal studies. In the retrospective study, adult personality is measured by questionnaire or projective test, and related to information about child-rearing from the subject or his or her parents. The snag is that few people have any idea when they were weaned or toilet trained. In fact, Freudian theory specifically predicts memory of both will have been repressed, not simply forgotten. Parental recollections, although not subject to repression, prove equally unreliable; parents can't give an accurate report of their ways of dealing with the child even 1 year later, let alone 10 (Robbins, 1963). Therefore only the longitudinal study can provide conclusive proof; child-rearing is studied at the time, adult personality is measured later, and the two are correlated. The cost and difficulty of such studies ensure that few have been carried out, of which only one (Hernstein, 1963) tests a Freudian hypothesis.

Studies of adult personality

Kline (1982) reviews factor analyses of inventories like 16PF, and goes to some trouble to try to equate Cattell's factors with psychosexual traits. Three factors of the 16PF—G: super-ego control, 'persevering, conscientious', Q3: will control; and Q4: id demand—'might be related to the anal character'; another three—Q2: self-sufficiency; F: surgency, 'cheerful, sociable, energetic', and E: dominance, confident, boastful, aggressive'—'could be related to orality'. The other 10 can't claim even these tenuous links with the Freudian account of personality. Kline's survey of 50 surface traits and 22 source traits (including 8 that aren't in the published 16PF) concludes that 56 of Cattell's source and surface traits are not remotely psychosexual, which means a lot of adult personality is completely unaccounted for by psychosexual theory.

Some personality tests were designed specifically to measure Freudian themes. The Dynamic Personality Inventory (DPI) measures a variety of Freudian themes, including no less than five scales of anal personality: anal hoarding, anal attention to detail, anal conservatism, anal submission to authority, and anal sadism. The DPI can differentiate homosexual men from heterosexual (homosexual men higher on need for warmth, narcissism, and feminine identification), but otherwise hasn't confirmed any psychoanalytic hypotheses. Kline's (1969) own Ai3q test finds meanness, orderliness and obstinacy go together, confirming the existence of the anal triad. Factor analysis of the DPI and other tests also confirms the existence of oral-optimist and oral-pessimist personalities (Kline and Storey, 1980). Showing that anal and oral personality traits exist and can be measured by questionnaire is a first small step for Freudian theory. However, showing that some adults are very concerned about cleanliness proves nothing about hypothesized origins in toilet training.

Kline makes one last attempt to verify oral hypotheses from questionnaires completed by adults, by trying to show that oral adults have preferences that only Freudian theory could predict. For example, pen-chewers and smokers score higher on oral pessimism, even though the questionnaire contains no direct reference to chewing, smoking, eating or the mouth. Pen-chewing and smoking are obviously oral behaviours, and often reflect strong anxiety, so could well have a psychodynamic origin. Other predictions, however, weren't confirmed; members of a Dracula society were neither oral optimists nor oral pessimists, and dentists aren't oral sadists (Kline and Storey, 1980).

Studies of child-rearing and child behaviour
The theory of the Oedipus complex generates six hypotheses testable by observation, survey and experiment (Kline, 1972), namely:

1. boys have an overt love for their mothers, which is later repressed;

2. boys are hostile towards their fathers;

3. girls have an overt love for their fathers, which is later repressed;

4. girls are hostile towards their mothers;

5. boys fear castration;

6. girls greatly desire a penis and regret their lack of one.

Earlier research, reviewed by Sears (1940), used survey methods, simply asking children what they felt for their parents, what they thought about physical gender differences, etc. The results didn't support any of the six predictions. Nearly all 4–5-year-olds, of either sex, liked their mothers, and either liked or were indifferent to their fathers. Only 4 per cent showed the predicted Oedipal pattern. No boys expressed any fear of castration; no girls supposed they'd ever had a penis, or said they would like to have one. Similarly negative results emerge from studies of breast-feeding, weaning and toilet training (Orlansky, 1949; Sewell, 1952; Sears *et al.*, 1957); the child's behaviour at the time and shortly afterwards wasn't affected (Freud didn't, however, specifically predict an effect until adulthood).

Some studies suggest severe toilet training is part of a broader pattern of parental behaviour. One study found parents who toilet trained severely also tended to have unsympathetic attitudes to their children and to reject them; the children reacted with aggressive and competitive traits and phobias (Wittenborn, 1956). Another study used 10 behavioural tests of anal tendencies in 5-year-olds – messiness in finger painting, persistence in trying to solve insoluble puzzles, hoarding supplies of free gravel generously supplied by the experimenters, etc. The tests didn't really confirm the existence of the anal triad, and were quite unrelated to severity, duration or earliness of toilet training; however, scores did correlate modestly with a questionnaire measure of the children's parents' anal personality (Hetherington and Brackbill, 1963).

Projective and percept-genetic techniques

One doesn't need to be a committed Freudian to regard survey methods as a little simple-minded. Asking children what they think about their parents invites a conventional, socially desirable answer. It also fails to take account of repression. The 4–5-year-old-cannot admit his or her true feelings, and may not know what they are at the conscious level. The analyst uses free association, dreams and resistance to infer the child's true feelings, but the analyst hasn't a monopoly on techniques of getting information people are reluctant to give. In projective tests, people read meanings into inkblots or deliberately vague drawings, and so project their conflicts into what they see. A paranoid woman might see in a Rorschach blot something with eyes that watch her; a homosexual man might see a crab, capable of castrating him. The Blacky Pictures portray dogs instead of people to make the test less threatening, but are otherwise rather obvious in purpose – castration anxiety is measured by a picture of a large knife threatening to cut off the dog's tail.

Projective methods have been used to test the central Oedipal hypotheses that 5-year-olds want sexual relations with the opposite-sex parent, and that 5-year-old boys fear castration (Friedman, 1952). Hidden incestuous desires were detected by a picture of a small girl standing near the bottom of a flight of stairs with a man. When asked what would happen next, girls tended to say the two went up the stairs together more frequently than did boys. How does this confirm the Oedipal incestuous desire hypothesis? Because mounting the stairs is a Freudian *dream symbol* of sexual intercourse, so girls who chose this outcome were symbolically expressing incestuous desires. Boys chose it less often, because they experienced no such desires.

To test the hypothesis of the castration complex, children of both sexes and various ages up to 15 completed stories about animals losing their tails. Boys at ages 5 and 13–14 were less likely to say the animal lost its tail than boys at other ages (Figure 9.1); no effect of age was found in girls. For tail, read penis, and the inference is clear: 5-year-old and 13–14-year-old boys fear castration, which causes them to avoid the obvious tail-loss ending to the story, whereas boys in pre-Oedipal and latent periods, and girls at all ages, have no such fear to project into the animal's tail story. Friedman also detected negative feelings towards same-sex parents in a story-completion task, even though the children, when asked directly, admitted to no hostility.

Studies like this are convincing to the extent that more mundane interpretations can be excluded; Friedman's study remains one of the best single proofs of the Oedipal hypothesis, because it's difficult to think of a convincing non-Freudian explanation of his results. Other studies are less convincing, and a few are openly frivolous. For example, Johnson (1966) noted that more women than men took away his pencils, equated pencil with penis, and claimed to have proved the existence of penis envy in women. Possibly, so long as one can exclude several much more boring explanations: that women are more forgetful, or found the experiment more stressful, or had less money to buy their own pencils, or even that women are less honest.

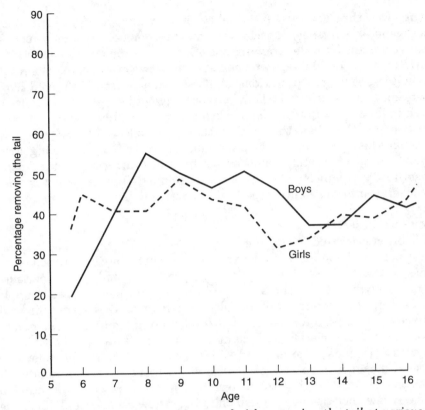

Figure 9.1 *The percentages of boys and girls removing the tail at various age levels (Friedman, 1952).*

In percept-genetic technique, a potentially threatening picture is shown a number of times, initially for too short a time to be perceived, then for longer periods, until it is exposed for long enough to be clearly seen. After each exposure, subjects describe or draw what they think they saw (Kragh and Smith, 1970). Kline used the method with a picture of a suckling pig – clearly an oral theme – and found what he considers clear evidence of Freudian defences; one subject twice described the piglet suckling, then on the next, longer, exposure of the same picture, said it wasn't suckling (Kline and Cooper, 1977). Another subject variously didn't mention the suckling (repression), said the piglet was feeding at a trough (displacement) and didn't mention the piglet at all (repression again).

Retrospective and longitudinal studies
One or two early researches using the retrospective method are often cited as confirming Freudian hypotheses. Goldman-Eisler (1950) found a low positive correlation – around $r = 0.30$ – between a questionnaire measure of oral pessimism in young adults, and early weaning reported by their mothers. Beloff (1957) found no direct link between toilet training and subsequent anal personality, but reported a large ($r = 0.51$) correlation between parent's and child's anality.

This suggests that the anal personality, if it exists, may be formed by the parents' general attitudes, especially to matters vaguely indecent such as sex and excretion, not by toilet training specifically. The one and only longitudinal study (Hernstein, 1963) reports no correlation between 18-year-olds' oral preferences in Rorschach interpretations or dependency in the TAT, and length of breast-feeding or nursing. It isn't a true longitudinal study, but uses data collected in infancy, as part of the Berkeley Growth Study. This ingenious form of time travel suffers from the problem that data collected for one purpose may not suit another, especially not something as specialized as testing Freudian theory. The oral character hypothesis mentions gratification and frustration in breast-feeding, which isn't the same as length – but length was the only breast-feeding information recorded in the Berkeley Growth Study.

Cross-cultural research

Freud is often criticized for basing his psychology on a handful of middle-class Viennese neurotics – much as modern academic psychology bases itself on college students and white rats. Might not child-rearing and family relations take such different forms in other cultures that Freud's account simply doesn't apply? Or might the differing customs of other cultures help prove or disprove his theories? One survey extracted information about upbringing from anthropological files on 75 very varied societies, and compared it with data on white, American, middle-class methods (Whiting and Child, 1953). Weaning and toilet training practices differ enormously across cultures, with the American middle class – back in the 1940s – tending to be one of the most restrictive and punitive societies. A few societies never wean children. A few seem entirely unconcerned with toilet training. Freudian theory predicts an absence of anal personalities in the latter, and a lot of oral optimism in the former. Unfortunately the anthropological files don't include any measures of either. Kline (1969) finds that Ghanaians, whose toilet training Kline thinks is very strict, get higher scores on his questionnaire measure of anal personality. Whiting and Child were able to show that explanations of disease and illness were linked to Freudian aspects of child-rearing. For example, a society that believed kissing caused illness tended to worry a lot about weaning, showing that oral frustration produced later anxiety centred on the mouth. The link was strongest for weaning, weak for toilet training, and non-existent for the Oedipal/Electral phase. No effect of excessive gratification at any phase could be found.

Closeness of child to parents also varies from society to society. Sometimes there are always a lot of relatives in the home – and in some societies as many subordinate wives as the man can afford. Some societies live communally, while some, notably modern Israel, raise children communally. The Western pattern of parents and children living in the privacy of their brick box stands out in contrast. This implies that Oedipal pressures will be greater in Western society, and reduced, possibly absent, in others. In fact, Oedipal pressures should be greater today than in Freud's time, because people have fewer children, no servants, and often move away from the extended family of in-laws, grand-parents, etc., so the preschool child gets a much more concentrated dose of parental influence. Whiting and Child tested hypotheses about the number of relatives in the home and strength of identification with the parents, but failed to find evidence of a link. A study of Israeli kibbutzim (Rabin, 1958) found that communally reared children showed less Oedipal conflict on a projective test, which is consistent with Freudian theory, but, as Kline (1982) points out, equally consistent with the common-sense proposition that the less you see of your parents, the smaller will be the emotional attachment to them. A long-term follow-up that showed altered rates of crime (= evidence of lack of identification) or homosexuality (= unresolved Oedipus complex) might be more convincing. The only evidence (Maccoby and Feldman, 1972) finds kibbutz children as well adjusted as children reared in conventional homes.

CONCLUSION

Attempts to verify Freudian theory by experiment and survey have been largely unsuccessful. Attempts to verify it by cross-cultural data have been inconclusive. In part this reflects the general difficulty of proving any link between early childhood experiences and later adult personality. In part, however, the failure reflects the nature of the theory itself. Some of its defects have been noted: vagueness, overinclusiveness, suspect claims to special forms of knowledge, and devices such as repression, resistance and reaction formation that 'explain' any apparent contradiction. But Freudian theory is also absurdly overambitious, the last word in very long-range determinism. The fact that one dreams about bats, or types 'Oedipud' for 'Oedipus', or arrives two minutes late for a lecture can all be interpreted as the inevitable outcome of forces set up many years ago. People are like mechanical toys that have been wound up, and left to perform their in-built routines. This is obviously very unlikely. Even if Freud's theories were correct, the link between early childhood experience and adult personality could never be more than indirect and statistically small. Freudian theory claims everybody who collects old railway timetables, or stamps, or beermats, or who is careful with their money (or spendthrift) had a particular type of toilet training; everybody who had that type of toilet training will collect things, be mean etc. Can there be no other outcome of frustrating toilet training (such as nothing in particular, as the evidence strongly suggests)? Can there be no other cause of the urge to collect, or of meanness?

Invert the relation between toilet training and collecting, and another defect becomes apparent: psychoanalysis explains too much, too easily. The range of possible predictions from the theory of the anal personality is enormous; with the aid of reaction formation, Freudian symbolism and sublimation, virtually any adult behaviour can be interpreted as evidence of anal fixation. This unlimited power of explanation seemed to some analysts proof of the theory's value; Karl Popper (1963) agreed that he 'could not think of any human behaviour which could not be interpreted in terms of either [Freudian or Adlerian] theory', but drew a very different conclusion. A theory that can explain everything explains nothing. The all-embracing nature of Freudian theory was one of the things that helped Popper devise his well-known criterion of *falsifiability*; a theory that can explain everything cannot be falsified, therefore it cannot be tested, therefore it isn't a scientific theory.

THE Bradshaw used in the example at the beginning of this chapter isn't an original 1938 edition; it's a modern facsimile reprint. Enough people in Britain want to collect old railway timetables to make it worth a publisher's while to print more copies. Which perhaps goes to prove an assertion that some of Freud's followers – whose claims often make Freud appear a model of precision, clarity and moderation – put forward: we live in an anal society.

Four Examples

THE motivational line's first station – motives – finds a fixed set of inherited and/or physiological forces, variations in the profile of which create individual differences. Motives lie some distance below the surface of behaviour, but their existence can be inferred from comparative data, both cross-cultural, anthropological comparisons, and comparisons between humans and animals. In theory, motives could be measured behaviourally, or even physiologically, but in practice large-scale research tends to rely more on paper-and-pencil, questionnaire methods. But since a questionnaire measure of motives resembles very closely indeed a questionnaire measure of traits, one wonders again whether the journey was really necessary, and whether it has taken one to a genuinely different destination.

Psychoanalysis explains personality by the interplay of a few all-embracing and very powerful forces, shaped by very early experience. Psychoanalysis undoubtedly succeeds in travelling far below the surface of behaviour, and certainly arrives at a genuinely different destination from any other account of personality. Its problem is that it may have travelled too far, and may have left the realm of psychology altogether. Much of psychoanalysis has more in common with metaphysics or mythology. Psychoanalysis also succeeds where other theories fail; it develops a set of entirely new measures and doesn't simply rely on questionnaires with different titles but the same central content. Unfortunately, the new measures psychoanalysis has invented – dreams, free association, resistance – have moved so far from conventional methods of measurement that they are beyond the ken of the scientific psychologist.

This final section looks at four examples of human personality: aggression, sexual deviation, alcoholism and resilience. The aim is to give the reader some idea of how the various approaches to personality deal with four important issues.

CHAPTER 10

The School Bully

Aspects of Aggression

BULLYING goes on in schools throughout the Western world. It's been a feature of British schools since *Tom Brown's Schooldays*, set in the 1830s. It's usually accepted as 'one of those things', but sometimes gets noticed by the press; the ensuing discussions are dominated by sociologists, politicians and miscellaneous pundits, and rarely include a psychologist.

Bullying caught the public eye in Sweden in the 1970s, and was variously blamed on large schools, large classes, resentment of bright pupils by 'underachievers', frustration and failure engendered by the educational system, or deviance (in the bullied, not the bullies). The prevailing Swedish orthodoxy thought bullying was caused by inequality and deprivation, still not finally solved by 40 years of uninterrupted socialist government. Anyone who bothered to consider the bully said he (or more rarely she) was 'basically' insecure and anxious, projecting his/her inadequacies on deviant co-pupils.

In the midst of this clamour of speculation, much of it clearly motivated by ideology or professional interest (smaller classes require more teachers), a lone Norwegian psychologist, Dan Olweus, actually went out and collected some evidence. He found that 1 in 20 of Swedish schoolboys are bullies, and 1 in 20 gets bullied. The problem doesn't 'sort itself out' if the school ignores it; three years on, the same bullies were making life miserable for the same victims. Bullies weren't victims of the school system of social deprivation; their intelligence and achievement were average, as was their social background. The same was true of their victims. Bullying was unrelated to class or school size. Bullies didn't pick on 'deviant' children–the fat, the immigrant, the handicapped.

Olweus concluded that bullying is caused by bullies, who bully others because they like bullying; bullies are raised by parents who give their sons too little love and too much freedom. Bullies are not unpopular–girls quite like them–nor are they insecure or secretly anxious. Olweus made very sure of this last point; he supplemented questionnaire measures with teachers' and parents' reports, projective tests and even urine analyses–bullies secreted less adrenalin under stress (Olweus, 1980b).

Olweus's conclusions may not seem very surprising to the general public, who usually explain how people behave by what they're like. But Olweus directly contradicts received opinion in the social sciences on aggression and other social problems. Olweus says bullying is caused by persons and personalities, not social forces; some boys are bullies, not because they're deprived or frustrated or discriminated against, but because they enjoy it. And they enjoy it because of the way they were brought up–badly, in Olweus's opinion.

Definitions

Aggression is the act, *aggressiveness* is the trait and *anger* is the emotion (recall that McDougall and Cattell matched an emotion to every motive). Most definitions of aggression first say what it is, then what it isn't. Buss (1961) defines aggression as 'delivering a noxious stimulus to another person in an interpersonal context', then qualifies his definition with a list of exclusions. Aggression doesn't include useful acts that cause pain, which excuses the dentist and the surgeon. Aggression is deliberate, which excludes clumsiness and (most) accidents. Buss excludes damage to objects, which is odd, for most people consider vandalism a form of aggression. Many definitions exclude *predation*: the bird that gets its worm, or the cat that kills the bird. Buss includes *verbal aggression*–where the 'noxious stimulus' is an insult. Laboratory studies have to rely heavily on verbal aggression, especially as the independent variable. Olweus (1979) offers a longer definition: 'any act or behavior that involves, might involve, and/or to some extent can be considered as aiming at, the infliction of injury or discomfort; also manifestations of inner reactions such as feelings or thoughts that can be considered to have such aim'. This includes verbal aggression, excludes accidents and clumsiness, but seems to include the dentist and surgeon.

Some researchers distinguish *prosocial* aggression–on the part of the good and the just, in the shape of parent, teacher, policeman–from *antisocial* (Sears, 1961). Rosenzweig (1945) distinguishes *intro-punitive* aggression, which is directed inwards towards the person him or herself, from *extra-punitive* aggression, which is directed outwards at other people. Other researchers contrast *instrumental* aggression, where goals are obtained by attacking someone, with *hostile* aggression, where the goal *is* attacking someone. Instrumental aggression is a way of getting things. The animal gains territory, food, a mate and uninterrupted enjoyment of them. The human gains territory, food, a mate, money, status. Instrumental aggression is a habit, created by reward and eliminated by punishment or non-reward (Buss, 1961). Dodge and Coie (1987) distinguish *reactive* and *proactive* aggression. Reactively aggressive children strike back when teased, and over-react angrily to accidents; they see others as hostile when in fact they aren't. Proactively aggressive children use physical force to dominate, threaten and bully their peers; teachers see them as leaders and as having a good sense of humour.

MEASURING AGGRESSION

Measures of aggression in children
'Real life' aggression can be observed easily in children, who form a captive audience at school, used to being watched by adults. Olweus (1979) reports high reliabilities ($r = 0.80$) for observing aggression in 3- and 4-year-old children, in three separate studies. Olweus (1980b) also finds that teachers can reliably identify which children in their classes are bullies, and which are bullied. Ratings of children's aggressiveness by other children are also very reliable. The Peer Nomination Inventory (Winder and Wiggins, 1964) includes 12 aggression items such as 'He likes to pick on little kids'; children list which of their classmates fits each description. Wiggins also devised a special game that afforded unusual scope for aggression. The boys played in teams of four, each team in a 'court' of four squares, hitting a hard rubber ball from square to square. There were twice as many boys as squares, so half the boys at any given time had to wait their turn to play; players and non-players switched roles every two minutes. Levels of physical and verbal aggression, 'resistant and oppositional behaviour' (breaking the rules, ignoring instructions) and 'ease of provocation' are extremely high, but predictable from peer nominations. Children's fantasy aggression is sometimes measured by the way they play with dolls (Lesser, 1957).

Measures of aggression in adults
In civilized circles, adults don't usually punch or push each other; they channel their aggression into gossip, insult, plots or fantasy. Adult aggression can be measured by questionnaire and Q sort. Aggression items in Block's Q sort included 'over-reactive to minor frustrations: irritable', 'expresses hostile feelings directly' and 'is alert to real or fancied differences between self and other people'. Q sorts achieve excellent reliabilities in long-term follow-ups; Block (1961) reports up to 0.80 over 18 years. Questionnaire measures include the Buss–Durkee Inventory, which covers *assault, indirect aggression* – 'I sometimes spread gossip about people I don't like' – *irritability, negativism, resentment, suspicion, verbal aggression* 'When I get mad, I say nasty things' – and *guilt* (Buss and Durkee, 1957; Velicer *et al.*, 1985). These days a lot of adult aggression is expressed on the road; Parry's (1968) questionnaire includes items like 'I swear under my breath at other drivers' (endorsed by 84 per cent of men) and 'on occasion I have tried to edge another driver off the road' (endorsed by only 4 per cent of males).

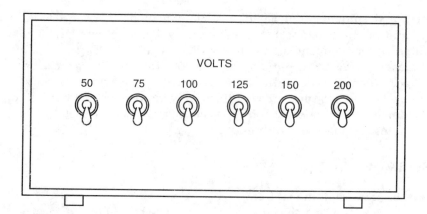

Figure 10.1   *The aggression machine. The subject is led to believe that operating the switches causes an electric shock of the stated voltage to be delivered to the victim.*

'Real-life' adult aggression includes murder, assault, rape and lynching. Many social scientists are wary of crime statistics, arguing that even serious crimes like rape may go unrecorded. Many social scientists are also reluctant to see crime as a pure expression of the criminal's personality, but prefer explanations in terms of peer pressure, deprivation, protest etc.

Two researchers simultaneously but independently invented the 'aggression machine' (Figure 10.1), in which the subject presses buttons to deliver electric shocks of varying intensity to a victim; aggressiveness is defined as the number and voltage of shocks delivered. In Buss's (1961) version, subjects are ostensibly training the victim to perform a simple task, and can use shock if they think the victim isn't trying hard enough. (The shocks never reach their target, even though the victim sometimes groans and gasps realistically.) Milgram (1965) simply ordered his subjects to administer electric shocks of increasing intensity – well past a level most people should know would be dangerous. Critics claim the aggression machine doesn't really measure aggression because the shocks are justified as training incentives, or 'in the interests of science', which makes them as legitimate as the pain the dentist or surgeon causes (Tedeschi *et al.*, 1974).

Many experimenters prefer projective techniques. The TAT can be coded for obvious and subtle signs of aggression. Obvious signs include violence, forceful language, and aggressive thoughts and wishes, while subtler signs include failing to mention the guns included in two pictures: 'The gun is an aggressive object and the fact that the patient avoids it suggests the possibility he may have difficulty in handling aggression' (Lindzey and Tejessy, 1957). People who cannot express their aggression directly tell stories in which people 'die . . . because of natural causes or as a result of an accident'. Projective tests specifically for aggression include Zaks's (1960) 'Draw-a-Man-with-a-Club – the bigger the club the more aggressive the artist – and Rosenzweig's Picture Frustration measure, where subjects write into cartoon bubbles what they think people being frustrated in various ways might say. Mischel (1968) argues that self-ratings of physical aggressiveness work just as well as aggression machines, observations, interviews or projective tests, and are of course much quicker. Mischel evidently doesn't share other researchers' pessimistic assumption that people will be ashamed to admit to being aggressive.

AGGRESSION AS STABLE PERSONALITY TRAIT

Critics listed aggression as one personality trait that doesn't stand up well to close inspection (Mischel, 1968); aggression, they argue, is specific to particular times and places, and isn't a generalized tendency. Sears (1961) found that five measures of aggression correlated moderately well in boys, but not in girls (an interesting difference). Another study found boys were aggressive at school, but not at home (Bandura and Walters, 1963). Later reviews of correlation between different measures of aggression – peer nominations, observations, teacher ratings, self-report, convictions for violent offences – conclude they are consistently positive, and not as low as the 0.30 Mischel argued was typical (Olweus, 1979). Olweus also finds measures of aggression are very stable over time. For children under 6, teacher ratings and observations are highly reliable in the short term, and predict aggression as adults, 18 or 21 years later, to a modest ($r = 0.26$ or 0.36) extent. After age 6, teacher ratings, clinical ratings and peer nominations remain highly reliable in the short term – up to 3 years – and show reasonable stabilities across 10, 14 or 18 years (median $r = 0.53$). Olweus concludes that aggressiveness is almost as stable as intelligence (Figure 10.2)

Several long-term follow-ups show how childhood aggression develops into adult aggression. Kagan and Moss (1962) define adult *retaliation* as 'direct verbal aggression or blatant resistance when attacked, teased, frustrated or restricted by the social environment', and code it from 'open refusal to co-operate with the request of an employer and outbursts of verbal aggression to a spouse, parent, friend or stranger'. Adult retaliation correlates with childhood *aggression to mother, behavioural disorganization* (irritability, tantrums, destructive behaviour) and *dominance*, but only in males; girls who attacked other children became women who showed *less* aggressive retaliation. *Ease of (adult) anger arousal* also correlates with childhood aggression to mother, behavioural disorganization and dominance, also only in males. *Competitive behaviour* in adults is a 'socially more effective method of expressing hostility', and correlates with all forms of childhood aggression, again for males only. *Aggressive conflict* in adults is a composite of worrying about aggression and trying to repress aggressive thoughts and feelings; it correlates negatively with childhood aggression towards mother and behavioural disorganization, this time for both males

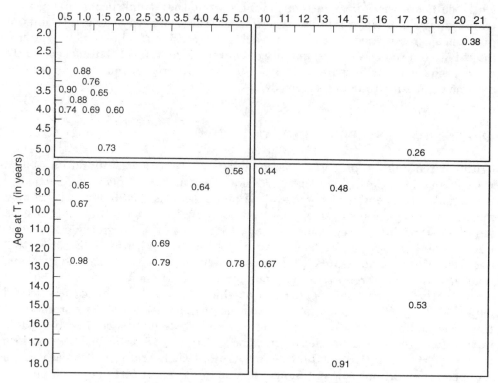

Figure 10.2 *Summary of stability correlations for aggression, corrected for attenuation, plotted against age at time of first assessment (T_1) and against interval between assessments T_1 and T_2 (Olweus, 1979).*

and females. The aggressive, bad-tempered child tends to become an adult who worries less about aggression and doesn't try to control aggressive thoughts.

A 22-year follow up, spanning three generations, finds that children who were punished severely by their parents grow into aggressive 18-year-olds, then aggressive 30-year-olds who punish their children, who in turn become more aggressive (Huesmann *et al.*, 1984). The same follow-up reports that aggressive 8-year-olds grow into less intelligent 30-year-olds (Huesmann *et al.*, 1987), apparently because they get on less well with parents and school. A London follow-up survey of 400 mainly working-class boys finds teacher ratings of aggressiveness correlates ($r = 0.41$) with self-reported aggression (in answers to questions as direct as 'carrying and using weapons in fights'), and also distinguishes very clearly the minority who had by age 21 acquired violent criminal records (West, 1969). The Berkeley Growth Study analysed the later careers of bad-tempered children (Caspi *et al.*, 1989), and found the men did less well in their careers, while the women 'apparently fared less well ... in the marriage market'. Twice as many ill-tempered men were downwardly socially mobile (53 per cent v. 28 per cent); twice as many ill-tempered women got divorced (26 per cent v. 12 per cent).

Results like these support a *genotype* model of lasting dispositions to aggressiveness, expressed in different forms at different ages; the boy who hits other children, teases and threatens them, dominates them, and screams and shouts a lot, becomes the man who competes in games and college grades. But the genotype model may not apply to women. Recall that Sears (1961) found moderate correlations between measures of aggression in boys, but not for girls. Social learning models argue that women are taught not to behave aggressively, hence fail to develop generalized aggressive tendencies like males. Biological models argue that women are 'naturally' less aggressive.

Projective tests of aggression also confirm the genotype model. There is no overall correlation between projective aggression and observed aggressiveness in the school playground (Lesser, 1957); taking account of maternal permissiveness – the factor Olweus found important in producing school bullies – a more complex picture emerges: a negative ($r = -0.41$) correlation in boys whose mothers disapproved of aggression, but a positive correlation ($r = 0.43$) in boys whose mothers approved. The implication is that boys whose mothers disapprove of aggression can only express it indirectly, in fantasy. Another researcher reports similar results – high positive correlations between overt and fantasy aggression in boys with no inhibitions about aggression, but fairly high negative correlations for boys with strong inhibitions (Olweus, 1974).

Anger

It's a common observation that some people have hotter tempers than others. It's also probable that some people have better control of their tempers, giving a two-dimensional model, but only three quadrants: very hot temper but very well controlled, very hot temper quite uncontrolled, and those so even-tempered they don't need control (Figure 10.3). Psychophysiological and behavioural measures of emotions like anger are cumbersome, and give inconsistent results. In animals anger is usually clearly expressed by instinctive mechanisms. The dog stands rigidly, tail outstretched and unmoving, head stretched forward and neck rigid, hair on the back erect; it growls or snarls, and shows its teeth. Anger is caused by a restricted and easily specified set of events – such as trying to take the animal's food away – and has a fairly predictable outcome – the dog bites you. The comparative argument, advanced by McDougall and Cattell, says that if dogs have innate anger displays, humans probably have too. Children react with scowls or temper tantrum when frustrated, but adults have usually learned to keep their emotions under control. Ekman's research (1972) shows facial expressions look much the same and can be recognized across different cultures, suggesting an innate basis. Children born blind and deaf, who could not have learned expressions from seeing or hearing others, still exhibit some

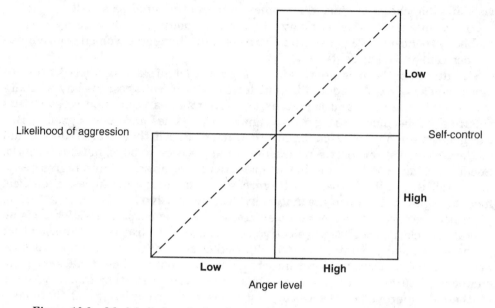

Figure 10.3 *Model of the relationship between anger, self-control and aggression.*

aggressive behaviour patterns: stamping their feet, clenching their teeth and making a fist (Eibl-Eibesfeldt, 1977). Ekman also cites *micro-momentary expressions* – changes of facial expression so fleeting they can only be detected by slowed down film; he interprets them as a momentary slipping of the culturally imposed mask to reveal the individual's true feelings.

Numerous questionnaire measures of emotional control have been devised, e.g. Roger and Najarian's (1989) Emotion Control Questionnaire, or Siegel's (1986) Multidimensional Anger Inventory. Megargee (1966) used the California Psychological Inventory to distinguish extremely assaultive males from moderately assaultive males and property offenders. The extremely assaultive group get 'better' CPI profiles – greater self-control, more responsible, higher achievement, greater tolerance, etc. Extremely assaultive males had tried to murder someone, whereas moderately assaultive men had only hit or kicked someone. But why do extremely aggressive males have 'better' personalities than moderately aggressive ones? Megargee suggested the moderate group are *undercontrolled*, and had never learned to control their aggression. The extreme group, by contrast, are *overcontrolled*, and had always stifled all feelings of anger and aggression – until one day they lost control suddenly and completely. Overcontrolled aggression is more dangerous because it's masked, and unpredictable. Other research suggests that anger, especially bottled-up anger, is linked to cardiovascular problems (Harburg *et al.*, 1979).

AGGRESSION AS MOTIVE

An aggression motive is postulated by (some) psychoanalysts, and by ethologists (Lorenz, 1966); both schools of thought favour *hydraulic* or *energy* models of motivation. If aggression can't find expression directly, it may affect behaviour indirectly. (A psychoanalyst who noticed that his patients occasionally broke wind or fell asleep during analysis interpreted both as signs of deep unconscious hostility towards the analyst.) Ethologists also favour a *deficit* model, which implies aggression increases, like hunger or thirst, until a target is found and attacked, whereupon aggression subsides to baseline level. As aggression mounts, the organism settles for less and less appropriate targets (*displacement*), and may eventually display a *vacuum reaction* by going through the motions of attacking a non-existent enemy. Vacuum reactions have been described in animals; Lorenz cites the example of a well-fed, caged starling going through the motions of catching and killing a non-existent fly. Krujit (1964) shows that fighting cocks get more and more likely to perform aggressive acts as time passes. However, evidence that all or any humans cannot go for a day, or a week, or a month without attacking someone is lacking. Some ethologists get around this by postulating forms of indirect or symbolic aggression, which creates a dangerously circular argument.

Aggression as instinctive reaction.
Plotting the aggressive behaviour of a dog – snarling, barking, biting – over time shows it doesn't follow the cyclical pattern of eating and drinking. If someone threatens to enter its owner's house or garden every 30 minutes, the dog will growl and bark every 30 minutes. If no one trespasses, or tries to take the dog's food, or evicts it from its favourite sleeping place, it may not bark even once in 24 hours. Canine aggression isn't internally regulated, but driven by outside events. In animals aggression is commonly linked to territory and/or dominance, and in lower species can be related to hormone levels. The evidence for innate mechanisms is very strong. Mice start fighting at 28 days. From a very early age, cats display *fixed action patterns* of stalking prey, striking, worrying and killing it, which can be easily elicited by trailing bits of string. But while the mechanisms are innate, the behaviour isn't fixed; mice that keep losing fights stop fighting; cats raised with rats don't attack rats, whereas cats who see their mothers killing rats are much more likely to do the same (Hinde, 1966).

In animals, aggression is related to territory, dominance and predation. Are there any comparable innate mechanisms in humans? Does the hypothetical Mr Savage, in Chapter 3, want to attack the postman because he's invading Mr Savage's territory? Does Mr Savage want to punch his neighbour in order to become dominant male in the street? Does he kick the office cat to satisfy a hunting instinct? It's impossible to prove any of these hypotheses, and equally impossible to disprove them. One can 'prove' the existence of innate aggression in humans by arguing that it's manifested in subtle, symbolic forms; the chairman of the local pigeon-fanciers' club has symbolically established dominance, the man who gets out of his car to talk to the policeman has 'appeased' him by voluntarily leaving his own territory.

Some ethologists add yet another aggressive instinct – the *expulsion reaction*. Any member of the species that doesn't look right is driven out or killed, serving the biologically useful purpose of eliminating sick or mutated individuals. The chick with an unusual comb is constantly attacked; the penguin that's a slightly different colour likewise. Eibl-Eibesfeldt (1970) sees evidence of the expulsion reaction in human societies that kill off deformed infants, or twins, albinos or children born with teeth. But the expulsion reaction clearly isn't universal, so there's no grounds for supposing it's innate. Eibl-Eibesfeldt explains bullying as an expulsion reaction, on the argument that it's directed at people with discernible oddities – a hypothesis Olweus has disproved.

HERITABILITY OF AGGRESSION

Aggression is definitely heritable in animals; varieties within some species are bred for it (e.g. terriers, fighting bulls). As usual, proof of heritability in humans has to rely on less conclusive evidence: twin studies of questionnaire measures, adoption studies of psychopathic personality and criminal convictions, and the XYY man.

Questionnaire aggression
Conventional twin studies find clear evidence of heritability for questionnaire measures of aggression. The Minnesota Twin Study (Tellegen *et al.*, 1988) reports correlations of 0.43 and 0.46 for identical twins, reared together and apart, and 0.14 and 0.06 for fraternal twins, reared together and apart. A second study in London (Rushton *et al.*, 1986) reports very similar results for identical and fraternal twins, all reared together. Both studies conclude that shared family environment, being brought up in the same home by the same parents, apparently contributes nothing to aggression.

Psychopathic personality
Two studies of heritability of psychopathic personality both use adopted children. One study started with psychopathic mothers, as *index cases*, and compared their children with a control group of adopted children whose mothers weren't psychopathic (Cadoret, 1978). The other study worked back in the other direction, starting with psychopathic persons who had been adopted, and tracing their biological parents (Schulsinger, 1972). Both studies found evidence of heritability, but the trends were small and only just significant; for example, 5 out of 54 biological fathers of adopted index persons had psychopathic symptoms, compared with 1 out of 56 biological fathers of adopted, non-psychopathic controls.

Criminality

Earlier twin studies of criminal tendencies generally produce weak evidence of heritability (K.O. Christiansen, 1974); Christiansen's own data, on a large Danish sample, found evidence of heritability for both aggressive offences and property offences. Research on adopted children in Iowa has compared adopted offspring of criminal and non-criminal mothers (Crowe, 1972), and found more arrests among the former – again suggesting an inherited element in criminal tendencies. Most research on adoption comes from Denmark, where centralized records make research on inheritance easier. Hutchings (1974) compares the fathers of adopted men who had criminal records with the fathers of ones that didn't. Criminal adoptees have biological fathers with criminal records nearly twice as often as non-criminal adoptees; the biological father contributes nothing to his son's development but his genes, some of which apparently predispose to criminality. However, criminal adoptees also had criminal adoptive fathers more often, which makes interpretation of the results difficult. It implies children from criminal homes were somehow selectively placed in criminally disposed adoptive homes – not, presumably, on purpose. Mednick *et al.* (1984) have a large enough sample to separate violent offenders from property offenders; they report that only property offending passes from biological father to adopted-away son.

XYY men

In the 1970s, the idea of the 'super-male XYY man' got a lot of publicity. One in a thousand males is born with an extra male Y chromosome, which makes him taller than average, duller than average and, it was supposed, more aggressive, criminal and dangerous. Research in Denmark reports a just significant tendency for XYY men to get into trouble with the law more often, but in trivial, un-aggressive ways, mostly petty thefts (Witkin *et al.*, 1976). This looks more likely to reflect the XYY man's limited intelligence than his supposed uncontrollable aggression.

If human aggression is heritable, eugenic speculations may have some substance. McDougall (1908) explained the differences between the very warlike people of central Borneo and the more peaceful inhabitants of the coast by arguing that the central tribes had experienced 'stricter weeding out of the more inoffensive and less energetic individuals'. Klineberg (1940) argued that in wartime more aggressive males volunteer for the army, leaving the less aggressive to await conscription. There have been enough wars during the twentieth century to test both hypotheses – an opportunity psychologists have missed.

UPBRINGING AND AGGRESSION

Frustration–aggression

The frustration–aggression hypothesis proposes that frustration causes aggression, and that all aggression is the result of frustration (Dollard *et al.*, 1939).

The hypothesis was very influential in its day, not least in helping to cause whole generations of children to be unusually badly brought up. Various lines of evidence were adduced: a survey showing that what people said frustrated them they also said made them angry, and studies of deprivation of sleep, food and tobacco. Dollard's group also reported the famous correlation between low price of cotton (economic frustration) and blacks lynched (aggression) in the Southern USA; recent reanalysis of the data concludes a significant correlation exists (Hepworth and West, 1988). On closer inspection, however, the frustration–aggression hypothesis turns out to be completely circular. How people interpret events determines how they react; a bus that doesn't stop necessarily frustrates the desire to travel, but if the bus clearly isn't in service, most people aren't angered (Pastore, 1952). But defining frustration subjectively robs the hypothesis of predictive power: if people don't react aggressively, they didn't see the event as frustrating. And some aggression clearly isn't caused by frustration. Aggression can be evoked in humans by insults, and in animals by mild pain. What need is frustrated by being insulted or hurt? It is the need to maintain self-esteem, and the desire for comfort. Hence aggression can be always be 'explained' by inventing corresponding needs that have been frustrated.

The parents' contribution
Sears *et al.* (1957) report a survey of how 379 American families brought up 5-year-olds. One of their findings has been very widely quoted; the child is more aggressive if mother is cold, if mother permits aggression, and if the family use physical punishment. The third link is often cited as proof that physical punishment is counterproductive; a child sees its parents imposing their will by force, and follows their bad example by acting aggressively. However, Sears *et al.*'s survey has its limitations; a critical student once asked if he'd been told to read it as an example of how *not* to research development. (But he was a 'rat man', who liked everything precisely controlled, from 50+ generations' heredity to the exact humidity of the lab; studies of upbringing, to be fair to Sears *et al.*, are always messy by comparison.) The main defects are their use of interview to collect data on both upbringing and child's behaviour, exposing them to the criticism that they are recording parents' theories of upbringing, not their actual practice, and failure to demonstrate direction of cause. The 'bad example' argument assumes parental punishment causes aggression in the child, but the correlation could equally plausibly be interpreted as showing that aggressive children 'attract' more punishment, or even that aggressive (physically punishing) parents pass on aggressive genes to their children.

Follow-up studies
Subsequent studies have improved on Sears *et al.*'s methodology by measuring parent and child behaviour independently, and by allowing the passage of time to show direction of cause. The Cambridge Somerville Youth Study recorded information about the home life and upbringing of 325 boys between 1939 and

1945, then followed them up in later years (W. McCord *et al.*, 1961). The first follow-up, when the boys were about 9 years old, identified an aggressive group, who bullied younger children, were always fighting, were vandals, and reacted to any frustration by abuse, rage and destructive outbursts. Observations of their earlier upbringing noted rejection by mother, permissiveness and parental use of *power-assertive discipline*. The mother sometimes neglected to control the boy, but sometimes overcontrolled him. Aggressive boys do not simply follow father's example; paternal aggression doesn't predict son's aggression at all. The second follow-up identified 53 property criminals and 34 violent criminals (assault, rape, murder, kidnapping), from court records (J. McCord, 1979). When the aggressive criminals were children, their parents had quarrelled, behaved aggressively and not supervised them. Their mothers had lacked self-confidence. When the thieves were children, they too had lacked parental supervision and had mothers who lacked self-confidence; they also had fathers who were criminals and/or alcoholics, and mothers who weren't affectionate. The Cambridge Somerville study used a largely slum area of Boston, Massachusetts, which commentators today would call 'deprived'. Such commentators often assume deprivation provides a complete, exhaustive explanation of criminal behaviour, and dismiss explanations in terms of individual differences as irrelevant or misguided. The McCords' work compares criminals with non-criminals, raised in the same deprived area, and shows that differences between families do account for aggressive or criminal behaviour.

More recent research links aggression at school to upbringing, using *path analysis* (Olweus, 1980b). (This is essentially a correlational analysis, where the researcher is prepared to make assumptions about direction of cause; thus Olweus assumes that maternal negativism can affect aggression at school, but not vice versa.) A combination of mother's negativism, mother's permissiveness for aggression, and both parents' use of power-assertive discipline predicts aggression at school. Another dozen or so studies confirm that harsh, punitive, power-assertive upbringing contributes to aggression, in both sexes, and in delinquents and non-delinquents (Martin, 1975).

However, all the research on upbringing and aggression is challenged by recent twin studies, which find that identical twins brought up apart resemble each other in aggression as much as identical twins brought up together (Tellegen *et al.*, 1988), which implies upbringing doesn't affect aggression at all. Perhaps twin studies of questionnaire aggression are measuring a different aspect of aggression. or perhaps what look like the effects of upbringing are really the effects of heredity, expressing itself in successive generations.

Gender differences
Research on aggression consistently finds very large gender differences. Most social scientists attribute such differences to gender-role learning: males are expected to act aggressively, while females are taught 'it isn't ladylike'. Maccoby and Jacklin (1980) note that gender differences are present before children start

school, and argue this makes social learning explanations a little less plausible. Some research suggests that females express aggression indirectly; 11- and 12-year-old girls show they 'are angry with another' child by gossip, sulking, ostracizing, changing allegiance, not by swearing, kicking, hitting and shoving, like boys (Lagerspetz *et al.*, 1988).

THE CONTRIBUTION OF TELEVISION

The average American child, watching an average amount of television, will see portrayed between its fifth and fourteenth birthdays 13,000 violent deaths. Opinions differ sharply as to what the effect will be. Bandura (1977)'s model of learning by observation clearly implies that children will imitate what they see on television, just as they imitate the videotaped model in the Bobo Doll experiment. Observed aggression will cause actual aggression. (To be precise, aggressive acts will be imitated only if seen to be successful; in theory, television could eliminate aggressive tendencies if aggression were always shown not to pay.) Bandura's prediction is challenged by an opposing school of thought, which includes Freud, Aristotle and apologists for the cinema and television industry. They argue that watching aggressive acts safely discharges, or *catharts*, the individual's aggression. The child who watches one person attacking another is less likely to do the same in real life. Critics dub this the 'pus' theory of aggression: watching other people's discharges your own.

   Numerous laboratory and field studies have researched the effects of watching violence on television. Many studies use self-reports of viewing habits or preferences, usually in children or adolescents, and find these correlate modestly ($r = 0.10$–0.20) with self-reports of aggressiveness (Freedman, 1984). This type of research isn't very conclusive because it can't prove direction of cause; perhaps 'naturally aggressive' children like violent programmes. Some researchers (Eron, 1980; Huesmann, 1982) collect data from children at various ages. If violent programmes create aggression, the effect should be cumulative, so the correlation between watching violence and behaving aggressively should increase with age. In fact, the correlation stays the same, disproving the cumulative effect hypothesis. Other researchers report follow-up studies, relating television watching at an early age to violence at a later age; a liking for violent television at age 8 predicts aggressiveness at age 18, but only in males (Eron *et al.*, 1972).

   Other researchers avoid self-reports, and seek a link between televised aggression and 'real-life' aggression recorded by observers or in crime statistics. Some studies control what programmes their subjects, usually delinquents, are allowed to watch; others rely on *natural experiments*. The results of controlled viewing studies with children and delinquents are inconsistent. Some report more aggressive behaviour (Parke *et al.*, 1977); some report no change; Feshbach and Singer (1971) report that boys who watched only violent television programmes became progressively less violent towards their peers week by week. One natural experiment analysed crime statisics from American cities that had television in 1949–52, and from those that hadn't got it yet; there was no difference (Hennigan *et al.*, 1982). Another natural experiment reported that murder increased after heavyweight boxing contests had been shown on American television (Phillips, 1983), but not until the third day after the broadcast, and only if the contest had been fought outside the USA, neither of which facts makes a great deal of sense. Watching a lot of violent television constructs a 'mean phenomenal world' for the watcher; the heavy viewer overestimates the number of policemen in the USA, overestimates his or her own chances of being involved in violent crime, and develops a cynically distrustful outlook (Gerbner *et al.*, 1976).

CONCLUSIONS

Research on aggression supports a number of reasonably definite conclusions:

- Aggressiveness can be measured in children and adults.
- Aggressiveness is a 'real' personality trait.
- Aggressive children tend to become aggressive adults, although their aggressiveness manifests itself in different ways.
- Aggressiveness has a heritable element, but is also probably affected by upbringing.
- Patterns of child-rearing that appear to increase aggression in the child include rejection by parents, permissiveness or inconsistency, but not direct encouragement of aggressiveness by the parents.

CHAPTER 11

The Most Unwelcome Visitor

Aspects of Sexual Variation

In 1977 I organized a conference on sexual attraction, which included sessions on infant and child sexuality and paedophilia (sexual interest in children). The greater part of the paedophilia symposium was contributed by psychologists from Broadmoor Special Hospital. Not long before the conference began, one Tom O'Carroll, Press Officer for the Open University and Chairman of the Paedophile Information Exchange (PIE), registered to attend the conference—an event which should have rung an alarm bell in my mind, but didn't. I thought—in so far as I thought about it at all— that O'Carroll might add a consumer's voice to the discussion of treatment, which can get as drastic as castration.

News of his plans to attend became known—from him—about a week before the conference, and began attracting a lot of attention, locally and nationally. A local newspaper, husbanding its resources carefully, sought opinions in turn from the local MP ('CHILD SEX MAN TOLD YOU'RE NOT WELCOME'), the college ('NOW PRINCIPAL JOINS IN ROW ON CHILD-SEX'), the porters' and cleaners' union ('COLLEGE STAFF TO BOYCOTT O'CARROLL'). The college principal 'gave his full backing to college staff who . . . threatened to boycott . . . O'Carroll' and asked me and the other conference organizers to prevent O'Carroll coming, which we decided we couldn't do.

He arrived, along with a large contingent from the press, and we spent the first day trying to keep the two apart, instead of talking to all the people at the conference we'd been looking forward to meeting. The union, beginning to lose patience, announced a strike to start at 10 on Wednesday, whereupon the college threatened that if O'Carroll didn't leave immediately, '1. Your conference will be cancelled forthwith. 2. Immediate steps will be taken by the College to eject participants to the Conference from the College Campus.'

Later on Tuesday two College officials escorted him from the premises. The paedophilia symposium went ahead on Friday, attended by myself, my wife, three or four students, two or three conference delegates, and a policeman trying to find the person who had punched O'Carroll and poured beer over him.

The whole affair afforded renewed insight into the yawning gap between what one reads in the newspapers and what actually happens. It also made everyone wonder about O'Carroll's own reasons for seeking to make himself so highly unpopular, and about the extreme reactions he aroused in otherwise very ordinary people. As Freud had discovered 90 years earlier, anyone who uses the words 'children' and 'sex' in the same sentence is asking for trouble.

Paedophilia is called a *sexual deviation*; if paedophiles ever succeed in winning public acceptance, paedophilia will be renamed a 'sexual variation' or an 'unconventional sexual behaviour', and anyone who calls it a 'deviation' in public will be rebuked. Past attempts to define the essence of a sexual variation have generally failed. 'Behaviour that offends public decency' doesn't include anything done in private. 'Behaviour that is pathological' begs the question. 'Behaviour that doesn't lead to procreation' is thought too narrow, although Gosselin and Wilson (1984) argue that 'the sex drive has clearly evolved for reproductive purposes', so that behaviour which is non-reproductive suggests 'something "going wrong" in the course of development'. Gosselin and Wilson's views make them unpopular with homosexuals in particular and social scientists in general.

A safer definition of sexual variation is 'any form of sexual expression not permitted within a given society', which allows for the very wide variations in standards across different societies and over time. Anthropological data show that homosexual behaviour is permitted – indeed, on occasion obligatory – in 49 of 76 societies documented (Ford and Beach, 1952; Quinsey, 1986). Societies which forbid it, as Britain and the USA did until quite recently, are in the minority. Attitudes to very young partners also vary widely; the age of consent in other societies is often much lower than in Britain (where it was raised for girls from 13 to 16 in 1885). Britain and the USA are more liberal when it comes to adultery, which is forbidden in most societies, and punishable by death in many. Only one prohibition is universal; no society, with the oft-noted exception of the ancient Egyptian royal family, permits incest. High rates of mental and physical handicap among children of incestuous liaisons suggest that a society which doesn't evolve controls of incest will not survive.

Attitudes have shifted a lot over the last 100 years. Eminent Victorians thought masturbation a sexual deviation and recommended tying the child to the bed or using bizarre electrical contraptions to prevent it. Medical men claimed masturbation caused blindness, enfeeblement and insanity, employing the not-very-sound reasoning that all the blind, feeble or insane patients they'd ever examined had masturbated at some stage. Oral sex remained listed as a deviation as late as Allen's (1962) *Textbook of Psychosexual Disorders*. Homosexual behaviour between males was illegal in Britain between 1885 and 1968. It was also regarded as a psychiatric illness; Quentin Crisp (1968) records in his memoirs being given a medical certificate declaring him unfit for military service in World War II, because he was 'suffering' from sexual perversion. Homosexual behaviour is still forbidden in the armed services, but has otherwise become acceptable in Britain and the USA. Homosexuality was officially 'demedicalized' and struck off the list of psychiatric illnesses in the USA in 1974. It was perhaps the impression of an irresistible tide of sexual liberation that caused PIE to attempt to make itself respectable in 1977; if so, the impression was seriously mistaken. The British public, with the eager assistance of the press, made it clear they weren't prepared to consider such an idea, let alone agree to it.

Other forms of sexual variation – transvestism and transexualism, assorted fetishisms, sado-masochism – are tolerated, provided with psychiatric help if needed, and have established societies, such as the Mackintosh Society for rubber fetishists and the Beaumont Society for transvestites. These societies provide social contacts for their members, and provide researchers with access to groups of reasonably well-adjusted people with unusual sexual preferences.

It's difficult to estimate the frequency of most sexual variations, because people are reluctant to admit ones that are still illegal, but offer inflated estimates once they have 'come out'. Homosexual pressure groups are fond of quoting figures derived from the Kinsey reports (Kinsey *et al.*, 1948, 1953). Kinsey used seven categories, from 'exclusively heterosexual with no homosexual experience' through 'equally heterosexual and homosexual' to 'exclusively homosexual with no heterosexual contact' (Figure 11.1). By age 18, nearly 40 per cent of American males had recorded some homosexual behaviour, apparently justifying a claim of '1 in 3', which would be very misleading, because the 40 per cent includes any childhood experience, even if unenjoyable and not repeated. A '1 in 5' figure is more realistic, based on 'predominantly homosexual but incidentally heterosexual' activities for a period of at least three years betwen age 16 and 55. Lifelong exclusively homosexual behaviour, sometimes called primary homosexuality, is much less frequent, reported by only 4 per cent ('1 in 25') American males. Kinsey's second report found homosexual behaviour slightly less frequent in American women.

Kinsey also reports data on the frequency of less socially acceptable behaviours such as bestiality. Sexual contact with animals is surprisingly common in some sections of the population: 'ultimately about 17% of . . . farm boys have complete sexual relations with animals' – another (nearly) '1 in 5' figure.

CAUSES OF SEXUAL VARIATION

The psychologist searching for causes of sexual variation faces all the usual problems of personality research, as well as two novel ones:

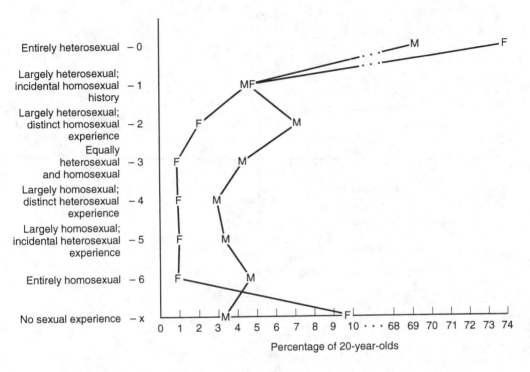

Figure 11.1   *Proportion of male and female 20-year-olds falling into each of seven categories of homosexual–heterosexual orientation (data from Kinsey et al., 1953).*

1. There is unlikely to be a single general explanation of all types of sexual variation. Even the same behaviour may have many different causes; Plummer (1981) emphasizes the immense variety of paedophile behaviour: 40-year-old man raping 5-year-old girl, 17-year-old caressing 13-year-old, 70-year-old woman and 10-year-old boy, 20-year-old man exposing himself to 9-year-old girl, etc.

2. Homosexuals in particular, now that they have gained a measure of acceptance, object to 'being explained', and distrust psychologists. They also dislike being categorized with paedophiles or men who steal underwear off washing lines.

   Critics argue there's nothing to be discovered; the psychologist might as sensibly collect data on people who like playing football, the implication being that homosexuality is simply another leisure preference. Critics particularly object to any explanation that implies homosexuality is pathological.

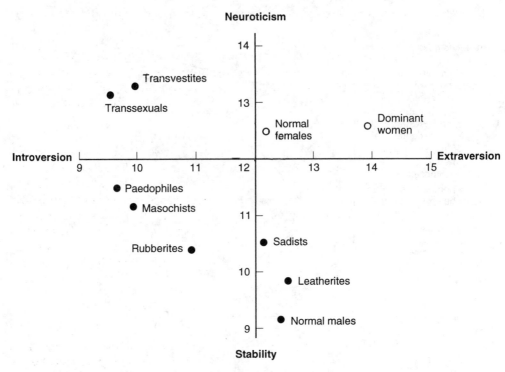

Figure 11.2   *Scores on the Eysenck Personality Inventory (extraversion and neuroticism) for normal males and for various sexually deviant groups (after Gosselin and Wilson, 1984, and Wilson and Cox, 1983).*

Familiar problems of direction of cause, narrow or unrepresentative samples, and proving anything about upbringing also arise:

- Research often uses offender samples, who may be typical offenders, not typical paedophiles, etc. The same goes for groups recruited from the researcher's patients, who may be typical people with problems, not typical paedophiles, etc. Some recent researchers have avoided these biases by recruiting larger samples from groups organized around a common sexual preference, but this may introduce other, subtler biases.

- Direction of cause is a particular problem when studying people who belong to an unpopular secret minority. Eysenck Personality Inventory data from organized rubber and leather fetishists, transvestites and transsexuals, and sado-masochists in London (Figure 11.2) found they score slightly introvert and slightly anxious (Gosselin and Wilson, 1984). But are 'rubberites' fond of rubber because they're introvert and anxious, or are they anxious and introvert because they're fond of rubber, which makes them a bit wary of others and afraid of being 'found out'?

- Retrospective accounts of upbringing are virtually the only practical source of data, but suffer distortion in many different ways: parents trying to explain why their child is different; 'normal' people censoring childhood recollections; attempts to present deviant behaviour as frequent and normal, etc.

There follows a review of research on sexual variations, both those presently socially acceptable, such as adult homosexuality, and those presently socially unacceptable, such as paedophilia. It isn't the intention to equate these in any way; they are reviewed together because many of the methodological problems are common. Homosexual men and women are also sufficiently numerous to make it possible to assemble large enough samples to establish trends, whereas it is often difficult to find enough paedophiles to prove anything about the origins or development of the problem. One thing homosexual men and paedophiles do have in common, however, is a high level of unpopularity, in former times for homosexuals, but very definitely in the present for paedophiles.

Heritability

Evidence for heritability of sexual variations in general, or homosexuality in particular, isn't very conclusive. Pillard and Weinreich (1986) report that homosexual men are more likely to have homosexual brothers. Kallman (1952) reported 100 per cent concordance for homosexuality in 37 identical twin pairs, compared with under 50 per cent in fraternal twins; Kallmann, and commentators since, think 100 per cent concordance is improbably high and must reflect some sampling error. Subsequent twin studies (Heston and Shields, 1968) have found too few twin pairs to give conclusive results. The Minnesota Twin Study includes six pairs of separated identical twins, where one was homosexual; one pair was definitely concordant, two were possibly concordant, the rest definitely weren't (Eckert *et al.*, 1986). The Minnesota data reveal one interesting fact about identical twins that no other twin study could have discovered; the concordant pair met without knowing they were twins, and were strongly attracted to each other. No study of adopted children has appeared to date.

Biology

It was long assumed that sexual variations had a biological origin, befitting their status as forms of illness. Micro-organisms being implausible, researchers looked to hormones. Homosexuals, it was argued, have hormone balances more properly characteristic of the opposite sex. Hence male homosexuals would be weak, effeminate, beardless, unable to whistle, wide in the hips, and attracted to males; female homosexuals, by contrast, would be gruff, broad-shouldered, moustached, and attracted to women. Research on a fairly large sample of well-adjusted homosexual men contacted through homosexual organizations found them on average taller, lighter, less muscular than heterosexual controls, and with lower levels of male hormones (Evans, 1972). Subsequently, however, numerous studies of homosexual males (Meyer-Bahlburg, 1977; Ellis and Ames, 1987) have failed to find any difference in circulating levels of testosterone. Research on hormone levels of homosexual women, by contrast, has concluded that about one-third show elevated levels of masculine hormones (Meyer-Bahlburg, 1979). Data on the physique of homosexual women show a slight tendency for them to be taller or heavier.

Some years ago Feldman and McCollough (1971) argued that primary homosexuality results from hormone imbalance in the womb, which sets the child's sexual orientation for life. They based their argument on experiments with rats, where early alteration of hormone levels affects later sexual behaviour. This is a *congenital* effect, the result of neither heredity nor environment, in the usual sense of upbringing, nutrition, etc. Some psychologists are impressed by rat research, but most other people preferred to wait for data from human beings. Dorner *et al.* (1975) gave homosexual men an oestrogen challenge, and reported that their physiological reaction followed the female pattern, which is consistent with the hypothesis that their brains had been feminized in the womb. The finding has been replicated (Gladue *et al.*, 1984; Gooren, 1986); Figure 11.3 shows how homosexual males' reaction to oestrogen falls between that of heterosexual women and that of heterosexual men.

Meyer-Bahlburg's (1979) review of prenatal hormone abnormalities in women concluded they didn't cause homosexuality. Subsequently congenital adrenal hypertrophy (CAH) has been put forward as a candidate. A few females get partly masculinized during foetal development, and subsequently show more masculine behaviour and preferences, including attraction to other women (Money, 1987). The masculinization extends to being born with partially masculine genitalia, which need surgical alteration, so extrapolation to homosexual women in general may be inadvisable.

Why should hormone balance during pregnancy get disturbed? Numerous experiments on animals show stress is one reason. Two surveys, both by Dorner's team, suggest the same may happen in humans. The first survey asked women if they had experienced bereavement, separation, money trouble, etc. during pregnancy, and found an enormous effect: nearly two-thirds of mothers of homosexual men reported some stress, but fewer than 1 in 10 mothers of heterosexual men (Dorner *et al.*, 1983). Critics will argue this shows how keen mothers of homosexual men are to find a reason for their behaviour. Dorner's second survey (Figure 11.4) showed that more homosexual men were born in Germany during the stressful bombing and invasion period of 1941–46, than before or after (Dorner *et al.*, 1980).

Some psychologists now think Feldman and McCollough's hormones-in-the-womb hypothesis is definitely confirmed as the principal explanation of homosexuality (Ellis and Ames, 1987). Others, however, strongly disagree, and point

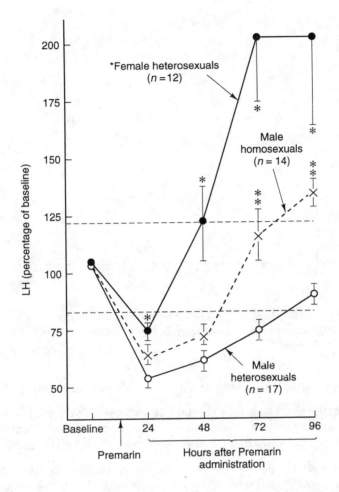

Figure 11.3 *Changes in LH in response to a single injection of Premarin. (Gladue et al., 1984).*

to Kinsey's conclusion of 40 years ago that homosexuality is a dimension, not a category. Many men and women experience homosexual feelings at some time, but most presumably were not feminized or maculinized before birth (McConaghy, 1987).

Psychodynamic factors
At the oedipal phase the boy experiences a desire for his mother, which is normally repressed because he's afraid of his father's wrath. Three linked aspects of the Oedipus conflict combine to cause homosexuality in the male:

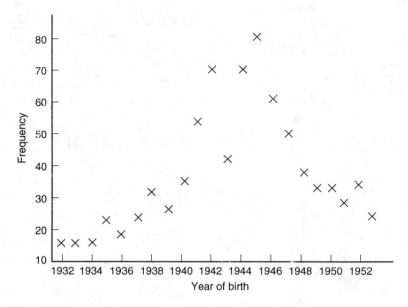

Figure 11.4   *Frequency of registered homosexual males born each year from 1932 to 1953, expressed as frequency per 10 of all males born (data from Dorner et al., 1980).*

1. The mother increases the son's desire for her by acting seductively.

2. The father fails to cause the boy to repress the desire by being so cold and distant the boy makes no effort to appease him. Hence the boy doesn't identify with his father, and doesn't learn the male sex role.

3. The boy also continues to be troubled by incestuous desires for his mother, which make all women threatening to him. Consequently the homosexual male is afraid of intercourse, and the sight of a naked woman triggers castration anxieties.

Note the characteristic lack of parsimony of Freudian theory, which describes three different ways male homosexuality develops. Gosselin and Wilson (1984) argue that sexual variations often are 'overdetermined' in this way, which helps explain their force and persistence.

One survey tested psychoanalytic hypotheses about homosexuality, and obtained impressive confirmation (Bieber *et al.*, 1962). The male homosexual was too close to his mother, who was too intimate, even seductive, when he was a child. The male homosexual's father, by contrast, was detached, even hostile, failing to provide a model for the boy. The male homosexual develops homosexual tendencies by default because he's afraid of heterosexual contact, fearing disease or injury to his genitals, and because he's afraid of, and repelled by, the female genitals. Bieber concludes that 'maternal close-binding intimacy and paternal detachment–hostility' is 'most conducive to promoting homosexuality', so any boy exposed to it is very likely to become homosexual. However Bieber's data were 'collected on the couch' by psychoanalysts. The accounts of upbringing were inferred by the analyst, not directly reported by the homosexual man. Analysts know what they expect to find in a homosexual patient, and the method's critics argue the patient is brain-washed into producing it. A second survey reports a non-analytic replication of Bieber's study; 43 well-adjusted homosexuals recruited from a homosexual organization completed a 27-item questionnaire (Evans, 1969). The results are an amazingly strong confirmation of Bieber *et al.*: a mother who was cold, puritanical, dominating, seductive, who allied with son against father, preferred son to father, was cold towards men, discouraged heterosexual activity in the boy, and encouraged feminine attitudes not masculine ones; and a father who spent little time with his son, who didn't encourage masculine activities, whom the son didn't respect or accept but often hated or feared, and who didn't show much mutual acceptance. Evans's data can't be faulted on grounds of analytic distortion, but they are retrospective self-reports.

Other studies of male homosexuality, reviewed by Feldman (1973), report comparable results: poor relationship with father and close relationship with mother. Whitam (1980) reports that 97 per cent of male homosexuals report one or more of the following in childhood: interest in girl's toys, cross-dressing, preference for girls' games, preference for the company of girls, being seen as a sissy, preferring sex play with boys. Only 20 per cent of heterosexual males report one or more, and the relation holds good in the USA, Guatemala, Brazil and the Philippines. The difference is large enough and consistent enough to regard childhood 'cross-gender' behaviour as diagnostic of adult homosexuality. Research on family dynamics and female homosexuality is less extensive. Kenyon (1968) reports generalized evidence of disturbed childhood: poor relationships with parents, death of mother, parental discord, and homosexuality within the family. Bene (1965) reports weak, incompetent fathers whom the subjects disliked and feared, but normal relations with their mothers.

Critics argue that these retrospective studies are biased; intelligent homosexual men and women read psychodynamic analyses of homosexuality and project them onto their own childhood. Or else they willingly report childhood experiences, like cross-dressing, that heterosexuals share equally, but repress or censor. Only one study has reported independent, contemporary data on upbringing. The Cambridge Somerville Study identified three patterns of sexual behaviour in adult males: *anxious inhibited*; *perverted*, meaning indiscriminate; and *feminine*, which included some who were overtly homosexual. Contemporary accounts of their upbringing reveal a common pattern of sexual anxiety and prudishness at home, maternal authoritarianism, quarrels between parents, father absent, father 'openly despised or neglected' son (W. McCord *et al.*, 1962). Unfortunately, none of the three patterns of adult behaviour is at all typical of homosexual men in general. The new school of neuro-endocrine theorists agrees that homosexual men and women have less harmonious relations with their parents, but thinks the direction of cause quite different. Ellis and Ames (1987) argue that parents react unfavourably to the 'partially inverted mannerisms, interests and behaviour' of their biologically homosexual children. Whitam finds homosexual men in USA, Brazil, Guatemala and the Philippines all report *cross-gender* behaviour as a child, but only American men also report detached, hostile fathers (Whitam and Zent, 1984); he concludes the cross-gender behaviour causes poor relations between father and son in cultures where homosexuality isn't accepted.

Critics argue that psychodynamic theory confuses *sexual orientation* (including homo/heterosexuality) and *sex role* (often called *gender role* to avoid such confusion). The theory assumes the boy who fails to learn to be a man, because his father doesn't provide a good model, finds men sexually attractive. But failing to learn the male gender role doesn't necessarily imply failing to acquire a sexual interest in women. Nor does it imply developing sexual interest in males. The psychodynamic model can be extended to women, changing gender throughout; rivalry with mother for affection of father is not resolved by identification with the mother, so the woman doesn't adopt female gender role and doesn't find men sexually attractive. There's an extra problem here; nearly all children identify with the mother, but only boys have to transfer identification to father to learn their gender role. This implies hardly any women will have gender problems, so hardly any will have homosexual interests. Hormone and physique theories of homosexuality also confuse gender and sexual orientation, and assume that saying a woman is masculine implies she is attracted to women.

Conditioning

McGuire *et al.* (1965) offer three, progressively more indelicate, hypotheses about the conditioning of sexual desires. The first simply states that an enjoyable sexual experience is very reinforcing, and that whoever or whatever provides it may become a conditioned stimulus for sexual arousal. If a male's first sexual experience is with another male, males may become cues to sexual arousal (though not just any male – the whole fascinating question of people's preferences for 'their type' of partner has barely been scratched by research). Maguire cites cases of two patients who started exposing themselves after being overlooked while urinating, and another who developed an underwear fetish after happening to look through a window and see a woman in her underwear. Gosselin mentions that some rubberites are engineers who wear protective suits at work; the implication is that sexual arousal caused by something else gets associated with the suit.

McGuire's second hypothesis restates the psychoanalysts' *heterophobia* argument; a sexual encounter with the opposite sex goes badly wrong and puts off the first-timer, which subsequently points him or her towards same-sex partners. Feldman and McCollough (1971) add the suggestion that an unpleasant experience may *incubate*; if the person broods about it, his or her aversion to that class of partner may increase. McGuire's first two hypotheses imply chance plays a large part in sexual development; it all depends how the first experience turns out, and who it's with. Gosselin and Wilson's London rubberites were typically aged 45 to 50, and most had been keen on rubber since they were between 4 and 10 years old. The origin of their interest in rubber coincided with the start of World War II – anxious times, with fathers absent, mothers overprotective, children evacuated to the country, and every single Briton issued with a rubber gas-mask. The idea sometimes crosses the mind of sex educators that many problems could be avoided if they could somehow ensure first encounters went off smoothly. Aldous Huxley's *Brave New World* (Chapter 4) anticipated modern thought; in its fictional twenty-second century, sex education starts very early, and emphasizes practice not theory.

Sexual learning may be largely a matter of luck, but there may also be predisposing factors that set people on one path rather than another. Recall that Bieber and Evans both found homosexual males tended to have a frail physique as a child; they were also fearful of injury, avoided fights, didn't play competitive games or baseball, played with girls or were 'lone wolves'. These men mostly grew up during the 1940s and 1950s when American culture valued masculinity. Gosselin and Wilson (1984) suggest that 'any genes predisposing to difficulty in competing for access to females (attributes such as shyness and submissiveness) might also be associated with the adoption of alternative sexual outlets'. Social Darwinism is rarely well received, and Gosselin and Wilson's views are no exception; homosexual men naturally dislike the suggestion they are all failed heterosexuals.

McGuire's third, and definitely most indelicate, hypothesis proposes that some sexual variations develop by *self-reinforced fantasy*. As McGuire notes, masturbation forms an almost perfect conditioning paradigm, with a strong reward following at exactly the right interval after whatever fantasy the masturbator employs. McGuire suggests that fantasies drift; parts of the old fantasy lose their appeal and new, possibly more deviant, elements are added. Hence people can condition themselves to unusual and complicated sexual images they'd never encounter in real life. Other authors (Gagnon and Simon, 1973; Storms, 1980) suggest self-reinforcement is particularly likely to shape sexual preferences in early puberty, when sex drives are strong and actual experience limited. Another factor, at least in former times, might have been ignorance. Binet (cited by Krafft-Ebing, 1886/1965) describes the unusual case of a French youth who supposed the nostril was the female sexual organ, and fantasized about, and drew sketches of, women with enormous noses and nostrils. McGuire's third hypothesis resurrects a familar argument about the relation between fantasy and behaviour. If a man indulges in fantasies of being whipped by women dressed only in thigh-length leather boots, is he more likely or less likely to try to perform such acts in real life? Or does it depend on how well-socialized or how afraid of the consequences he is? Verification of McGuire *et al.*'s hypotheses proceeds along three lines: survey data, laboratory studies of conditioning sexual responses, and clinical work on unconditioning actual sexual variations.

EARLY SEXUAL EXPERIENCE.   The conditioning hypothesis clearly implies the first sexual experience is critically important, but few researchers have enquired about it. Schofield (1965) found a high proportion of males and females didn't particularly enjoy their first experience of intercourse, and a minority found it definitely unpleasant. Two studies (Kenyon, 1968; Gundlach and Riess, 1968) found homosexual women had been frightened by a male, or been raped, more frequently than heterosexual women, confirming the heterophobia hypothesis. Another researcher found homosexual men and women report more pre-adolescent experience (Manesovitz, 1970); assuming precocious sexual experience is more likely to involve one's own sex, this confirms the conditioning hypothesis. One obvious prediction has, surprisingly, never been confirmed; there's no evidence single-sex schools lead to homosexuality.

CREATING SEXUAL PREFERENCES.   For obvious reasons, psychologists do not try to create by conditioning bizarre or antisocial perversions. However, Rachman and Hodgson (1968) did go as far as creating a mild boot fetish in volunteer male subjects, by pairing pictures of a boot with pictures of nude females. LaTorre (1980) produced a laboratory analogue of heterophobic fetishism in college males, by telling them a potential female date they'd selected from a photo album had turned them down; the rejected males found pictures of underwear, feet and legs more attractive but pictures of women less attractive. Critics of the conditioning hypothesis argue that if sexual arousal gets conditioned to whatever people happen to be looking at just before orgasm, there ought to be a lot of sheet, blanket and ceiling fetishes about. Fetishes tend, however, to fall into a few clearly defined categories: rubber/leather/plastic/fur, clothing, especially underwear and shoes, and smells. This suggests an element of *preparedness*, as in phobias; a few special things are easily conditioned to sexual arousal, while others are difficult or impossible. Critics also note that indecent exposers, transvestites, fetishists, paedophiles and sado-masochists are seldom, if ever, female. Why don't women learn these variations?

Other critics argue that conditioning simply can't explain the force and persistence of sexual variations. Why did people persist in homosexual behaviour when it was illegal and generally despised? And why do paedophiles persist in their preference when it makes them so unpopular, or even gets them imprisoned, with all the risks this creates for sex offenders? Gosselin and Wilson (1984) suggest overdetermination — that some variations satisfy a variety of needs or have been learned in several different ways. They also suggest minimal brain damage, affecting the dominant temporal lobe, as a possible cause of compulsive sexual variations like fetishism, transvestism or psychopathic sexual impulses (but not homosexuality).

CRITICAL PERIODS.   Several authors have hypothesized a *critical period* when sexual preferences are readily, and permanently, shaped. Most (Feldman and McCollough, 1965; Gadpaille, 1980) suggest adolescence, which is plausible, but contradicted by Saghir and Robins's (1973) finding that many homosexual men and women report being attracted to their own sex well before adolescence.

Gosselin and Wilson's rubberites similarly developed their taste for rubber long before puberty. Storms (1981) sets the critical period earlier, and suggests some children experience strong sexual drives while they're still in a 'period of strong homosocial bonding' that provides an 'unusually rich source of same sex stimuli'; this critical period lies between ages 8 and 13. Wilson suggests an even earlier critical phase, in infancy, when *imprinting* may occur; but true imprinting only occurs in certain species of bird.

Perhaps conditioning *can* explain the persistence of some sexual variations. A single electric shock or suffocating injection creates a lasting fear, so why shouldn't a single intensely enjoyable experience create a lasting preference? Or why can't a single humiliating experience with the opposite sex create an enduring fear and distrust, so that whatever preference develops, it isn't heterosexual? Or perhaps the answer lies in the schedule of reinforcement. Sexual acts are almost always rewarded, quickly and strongly, more rarely punished. Even illegal acts like indecent exposure can go unpunished for weeks, or months, so the threat of punishment recedes into the distance. Two classes of person might be more swayed by immediate reward than distant punishment: extreme extraverts, slow to socialize, and the intellectually limited. Virkkunen (1976) distinguished two types of paedophile: the antisocial psychopathic, and the merely unintelligent. *CHANGING SEXUAL PREFERENCES.* Behaviour therapy's slogan is 'what has been learned can be unlearned'. While there are limits on what researchers can do in the way of creating sexual variations, there seem fewer limits to what clinicians can do by way of 'curing' them. Feldman and McCollough (1971) describe a sophisticated, multi-stage programme using escape and avoidance learning. In the first stage, male subjects were presented with pictures of males; the man had eight seconds to press a button to remove the picture, or he received a painful electric shock. At first the men pressed the button to end the shock (*escape*), then to remove the picture before the shock came (*avoidance*). In the second stage *partial reinforcement* was used to help learning transfer to the outside world; the escape button sometimes didn't work straight away, and sometimes didn't work at all. In the third stage, when the male pictures disappeared, they were replaced by a picture of a female. By this time the men were beginning to feel relief whenever the male picture, with its implied threat of shock, disappeared. The third stage was intended to condition this feeling of relief to the sight of females. By this time, even the sight of a blank screen was beginning to become threatening, because it might be followed by a male, and then by a shock. The subjects were given a second button, which would (sometimes) cause a picture of a female to be projected; this was intended to reinforce approaches towards females. It's an irony of history that Feldman and McCulloch perfected their methods at just the time no one wanted 'cures' for homosexuality any more.

While homosexual men are no longer regarded as a 'suitable case for treatment', and homosexual women never were, paedophiles most certainly are. Castration has been used in Denmark, and brain surgery to eliminate the sex drive in West Germany (Crawford, 1981). Aversion treatment has been used, but is losing popularity, partly because of doubts about its effectiveness, and partly because psychologists find it distasteful. A treatment of some theoretical interest is politely called *fantasy modification*, and derives its inspiration from McGuire's third hypothesis, on the role of masturbation in shaping sexual variations. The patient is instructed to change his fantasy just before orgasm, so a different, more acceptable, fantasy gets conditioned instead. Crawford describes a variation of fantasy modification, intended to reverse the drift to increasingly deviant preferences; paedophile males continued fantasizing about under-age targets, but over a period of months moved the target's age upwards by 'sequentially eliminating the youngest fantasy currently used'. *Covert sensitization* also uses fantasies, to create an aversion for under-age boys and girls. The paedophile is instructed to imagine himself approaching a child, then starting to feel sick, vomiting all over the child, and finally running away; Barlow *et al.* (1969) found it quite successful.

THE PAEDOPHILE

Until recently most people thought adult sexual interest in children was very rare. Evidence that it's quite frequent was available, but got overlooked. The Kinsey Reports recorded 40 years ago that 24 per cent of women recalled a sexual approach from an adult before the age of 14. Two recent North American opinion polls confirm Kinsey's high figure for women and add data for males. Finkelhor *et al.* (1990) find that 15 per cent of males and 27 per cent of females report sexual approaches in childhood. A Canadian poll found 31 per cent of males and 54 per cent of females had experienced unwanted sexual attention at some time, mostly before age 18 (Commission on Sexual Offenses, 1984).

Data on how many adults have a sexual interest in children are harder to come by. A survey of American college men found 7 per cent wouldn't entirely exclude the possibility of 'sex with a child' if they could be guaranteed not to be found out or punished (Briere and Runtz, 1989). Two other lines of evidence suggest paedophile tendencies could be quite widespread in males. The first argues that the man often knows the child he approaches, so if one in four girls get approached, there must be a lot of men doing the approaching (whereas if the men were always strangers, a few could approach a lot of different girls). The Canadian survey found only 18 per cent of men who made unwanted sexual attentions were strangers, while 48 per cent were friends and acquaintances, and 21 per cent were family. The second line of evidence comes from *penile plethysmography*; surveys can be faked, but sexual response is harder to control. Freund (1981) reports plethysmography reliably distinguishes paedophiles from other men; his data (Figure 11.5) also show most males show some penile response to nude pictures of under-age females, which implies latent paedophile impulses could be very widespread.

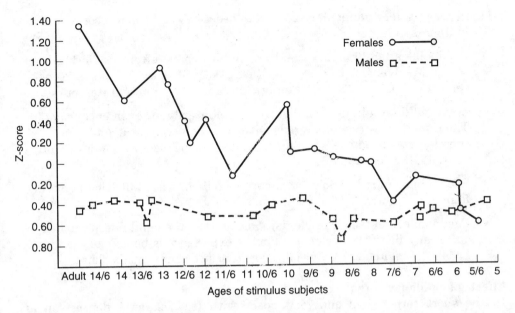

Figure 11.5　*Responses of normal males to nudes of adults, pubescents and children (Freund et al., 1972).*

The public image of the paedophile is of a 'dirty, dangerous "old man" who attacks innocent young children in isolated spots, rapes them and then leaves the child in a permanent state of shock and damage', says Plummer (1981), who argues that virtually every part of the image is wrong:

- The paedophile, like the homosexual before him, claims that he's not 'dirty', sick, or different in any way except happening to be unusually fond of children. The only survey of paedophiles not in hospital or prison found most fairly well-adjusted, but a minority showing psychotic tendencies (G.D. Wilson and Cox, 1983).

- Paedophiles aren't old, but most typically in their late thirties, according to Mohr *et al.* (1964); Wilson and Cox (1983) report a more even age distribution.

- Paedophiles are almost always male – but why? Plummer argues that women's role in Western society allows them to express affection to children in ways forbidden to men. Biologically minded psychologists like Wilson argue women's different sex drive means they just aren't interested in paedophilia (nor in fetishisms, transvestism, sado-masochism, etc). Or do people find the idea of women being sexually interested in children so hard to accept that they cannot see

it when it does happen? Krug (1989) describes eight instances of mother–son incest.

- Paedophiles rarely attack children, or rape them, often restricting their sexual involvement to caresses. Russell's (1986) survey reports 20 per cent of contacts with girls involved actual or attempted intercourse.

- Some children join in sexual activity voluntarily, or even encourage it. The Canadian survey disagrees with this, reporting that physical coercion was used in 50 to 60 per cent of encounters (Commission on Sexual Offenses, 1984).

- Paedophiles mostly aren't strangers who lie in wait, but friends of the family, or family of friends, or even family.

- Paedophiles, and their apologists, argue that the child doesn't usually suffer any ill-effects, or even that the experience is beneficial (Sandfort, 1984). The evidence, reviewed below, doesn't confirm this claim.

Effects of childhood sexual experience

In the short term, boys and girls react with fear, anxiety, depression and hostility, and may show unusual sexual activity such as exposing themselves or excessive curiosity. Longer-term effects also include depression and anxiety, as well as nightmares, sleeplessness, feelings of isolation, low self-esteem and difficulty trusting others (Browne and Finkelhor, 1986; Finkelhor, 1990). Actual 'penetration' has more serious long-term effects than touching or fondling. It is true that most researchers also report that about one in three children show no detectable ill-effects of the experience. It's often said that the abused in turn become abusers: Goodwin *et al.* (1981) report that 8 out of 34 (24 per cent) of women in incestuous families had themselves been victims of incest as children, compared with only 3 per cent of women in 500 non-abusing families. But the women who'd suffered sexual abuse weren't committing the incest in their own families; the link must arise because they find unsuitable partners, or because their relationship somehow goes badly wrong. Other studies (Fields, 1981) appeared to find a very strong link between childhood abuse and adult prostitution, until inclusion of control groups matched for age, ethnicity and education, but who weren't prostitutes, found they too reported extraordinarily high (about 40 per cent) rates of childhood sexual abuse.

Paedophile groups aren't convinced by these data, and argue that ill-effects only result from family outrage, legal proceedings or insensitive psychiatrists. However, they first draw a careful distinction between paedophilia (which is consenting and affectionate) and child-molesting (which isn't), thereby rendering their argument circular; if the child is upset, it wasn't paedophilia. In fact, research shows force of parental reaction isn't a factor in determining the effects of sexual abuse; nor is whether the child tells others or keeps the guilty secret to itself, which doesn't support the argument that reaction to the experience, not the sexual contact itself, determines how the child reacts (Browne and Finkelhor, 1986). Critics argue that adults, especially in positions of authority, as teachers or youth leaders, find it so easy to influence the child that the notion of consent becomes meaningless.

Origins of paedophilia

Paedophiles are much more likely to report childhood sexual contacts with adults (Gebhard *et al.*, 1967; Groth, 1979); one-third of child-molesters report some early sexual experience, against only 3 per cent of controls. This could confirm a straightforward learning-by-experience hypothesis, or even a more sinister hypothesis of recruitment (of the next generation of paedophiles by the previous). Or it could result from willingness to report what others prefer to forget, or be an attempt at self-justification.

Many men who have sexual contacts with children aren't 'really' paedophile; their behaviour is *opportunist* or *regressive*. The man is under stress, typically because his marriage is breaking up (Gebhard *et al.*, 1967), is drinking too much, which clouds his judgement (Aarens *et al.*, 1978), and happens to have access to an under-age female. Often the man is schizoid, psychopathic or has a criminal record. The true or *fixated* paedophile is rarely married (Groth and Birnbaum, 1978), often isn't very bright (Virkkunen, 1976), tends to have repeated contact with the child, tends to have the child's consent, as evidenced by the child visiting the paedophile's home, may be interested in boys not girls, but tends to stick to one sex of partner.

Evidence on samples of paedophile offenders, who may be typical offenders, not typical paedophiles, is summarized by Howells (1981); they are isolated, dependent, timid, submissive and sexually inhibited. Wilson and Cox's survey of 77 members of the notorious Paedophile Information Exchange found them somewhat introvert, somewhat anxious, also shy, sensitive, lonely, depressed and lacking a sense of humour. Howells (1979) obtained Repertory Grids from paedophile offenders; they tended to see adults in terms of dominance/ submission, 'tells me what to do' and 'domineering', whereas their child victims were 'not domineering' and 'easy to get on with'. Children were also idealized: 'innocent', 'trusting' or 'spontaneous'. The men saw women only in sexual or physical terms, not as 'amusing', 'affectionate' or 'inspiring'. The implication is they can't relate to women as people, and find all adults threatening. Crawford and Allen (1979) have found social skills training useful for paedophile offenders. Another study reports 'fear of heterosexual contact' in 85 per cent of paedophiles (Hammer and Glueck, 1957); shown a TAT card of a semi-nude adult female, they avoid sexual themes and describe her as sick, dying or dead.

Howells (1981) points out that sex play – with girls or other boys – is common enough in pre-adolescent boys to be regarded as a normal part of development. About one in five are likely to find their first sexual satisfaction with another boy, and about the same again with an under-age girl, which implies paedophile tendencies should be very common. Clearly the great majority move on to adult partners, and relatively few continue to seek out the target of their first affections. Gosselin and Wilson (1984) state bluntly the hypothesis implied by others: paedophiles find they're 'not adequate for the task of competing with other men for adult heterosexual conquests' and revert to their first love. Hence the picture of the paedophile as socially and intellectually dim, and sexually inhibited (they actually read less pornography than the average male according to Goldstein (1973)); hence also Mohr *et al.*'s (1964) modal age in the late thirties, because it takes them until then to realize they're heterosexual failures.

There are, however, quite a few holes in this apparently neat explanation. Critics again question whether conditioning models can account for the compulsive nature of some paedophile impulses, or whether extra factors like brain damage, imprinting or psychodynamics are needed. (Freud, having discovered childhood sexuality, had surprisingly little to say about paedophiles.) Most data come from surveys of offenders, who are probably atypical. No data establish direction of cause; are men paedophile because they're shy and anxious, or shy and anxious because they're paedophile? And no research has studied paedophilia longitudinally, to demonstrate the hypothesized sequence of satisfying sexual experience with children as a child, unsatisfactory sexual experience with older partners in teens and twenties, reversion to child partners thereafter.

IN February 1978 Tom O'Carroll was dismissed from his job at the Open University. In March 1979 he lost a claim for unfair dismissal; it was revealed at the hearing that he had lost a job as a schoolteacher in 1970, when he became infatuated with a 14-year-old boy. In 1981 he was charged with conspiracy to corrupt public morals; PIE's newsletter was claimed to contain adverts which would encourage adults to have sexual contact with children, and to encourage its readers to exchange obscene material through the post. He was found guilty and sentenced to two years in prison.

CHAPTER 12

The Curse of the Drinking Classes

Alcohol Abuse

THE Victorian middle classes had a patronizing dictum: 'Drink is the curse of the working classes'. Oscar Wilde turned it inside out: 'Work is the curse of the drinking classes'. A century later, many people think alcoholism is the curse of the drinking classes.

Alcohol exerts a depressing effect on the central nervous system, causing people to react slowly, and eventually lose control of speech and limbs. On the way alcohol removes inhibitions – in the lay sense, not the Pavlovian sense – and so makes people more cheerful and sociable. Some drinkers, however, become suspicious, even violent. The ill-effects of alcohol are well known. Problem drinkers are absent from work two and half times more than average. Problem drinkers cost twice as much in health care, and shorten their own life expectancy considerably. Alcohol is linked to crime, industrial accidents, road traffic accidents, domestic violence and child abuse. Pressure groups estimate alcohol problems cost the USA many billions of dollars a year.

Prolonged excessive drinking causes psychological changes. It damages the brain, and causes deficits in abstracting ability, complex perceptual-motor skills, and learning and recall, which may be reversible if the person stops drinking (Grant, 1987). Sometimes *Korsakoff's psychosis* results, in which sufferers lose short-term memory altogether, and fill in the gaps by *confabulation*, describing what might have happened yesterday – but didn't. However, people who drink excessively, then stop too suddenly, risk *delirium tremens*, whose symptoms include a coarse tremor and hallucinations of small, rapidly moving animals.

Women who drink excessively during pregnancy risk giving birth to children with *fetal alcohol syndrome*, whose effects include mental retardation.

Different researchers and theorists talk about different aspects of the problem. It divides conceptually into three main areas:

1. *Drinking* – how much, of what, how often. This places people on a continuum from those who never drink alcohol at all, through occasional and social drinkers, to heavy or problem drinkers.

2. *Effects* – the effects of alcohol intake on physical health (morning shakes, liver trouble), performance at work (sickness, absence, employer complaints, multiple job losses), personal relations (complaints from friends, marital discord), and life in general (accidents, brushes with the law).

3. *Underlying conditions* – called *alcoholism* or *alcohol dependence*. Many alcoholics drink little or no alcohol for long periods of time, so aren't picked up by intake or ill-effects measures. Nevertheless, most theorists think such individuals somehow differ even if they are not presently drinking.

The disease model of alcoholism argues some people have an inherent weakness, which means they can never drink in moderation, so must never drink alcohol at all. Some attempts to characterize the inherent weakness are very vague, e.g. 'loss of control'. Nevertheless, clinicians agree very well about diagnoses of alcohol abuse (whereas they generally don't agree so well about schizophrenia, neurosis or psychopathic personality). The Alcohol Use Inventory (Wanberg and Horn, 1923) has 17 scales covering areas like perceived benefits of alcohol to the drinker, the disruptive consequences of drinking, acknowledgement of drinking problem, etc. The Inventory has been factor-analysed (H. A. Skinner, 1981); the largest of the four factors, alcohol dependence, suggests the concept of an underlying condition has some empirical validity. DSM-III, the official psychiatric diagnostic system in the USA, includes a list of nine criteria for identifying dependence on alcohol. Anyone who fits more than two of these criteria may be diagnosed as dependent.

1. The person uses more than he or she intends, or uses it for longer.

2. The person has tried to reduce consumption, and failed.

3. Most of the person's time is spent either getting it, or recovering from its effects.

4. The person is intoxicated or recovering when he or she should be working.

5. The person has given up, partly or completely, work, recreation or socializing.

Table 12.1 *Prevalence of alcoholism in three Scandinavian community surveys (data from Helzer, 1987)*

Community	Men (%)	Women (%)
Bornholm	3.5	0.1
Iceland	9.8	0.5
Rural Sweden	19.3	–

6. The person is experiencing problems in health, psychological functioning, etc.

7. Tolerance has developed (defined as needing a dose at least 50 per cent bigger to get the same effect).

8. The person has withdrawal symptoms.

9. The person uses alcohol, or another drug, to counter withdrawal symptoms.

Different approaches to defining alcoholism, and different definitions of how much is too much, mean that apparently similar studies may differ. Research on heritability of alcohol problems uses a range of criteria, from diagnosis of cirrhosis of the liver to being reported to a Swedish Temperance Board by police, health care workers, family or neighbours as someone who drinks too much.

Frequency of alcohol problems

Prevalence means the proportion of persons who have had drink problems within a specified period of time, e.g. one year or a lifetime. At least three community surveys have been reported in which virtually every adult, not just a sample or cross-section, is checked for alcoholism (Helzer, 1987). The surveys are all Scandinavian, and all report high rates of alcoholism in males (Table 12.1); the two studies that included women found their alcoholism rate a tiny fraction of the male rate. A series of 12 American surveys between 1946 and 1982 (Warheit and Auth, 1985) shows that up to one-third of American males are heavy drinkers, and about one in ten has alcohol problems. Up to a quarter, however, do not drink alcohol at all. The rates for American women are much lower, between 2 per cent and 5 per cent being heavy drinkers, and about 2–3 per cent having alcohol problems. The proportion of problem drinkers in the USA appears to be increasing steadily; in 1940 it was only 2 per cent, but by 1985 it had risen to 12 per cent (Caddy, 1983). Tht most recent American research is the Epidemiological Catchment Area prevalence survey (Robins *et al.*, 1984) in which 20,000 people in five separate places were interviewed twice. Prevalence rates based on six months were 19–29 per cent for males, and 4–5 per cent for females. In Britain 24 per cent of males and 9 per cent of females drink more than the medically recommended sensible weekly limit. Drinkers take four times as many days off work as other workers. Consumption is rising in Britain as elsewhere; annual per head consumption nearly doubled between 1960 and 1988.

Alcoholic's progress

Earlier theorists described the classic alcoholic's progress (Jellinek, 1952); alcoholics start as heavy social drinkers, then move into the *pro-dromal* phase, characterized by furtive drinking and occasional blackouts, by which time they are using alcohol as a drug, not a beverage. Next comes the *crucial* phase, in which they start losing control and find they can't stop once started; they drink during the day, neglect their food, and have their first *bender*, meaning several days spent continuously drinking. Even at this stage, however, they may be able to abstain for days, even months. Finally alcholics enter the *chronic* phase, in which they will drink meths if they can't get alcohol. Later research has modified this picture in several respects. Blackouts are rare in the early stages, and many alcoholics never experience them at any stage. Some alcoholics restrict their drinking to the weekends, making it easier to survive at work (Clark and Cahalan, 1976). Only a few alcoholics – around 5 per cent – end up right at the bottom, on 'skid row'. Women tend to start their alcoholic career later, often after a highly stressful experience such as a bereavement, but then progress through the stages more quickly. They are more likely to be steady, and solitary, drinkers and don't go on benders (Hill, 1980).

ORIGINS OF ALCOHOL PROBLEMS

Culture

Official statistics on alcoholism rates show big differences from one country to another; France leads, with rates over four times higher than Norway's (Table 12.2). Alcohol consumption in Britain and the USA is about the same, and places both countries in the lower half of the league table. Within the USA, large differences in drinking patterns and alcoholism rates were noted early on between immigrants from different countries and backgrounds. Italian Americans were said to have low rates, because they only drink alcohol with meals, introduce children to controlled moderate drinking within the family circle, and disapprove of drunkenness. Irish Americans were supposed to have very high rates, because they drink to relax, don't drink at home, and have few cultural restrictions on drinking. Follow-up studies in Boston, Massachusetts, confirms this, finding high rates for boys from Irish American homes and low rates for boys from Italian American homes, with North European and old American homes in between (W. McCord and McCord, 1960; Vaillant, 1983: these data describe men born in the 1920s and 1930s, many of whose parents were born outside the USA). An early paper (Dollard, 1945) claimed that lower-middle-class Americans

Table 12.2 *Alcohol consumption in litres of absolute alcohol per capita for those aged 15 years and older*

Country	1960	1973	Change
France	27.3	24.1	−12
Italy	19.1	21.1	10
Spain	11.9	18.5	55
Luxembourg	13.8	18.5	34
West Germany	10.2	16.8	65
Portugal	15.3	17.9	17
Russia	10.4	14.7	41
Switzerland	12.5	19.3	54
Austria	10.9	16.0	47
Belgium	11.7	14.5	24
Hungary	9.2	13.2	43
Australia	9.5	12.2	28
New Zealand	9.3	11.7	26
East Germany	7.8	12.3	58
Yugoslavia	8.0	10.5	31
United States	7.8	10.6	36
Denmark	6.1	11.0	80
Canada	7.8	11.1	42
Great Britain	6.8	10.0	47
Sweden	5.9	8.0	36
Netherlands	3.8	10.1	166
Poland	6.2	9.2	48
Republic of Ireland	4.9	9.0	84
Finland	3.9	7.8	100
Norway	3.6	5.4	50

Note: From deLint (1978). Copyright © 1978 by Pergamon Press. Adapted by permission.
* 1960 = 100.

strongly disapproved of alcohol (whereas upper-middle-class Americans were unconcerned). However, the McCords found middle-class children more likely than working-class children to become alcoholics.

As insurance companies know well, some occupations have a higher alcohol problem rate than others. Table 12.3 lists occupations where cirrhosis rates are average; drink trade jobs head the list, with sailors in second place. Jobs with higher than average alcoholism rates are very diverse. Alcohol Concern identify six very general common themes: availability of alcohol at work, social pressure to drink at work, very high or very low income, freedom from supervision, strains and stresses (danger, responsibility, lack of job security, and boredom), and separation from normal social and sexual relationships. In the USA, but not

Table 12.3 *Liver cirrhosis mortality among British males in different occupations (1979–80, 1982–3)*

Occupational group	Mortality rate
Average occupation	100
Publicans	1017
Foremen, ships, lighters and other vessels	900
Deck, engine-room hands, bargemen, lightermen and boatmen	873
Barmen	612
Managers of hotels, clubs, etc. and in entertainment and sports	553
Waiters and barstaff	461
Deck, engineering and radio officers and ship pilots	417
Electrical engineers (so described)	387
Hotel and residential club managers	342
Officers (ships and aircraft), air traffic planners and controllers	337
Innkeepers	315
Officers, UK armed forces	303
Catering supervisors	297
Fishermen	296
Bus conductors	277
Chefs, cooks	265
Restaurateurs	263
Authors, writers, journalists	261
General labourers	247
Travel stewards and attendants, hospital and hotel porters	245
Drivers' mates	225
Actors, musicians, entertainers, stage managers	222
Winders, reelers	202
Bakers, flour confectioners	157
Judges, barristers, advocates, solicitors	155
Salesmen, sales assistants, shop assistants, shelf fillers, petrol pump forecourt attendants	147
Other domestic and school helpers	141
Garage proprietors	140
Clergy, ministers of religion	131
Pharmacists, radiographers, therapists	127
Medical and dental practitioners	115
Nurse administrators, nurses	108

Britain, railway workers have a high rate of drink problems (Mannello and Seaman, 1979), 14 per cent drink on the job, 5 per cent come to work drunk or get drunk at work, and 20 per cent report to work with hangovers.

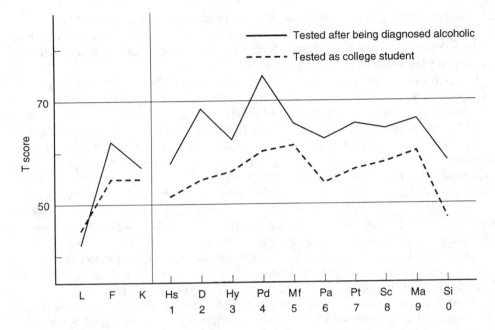

Figure 12.1 *MMPI profile of group of 38 college men, tested as college students, and again in later life after being diagnosed as alcoholic (Kammeier et al., 1973). (Scales 1 to 4 and 6 to 9 of the MMPI profile indicate various types of maladjustment: D for depression, Pd for psychopathic deviance, etc.)*

Personality
Several different personality patterns were traditionally supposed to precede, and predispose to, alcoholism. Depression and psychopathic tendencies were two, while insecurity, anxiety, dependency and low self-esteem made up the third. There is an extensive literature on the personality of alcoholics (Barnes, 1979), using measures like the MMPI. The results are confusing, in that no single profile or pattern emerges. For example, some results show problem drinkers are gregarious, while others find them solitary. Most researchers study clinical groups of alcoholics, who are likely to be as unrevealing as imprisoned paedophiles, for the same reason – direction of cause. If alcoholics have low well-being scores on the California Psychological Inventory, does this mean low well-being leads to alcoholism? Or that being alcoholic makes people feel wretched? Research on diagnosed or institutionalized alcoholics, while easy to do if the researcher works in the institution, tends to be uninformative; Keller's Law (1972) states that on any given measure, alcoholics differ from non-alcoholics. One group of researchers showed more enterprise, and managed to find some personality data collected on alcoholics before they became alcoholic (Kammeier *et al.*, 1973); in their college days the men had had normal MMPI profiles, but after they

developed alcohol problems they showed elevated depression, paranoia and psychopathic deviance (Figure 12.1) – in fact 'the neurotic patterns consistent with self-centred immature dependent resentful irresponsible people who are unable to face reality': Clear proof of *effect*, not *cause*.

Longitudinal and high-risk studies should prove more revealing. Five longitudinal studies contribute data on childhood antecedents of problem drinking: the Cambridge Somerville Study, the Oakland Growth Study, Robins's (1966) child guidance study, and Vaillant's (1983) Core City sample and his College sample. All five studies collected baseline data on a *cohort* of Americans, usually back in the 1920s or 1930s, and then related adult drink problems to childhood experiences. While a powerful way of determining direction of cause, longitudinal studies have some limitations. The number in the cohort who develop alcohol problems may prove small; some studies follow up at age 30, which is too soon to identify many alcohol problems. Two studies were concerned primarily with delinquency, so included only or mostly children from problem families, which makes it difficult to untangle alcoholism and general deviance. All five cohorts are American, and no less than three are located in the same city. The biggest limitation of all is not having collected the right data back at the beginning of the research. Only one study used any systematic measure of early personality; the rest relied on detailed case histories. The Oakland Study finds the small number of men who became problem drinkers or alcoholics had Q sorted, in adolescence, as undercontrolled, rebellious, expressing direct hostility, pushing the limits, manipulative, self-indulgent and sensuous (M. C. Jones, 1968). The study found no evidence they had been depressive, isolated or given to self-pity – personality traits said to be characteristic of alcoholics. Robins (1966) analysed child guidance records of alcoholics and non-alcoholics, and found the alcoholics had histories of truancy, theft, inattention and daydreaming, but showed no differences in impulsivity, depression or unhappiness.

High-risk studies assess people who are likely to become alcoholics, before alcohol problems develop. High risk is usually defined as having an alcoholic parent, so suitable subjects aren't too difficult to find. High-risk subjects are researched before they've had time to develop drinking problems (but not before having an alcoholic parent might have affected them). One study (Tartar *et al.*, 1984) found high-risk subjects scored higher on the 'neurotic triad' of the MMPI – hysteria, hypochondria and depression – while still falling within the normal range. Another study (Schuckit, 1987) found no differences in locus of control, trait anxiety, extraversion or neuroticism, but did find higher scores on an alcoholism scale of the MMPI. A large-scale follow-up study of high-risk men has been started in Denmark (Schulsinger *et al.*, 1986). Two hundred and twenty men, at risk for alcoholism because their fathers are diagnosed acoholic, were given an intensive neuropsychological, biochemical, biographical and psychological assessment in 1980, and will be re-examined periodically (and compared with a matched control group). Preliminary findings indicate the high-risk group are marginally more impulsive and less likely to spend time thinking or worrying about things. At present the study compares high-risk and low-risk subjects but, as alcoholism emerges in a proportion of the high-risk group, a move interesting comparison will become possible: high-risk alcoholic versus high-risk but not alcoholic. This may reveal what brings out an inherited risk, and what enables a person to overcome it.

Upbringing

Retrospective studies – asking alcoholics or alcoholics' parents to describe how they were brought up – abound, but aren't very useful, because the reports are inaccurate, biased, rationalizations, etc. More reliable data are available from the five long-term follow-ups. The Cambridge Somerville study tested various hypotheses about upbringing, and failed.to confirm most of them (W. McCord and McCord, 1960). For example, parents who approved of drinking, and who might therefore serve as an adult model to their children, weren't any more likely to raise an alcoholic. Parents who argued about alcohol showed an insignificant trend to have alcoholic children. Later alcoholism couldn't be linked to mothers who kept their sons 'tied to their apron strings', or to mothers who restricted boys' activity by selecting their friends and generally trying to shelter them from adversity. Later alcoholism wasn't related to 'strong inferiority feelings', or to phobias in adolescence. The Cambridge Somerville study did find later alcoholics twice as likely to have mothers who had responded to crises by escapism – hiding away, trying to ignore problems; perhaps these mothers gave their sons a model of facing problems by seeking escape, through drink.

Vaillant's Core City sample are the control group for the Gluecks' well-known study of juvenile delinquency (Glueck, 1950): 456 11–16-year-olds of the same age, intelligence, ethnicity and neighbourhood, but with no history of delinquency. The main differences between future alcoholics and future moderate drinkers were heredity and ethnicity; upbringing factors accounted for far less of the variance. Boys who lacked a cohesive family, who lacked a close relationship with father, and whose family environment generally lacked support were more likely to develop drinking problems. Relationship with mother, inadequate supervision by mother, social class and childhood emotional problems were quite unrelated to later alcohol problems. Vaillant also followed up 268 Harvard men, a much more privileged, intellectually able group. In the better-off college cohort, childhood environment didn't predict alcohol problems at all; an unhappy childhood preceded mental illness, low esteem or lack of friends, but not drink problems. Vaillant concludes that upbringing may not contribute as much to alcoholism as people suppose. Zucker and Lisansky Gomberg (1986) take issue with Vaillant's analysis of both his own and others' data. They argue he underestimates the importance of parents and upbringing in his Core City data. Their review of six follow-ups, including Vaillant's, concludes future alcoholics show more antisocial behaviour as children – rebelliousness, aggression, even sadistic behaviour – and have more problems with school – poorer performance, leaving school earlier, truancy. They may also be hyperactive.

Vaillant's Core City cohort contained 80 men who did not drink at all, which turned out not to be a sign of a well-adjusted adult, or of a happy childhood. On many variables the abstainers and the alcoholics had similar scores, while the moderate drinkers were more 'normal'. In particular, the abstainers had poorer average ratings than moderate drinkers for global mental health. The abstainers were more likely to have had alcoholic parents, and to have lacked warmth in early relations with them. This suggests they didn't drink because they had seen what it did to their parents or because they feared, consciously or unconsciously, that they couldn't handle it.

Motivation

McClelland *et al.* (1972) think men drink because 'drinking serves to increase power fantasies and that heavy liquor drinking characterises those whose personal power needs are strong and whose level of inhibition is low'. Drinkers are motivated by 'personal power' which is competitive and essentially selfish, whereas 'socialised power' seeks to exert influence over others for their own good. Excessive drinking is one outlet for the need for power in working-class men; others include gambling, aggressive behaviour and collecting prestige objects. Working-class men develop an excessive need for power, for various reasons to do with social expectations, effects of ageing, the fact that they aren't really very important persons; they may try to create a facade of strength to cover up feelings of weakness and powerlessness. McClelland *et al.* use the TAT to show how the need for power changes before and after taking a drink; Figure 12.2 shows that two drinks increase both social and personal power, but after three or more drinks social power themes declined, while the more selfish personal power themes increased. They also present cross-cultural data, using the same imaginative types of measure described in Chapter 8 (for example, the analysis of folk tales), and devise *power motivation training* treatment, designed to reduce or divert the need for power and consequently reduce the need for drink. Unfortunately their findings have not replicated very successfully (Cutter *et al.*, 1973); TATs completed by alcoholics before and after drinking show no evidence of changes in power motivation, only decreases in inhibition.

Psychoanalysis

Psycho-analytic explanations tend to focus on the oral-phase, because alcohol is taken by mouth. Latent homosexuality is another favourite theme. Fenichel (1945) proposes that the alcoholic drinks because of passive, dependent, oral urges. Adams (1978) argues that an overprotective mother creates a need to remain dependent; if this need is later frustrated, the man becomes angry, aggressive and guilty; he then drinks to reduce these impulses and to punish those who withhold affection. Fenichel also elaborates the homosexuality theme; a neglectful mother turns the boy towards his father, which produces unconscious homosexual impulses. Later in life the man goes to bars to drink with other men, to get the emotional satisfaction he did not get from his mother. Many alcoholics,

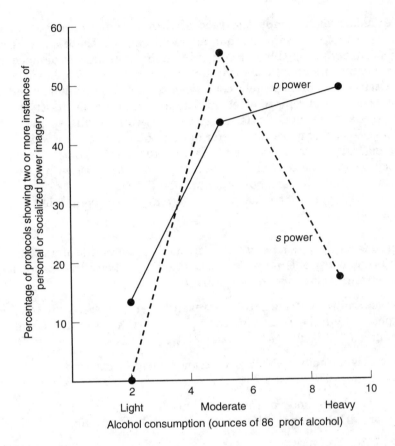

Figure 12.2 *Proportions of subjects writing stories containing personal (p) or socialized (s) power imagery with increasing alcohol consumption (after McClelland et al., 1972).*

however, drink alone, not in company. The Cambridge Somerville study casts doubt on both main psychoanalytic themes. Later alcoholics didn't show oral tendencies as children; they were no more likely than average to be thumb-suckers, to smoke too much at an early age, to indulge in orgies of eating, or to play with their mouths. Also boys with feminine tendencies (who played with dolls, wore girls' dresses, or wished they were girls) were significantly less likely to become alcoholics, although psychoanalytic thinking could see feminine behaviour in boyhood as evidence of repressed homosexuality, which should predispose to drink problems by creating hidden anxieties.

Social learning: tension reduction
Alcohol has been called 'the home remedy for anxiety'. Perhaps anyone who experiences a lot of fear, anxiety or tension and then discovers alcohol's ability

to reduce such feelings runs the risk of drink problems. Research on rats, monkeys and humans confirms that alcohol dampens the effects of stressful events (Levenson *et al.*, 1980). Being placed in approach avoidance conflicts results in increased alcohol consumption (Conger, 1951). People suffering from phobias often use alcohol to help cope with their fears (Mullaney and Trippet, 1987); alcoholics often relapse after misfortune hits them (Marlatt and Gordon, 1980). Analysis of official statistics suggests people living in more stressful parts of the USA drink more, and suffer more alcoholism (Linsky *et al.*, 1985). The State Stress Index is a composite of divorce, disaster, strikes, unemployment, bankruptcy, proportion on welfare, etc., and correlates well with death rate for cirrhosis (0.45), and with alcohol consumption (0.31).

However, this apparently neat *tension reduction* explanation has several limitations.

- It implies anyone who discovers alcohol's anxiety-dissolving properties will become a problem drinker or alcoholic. It doesn't allow for the existence of social or moderate drinkers.

- People, and rats, drink after a stressful event, whereas the tension reduction hypothesis implies they should drink before the event or during it (Volpicelli *et al.*, 1982).

- Alcohol is actually a fairly poor tranquillizer (Mello and Mendelson, 1978).

- There is a large body of research that shows that what people think they are drinking, not what they are actually drinking, reduces their anxiety.

Cognitive social learning

Simplistic tension reduction models of social learning of alcoholism were soon discredited when research showed the link between alcohol and stress is mediated by cognitions. The basic 'imaginary drink' paradigm has a two-by-two design. Half the subjects get a real drink, usually vodka and fruit-juice; half get a soft drink, fruit-juice without the vodka. Half are told they're getting a real drink; half are told they're getting fruit-juice. Hence a quarter of the subjects think they're getting a real drink but aren't – the 'imaginary drink' group. Another quarter think they're getting a fruit-juice, but are really getting a vodka as well. (All have previously agreed to face the possibility of drinking a large vodka.) This is a very easy experiment to do, so, as Cook's Law of Conservation of Experimenter Effort predicts, it has been done lots of times. It's also one of those experiments that almost always seem to 'work', in the sense that people who think they've drunk a large vodka, but haven't, usually react as if they have. Figure 12.3 shows that an imaginary drink has as much effect on male sexual arousal as a real drink (G. T. Wilson and Lawson, 1976), causing the same increase in penile volume

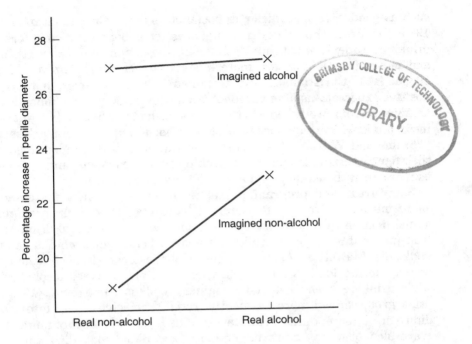

Figure 12.3   *Sexual arousal (increase in penis diameter) after viewing an erotic film, in subjects who have taken a real or imaginary drink (data from Wilson and Lawson, 1976).*

when subjects watched an erotic film. Imaginary drinks can relieve social anxiety, increase aggression on the Buss aggression machine (Lang *et al.*, 1975), reduce GSR, heart rate and forehead muscle tension (Levenson *et al.* 1980). However, Levenson's study also shows one limitation of the imaginary drink paradigm. People can imagine the effects of one drink; it's more difficult to imagine the effects of several. When Levenson doubled the dose from half a gram of alcohol per kilogram of body weight to a whole gram per kilogram, the real drinks started having effects the imaginary ones couldn't achieve, namely reducing people's physical reactions to the threat of a painful electric shock.

Following on from the imaginary drink paradigm, subsequent researchers have looked at the ability of people's beliefs about alcohol to predict their drinking. People have a whole range of beliefs about alcohol's effects which must be the despair of health educators. People think alcohol enhances social and physical pleasure, enhances sexual performance, increases power and aggression, increases social assertiveness and reduces tension (Brown *et al.*, 1980). These beliefs aren't necessarily based on experience with alcohol, because they're found in 10–14-year-olds who've never drunk any. People's beliefs about alcohol's effects predict their drinking patterns more accurately than demographic variables such as gender, age, ethnicity or social class (B.A. Christiansen and Goldman, 1983). Students who think drink enhances social behaviour go in for more social drinking; students who think alcohol relieves tension, or improves their cognitive and motor functioning, are more likely to develop problem drinking (Brown, 1985a; B.A. Christiansen and Goldman, 1983). However, not everyone has positive expectations about alcohol. Men who think they've had a drink are less anxious; but one study reports that women who have had an imaginary drink get more anxious, perhaps because they associate it with male loss of control (Abrams and Wilson, 1978). This expectation is well-founded; men who know their female companion has been drinking do feel less social anxiety, and view her as more open to sexual advances (G.T. Wilson *et al.*, 1981).

Many treatment programmes tell alcoholics they must abstain completely: 'one drink and you're lost'. Research with the imaginary drink paradigm suggests a qualification to this principle. Alcoholics who drank a real drink disguised as fruit-juice didn't go on to drink a lot more, whereas ones who had an imaginary vodka did (Marlatt *et al.*, 1973). If the alcoholic doesn't know he's had 'one drink', he may not be 'lost'. A later replication minutely analysed alcoholics' reactions while drinking their real and imaginary vodkas (Berg *et al.*, 1981). The real drink group sipped more frequently, rated themselves more intoxicated. They didn't drink more, didn't drink faster, didn't mention alcohol more often, didn't crave alcohol more, didn't fidget more, and didn't look different to watching psychologists. Alcoholics' beliefs about drinking and tension reduction are the best predictor of treatment outcome, better than demographic and treatment variables, such as marital status, being in work, stress levels and social support (Brown, 1985b).

HEREDITY AND ALCOHOL

There is a large body of research on the heritability of alcoholism, using all the usual research paradigms from selective breeding (of rats) to adoption. Most studies restrict themselves to male subjects, because female rates of alcoholism are so much lower. As long ago as 1878, research had shown that alcoholism runs in families. About 25 per cent of alcoholic men have alcoholic fathers (Cotton, 1979), which doesn't in itself prove heritability. Earlier twin studies, comparing identical and fraternal twins, were not all that conclusive. A more recent study (Hrubec and Omenn, 1981) used very large samples (5932 identical and 7554 fraternal twin pairs), all past the risk period for alcoholism, and had access to complete medical histories; concordance for alcoholism is much higher for identical twins (26 per cent) than for fraternal twins (12 per cent), as is concordance for cirrhosis (12 per cent v. 5 per cent).

Adoption studies
The main burden of proof rests, however, on adoption studies, in particular Goodwin's Danish study, and Cloninger's Swedish study. Research on herita-

bility is much easier in Scandinavia because there are centralized records of health, adoption and kinship, and in Sweden there are Temperance Boards, which gather information about problem drinking. Two smaller adoption studies in the USA (Cadoret *et al.*, 1980; Roe, 1944) give less conclusive results, partly because information about the true or biological parents of adopted children is harder to get at, possibly also because their index cases were problem drinkers, not alcoholics.

The Danish study (D.W. Goodwin *et al.*, 1974) looked at alcohol problems in three groups of men:

- 55 adopted men, one of whose biological parents was alcoholic;

- 30 brothers of the 55 adopted males, who had not been adopted, but were brought up by their biological parents (one of whom in every case was therefore alcoholic);

- 78 controls who had been adopted, but whose biological parents had no alcohol problems.

The 55 sons of an alcoholic biological parent had higher rates (18 per cent v. 5 per cent) of alcoholic symptoms (morning drinking, hallucinations, loss of control, need for treatment). They also had higher rates of divorce, psychiatric illness and psychiatric treatment. The 30 men brought up by biological parents one of whom was alcoholic had the same rates of alcohol problems – around 5 per cent – as the 55 adopted away. Being brought up by an alcoholic parent didn't increase the risk; Goodwin's data provide no evidence for a contribution from upbringing or social learning. This research also assessed depression, personality disorders and criminality, and found no differences between the groups, which suggests alcoholism specifically is inherited, not a general tendency to social deviance. A replication with adopted women found much lower rates of alcoholism, and no evidence of heritability (D.W. Goodwin *et al.*, 1977).

In the Swedish study (Cloninger *et al.*, 1981), the outcome in the adopted persons was graded from no alcohol abuse, through mild and moderate abuse, to severe abuse. The results for adopted men are rather strange. Figure 12.4 shows that the likelihood of having a biological father who abused alcohol rose steadily from the no abuse group, through the mild abuse group, peaking for the moderate abuse group, indicating a role for heredity. However, for the 51 severe abusers, the likelihood of true father abusing alcohol was no greater than for the adopted men with no alcohol problems. Hospitalizations and registrations with Temperance Boards showed a similar pattern. The severe abusers were defined by histories of hospitalization or compulsory treatment for alcoholism – yet drink problems didn't seem to run in their families, at least not back to their biological fathers. Cloninger *et al.* also found more criminal behaviour in the biological fathers of the moderate abuser group, and some differences in 'adoptive home and preplacement experience' variables. On the strength of these results, Cloninger *et al.* proposed two patterns of transmission of alcoholism,

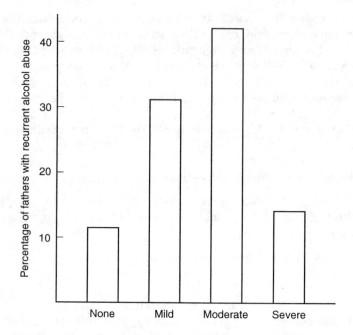

Figure 12.4   *Recurrent alcohol abuse in fathers of men with varying levels of alcohol abuse (data from Cloninger* et al., *1981).*

called *male-limited* and *milieu-limited*. The former was said to be entirely inherited and unrelated to any aspect of the adopting family, while the latter could be linked to both heredity and environment. The male-limited pattern results in moderate abuse, while the milieu-limited pattern results in mild or severe abuse. Cloninger's conclusion has been widely quoted, but it amounts to not a lot more than Figure 12.4 reveals – that Cloninger *et al.* found moderate alcohol abuse runs in families while mild *and severe* abuse doesn't. Three of the four environmental variables that are supposed to help explain milieu-limited abuse don't look very important: length of time in hospital at birth, age in days when adopted, and occupational status of adoptive father. The four variables certainly don't give any comprehensive picture of the adoptive homes of the four groups. Searles (1988) points out nearly half (45 per cent) the adopted men who became alcoholic had neither alcoholic biological parents, nor any sort of unfavourable environment, according to Cloninger's data, so his data cannot account for their problem at all. Cloninger *et al.*'s results need replication before they are accepted as a definitive account of the transmission of alcoholism.

Cloninger's group also report data on heritability of alcoholism in women (Bohman *et al.*, 1981). Table 12.4 shows how rare alcoholism is in women; only 3.4 per cent of a sample of over 900 adopted women became alcoholics. Of the 31 who did so, 10 had an alcoholic true father – as did 1 in 3 of the adopted women

Table 12.4   *Alcoholism in adopted women (data from Bohman et al., 1981)*

Category	Alcoholic	Not alcoholic	% Alcoholic
True father only alcoholic	10	275	3.5
True mother only alcoholic	3	26	10.3
Both true parents alcoholic	2	20	9.1
Neither true parent alcoholic	16	561	2.8
Total	*31*	*882*	*3.4*

Table 12.5   *Alcoholism in half-siblings, according to alcoholism in true and adoptive parents (data from Schuckit et al., 1972)*

True parent	Foster parent alcoholic	Foster parent not alcoholic
Alcoholic	11/24 (46%)	22/44 (50%)
Not alcoholic	2/14 (14%)	8/104 (8%)

who weren't alcoholics. The proportion of adopted women alcoholics who had an alcoholic mother (or alcoholic mother and father) was higher, suggesting *maternal transmission*, but the trend is very small and only marginally significant. Half the alcoholic women had no history of alcoholism in either biological parents; Cloninger's group tried to find factors in either the true parents' background or the early life of the adopted women that might help explain their problem. They found small trends, e.g. for alcoholics' true mothers to be of lower social class, but of better character, or for the adopted women to have been raised in the countryside. Given the very small trends, in very small samples, it would be a mistake to read too much into these data.

Another study (Schuckit *et al.*, 1972) takes as its index cases two groups of half-siblings, the first group alcoholics, the second group not. By their nature, half-siblings are often brought up by someone who isn't a biological parent, allowing a two-by-two cross-fostering design (Table 12.5). Being brought up by an alcoholic parent didn't increase the risk of developing alcoholism, but having an alcoholic biological parent did. However, the most critical cell in the two-by-two design – raised by alcoholic foster parent, biological parent not alcoholic – does not contain very many subjects.

Critics (Searles, 1988) have noted some puzzling features and possible weak points of adoption studies:

- The father of an adopted-away child may give it literally only his genes; the mother necessarily provides an environment for at least nine months. An alcoholic mother may affect her adopted-away child in the womb, or during birth, creating a congenital effect rather than an inherited one. In the Danish study, 15 per cent of the biological parents of the adopted sons were mothers, a large enough proportion possibly to account for the elevated rate of alcohol problems in the adopted men. Similarly, in the Swedish data, adopted women only 'inherit' alcoholism from their mothers.

- The outcome data of the Danish study used a graded continuum of alcohol abuse, including heavy or problem drinking as well as alcoholism. The results, however, were 'all or nothing'. There was no contribution of heredity to problem drinking, only to alcoholism, which is odd and the opposite of the Swedish study's data, where heredity contributed to moderate abuse but not to severe abuse. If the data for Danish heavy and problem drinkers are combined with the data for alcoholics, the evidence for heritability vanishes.

- In the Swedish study, the rates of alcoholism were extremely high – 35 per cent in the biological fathers – which suggested either a very strange sample, or an over-inclusive definition of alcohol abuse.

BIOLOGICAL VULNERABILITY

If alcoholism is inherited, there must be a physical difference between alcoholics and non-alcoholics, from birth – some reason why one group can control their drinking, while the other group cannot. The main thrust of recent research has been to uncover this difference, mostly using the high-risk method. The sons of alcoholic fathers are compared with controls with no familial alcoholism. Most researchers are looking for *biological markers*, something that distinguishes the future, something which can be detected by a laboratory test, something perhaps that cannot be concealed or faked.

The obvious first hypothesis to test is a difference in physical reaction to alcohol. Perhaps people who react more to alcohol are at greater risk for alcoholism. However, high-risk men show no differences in blood alcohol absorption and clearance rates (Schuckit, 1987). A high proportion of Japanese people experience an unpleasant flush if they drink alcohol, so tend not to (Suwaki and Ohara, 1985). There is some evidence that sons of alcoholics are less affected by a standard dose of alcohol, rating themselves less intoxicated by it (Schuckit, 1987). Clearly if alcohol has less impact on someone, they might drink more of it, without realizing its effects. The effect is greater for smaller doses of alcohol; this implies high-risk subjects could get further into an evening's drinking before feeling intoxicated, so might have greater difficulty knowing when to stop. If bad luck then places the high-risk person in a 'heavy-drinking milieu', he could be on the slippery slope to alcoholism.

Acetaldehyde hypothesis

Alcohol is broken down by alcohol dehydrogenase (ADH) to *acetaldehyde*, a psycho-active substance. More acetaldehyde is produced in alcoholics; acetaldehyde in turn produces norepinephrine, and may create greater euphoria. It may also possibly create opiates. High-risk research has found higher acetaldehyde production as a pre-alcoholism difference in sons of alcoholics, suggesting a different physical reaction to alcoholism may cause alcoholism (Schuckit and Rayses, 1979). Acetaldehyde is in turn destroyed by aldehyde dehydrogenase (ALDH); ALDH has four isoenzymes. One of these four isoenzymes of ALDH is more sensitive to low doses of alcohol, and is also the one a high proportion of Japanese persons do not have, which could explain why they get an adverse reaction to alcohol, in the shape of an unpleasant facial flush (Suwaki and Ohara, 1985).

Brain waves and body sway

Several studies (e.g. Pollock *et al.*, 1983) have shown that alcoholics have lower levels of alpha (slow) waves, before they have taken any drink. Another study (Propping *et al.*, 1981) reports increased alpha activity after they have drunk alcohol. High-risk studies have found similar trends (Schuckit, 1987). Schuckit suggests alcohol somehow corrects for the lower level of alpha, and produces feelings of relaxation. Begleiter *et al.* (1984) report another brain wave difference, in *P300 amplitude*. Approximately 300 milliseconds after people experience an anticipated but rare event, a positive wave is recorded in the brain, which is thought to have something to do with capacity for selective attention. In alcoholics this P300 wave is flatter. Begleiter *et al.* report flatter P300 in high-risk subjects, suggesting P300 may be a possible biological marker. Several studies report that high-risk subjects show more body sway, or even that they sway more when sober, but less after a drink (Hegedus *et al.*, 1984). Searles (1988), however, concludes results are inconsistent.

CONCLUSION

Alcoholism probably has a strong heritable element, although some research is less conclusive than many commentators have assumed. A heritable component implies also a biological basis, indications of which are being discovered; research is tending to produce somewhat inconsistent results. The role of upbringing is less certain; some research concludes parents play a definite role in causing alcoholism in their children by failing to provide them with security. Other researchers, notably Vaillant, argue that an unhappy childhood doesn't lead to alcoholism, although the tendency of researchers to focus on problem families may create the illusion it does. American research finds very strong cultural influences on alcohol problems, which may have useful lessons in helping people control their alcohol use. One thing does emerge fairly clearly, however;

personality differences are found in alcoholics, but they are definitely an effect of alcoholism, not its cause.

OSCAR Wilde had another witty observation to make about drink: 'I have discovered that alcohol taken in sufficient quantity produces all the effects of drunkenness'. Wilde faced many problems in his last five years, so it's unlikely his 'discovery' is the only reason he died at the age of 46, but it probably didn't help.

CHAPTER 13

Bouncing Back

Resilience

'WHAT happens to you here is for ever. . . . Things will happen to you from which you could not recover, if you lived for a thousand years' (Orwell, 1949).

George Orwell's *Nineteen Eighty-Four* describes Winston Smith being 'brain-washed' by O'Brien of the Thought Police. Winston is repeatedly beaten up, interrogated for days on end, and forced to confess to innumerable crimes he couldn't possibly have committed (such murdering his wife, who is still alive). He is connected to what sounds like a very early electroconvulsive therapy machine that reprograms his memories, then finally taken to Room 101 to be threatened with 'the worst thing in the world' — having starving sewer rats let loose on his face.

This chapter describes some lines of research an how people cope with adversity; what sort of person copes best; how people learn to cope, and develop resilience. Most psychologists spend a lot of their time dealing with life's casualties; happy, well-adjusted people have less need of their services. This creates the impression that psychology is all about maladjustment, abnormality, immaturity, mental illness. This chapter tries to focus on the other end of these dimensions: maturity, normality, mental health, ego strength, hardiness, positive adjustment.

The Harvard Study of Adult Development was set up in the late 1930s, by people who complained that 'Large endowments have been given and schemes put into effect for the study of the ill, the mentally and physically handicappped. Very few have thought it pertinent to make a systematic enquiry into the kinds of people who are well and do well'. Accordingly they set up a cohort of 268 men, selected as likely to graduate, as being neither physically ill nor maladjusted, and as creating a favourable impression on the dean; 'boys we were glad we had admitted to college'. Vaillant (1977) sees the cohort as similar to Terman's Gifted Children (Terman, 1926, 1947, 1959), with one difference: they were selected for achievement, not intelligence. At baseline, they proved good physical specimens: above average height, with a preponderance of mesomorphs. They came from stable families, with the first-born over-represented. The cohort were bright themselves; their Scholastic Aptitude Test scores placed them in the top 5–10 per cent of American high school pupils. Unfortunately the study didn't collect any other baseline personality data. During World War II, the cohort did well, most getting commissioned; in combat they suffered less than average from nausea, incontinence, palpitations, tremor and giddiness. Vaillant's later follow-ups compared the cohort with the rest of their class — the ones less likely to graduate, in less perfect health, who hadn't caught the dean's eye. By comparison, the cohort were happier, fitter, healthier and more satisfied with their jobs. The cohort collectively have a liberal outlook on life: pro-civil rights, anti-Nixon.

Adversity is a very broad concept, covering a wide range of threats and problems, from the fairly trivial to the catastrophic. There is a lot of research on reactions to physical danger — especially combat — including information about who survives, and how. At the other extreme there is research on coping with 'everyday hassles', on the problems of adapting to daily life. On a longer time scale, there is research on the effects of ageing and ill health. The area that interests psychologists most is how people cope with themselves and their own impulses. Finally, research on intelligence suggest that more intelligent people tend to be more resilient.

RESILIENCE AND PHYSICAL STRESS

During the trench warfare of World War I, soldiers needed a lot of resilience; those who didn't have enough succumbed to 'shell shock'. In World War II, the American armed services employed a lot of psychologists, who collected volumes of information on what they now called *combat stress* (Grinker and Spiegel, 1945). World War II also gave psychologists the opportunity to observe how civilians react to being bombed, and to being imprisoned in concentration camps. The effects of *combat stress reaction* (CSR) include palpitations, dryness of mouth, sweating, stomach pains, excessive urination, trembling, tension and irritability. CSR may result in total withdrawal. The most frightening experiences for bomber crews were reported to be being fired on with no chance to shoot back, hearing reports of enemy aircraft that you cannot see, and the sight of enemy tracer bullets. CSR is short term, its symptoms usually disappearing within a few days. A proportion of people suffer longer-term effects, now generally referred to as *post-traumatic stress disorder* (PTSD). PTSD's symptoms include nightmares, sleep disturbance, hyper-alertness, memory and concentration difficulties, survivor guilt, and reliving: recurrent intrusive recollections of the traumatic event.

World War II bomber crews were exposed to danger on a regular, predictable basis. During a 'tour of operations' they would leave the safety of their base 20 or 30 times to fly bombing missions, knowing that each time a proportion of their number would be shot down (sometimes 5 per cent, which meant the probability of surviving the tour was zero). Other servicemen faced equal danger, but not so predictably, nor were they assessed so regularly between the dangerous times. Hence research on bomber crews provides a unique insight into combat stress. As the tour progressed, men developed insomnia, loss of appetite, tremor, irritability and tension. The most prominent manifestation of 'erosion of courage' was fatigue plus restlessness. By the end of the tour, 52 per cent of bomber crews were suffering sleep disturbances, compared with only 13 per cent at the beginning (Grinker and Spiegel, 1945). Men also developed extreme startle reaction; Grinker and Spiegel suggest anxiety spread from danger points, until it was continuous, capable of being evoked by 'only trivial sounds'. Ruminations and nightmares also became common. Extreme reactions in a few men included depression, seclusiveness, forgetfulness, preoccupation and brooding. Despite the mounting stress, most men stuck at it. As the tour progressed, men got more and more afraid of being killed or wounded, and felt growing pessimism about their chances of surviving.

How do men cope with such extreme pressure? A very small minority experience no fear; 1 per cent of USAAF personnel reported no fear in combat (Flanagan, 1948). The rest felt fear, but managed to carry on. This leads Rachman (1978) to define courage as the ability to cope with fear, not the absence of fear. Attempts to predict who would be able to cope with combat stress in World War II weren't very successful. Test data collected on the men before combat failed to predict their anxiety reactions during or after combat (Wickert, 1947), except that 'men with greater intellectual ability are better able to control their emotional reactions'. (Note, however, that air crew were very highly selected so the data would have suffered severe restriction of range.) On the other hand, ratings of the men's flying skill predicted combat ratings very well (Lepley, 1947). Current US military screening for high CSR risk uses three criteria to exclude: history of psychiatric illness, history of criminality, and low intelligence. Their assessments aren't very accurate; they miss as many unsuitable persons as they exclude, and they exclude twice as many suitable persons as they accept (P. Watson, 1978).

During the Korean War of 1950–52 many Allied prisoners of war were 'brainwashed' into signing confessions that the USA had used biological warfare, or even into publicly espousing communist ideology. At the end of the war, the return of the PoWs, except for 21 who chose to stay in China, gave psychologists the opportunity to compare those who resisted, those who collaborated, and those who did neither. Background factors didn't differentiate. Segal (1956) reports a small trend for collaborators to be of lower intelligence. Schein *et al.* (1957), however, found both collaborators and resisters less intelligent than the majority who managed to keep a low profile. Segal reports that a strong interest in material rewards was the main predictor of collaboration. Schein *et al.* again found collaborators and resisters were alike, and differed from the majority, with higher scores on the MMPI Psychopathic Deviance scale.

The Pueblo Incident in 1968 gave military psychiatrists another opportunity to observe individual reactions to stress. A US Navy ship, the *Pueblo*, was seized off the Korean coast and its crew of 82 were held in North Korea for 11 months, during which time they were interrogated, beaten and forced to sign false confessions. On their return, navy psychiatrists divided the crew into three, according to how well they had coped with captivity. Biographical factors, age, length of military service, education, psychiatric history and criminal record didn't distinguish, but personality factors did. Of those who coped poorly, more than one-third had passive-dependent personalities; of those who coped well, two-thirds were either healthy or 'schizoid'. The group who coped well had twice as many defence mechanisms, and they favoured different ones: reality testing, rationalization, faith, denial and humour, whereas the captives who coped poorly were more likely to defend themselves with obsessive ideation (P. Watson, 1978).

One of the big surprises of World War II was civilian reaction to being bombed. All through the 1930s everyone expected air raids to be massively destructive, which they eventually were, and to cause hundred of thousands of nervous breakdowns, which they didn't. This is not to say that people weren't affected; most experienced short-term reactions, a minority suffered longer-term (days, weeks) reactions: jitteriness, sensitivity to noise, excessive fatigue, trembling hands and terrifying nightmares re-experiencing the traumatic situation (Janis, 1951). However, the Blitz in Britain caused virtually no psychiatric casualties (Vernon, 1941), and the facilities set up to deal with them remained unused. In the Blitz, those most closely involved and most at risk were least affected: firefighters, police, ambulance crews, civil defence and bomb disposal (Lewis, 1942).

Rachman (1978) finds several themes running through these World War II findings:

- *Knowing how to cope:* men who were good fliers stood the pressure better, perhaps because they felt they had some control over their fate. Similarly, men and women who had been trained to deal with emergencies stood the pressure better.

- *Required helpfulness,* having a job to do: firefighters and the rest couldn't break down because everyone else one was depending on them.

- *Not letting the team down:* in the early stages, flying crew members were afraid of being cowards, or of letting down the rest of the crew. Training in the armed services concentrates on creating a cohesive group, to maximize these pressures.

Being a prisoner in a concentration camp is probably the ultimate in stressful experiences. Surveys in the 1950s and 1960s found survivors experiencing survivor guilt, depression, sleep problems, emotional lability, blunted affect, nightmares and reliving: 'These patients communicated an uncanny feeling that nothing of real significance had happened in their lives since their liberation, as they reported their experiences with a vivid immediacy and wealth of detail which almost made the walls of my office disappear, to be replaced by the bleak vistas of Auschwitz or Buchenwald' (Chodoff, 1963). It was generally thought the experience marked people indelibly. However, by the end of the 1970s one sample of survivors seemed to have recovered (Leon *et al.*, 1981), and showed no signs of survivor guilt or emotional blunting.

STRESS, RESILIENCE AND HEALTH

The idea that some people behave in ways that increase their chance of certain illnesses, or of illness in general, is not new – it dates back to the time of Galen and Hippocrates. Research on personality traits that may help people resist illness has flourished in the last 10 to 15 years.

Type A personality

People with *Type A* personalities are not resilient; they find themselves driven to behave in ways that increase their risk of coronary heart disease. They show exaggerated competitiveness, intense ambition, easily evoked hostility and a strong sense of time urgency (the very characteristics many employers value highly and seek to select for). *Type Bs* are more relaxed and easy-going, less hostile and overtly competitive; they are free of stress, but confront challenges and threats less frenetically. They don't try to do two or more things at once, e.g. reading while shaving. Type As are easily recognized; their verbal flow is staccato, and they hurry along the conversation with 'mm-hm' or 'yes yes', whereas the Type B's verbal expression flows more smoothly. Type As are characterized by short explosive laughs, tense energetic movements, fidgeting, drumming fingers and hyperactive facial expressions. The Type A personality is assessed by a structured interview or, less accurately, by a questionnaire, the Jenkins Activity Survey (Booth-Kewley and Friedman, 1987). A medical follow-up study, the Western Collaborative Group Study, confirms that Type As are more likely than Type Bs (11.2 per cent v. 5 per cent) to suffer coronary heart trouble (Rosenman *et al.*, 1975). Possibly Type A behaviour leads to increased activity of the sympathetic side of the autonomic system, which has structural effects that lead to coronary heart disease (K.A. Matthews, 1982).

Hardiness

The more stressful events people experience in one six-month period, the greater the likelihood of their being ill in the following six months (Holmes and Rahe,

1967). Kobasa (1979) found a group of 86 exceptions to the rule, then looked for questionnaire measures that differentiated *hardy* people from people who fell ill after stress. The Hardiness Test has three component scales: control, commitment and challenge. Challenge is the 'belief that change rather than stability is normal in life, and that the anticipation of changes are interesting incentives to growth rather than threats to security'. Commitment is the 'tendency to involve oneself in (rather than experience alienation from) whatever one is doing or encounters'. Control is the 'tendency to feel and act as if one is influential (rather than helpless) in the face of the varied contingencies of life'. Kobasa next reported a prospective study of hardiness, stress and illness, showing that personality measured at year one predicted reaction to stress in year two, thereby excluding the possibility that stress and illness affect how people answer the personality questionnaire (Kobasa *et al.*, 1982). Other research showed that hardiness predicted immunity to stress, independently of Type A personality, previous illness or inherited liability to illness (Kobasa *et al.*, 1981). Critics argue that hardiness is not a unitary concept; that commitment and control predict immunity to stress, but challenge doesn't (J.G. Hull *et al.*, 1987), or that hardiness is just another name for the absence of maladjustment (Funk and Houston, 1987).

Inhibited power motive

McClelland (1979) hypothesizes that people who have a strong need for power which they are inhibited from expressing directly are prone to develop high blood pressure; he describes these individuals as chronically angry but unable to express their anger. Need for power is assessed by projective test, and its 'inhibition' by the number of times the person says 'not' while describing the pictures. McClelland used Vaillant's Study of Adult Development cohort, assessing their inhibited need for power in 1952, and measuring their blood pressure in 1972. A correlation of 0.34 resulted, confirming McClelland's hypothesis.

Pessimistic explanatory style

Misfortunes beset everyone. What varies – perhaps importantly – is how people explain them. *Pessimistic explanatory style* (PES) means people explain misfortunes as:

- stable – 'never going to go away';
- global – 'will ruin everything';
- internal – 'my fault'.

PES can be measured by the Attributional Style Questionnaire (ASQ) or by Content Analysis of Verbatim Experience (CAVE). CAVE is a versatile measure that can extract estimates of PES from interviews, diaries or press cuttings. Burns and Seligman (1989) report a retrospective longitudinal study, correlating

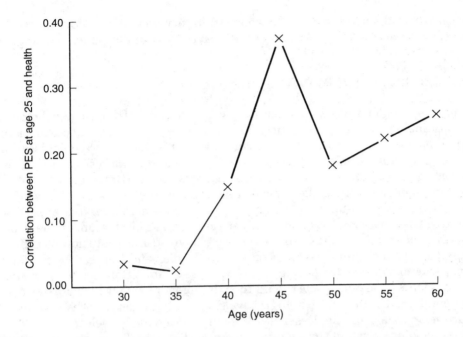

Figure 13.1 *Correlation between pessimistic explanatory style in early life, and illness at various ages from 30 to 60 (data from Peterson* et al., *1988).*

CAVE from 50-year-old letters and diaries with CAVE in current accounts of pleasant or upsetting events. Peterson *et al.* (1988) use CAVE to establish a baseline for PES in 1946 by analysing accounts of difficult wartime experiences, written as part of the Study of Adult Growth – the men 'who are well and do well'. The rest of the follow-up provides data on the cohort's health between ages 30 and 60, at five-year intervals. As the cohort ages, correlation between PES at age 25 and poor health increases (Figure 13.1). Possibly the pessimistic style leads to people neglecting themselves and not seeking medical help. Peterson and Seligman (1987) use CAVE to analyse press quotes from 1900 to 1950 by America's Baseball Hall of Fame. PES predicted shorter life span, especially when players made pessimistic comments about events that went well for them. Peterson and Seligman also report that PES, measured by the ASQ, correlated 0.27 with self-reported illness.

Conclusions
Type A behaviour reliably predicts coronary heart disease, implying Type Bs are more resilient. Otherwise, according to Krantz and Hedges (1987), 'few personality variables have as yet been demonstrated convincingly to be consistent predictors of health and disease'. Research has been characterized by weak associations, poor replicability and a confusing multiplicity of unreliable

measures. Epidemiologists, used perhaps to 'harder' data like occupation, income, address, age and weight, are said to find psychological data unconvincing.

RESILIENCE AND EVERYDAY HASSLES

Combat stress as a research topic isn't very accessible to most psychologists; longitudinal studies of personality, health and resilience take time and money. Hence it probably isn't all that surprising that a lot of psychologists have investigated how people cope with everyday hassles or *micro-stressors*, such as 'preparing meals' and 'getting on with fellow workers' (DeLongis *et al.*, 1982). These are not remotely in the same league as being shot at, bombed or sent to a concentration camp – but they do happen, and what's more, everyone experiences them, so they are easy to research. Most research is reported under the general title of *coping*, and the last 10 to 15 years have seen a profusion of different questionnaire measures of how people cope (Endler and Parke, 1990). Another minor-league stressor for people in the West is exams. Bolger (1990) examines how students cope during the run up to an important exam, which creates mounting anxiety. Students with high levels of trait anxiety, measured by the neuroticism scale of the Eysenck Personality Inventory, selected ineffective ways of coping – wishful thinking, self-blame – that actually caused their anxiety to increase more. However, high neuroticism scorers and ineffective copers fared no worse in the exam itself.

Instrumentality

This is a broad-band trait whose main strands are self-assertiveness, independence and task-orientation; it's measured by the Personal Attributes Questionnaire (Towbes *et al.*, 1989). Instrumentality is seen as a *stress buffer* for adolescents, enabling them to cope better with a wide range of 'negative life events'. The research has three elements: causes of stress, effects of stress, and the buffer between the two (Figure 13.2). Life stress for the American adolescent consists of 'flunk[ing] a grade' (poor marks at school) 'br[eaking] up with boy/girl friend', etc. The effects of stress are self-ratings of anxiety, depression and self-esteem. The buffer is instrumentality. The prediction is that adolescents with high instrumentality, i.e. a strong buffer against stress, will be less affected by stressful life events, so that the correlation between stress and resulting anxiety, depression, etc. will be lower. The prediction is confirmed for girls but not for boys, and for controllable stressful events ('I ran away from home') but not for uncontrollable ones (death of parent).

EGO RESILIENCE AND INNER STRESS

Some psychologists think the major threat to most people's well-being comes from within – from impulses and motives they can't control or won't admit.

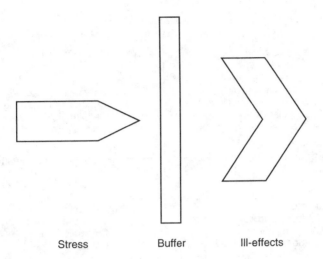

Stress   Buffer   Ill-effects

Figure 13.2 *The concept of stress buffering, e.g. by instrumentality.*

Resilience consists of being able to cope with oneself, as much as with outside pressures. Some people have strong *ego controls*; they manifest their needs and impulses indirectly, delay gratification unduly, and show minimal expression of emotion. At the other extreme are undercontrolled people, who seek immediate gratification of their desires, and experience many but short-lived enthusiasms and interests. Data from the Berkeley Growth Study show that overcontrolled adults come from homes that emphasize structure, order and conservative values (Block, 1971). Undercontrolled adults come from conflict-ridden homes, where the parents' basic values are discrepant, where parents place less emphasis on socialization of children, where parents make fewer demands for achievement, where parents neglect teaching roles, and where parents require children to assume fewer personal and family responsibilities.

Both ends of the ego-control dimension create problems; neither constitutes perfect adjustment or ideal mental health. *Resilience* is a second dimension, independent of ego control (Figure 13.3). The resilient person can change ego control, allowing impulses freer expression if appropriate or, equally easily, controlling them more tightly it needed. Resilience is defined as the 'dynamic capacity of an individual to modify his/her modal level of ego-control, in either direction, as a function of the demand characteristics of the environmental context' (Block and Block, 1980). Resilience means resourceful adaptation to changing circumstances and environmental contingencies; its opposite is, *ego brittleness*. Resilience–brittleness is primarily measured by Q-sort technique; Figure 13.3 gives some illustrative items.

Ego-resilient people are resourceful in the face of new, unmastered situations, maintain an integrated performance under stress, are better able to process two or more competing stimuli, and are better able to resist sets or illusions. They can,

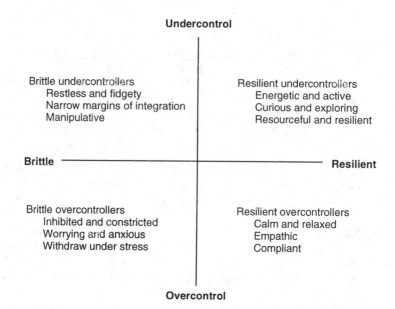

Figure 13.3 *Ego control and ego resilience as two independent dimensions, dividing people into four quadrants, with sample Q-set items describing 4-year-olds in each quadrant (data from Block and Block, 1980).*

however, equally well become highly organized, even compulsive, as circumstances demand. Brittle people tend to perseverate or become disorganized under stress or changed circumstances, and have difficulty recovering after traumatic experiences. They are stereotyped in responding to new situations, and liable to become immobilized, rigidly repetitive or behaviourally diffuse under stress. They are made anxious by competing demands, and take time to recover from stress. They are unable to resist sets or illusions; they cannot modify their personal tempo. The Berkeley Growth Study shows that ego-resilient adults come from homes with loving, patient, intelligent, competent, integrated mothers, where there is free interchange of problems and feelings (Siegelman *et al.*, 1970). Their parents are sexually compatible, agree about values, and express concern about philosophical and moral issues. Ego-brittle persons, by contrast, come from homes that are conflictful, discordant, and lack any philosophical or intellectual emphasis; they have neurotic, anxious mothers, who are ambivalent about their maternal role and very concerned with status and wealth. Most men in the Berkeley and Oakland Growth Studies joined the armed services in World War II; Elder and Clipp (1989) divided them according to amount of combat experience, based on duration, exposure to fire and having killed someone. Men with 'heavy' combat experience mostly still remembered the unpleasant side, and some still suffered anxiety, sleep disturbance or intrusive memories. However, they also said it helped them learn to cope with adversity, and to value life more. At age 40, their Q-sort resiliency index is higher than it was when they were adolescents. They also show more goal-orientation and more assertion, but less helplessness.

Block set up another longitudinal study, specifically to study ego resilience (Block and Block, 1980). From a baseline in 1968, 130 children were studied at ages 3, 5, 7, 11, 14 and 18. The research uses a special California Child Q-Set, based on criterion definitions of the ego-undercontrolling and ego-resilient child, generated by three clinical psychologists. Ozer and Gjerde (1989) cluster-analyse the cohort using the successive Q sets. Two of the large clusters in males define resilience–brittleness, showing how the resilient 3- or 4-year-old grows into the resilient 18-year-old. The research also uses a very large number of measures of behavioural and laboratory tests of ego control and ego resilience. The experiment based index of ego resiliency included ability to change tempo under instruction in three motor inhibition tasks, ability to process two sorts of information simultaneously in dual focus tasks, ability to profit from feedback as manifested in successive estimates in a level of aspiration task, ability to perceive communalities among diverse stimuli, repetition of digits in reverse order, ability to generate alternative solutions, and ability to work under conditions of distractibility. The two types of data, and the two dimensions of ego control and resilience, achieve reasonable convergent-discriminant validity data. Q-set and experimental measures of the same dimension correlate, as they should; Q-set ego control and Q-set resilience don't correlate, which they shouldn't. The two dimensions of control and resilience generate four quadrants (Figure 13.3), whose Q sets at age 4 look quite different. Surveys of favourite TV programmes at age 7 shows children in the resilient undercontroller quadrant prefer family situation shows, whereas brittle undercontrollers prefer more aggressive shows.

Longer-term follow-ups of the second Berkeley cohort are now beginning to appear. Gjerde *et al.* (1986) show that egocentrism at age 3 or 4 predicts Q-sort resilience at ages 7, 11 and 14, but only for boys. Egocentrism was defined as being unable to work out how something will look from another person's point of view. Block *et al.* (1988) describe links between early personality, resilience and drug use at age 14, by which time 10 per cent were using marijuana regularly, and between 5 per cent and 12 per cent had experimented with hard drugs. Ego undercontrol at age 3 predicted drug use 11 years later for boys and girls, but for girls the undercontrol had a tinge of 'anticipations of deprivation leading to self-aggrandizement'. Ego resilience predicted drug use in girls, but not boys. The third follow-up yielded some very strange data; ego undercontrol in boys — impulsiveness, aggression, abundant but misguided energy — predicted the parents' marriage splitting up (Block *et al.*, 1986); Block *et al.* interpret this as tension between the parents making itself felt before the marriage breaks up, thereby changing the boy's behaviour, and don't discuss whether the boy's behaviour affects the success of the marriage, or whether impulsive, undercontrolled parents have impulsive, undercontrolled children.

INTELLIGENCE, CREATIVITY AND RESILIENCE

Most personality theorists have little to say about intellectual abilities, and few recent researchers on resilience have included any measures of them (with one notable exception – Block and Block (1980) suggest that resilience and intelligence have a lot in common). Research during the 1980s, and reanalysis of earlier research (Cook, 1988), shows that intelligence predicts ability to cope with work very well, certainly much better than any measure of personality. From ability to cope with work to ability to cope with life in general, or with stressful events, isn't a very large step. One or two pointers earlier in the chapter suggests more intelligent persons are better able to cope with combat stress or captivity.

One of the earliest, largest and longest cohort studies focused on intelligence. In 1921, Lewis Terman started the Genetic Study of Genius, a life-time follow-up of 1000 Californians with IQs of 130 or more (Terman, 1926). The title proved overambitious; the cohort contains no famous authors, inventors, politicians, philosophers or captains of industry. In later reports (Burks *et al.*, 1930; Terman and Oden, 1947, 1959), the authors refer more modestly to the 'Gifted Group'. The cohort matured earlier, learning to walk and talk sooner than average and showing greater maturity of interests in childhood. They enjoyed better health in childhood, and slept almost an hour longer than the average child. On a range of tests of 'character' they scored far above the general average. They expressed fewer 'questionable social attitudes', cheated less, had more 'wholesome' reading preferences, and greater emotional stability on a version of Woodworth's Personal Data Sheet.

At school, ratings of their temperament and personality by teachers showed them to be better adjusted, not poorly adjusted as the lay person sometimes supposes. They were as popular as other children, but preferred to make friends with older children. They scored well above average on tests of social intelligence, disproving the argument that very intelligent people are socially inept or cannot relate to others. They read a lot, but also liked games that required a lot of exercise, and made as much contribution to the non-academic side of school as to the academic. In their teens, the females in the cohort expressed a less stereotypically feminine outlook. The Gifted Group were less likely than average to have died by 1940 or 1955. They enjoyed excellent health, and were generally very well adjusted. The few that had been rated maladjusted at one of the follow-ups seemed better than averagely able to recover by the next. In the 1955 follow-up, when they were 45, only 1.3 per cent of the males and 0.5 per cent of the females were alcoholics, compared with 7 per cent of American men and 1 per cent American women.

Given the way the cohort were selected, it's perhaps unsurprising they were seven times as likely as the average Californian to enter college, or seven times likelier to enter one of the professions. Few were unemployed, and relatively few had unskilled or semi-skilled jobs. Few had got into trouble with the law. In 1940,

91 per cent voted regularly, against a national average of 65 per cent. By 1945 a higher than average proportion were married (84 per cent). They generally married very intelligent, college-educated persons like themselves, and their marriages were slightly happier than average. The cohort have generally been very successful in their chosen careers, and have produced collectively some 2000 scientific patents, 230 patents and 33 novels.

The size of the cohort allowed Terman *et al.* to distinguish a sub-group who did less well: 92 males whose careers by 1945 hadn't prospered. They were mostly doing jobs that they'd drifted into, that they didn't want to be doing, and that didn't suit their vocational interests; they were less likely to have got married, more likely to have married poorly educated women of lower social class, and much more likely to have got divorced. The rot had set in long before. They'd done as well as the rest at primary school, but started falling behind in high school, and shown a slump of 'alarming proportions' in college. Their physical health was as good as the rest of the Gifted Group, but they exhibited increasing nervousness and instability as time passed. During the same time, their social adjustment grew poorer, and they took less and less part in extra-curricular activities. What had prevented them their fulfilling their promise? Terman's data suggest two possibilities: personality, and background. The 92 men were rated lower, by self, spouse and parent, on a long list of personality traits: appearance, attractiveness, poise, alertness, friendliness, perseverance, self-confidence, integration and absence of inferiority feelings. These differences got bigger as the years passed. The 92 men also came from different homes, of lower social standing, with less emphasis on the value of education, where parents were less likely to be employed in professional capacities.

Creativity

The Institute of Personality Assessment and Research (IPAR) report intensive studies of creative architects, writers and mathematicians (Barron, 1969). The results contain an interesting paradox; the creative people get more deviant profiles on the MMPI, consistent with the idea that 'genius is akin to madness', but they also get higher ego-strength scores. On the California Psychological Inventory, the creative groups score higher on flexibility, psychological-mindedness and self-acceptance, but lower on socialization, self-control, well-being and desire to create a good impression on others. Barron concludes 'they are much more troubled psychologically, but they also have far greater resources with which to deal with their troubles'.

Several studies have been reported of resilience and general ability to cope with life at the opposite end of the general intelligence dimension. Charles (1953) describes a cohort of 205 persons who'd been allocated to the 'opportunity room' at school, when their tested IQ averaged at 60. Fourteen years later, most (83 per cent) were employed, not necessarily full time; most had low-status jobs, labouring for the men and domestic service for the women, although a few had supervisory or skilled posts. In the hard days of the 1930s, 24 per cent were largely dependent on relief (social security), but in the prosperous 1940s and 1950s fewer than one in ten needed major support. Charles visited nearly 50 of their homes, and found two or three were very pleasant, most reasonably comfortable if cramped, but nine or ten were 'squalid' and 'unbelievably dirty'. The men showed more evidence of limited resilience. Many had brushes with the law, mostly for drunkenness and petty offences such as not having a dog licence. By age 35, about twice as many had died as average for their age, mostly in accidents or by violence. Other studies of groups of persons of very low intelligence suggest more limited ability to cope: Gazaway (1969) describes the 'hillbilly' inhabitants of 'Duddy's Branch', in a remote, impoverished part of the USA, as unable to count money, observe any standards of hygiene, obtain any work, use simple tools such a hammer or saw, or limit their own fertility. They live extremely squalid lives.

IN Orwell's novel, Winston Smith doesn't bounce back. The last chapter of *Nineteen Eighty-Four* portrays him leading an aimless, gin-sodden existence, hanging on to every word of the propaganda he used to despise, trying to shut out of his mind the smell of those . . .

CHAPTER 14

The Line Ahead

The Future of Personality Research

PAUL Meehl is a leading world expert on personality and its measurement; his experience stretches as far back as the construction of the MMPI in the late 1930s. Over ten years ago (1978) he wrote despairingly about 'the slow progress of soft psychology'; the study of personality 'shows a disturbing absence of that cumulative character that is so impressive in disciplines like astronomy, molecular biology, and genetics'. The astronomer of today knows things the astronomer of 1940 couldn't begin to think of. The geneticist of today is performing incredible and frightening feats of genetic engineering. But what about personality theorists? They're still using the MMPI, and still writing papers saying how limited is the measure and the approach it represents. Soft psychology hasn't progressed noticeably since before the Second World War. Indeed, to Meehl's pessimistic eye it seems to be floundering round in circles. A new theory is put forward; there is a period of enthusiasm, . . . a period of attempted application to several fact domains, a period of disillusionment as the negative data come in, a growing bafflement about inconsistent and unreplicable empirical results, multiple resort to ad hoc excuses, and then finally people just sort of lose interest in the thing and pursue other endeavours.'

Topics that 'just kind of dried up and blew away' include *authoritarian personality* and *the good judge of personality*. Following the publication of Adorno *et al.*'s work on *The Authoritarian Personality* in 1950, there was a flurry of research on the issue. By 1965, no one was researching authoritarianism any more; now no one even teaches it. The early 1950s also saw a lot of research on the good judge of personality, until interest in the topic was killed outright by Cronbach's (1955) critique. Little research is reported these days on why some people are better at summing up their fellows, despite the obvious practical significance of the issue.

Students often share Meehl's doubts about the state of personality theory and research. There's an awful lot of it, but it doesn't seem to add up to very much. For every theory, there's a counter-theory. For every interesting and socially significant result, there are a dozen non-replications, half-replications and qualifications. For every researcher who's trying to prove something, there are half a dozen waiting to pick holes in his or her work. The journals are full of incomprehensible papers researching issues of no imaginable importance whatever. And no personality theorist can begin to answer any single one of the practical questions the lay person insists on asking: Why do people in Northern Ireland keep blowing each other up? How can I recruit efficient sales staff? Why do I have nightmares? Why does my 5-year-old keep wetting his bed? What sort of man is the Yorkshire Ripper? ('Aggressive and hostile to women' was the astounding insight of one expert, before Sutcliffe was caught.) This last chapter considers two questions: why hasn't the study of personality gone forwards faster? And how can it keep moving in the future?

REASONS FOR SLOW PROGRESS

The picture painted in the preceding paragraphs is of course far too black. The study of personality has achieved a great deal; the research on aggression, sexuality, alcoholism and resilience reviewed in Chapters 10–13 proves that. Personality theorists have, moreover, developed a technology, a practical proof they have gained some understanding of the field. In fact, personality research has given rise to two fairly successful technologies: psychological assessment and behaviour modification. The occupational psychologist can help the employer who wants to select better sales staff. The behaviour therapist can stop the 5-year-old wetting the bed. Even, here, though, personality theorists find it's 'heads I win, tails you lose'; as soon as these technologies prove successful, they're attacked as divisive, elitist or coercive.

But there is a lot wrong with personality research. Meehl (1978) comes up with a list of 20 reasons for its slow progress, which he apparently generated at the rate of one every 30 seconds, for he says the whole list took only 10 minutes to write. Meehl's list divides into two: the practical problems of studying personality, and the inherent difficulties. There are also ethical problems, and a subtler set of limitations ('empire building') arising from who does personality research, and why.

Practical problems
The personality researcher faces a lot of practical difficulties, some of which have been mentioned in previous chapters. Meehl lists about half a dozen more, which are outlined briefly here, using Meehl's own labels.

RESPONSE CLASS PROBLEM.   Or defining one's units of analysis: getting a degree? Sitting an exam? Answering a question? Writing a sentence? Writing a letter? Firing a motor neuron in arm or hand? This problem exists even in such a structured environment as the Skinner box, and 'reaches unmanageable proportions' in studying human behaviour.

SITUATION-TAXONOMY PROBLEM.   This is the response class problem applied to stimuli or situations. Every theory of personality, explicitly or implicitly, defines behaviour as a function of the person and the situation, so a comprehensive classification of situations is needed. This too has to define its units: a whole culture? A region? A town? A street? A house? A room? An election? A political meeting? A question asked at the meeting?

SHEER NUMBER OF VARIABLES.   How many facts would the psychologist need for a complete understanding of an individual personality? Meehl thinks the most exhaustive enquiries by psychologist or analyst 'so thin and spotty and selective as to border on the ludicrous'. Meehl lists some important facts the psychologist might not know: never-diagnosed sub-clinical TB, a mutated gene, a mother who absented herself the day after the person fantasized a brutal father would disappear. The total assessment team should include a geneticist and a chest specialist as well as a psychoanalyst.

UNKNOWN CRITICAL EVENTS.   Even if psychologists had access to every fact there was to be known about a person, they still mightn't understand that person's personality. The outsider just can't see some critically important events, such as fantasies, resolutions or shifts in cognitive structure (for example, catching sight of oneself unexpectedly in the mirror coughing, and being so revolted by the sight that one decides to give up smoking).

DIVERGENT CAUSALITY AND RANDOM WALK.   Any minor event can set one on a different path, and change the rest of one's life. A lot of students marry other students, but which other students they meet depends on which college makes them an offer, what subject they study, what room in hall they get allocated, etc.

AUTOCATALYTIC PROCESSES.   A chance event, or a hard-to-detect inner event, can sometimes start an autocatalytic process or 'vicious circle'. Mednick (1958) proposed that schizophrenia results from *reciprocal augmentation* of anxiety; anxiety increases the range of things the person fears, so more things make him or her anxious, which creates still more things he or she's afraid of, which makes him or her even more anxious . . . Eysenck's incubation hypothesis of neurosis (Chapter 5) also postulates an autocatalytic increase in anxiety.

IDIOGRAPHIC PROBLEM.   Personality is shaped by the interplay of countless factors that interact complexly. Hence every individual personality is unique. But then so is every tree, rock formation or day's weather. The scientist can still investigate the general principles of their development.

NUISANCE VARIABLES.   A random variable, by definition, is as likely to affect behaviour in one direction as the other, so its effect cancels out, given a sufficient number of observations. But some variables aren't random, and can't be cancelled out. One of the biggest nuisance variables in personality research is social class, which 'gets in' everywhere, and is very difficult to control for.

Ethical constraints

As Meehl says, a definitive answer to the 'IQ–heredity controversy' could have been given long ago, if experimenters could treat children the way they treat rats. As psychologists' consciences grow ever more delicate, the limits on the research they can do get tighter. The very act of hypothesizing that something might be harmful to a child is sufficient to proscribe experiments that include it, even if it's a daily occurrence outside the laboratory, and would in fact prove entirely harmless.

The late Stephen Potter missed the chance to describe 'non-researchmanship' – the art of never doing any research without appearing to be lazy or incompetent. This is what he might have said:

> The Ethicsman expresses an exaggerated concern for the privacy, feelings or self-esteem of his subjects. The subjects whose privacy he can never bring himself to invade are always people, often children; animal researchers can't use the Ethics ploy. The Apparatusman waits forever for his impossibly complex all-purpose equipment to be built, aided in many universities by idle and incompetent technicians. The Designman worries about controlling every microscopically tiny factor that might contaminate his results, so limits himself to the occasional notes picking holes in other people's research. The Paradigmman has more fundamental doubts; should psychologists try to ape the physical sciences or should they develop their own special methods of enquiry? Questioning the very nature of knowledge in the social sciences excuses him from the tedious task of adding to it.

Empire building: the psychology of the personality theorist

Meehl neglects – through tact, perhaps – to analyse why theories come and go like crazes for skateboards or hula-hoops, instead of building a permanent and extending structure of knowledge. Six linked pressures contribute to the faddiness of personality research; five are general to all academic fields, but one is more specific to psychology.

PUBLISH OR PERISH.   All academics are under pressure to publish, because they want a 'good CV', or need 'something for the annual report', or the like. Unfortunately these pressures often favour quantity not quality. Reading some of the earliest researches on personality, for example Dudycha's work on punctuality, one is struck by the number of subjects and the amount of 'real' behaviour studied; whereas much research published these days tends to look like pilot studies for the real research. Where the researcher has completed a substantial project, he or she splits it up into half a dozen separate papers.

NIT-PICKING.   If one's goal is quantity, it's tempting to complete one's quota of published work by picking holes in other people's work, which is often easier than doing one's own. This is not to say that defective research shouldn't be criticized, but how much better if people didn't publish so much in the first place.

PSEUDO-CONTROVERSY.   Another negative way of boosting one's list of published works is to take a side in whichever pseudo-controversy is raging at the moment. An endless, published, argument about a non-issue, like 'person/ situation', doesn't just improve the researcher's CV; it also does wonders for his or her citation index (how often other psychologists refer to the researcher's work, widely taken as an index of its value).

CULTIVATE YOUR OWN GARDEN.   Personality researchers needlessly multiply concepts and measures, because it's easier to make a name for oneself by inventing a new concept or measure than by building upon someone else's existing work. Developing, or contributing to, a unified theory isn't in the psychologist's professional interest, unless he or she's the person at the top. Developing new theories or models, even if they are virtually indistinguishable from others already published, is the way to get on. A cynical observer might suggest the success of such ventures often owes more to the energy or charisma of the author than to the idea's merit. The same pressure applies to personality measures, which are legion, with the added bonus that one that catches on will make its owner a lot of money. And there are some really bad tests in widespread use.

DON'T VENTURE OFF CAMPUS.   A lot of research published in personality journals these days is very self-contained. It's based on paperwork of various sorts, completed by the researcher's students. Of course many interesting problems can be researched in this way—but many more cannot. However, it's much more difficult to get information about 'real' behaviour of 'real' people, and it means leaving the security of the campus.

COTTAGE INDUSTRY.   There is a structural difference between psychology and physics or cancer research. Most psychological research is small-scale and fairly cheap, so it can remain at the cottage-industry level, whereas the expense of research on e.g. nuclear physics forces people to work in large teams, carrying out a co-ordinated programme of research. It's much easier for personality researchers to go their own way and do their own thing. (There are some large collaborative projects: Murray's Harvard Psychological Clinic, Cattell's work and Eysenck's group at the Maudsley, to mention but three.)

INHERENT DIFFICULTIES

The obstacles listed so far could be overcome, at least in theory. Other obstacles are less easy to shift or get round; they are created by the fact that personality theorists' subject matter is human social behaviour.

Feedback loops

Early accounts of upbringing saw it as a one-way process; the parent moulds the child into the desired image. But children are not passive lumps of dough; their behaviour, right from birth, affects the parent. The parents influence each other. Other children influence each other and the parents, creating a highly complex set of feedback loops. Twin research suggests both parent and child are also influenced by heredity. Another complicating feedback loop involves the psychologist and his or her subjects; human beings react to being observed and measured.

Context-dependent stochastologicals

This finely crafted chunk of jargon refers to the baffling, often irritating, way correlations fluctuate for no apparent reason (unless, as Meehl notes, they happen to have been calculated by Cyril Burt). If Meehl's Mental Measure (fictional) correlates +0.50 with social class in Duluth junior high-school students, while Jones finds a correlation of +0.34 on Mexican American senior high-school students in Tucson, how can one explain the difference? Is it caused by age, ethnicity or place, or all three, or something else altogether? A comprehensive theory ought to be able to list the factors capable of altering the correlation, and a large enough sample ought to iron out random variation. Some progress has been made with this problem since Meehl's article was published. Meta-analysis and validity generalization help the researcher decide which differences in correlations may be real and are worth trying to explain, and which probably arise from random variation.

Open concepts and conceptual drift

Most concepts in personality are open, not rigorously and explicitly defined. Physicists know exactly what they mean by light; chemists know exactly what they mean by copper sulphate. Everyone knows what 'intelligence' or 'extraversion' mean, but everyone means something different. Meehl thinks this openness is intrinsic to personality, and doesn't just (or only) reflect personality theorists' laziness or sloppiness. Open concepts drift – they change meaning over time. Eysenck's idea of extraversion is quite unlike Jung's. The sociologist's concept of intelligence – a myth invented by the middle class to justify continued oppression of the working class – is far removed from Cyril Burt's elegant definition 'innate general cognitive ability'.

Reliance on human judgement and on words

Fiske (1974) agrees with Meehl that the 'conventional science of personality' has reached its limits. Conventional personality researchers are so 'preoccupied with global variables' that they simply fail to notice when their data don't confirm the global variables' existence. Hence theories aren't rejected because they're falsified, but just die a death when they fall out of fashion. Personality research will always yield inconsistent results, only tenuously related to theory, because it relies on the human observer; to rate others' behaviour, or to rate his or her own. Personality is social behaviour, so can only be defined by a human observer. (This is why personality concepts are intrinsically open.) The human observer describing own or others' behaviour is summarizing extended and diverse perceptions, so cannot be expected to agree with another observer, or with him or herself on a later occasion. Fiske's second point is closely related to his first. Human observers of personality use words to describe what they see in themselves or others: their own words, or those on rating scales or in questionnaires. Hence personality concepts, defined in words, will inevitably be vague and open.

THE LINE AHEAD

Everyone agrees the study of personality is in danger of losing direction. Kline (1983) complains it's also losing research funding, so telling have been the attacks of its critics. The 25 years since Mischel's critique have seen attempts to repair the trait model, further attacks upon it, the diversion into studying 'situations', but no line that personality research can usefully follow. Meehl offers one, rather odd, suggestion: Fiske offers three; and Eysenck points to a fifth.

Stop tabulating asterisks

The traditional psychology experiment states a *null hypothesis*: there will be no significant difference between massed and spaced Muller–Lyer trials. Meehl thinks stating null hypotheses – there is no significant difference between middle and working class in use of physical punishment – is the wrong appproach for personality, because null hypotheses are trivial, because they're always false in personality studies, and because they're uninformative. The null hypothesis is always false, because any pair of groups of people – Conservative/Labour, black/white, male/female – will always differ. Null hypothesis studies are uninformative because a difference doesn't confirm any particular theory. Attempts to prove Freudian theory illustrate this clearly; Johnson's penis envy experiment (p. 160) found a sex difference in taking pencils, which is consistent with Freudian theory, but with half a dozen others as well. Finally, the null hypothesis is often trivial, because it's often so obvious that a difference will be found that it's a waste of time and money collecting the data. Meehl draws the analogy of a theory of weather that solemnly proves, by a test on two sets of 30 days' rainfall, that it rains more in April than in May.

The final stage of 'tabular asterisks' game is the *Psychological Bulletin* review, when all the studies comparing, say, sadistic murderers' fantasies with clergymen's fantasies are summarized in a table, and awarded three asterisks for a difference significant at the 0.1 per cent level, two for the 1 per cent, one for the 5 per cent, and none for no significant difference. (Soft psychology often goes one step beyond proving the blindingly obvious – and fails to prove the blindingly obvious.) The reviewer then 'counts noses', and finds seven of the ten studies confirm the hypothesis that sadistic murderers have more aggressive fantasies than clergymen. Other sciences, such as physics or chemistry, don't test significance of differences, nor do they exhibit the 'pretentious and stuffy . . .

verbal pseudorigor of the soft branches of social science' (Meehl, 1978). What do they do? And what, according to Meehl, should psychology and personality theory be doing? He offers several alternatives to tabular asterisks:

- Make precise predictions. A theory of weather that says it rains more in April than in May is trivial; one that can predict which days in April will be wet commands respect.

- Make numerical predictions. The hard sciences can predict how fast an object will be falling 1.75 seconds after it is dropped from a great height.

- Plot one variable as a function of another. Physics texts are full of graphs plotting x against y for n different values of z.

Personality theory is some way from making precise or numerical, predictions for individuals. Might it be possible one day to predict that a person with a particular inheritance, brought up in a particular way, will score 20 on Eysenck's extraversion scale? It seems unlikely. Meehl emphasizes the almost infinite number of factors contributing to an individual personality. Predicting the speed of falling objects is very simple by comparison. Personality theorists can say that people brought up in particular ways are more likely to have particular personalities, but they can't make numerical predictions, nor can they predict with complete confidence how particular individuals will behave. Plotting the function of one quality against another was the starting point of experimental psychology; psychophysics states general principles relating perceived stimuli to actual stimuli. The analogy in personality research is plotting absolute auditory threshhold against extraversion, or – ethics permitting – stress tolerance against neuroticism, in place of the present extreme groups paradigm. Plotting a graph of threshold against extraversion is perfectly feasible; it would entail testing a vast number of persons, and – unless the relation were curvilinear – would add little to Eysenck's theory.

In fact, research on individual differences has solved the tabular asterisks problem, in a different way. The traditional *Psychological Bulletin*, narrative review approach is confusing and unhelpful, and has been largely replaced by meta-analysis and validity generalization analysis (VGA), which allow the researcher to state a single relationship between e.g. sadistic fantasizing and murder. Neither meta-analysis nor VGA, however, achieves Meehl's goal of making precise predictions.

Personality as naturalistic molecular acts

Fiske (1974) suggests videotaping behaviour and deriving personality measures from the recording. This eliminates the human observer, whom Fiske sees as the origin of personality research's difficulties; behaviour can be coded from videotapes with such high inter-observer reliability that the measures can be considered objective.

What behaviour can be coded from videotapes? Fiske seems to be thinking of non-verbal communication – tone of voice, posture, gaze, facial expression – which has been extensively researched since the 1960s (Argyle, 1975). Fiske's suggestion is hardly new; Allport and Vernon reported an extensive study of what was then called 'expressive style' in 1932. Research on non-verbal communication suffers from Meehl's 'unit-of-response' problem; should one code paragraphs, sentences, words, syllables or 10-millisecond slices of sound? It's very laborious, especially at the finer time scales, and doesn't relate very well to other personality measures (Argyle and Cook, 1976). Or perhaps Fiske is proposing that personality be defined in terms of posture, tone of voice or amount of eye-contact. Farber (1980) notes that the voice and speech patterns and 'body language' of identical twins were strikingly similar, even where the twins were reared apart, which suggests non-verbal behaviour is a stable individual difference, and may be a good measure of temperament. Applied psychologists implicitly agree with Fiske and Farber; interviews are almost always used for selecting staff, even though their only function that couldn't be carried out more efficiently by other means is finding out what the person looks and sounds like.

Personality as experimental observations

Fiske also suggests laboratory measures, which eliminate the human observer and achieve greater reliability. Fiske does not mention Eysenck or Cattell in his paper, but presumably cannot be unaware that both have been doing precisely what he suggests for some 40 years. Laboratory measures may eliminate the human observer and the reliance on words, but don't automatically achieve high reliability. Some – notably eye-blink conditioning – are difficult to set up, and give very inconsistent results.

Personality as perceptions

Fiske's third suggestion doesn't dispense with the human observer and his or her reliance on words, but tries to make the best of a bad job and regard the study of personality as the study of how people see personality. But there's already a field of psychology concerned with how people perceive others' personality; it's called *person perception*. Its findings (Cook, 1979) include the discovery that people are generally very poor judges of personality and unable to agree among themselves or predict actual outcomes, so Fiske's suggestion condemns personality research to eternal vagueness.

Change the level of description

The final suggestion incorporates Fiske's first two suggestions, but derives from Eysenck (1972): if one level of description proves unsuccessful, try another. Eysenck suggests personality can be studied on five levels: the surface, special phenomena (such as crime or mental illness), psychological mechanisms (covering Fiske's 'experimental observation'), psychophysiology, and – the most basic level – its biological basis.

The advantages of the multi-level approach are threefold. At the higher levels, measurements depend on the human observer, who is inefficient and relies on words which are inherently vague; lower-level measures—(some) psychological measures and psychophysiology—are more objective. At the higher levels, behaviour is determined by a multitude of factors, many of them impossible to measure or identify; at the lower levels, there are some grounds for supposing that one is measuring something basic, which influences a wide range of higher-level behaviour. Finally, to the extent that measures at different levels confirm hypotheses, the theory gains strength and resembles theories in the hard sciences. As Meehl says, when something has been proved, or a number has been estimated, in half a dozen independent ways, one can be fairly certain of it.

Personality theory and research will progress by examining the person from all angles, and by every available technique. It will continue to stagnate to the extent that it sticks to narrow, 'pre-emptive' constructs: personality is the study of psychodynamic conflicts and all else is heresy, or personality is the phenomenal world and all else is meaningless, or personality is a bundle of habits. There is (some) virtue in every approach. And psychologists do not have a monopoly on scientific insight into the subject; personality psychologists should be ready to work with other disciplines, seeking always to find the links from one level of description to another. There's even a place somewhere for Meehl's chest specialist.

References

Aarens, M., Cameron, T. and Roizen, J. (1978) Alcohol and family abuse. In *Alcohol Casualties and Crime*. Berkeley, CA: Social Research Group.

Abraham, K. (1921/1965) Contributions to the theory of the anal character. In *Selected Papers of Karl Abraham*. London: Hogarth Press and Institute of Psycho-Analysis.

Abrams, D.B. and Wilson, G.T. (1978) Effects of alcohol on social anxiety in women: cognitive versus physiological processes. *Journal of Abnormal Psychology*, 88, 161–73.

Adams, J. (1978) *Psychoanalysis of Drug Dependence*. New York: Grune Stratton.

Adams-Webber, J.R. (1969) Cognitive complexity and sociality. *British Journal of Social and Clinical Psychology*, 8, 211–16.

Adler, A. (1930) Individual psychology. In C. Murchison (ed.), *Psychologies of 1930*. Worcester, MA: Clark University Press.

Adler, A. (1931) *What Life Should Mean to You*. Boston: Little, Brown.

Adorno, T.W., Frenkel-Brunswik, E., Levinson, D.J. and Sanford, R.N. (1950) *The Authoritarian Personality*. New York: Harper.

Alker, H.A. (1972) Is personality situationally specific or intrapsychically constant? *Journal of Personality*, 40, 1–16.

Allport, G.W. (1937) *Personality: a psychological interpretation*. New York: Holt, Rinehart and Winston.

Allport, G.W. (1961) *Pattern and Growth in Personality*. New York: Holt, Rinehart and Winston.

Allport, G.W. (1966) Traits revisited. *American Psychologist*, 21, 1–10.

Allport, G.W. and Odbert, H.S. (1936) Trait-names: a psycho-lexical study. *Psychological Monographs*, 47, no. 1 (whole no. 211).

Allport, G.W. and Vernon, P.E. (1932) *Studies in Expressive Movement*. New York: Macmillan.

Andersen, S.M. and Klatzky, R.L. (1987) Traits and social stereotypes: levels of categorisation. *Journal of Personality and Social Psychology*, 53, 37–54.

Argyle, M. (1964) Introjection: a form of social learning. *British Journal of Psychology*, 55, 391–402.

Argyle, M. (1975) *Bodily Communication*. London: Methuen.

Argyle, M. and Cook, M. (1976) *Gaze and Mutual Gaze*. Cambridge: Cambridge University Press.

Arkowitz, H., Lichtenstein, E., McGovern, K. and Hines, P. (1975) The behavioural assessment of social competence in males. *Behavior Therapy*, 6, 3–13.

Aronson, E. (1958) The need for achievement as measured by graphic expression. In Atkinson, J.W. (ed.), *Motives in Fantasy, Action, and Society*. Princeton, NJ: Van Nostrand.

Bandura, A. (1962) Social learning through imitation. In Jones, M.R. (ed.), *Nebraska Symposium on Motivation*. Lincoln, NE: University of Nebraska Press.

Bandura, A. (1977) *Social Learning Theory*. Englewood Cliffs, NJ: Prentice-Hall.

Bandura, A. (1986) *Social Foundations of Thought and Action: a social cognitive theory*. Englewood Cliffs, NJ: Prentice-Hall.

Bandura, A. and Rosenthal, T.L. (1966) Vicarious classical conditioning as a function of arousal level. *Journal of Personality and Social Psychology*, 3, 54–63.

Bandura, A. and Walters, R. (1963) *Social Learning and Personality Development*. New York: Holt, Rinehart and Winston.

Bandura, A., Blanchard, E.B. and Ritter, B. (1969) Relative efficacy of desensitisation and modeling approaches for inducing behavioral, affective and attitudinal changes. *Journal of Personality and Social Psychology*, 13, 173–99.

Bandura, A., Grusec, J.E. and Menlove, F.L. (1967) Vicarious extinction of avoidance behaviour. *Journal of Personality and Social Psychology*, 5, 16–23.

Bandura, A., Ross, D. and Ross, S. (1963) A comparative test of the status envy, social power, and secondary reinforcement theories of identificatory learning. *Journal of Abnormal and Social Psychology*, 67, 527–34.

Bandura, A., Taylor, C.B., Williams S.L., Mefford, I.N. and Barchas, J.D. (1985) Catecholamine secretion as a function of perceived coping self-efficacy. *Journal of Consulting and Clinical Psychology*, 53, 406–14.

Bannister, D. (1963) The genesis of schizophrenic thought disorder: a serial invalidation hypothesis. *British Journal of Psychiatry*, 109, 680–6.

Bannister, D. (1965) The genesis of schizophrenic thought disorder: re-test of the serial invalidation hypothesis. *British Journal of Psychiatry*, 111, 377–82.

Bannister, D. and Fransella, F. (1966) A grid test of schizophrenic thought disorder. *British Journal of Social and Clinical Psychology*, 5, 95–102.

Bannister, D. and Fransella, F. (1971) *Inquiring Man*. Harmondsworth: Penguin.

Bannister, D. and Mair, J.M.M. (1968) *The Evaluation of Personal Constructs*. London: Academic Press.

Bannister, D., Adams-Webber, J.R., Penn, W.I. and Radley, A.R. (1975) Reversing the process of thought disorder: a serial validation experiment. *British Journal of Social and Clinical Psychology*, 14, 169–80.

Barker, R.G. and Wright, H.F. (1954) *Midwest and Its Children*. New York: Harper.

Barling, J. and Beattie, R. (1983) Self-efficacy beliefs and sales performance. *Journal of Organisational Behavior Management*, 5, 41–51.

Barlow, D.H., Leitenberg, H. and Agras, W.S. (1969) The experimental control of sexual deviation through manipulation of the noxious scene in covert sensitisation. *Journal of Abnormal Psychology*, 74, 596–601.

Barnes, G.E. (1979) The alcoholic personality: a reanalysis of the literature. *Journal of Studies on Alcohol*, 40, 571–634.

Barr, R.F. and McConaghy, N. (1972) A general factor of conditionability: a study of galvanic skin responses and penile responses. *Behaviour Research and Therapy*, 10, 215–27.

Barrick, M.R. and Mount, M.K. (1991) The big five personality dimensions and job performance: a meta-analysis. *Personnel Psychology*, 44, 1–26.

Barron, F. (1969) *Creative Person and Creative Process*. New York: Holt, Rinehart and Winston.

Baumeister, R.F. and Tice, D.M. (1988) Metatraits. *Journal of Personality and Social Psychology*, 56, 571–98.

Baumrind, D. (1971) Current patterns of parental authority. *Developmental Psychology Monographs*, 4, 1–103.

Becker, W.C. (1960) The matching of behavior rating and questionnaire personality factors. *Psychological Bulletin*, 57, 201–12.

Becker, W.C. (1964) Consequences of different kinds of parental discipline. In Hoffman, M.L. and Hoffman, L.W. (eds), *Review of Child Development Research*, vol. 1. New York: Russell Sage.

Begleiter, H., Porjesz, B., Bihari B. and Kissin, B. (1984) Event-related potentials in boys at risk for alcholism. *Science*, 255, 1493–6.

Beloff, H. (1957) The structure and origin of the anal character. *Genetic Psychology Monographs*, 45, 141–72.

Bem, D.J. (1972a) Constructing cross-situational consistencies in behavior: some thoughts on Alker's critique of Mischel. *Journal of Personality*, 40, 17–26.

Bem, D.J. (1972b) Self-perception theory. *Advances in Experimental Social Psychology*, 6, 1–62.

Bem, D.J. and Allen, A. (1974) On predicting some of the people some of the time: the search for cross-situational consistencies in behaviour. *Psychological Review*, 81, 506–20.

Bene, E. (1965) On the genesis of male homosexuality: an attempt at clarifying the role of the parents. *British Journal of Psychiatry*, 111, 803–13.

Berg, G., Laberg, J.C., Skutle, A. and Ohman, A. (1981) Instructed versus pharmacological effects of alcohol in alcoholics and social drinkers. *Behaviour Research and Therapy*, 19, 55–66.

Bernard, L.L. (1919) *Instinct: a study in social psychology*. New York: Holt.

Bersh, P.J. (1980) Eysenck's theory of incubation: a critical analysis. *Behaviour Research and Therapy*, 18, 11–17.

Bieber, I., Dain, H., Dince, P., Dreelich, M., Grand, H., Gundlach, R., Kremer, M., Rifkin, A., Wilber, C. and Bieber, T. (1962) *Homosexuality: a psychoanalytic study*. New York: Basic Books.

Block, J. (1961) *The Q-sort Method*. Springfield, IL: C.C. Thomas.

Block, J. (1968) Some reasons for the apparent inconsistency of personality. *Psychological Bulletin*, 70, 210–12.

Block, J. (1971) *Lives through Time*. Berkeley, CA: Bancroft.

Block, J. (1977) Advancing the psychology of personality: paradigmatic shift or improving the quality of research. In Magnusson, D. and Endler, N.S. (eds), *Personality at the Crossroads: current issues in interactional psychology*. Hillsdale, NJ: Erlbaum.

Block, J.H. and Block, J. (1980) The role of ego-control and ego-resiliency in the organisation of behavior. In Collins, W.A. (ed.), *Development of Cognition, Affect, and Social Relations*. Hillsdale, NJ: Erlbaum.

Block, J. and Thomas, H. (1955) Is satisfaction with self a measure of adjustment? *Journal of Abnormal and Social Psychology*, 51, 254–9.

Block, J., Block, J.H. and Gjerde, P.F. (1986) The personality of children prior to divorce: a prospective study. *Child Development*, 57, 827–40.

Block, J., Block, J.H. and Keyes, S. (1988) Longitudinally foretelling drug usage in adolescence: early childhood and environmental precursors. *Child Development*, 59, 336–55.

Bohman, M., Sigvardsson, S. and Cloninger, R. (1981) Maternal inheritance of alcohol abuse. *Archives of General Psychiatry*, 38, 965–9.

Bolger, N. (1990) Coping as a personality process: a prospective study. *Journal of Personality and Society Psychology*, 59, 525–37.

Booth-Kewley, S. and Friedman, H.S. (1987) Psychological predictors of heart disease: a quantitative review. *Psychological Bulletin*, 101, 343–62.

Borkenau, P. and Ostendorf, F. (1987) Fact and fiction in implicit personality theory. *Journal of Personality*, 55, 415–43.

Bouchard, M., Lalonde, F. and Gagnon, M. (1988) The construct validity of assertion: contributions of four assessment procedures and Norman's personality factors. *Journal of Personality*, 56, 763–83.

Bowers, K. (1974) Situationism in psychology: an analysis and a critique. *Psychological Review*, 80, 307–36.

Breuer, J. and Freud, S. (1895/1955) *Studies on Hysteria*. Standard Edition, vol. 2. London: Hogarth Press and Institute of Psychoanalysis.

Briere, J. and Runtz R. (1989) University males' sexual interest in children: predicting potential indices of 'pedophilia' in a non-forensic sample. *Child Abuse and Neglect*, 13, 65–75.

Brodsky, C.M. (1954) *A Study of Norms for Body Form–Behavior Relationships*. Washington, DC: Catholic University of America Press.

Brown, S.A. (1985a) Expectancies versus background in the prediction of college drinking patterns. *Journal of Consulting and Clinical Psychology*, 53, 123–30.

Brown, S.A. (1985b) Reinforcement expectancies and alcohol treatment outcome after one year. *Journal of Studies on Alcohol*, 46, 304–8.

Brown, S.A., Goldman, M.S., Inn, A. and Anderson, R. (1980) Expectancies of reinforcement from alcohol: their domain and relation to drinking patterns. *Journal of Consulting and Clinical Psychology*, 48, 419–26.

Browne, A. and Finkelhor, D. (1986) Impact of childhood sexual abuse: a review of the literature. *Psychological Bulletin*, 99, 66–77.

Burgess, P.K. (1972) Eysenck's theory of criminality: a test of some objections to disconfirmatory evidence. *British Journal of Social and Clinical Psychology*, 11, 248–56.

Burks, B.S., Jensen, D.W. and Terman, L.M. (1930) *Genetic Studies of Genius, Vol. 3. Follow-up studies of a thousand gifted children*. Stanford: Stanford University Press.

Burns, M.O. and Seligman, M.E.P. (1989) Explanatory style across the life span: evidence for stability over 52 years. *Journal of Personality and Social Psychology*, 56, 471–7.

Burns, R.B. (1975) Attitudes to self and to three categories of others in a student sample. *Educational Studies*, 1, 181–9.

Burns, R.B. (1979) *The Self Concept: theory, measurement, development and behaviour*. London: Longman.

Burton, R.V. (1963) Generality of honesty reconsidered. *Psychological Review*, 70, 481–99.

Burwen, L.S. and Campbell, D.T. (1957) The generality of attitudes toward authority and non-authority figures. *Journal of Abnormal and Social Psychology*, 54, 24–31.

Buss, A. (1961) *The Psychology of Aggression*. New York: Wiley.

Buss, A.H. and Durkee, A. (1957) An inventory for assessing different kinds of hostility. *Journal of Consulting Psychology*, 21, 343–9.

Buss, A.H., Plomin, R. and Willerman, L. (1973) The inheritance of temperament. *Journal of Personality*, 41, 511–24.

Byrne, D. (1966) *An Introduction to Personality*. Englewood Cliffs, NJ: Prentice-Hall.

Caddy, C.R. (1983) Alcohol use and abuse. In Tabakoff, B., Sutker, P.B. and Randell, C.L. (eds), *Medical and Social Aspects of Alcohol Abuse*. New York: Plenum.

Cadoret, R.J. (1966) Relationship between autonomic response patterns and conditioned learning. *Perceptual and Motor Skills*, 16, 67–85.

Cadoret, R.J. (1978) Psychopathology in adopted-away offspring of biologic mothers with antisocial behavior. *Archives of General Psychiatry*, 35, 176–89.

Cadoret, R.J., Cain, C.A. and Grove, W.M. (1980) Development of alcoholism in adoptees raised apart from alcoholic biologic relatives. *Archives of General Psychiatry*, 37, 561–3.

Campbell, D.T. and Fiske, D.W. (1959) Convergent and discriminant validation by the multitrait-multimethod matrix. *Psychological Bulletin*, 56, 81–105.

Campbell, D., Sanderson, R.E. and Laverty, S.G. (1964) Characteristics of a conditioned response in human subjects during extinction trials following a single traumatic conditioning trial. *Journal of Abnormal and Social Psychology*, 68, 627–38.

Cannon, W.B. (1932) *Wisdom of the Body*. New York: Norton.

Cantor, N. and Kihlstrom, J.F. (1987) *Personality and Social Intelligence*. Englewood Cliffs, NJ: Prentice-Hall.

Cantor, N. and Mischel, W. (1979) Prototypes in person perception. *Advances in Experimental Social Psychology*, 12, 3–52.

Carey, G., Goldsmith, H.H., Tellegen, A. and Gottesman, I.I. (1978) Genetics and personality in inventories: the limits of replication with twin data. *Behavior Genetics*, 8, 299–313.

Carlson, R. (1971) Where is the person in personality research? *Psychological Bulletin*, 75, 203–19.

Caspi, A., Bem, D.J. and Elder, G.H. (1989) Continuities and consequences of interactional style across the life course. *Journal of Personality*, 57, 357–406.

Cattell, R.B. (1937) *The Fight for Our National Intelligence*. London: P.S. King.

Cattell, R.B. (1946) *Description and Measurement of Personality*. Yonkers, NY: World Book Co.

Cattell, R.B. (1957) *Personality and Motivation Structure and Measurement*. Yonkers, NY: World Book Co.

Cattell, R.B. (1965) *The Scientific Study of Personality*. Harmondsworth: Penguin.

Cattell, R.B. (1973) *Personality and Mood by Questionnaire*. San Francisco: Jossey Bass.

Cattell, R.B. (1979) *Personality and Learning Theory. Vol. 1: Structure of personality in its environment*. New York: Springer.

Cattell, R.B. and Child, D. (1975) *Motivation and Dynamic Structure*. London: Holt, Rinehart and Winston.

Cattell, R.B. and Kline, P. (1977) *The Scientific Analysis of Personality and Motivation*. London: Academic Press.

Cattell, R.B., Kawash, G.F. and DeYoung, G.E. (1972) Validation of objective measures of ergic tension: response of the sex erg to visual stimulation. *Journal of Experimental Research in Personality*, 6, 76–83.

Chapman, L.J., Chapman, J.P. and Raulin, M.L. (1976) Scales for physical and social anhedonia. *Journal of Abnormal Psychology*, 85, 374–82.

Charles, D.C. (1953) Ability and accomplishment of persons earlier judged to be mentally deficient. *Genetic Psychology Monographs*, 47, 3–71.

Chodoff, P. (1963) Late effects of the concentration camp syndrome. *Archives of General Psychiatry*, 8, 323–33.

Christiansen, B.A. and Goldman, M.S. (1983) Alcohol related expectancies versus demographic/background variables in the prediction of adolescent drinking. *Journal of Consulting and Clinical Psychology*, 51, 249–57.

Christiansen, K.O. (1974) The genesis of aggressive criminality: implications of a study of crime in a Danish twin study. In De Wit, J. and Hartup, W.W. (eds), *Determinants and Origins of Aggressive Behavior*. The Hague: Mouton.

Claridge, G. (1967) *Personality and Arousal*. Oxford: Pergamon.

Claridge, G. (1981) Psychoticism. In Lynn, R. (ed.), *Dimensions of Personality: papers in honour of H.J. Eysenck*. Oxford: Pergamon.

Clark, W.B. and Cahalan, D. (1976) Changes in problem drinking over a four-year span. *Addictive Behaviors*, 1, 251–9.

Cloninger, C.R., Bohman, M. and Sigvardsson, S. (1981) Inheritance of alcohol abuse: cross-fostering analysis of adopted men. *Archives of General Psychiatry*, 38, 861–8.

Coie, J.D. (1974) An evaluation of the cross-situational stability of children's curiosity. *Journal of Personality*, 42, 93–116.

Comfort, A. (1971) The likelihood of human pheromones. *Nature*, 230, 432–3, 479.

Commission on Sexual Offenses against Children and Youths (1984) *Sexual Offenses against Children*, Vols 1 and 2. Ottawa: Supply and Services Canada.

Comrey, A.L. (1978) Common methodological problems in factor analytic studies. *Journal of Consulting and Clinical Psychology*, 46, 648–59.

Conger, J.J. (1951) The effects of alcohol on conflict behaviour in the albino rat. *Quarterly Journal of Studies on Alcohol*, 12, 1–29.

Conley, J.J. (1984) Longitudinal consistency of adult personality: self-reported psychological characteristics across 45 years. *Journal of Personality and Social Psychology*, 47, 1325–33.

Cook, M. (1979) *Perceiving Others*. London: Methuen.

Cook, M. (1982) Perceiving others: the psychology of interpersonal perception. In Davey, D.M. and Harris, M. (eds), *Judging People: a guide to orthodox and unorthodox methods of assessment*. London: McGraw-Hill.

Cook, M. (1988) *Personnel Selection and Productivity*. Chichester: Wiley.

Cook, M. and Simukonda, F. (1981) Anhedonia and schizophrenia. *British Journal of Psychiatry*, 139, 523–5.

Cooley, C.H. (1902) *Human Nature and the Social Order*. New York: Scribners.

Coopersmith, S. (1967) *The Antecedents of Self-Esteem*. San Francisco: Freeman.

Cotton, N.S. (1979) The familial incidence of alcoholism. *Journal of Studies on Alcohol*, 40, 89–116.

Crawford, D.A. (1981) Treatment approaches with pedophiles. In Cook, M. and Howells, K. (eds), *Adult Sexual Interest in Children*. London: Academic Press.

Crawford, D.A. and Allen, J.V. (1979) A social skills training program with sex offenders. In Cook, M. and Wilson, G.D. (eds), *Love and Attraction: proceedings of an international conference*. Oxford: Pergamon.

Crisp, Q. (1968) *The Naked Civil Servant*. London: Cape.

Cronbach, L.J. (1955) Processes affecting scores on 'understanding of others' and assumed similarity. *Psychological Bulletin*, 52, 177–93.

Cronbach, L.J. (1970) *Essentials of Psychological Testing*. (3rd edn) New York: Harper.

Cronbach, L.J. (1990) *Essentials of Psychological Testing*. (5th edn) New York: Harper.

Crowe, R.R. (1972) The adopted offspring of women criminal offenders: a study of their arrest records. *Archives of General Psychiatry*, 27, 600–3.

Curran, J.P., Monti, P.M., Corriveau, D.F., Hay, L.R., Hagerman, S., Zwick, W.R. and Farrell, A.D. (1980) The generalisability of procedures for assessing social skills and social anxiety in a psychiatric population. *Behavioural Assessment*, 2, 389–401.

Cutter, H.S., Key, J.C., Rothstein, E. and Jones, W.C. (1973) Alcohol, power, and inhibition. *Quarterly Journal of Studies on Alcohol*, 34, 381–9.

D'Andrade, R.G. (1965) Trait psychology and componential analysis. *American Anthropologist*, 67, 215–28.

Davey, G.C.L. (1989) UCS revaluation and conditioning models of acquired fears. *Behaviour Research and Therapy*, 27, 521–8.

Davidson, P.O., Payne, R.W. and Sloane, R.B. (1964) Introversion, neuroticism, and conditioning. *Journal of Abnormal and Social Psychology*, 68, 136–43.

Davies, D.R. and Parasuraman, R. (1982) *The Psychology of Vigilance*. London: Academic Press.

Davis, B.M. and Gilbert, L.A. (1989) Effect of dispositional and situational influences on women's dominance expression in mixed-sex dyads. *Journal of Personality and Social Psychology*, 57, 294–300.

deLint, J. (1978) Alcohol consumption and alcohol problems from an epidemiological perspective. *British Journal of Alcohol and Alcoholism*, 13, 75–85.

DeLongis, A., Coyne, J.C., Dakof, G., Folkman, S. and Lazarus, R.S. (1982) Relationship of daily hassles, uplifts and major life events to health status. *Health Psychology*, 1, 119–36.

Digman, J.M. and Takemoto-Chock, N.K. (1981) Factors in the natural language of personality: re-analysis, comparison, and interpretation of six major studies. *Multivariate Behavioral Research*, 16, 149–70.

Dimond, S.J. (1970) *The Social Behaviour of Animals*. London: Batsford.

Dodge, K.A. and Coie, J.D. (1987) Social information processing factors in reactive and proactive aggression in children's peer groups. *Journal of Personality and Social Psychology*, 53, 1146–58.

Dollard, J. (1945) Drinking mores of the social classes. In *Alcohol, Science and Society*. New Haven: Quarterly Journal of Studies on Alcohol.

Dollard, J. and Miller, N.E. (1950) *Personality and Psychotherapy: an analysis in terms of learning, thinking and culture*. New York: McGraw-Hill.

Dollard, J., Doob, L.W., Miller, N.E., Mowrer, O.H. and Sears, R.R. (1939) *Frustration and Aggression*. New Haven: Yale University Press.

Dornbusch, S.M., Ritter, P.L., Leiderman, H., Roberts, D.F. and Fraleigh, M.J. (1987) The relation of parenting style to adolescent school performance. *Child Development*, 58, 1244–57.

Dorner, G., Schenk, B., Schmiedel, B. and Ahrens, L. (1983) Stressful events and prenatal life of bi- and homosexual men. *Experimental and Clinical Endocrinology*, 81, 83–7.

Dorner, G., Rohde, W., Stahl, F., Krell, L. and Masius, W.G. (1975) A neuro-endocrine predisposition for homosexuality in men. *Archives of Sexual Behavior*, 4, 1–8.

Dorner, G., Geier, T., Ahrens, L., Krell, L., Munx, G., Sieler, H. Kittner, E. and Muller, H. (1980) Prenatal stress as possible aetiogenetic factor of homosexuality in human males. *Endokrinologie*, 75, 365–8.

Dudycha, G.J. (1936) An objective study of punctuality in relation to personality and achievement. *Archives of Psychology*, 204.

Duncan, O.D., Featherman, D.L. and Duncan, B. (1972) *Socio-economic Background and Achievement*. New York: Harcourt Brace.

Dunn, J.F., Plomin, R. and Daniels, D. (1985) Consistency of mothers' behavior towards infant siblings. *Developmental Psychology*, 21, 1188–95.

Eckert, E.D., Bouchard, T.J., Bohlen, J. and Heston, L.L. (1986) Homosexuality in monozygotic twins reared apart. *British Journal of Psychiatry*, 148, 421–5.

Eibl-Eibesfeldt, I. (1970) *Ethology: the biology of behavior*. New York: Holt, Rinehart and Winston.

Eibl-Eibesfeldt, I. (1977) Evolution of destructive aggression. *Aggressive Behavior*, 3, 127–44.

Ekman, P. (1972) Universals and cultural differences in facial expressions of emotion. In Cole, J. (ed.), *Nebraska Symposium on Motivation*. Lincoln, NE: University of Nebraska Press.

Elder, G.H. (1988) Military times and turning points in men's lives. *Developmental Psychology*, 22, 233–45.

Elder, G.H. and Clipp, F.C. (1989) Combat experience and emotional health, impairment and resilience in later life. *Journal of Personality*, 57, 311–41.

Elliott, C.D. (1971) Noise tolerance and extraversion in children. *British Journal of Psychology*, 62, 375–80.

Ellis, L. and Ames, M.A. (1987) Neurohormonal functioning and sexual orientation: a theory of homosexuality and heterosexuality. *Psychological Bulletin*, 101, 233–58.

Endler, N.S. and Hunt, J.McV. (1966) Sources of behavioral variance as measured by the S-R inventory of anxiousness. *Psychological Bulletin*, 65, 336–46.

Endler, N.S. and Magnusson, D. (1976) Towards an interactional psychology of personality. *Psychological Bulletin*, 83, 956–74.

Endler, N.S. and Parke, J.D.A. (1990) Multidimensional assessment of coping ability. *Journal of Personality and Social Psychology*, 58, 844–54.

Epstein, S. (1979) The stability of behavior: I. On predicting most of the people much of the time. *Journal of Personality and Social Psychology*, 37, 1097–126.

Eron, L.D. (1980) Prescription for the reduction of aggression. *American Psychologist*, 35, 224–52.

Eron, L.D., Lefkowitz, M.M., Huesmann, L.R., and Walder, L.O. (1972) Does television violence cause aggression? *American Psychologist*, 27, 253–63.

Evans, R.B. (1969) Childhood parental relationships of homosexual men. *Journal of Consulting and Clinical Psychology*, 33, 129–35.

Evans, R.B. (1972) Physical and biochemical characteristics of homosexual men. *Journal of Consulting and Clinical Psychology*, 39, 140–7.

Eysenck, H.J. (1939) Critical notice of 'Primary Mental Abilities' by L.L. Thurstone. *British Journal of Educational Psychology*, 9, 270–5.

Eysenck, H.J. (1947) *Dimensions of Personality*. London: Routledge and Kegan Paul.

Eysenck, H.J. (1952) *Psychology of Politics*. London: Routledge and Kegan Paul.

Eysenck, H.J. (1953) *Uses and Abuses of Psychology*. Harmondsworth: Penguin.

Eysenck, H.J. (1957) *The Dynamics of Anxiety and Hysteria*. London: Routledge and Kegan Paul.

Eysenck, H.J. (1964) *Crime and Personality*. London: Routledge and Kegan Paul.

Eysenck, H.J. (1965a) *Fact and Fiction in Psychology*. Harmondsworth: Penguin.

Eysenck, H.J. (1965b) *Smoking, Health and Personality*. London: Weidenfeld and Nicolson.

Eysenck, H.J. (1965c) Extraversion and the acquisition of eyeblink and GSR conditioned responses. *Psychological Bulletin*, 63, 258–70.

Eysenck, H.J. (1966) Personality and experimental psychology. *Bulletin of the British Psychological Society*, 19, 1–28.

Eysenck, H.J. (1967) *The Biological Basis of Personality*. Springfield, IL: C.C. Thomas.

Eysenck, H.J. (1971) Hysterical personality and sexual adjustment, attitudes and personality. *Journal of Sex Research*, 7, 274–81.

Eysenck, H.J. (1972) Human typology, higher nervous activity, and factor analysis. In Nebylitsyn, V.D. and Gray, J.A. (eds), *Biological Bases of Individual Behaviour*. London: Academic Press.

Eysenck, H.J. (1976) *Sex and Personality*. London: Open Books.

Eysenck, H.J. (1979) The conditioning model of neurosis. *Behavioral and Brain Sciences*, 2, 155–99.

Eysenck, H.J. (1989) Personality and the prediction of success in industry and commerce. Paper given at conference on the Selection and Use of Psychometric Tests. London, July 1989.

Eysenck, H.J. and Eysenck, S.B.G. (1975) *Manual of the Eysenck Personality Questionnaire*. London: Hodder and Stoughton.

Eysenck, H.J. and Eysenck, S.B.G. (1976) *Psychoticism as a Dimension of Personality*. London: Hodder and Stoughton.

Eysenck, H.J. and Levey, A.B. (1972) Conditioning, introversion–extraversion and the strength of the nervous system. In Nebylitsyn, V.D. and Gray, J.A. (eds), *Biological Bases of Individual Behaviour*. London: Academic Press.

Eysenck, H.J. and Wilson, G.D. (1973) *The Experimental Study of Freudian Theories*. London: Methuen.

Farber, S.L. (1980) *Identical Twins Reared Apart: a reanalysis*. New York: Basic Books.

Farrell, B.A. (1963) Introduction. In Freud, S., *Leonardo*. Harmondsworth: Penguin.

Feldman, M.P. and McCollough, M.J. (1971) *Homosexual Behavior: therapy and assessment*. Oxford: Pergamon.

Feldman, P. (1973) Abnormal sexual behaviour – males. In Eysenck, H.J. (eds), *Handbook of Abnormal Psychology*. (2nd edn) London: Pitman Medical.

Fenichel, O. (1945) *The Psychoanalytic Theory of Neurosis*. New York: Norton.

Feshbach, S. and Singer, R.D. (1971) *Television and Aggression*. San Francisco: Jossey Bass.

Fields, P.J. (1981) Parent child relationships, childhood sexual abuse, and adult interpersonal behaviour in prostitution. *Dissertation Abstracts International*, 42, 2053B.

Fineman, S. (1977) The achievement motive construct and its measurement: where are we now?. *British Journal of Psychology*, 68, 1–22.

Finkelhor, D. (1990) Early and long term effects of child sex abuse: an update. *Professional Psychology*, 21, 325–30.

Fiske, D.W. (1974) The limits for a conventional science of personality. *Journal of Personality*, 42, 1–11.

Fiske, D.W. (1982) Schema-triggered affect: applications to social perception. In Clarke, M.S. and Fiske, S.T. (eds), *Affect and Cognition: the 17th Annual Carnegie Symposium on Cognition*. Hillsdale, NJ: Erlbaum.

Fiske, D.W. and Pavelchak, M.A. (1986) Category-based versus piecemeal affective responses: development of schema-triggered affect. In Sorrentino, R.M. and Higgin, E.T. (eds), *Handbook of Motivation and Affect*. New York: Guilford Press.

Ford, C.S. and Beach, F.A. (1952) *Patterns of Sexual Behaviour*. London: Methuen.

Forester, N.C., Vinacke, W.E. and Digman, J.M. (1955) Flexibility and rigidity in a variety of problem situations. *Journal of Abnormal and Social Psychology*, 50, 211–16.

Forgas, J.P. (1982) Episode cognition: internal representations of interaction routines. *Advances in Experimental Social Psychology*, 15, 59–101.

Fransella, F. and Adams, B. (1966) An illustration of the use of repertory grid technique in a clinical setting. *British Journal of Social and Clinical Psychology*, 5, 51–62.

Fransella, F. and Bannister, D.B. (1967) A validation of repertory grid technique as a measure of political construing. *Acta Psychologica*, 26, 97–106.

Flanagan, J. (1948) *The Aviation Psychology Program in the Army Air Forces*. USAAF Aviation Psychology Research Report 1. Washington, DC: US Government Printing Office.

Fransella, F. and Bannister, D. (1977) *A Manual of Repertory Grid Technique*. London: Academic Press.

Frcka, G. and Martin, I. (1987) Is there – or is there not – an influence of impulsiveness on classical eyelid conditioning? *Personality and Individual Differences*, 8, 241–52.

Freedman, J.L. (1984) Effect of television violence on aggressiveness. *Psychological Bulletin*, 96, 227–46.

Freud, S. (1905/1966) *Three Essays on Sexuality*. London: Hogarth Press and Institute of Psychoanalysis. (Standard Edition, vol. 7).

Freud, S. (1909/1966) *Analysis of a Phobia in a Five-year-old Boy*. London: Hogarth Press and Institute of Psychoanalysis. (Standard Edition, vol. 10).

Freud, S. (1914/1966) *History of the Psychoanalytic Movement*. London: Hogarth Press and Institute of Psychoanalysis. (Standard Edition, vol. 14).

Freud, S. (1933/1966) *New Introductory Lectures on Psycho-Analysis*. London: Hogarth Press and Institute of Psychoanalysis. (Standard Edition, vol. 22).

Freud, S. (1939/1966) *Moses and Monotheism*. London: Hogarth Press and Institute of Psychoanalysis. (Standard Edition, vol. 23).

Freud, S. (1940/1966) *An Outline of Psycho-analysis*. London: Hogarth Press and Institute of Psychoanalysis. (Standard Edition, vol. 23).

Freund, K. (1981) Assessment of pedophilia. In Cook, M. and Howells, K. (eds), *Adult Sexual Interest in Children*. London: Academic Press.

Freund, K., McKnight, L.K., Langevin, R. and Cibiri, S. (1972) The female child as surrogate object. *Archives of Sexual Behavior*, 2, 119–33.

Friedman, S.M. (1952) An empirical study of the castration and Oedipus complexes. *Genetic Psychology Monographs*, 46, 61–130.

Funk, S.C. and Huston, B.K. (1987) A critical analysis of the Hardiness scale's validity and utility. *Journal of Personality and Social Psychology*, 53, 572–8.

Furnham, A. (1989) Personality correlates of self-monitoring: the relationship between extraversion, neuroticism, Type A and Synder's self-monitoring concept. *Personality and Individual Differences*, 10, 35–42.

Gadpaille, W. (1980) Cross-species and cross-cultural contributions to understanding homosexuality. *Archives of General Psychiatry*, 37, 349–56.

Gagnon, J.H. and Simon, W. (1973) *Sexual Conduct: the social sources of sexual conduct*. Chicago: Aldine.

Gale, A. (1969) Stimulus hunger: individual differences in operant strategy in a button pressing task. *Behaviour Research and Therapy*, 7, 265–74.

Gale, A. (1973) The psychophysiology of individual differences: studies of extraversion introversion and EEG. In Kline, P. (ed.), *New Approaches in Psychological Measurement*. London: Wiley.

Gazaway, R. (1969) *The Longest Mile*. New York: Doubleday.

Gebhard, P.H., Gagnon, J.H., Pomeroy, W.B. and Christensen, C.V. (1967) *Sex Offenders: An analysis of types*. New York: Harper & Row.

Genero, N. and Cantor, N. (1987) Exemplar prototypes and clinical diagnosis: toward a cognitive economy. *Journal of Social Clinical Psychology*, 5, 59–78.

Gerbner, G., Gross, L., Eleey, M.F., Jackson-Beeck, M., Jeffries-Fox, S. and Signorielli, N. (1976) TV violence profile No. 8: the highlights. *Journal of Communication*, 27, 173–99.

Ghiselli, E.E. (1966) *The Validity of Occupational Aptitude Tests*. New York: Wiley.

Giese, H. and Schmidt, G. (1968) *Studenten-Sexualitat: Verhalten und Einstellung*. Reinbek: Rowohlt.

Gjerde, P.F., Block, J. and Block, J.H. (1986) Egocentrism and ego resiliency: personality characteristics associated with perspective taking from early childhood to adolescence. *Journal of Personality and Social Psychology*, 51, 423–34.

Gladue, B.A., Green, R. and Hellman, R.E. (1984) Neuroendocrine response to estrogen and sexual orientation. *Science*, 225, 1496–9.

Glueck, S. (1950) *Unraveling Juvenile Delinquency*. Cambridge, MA: Harvard University Press.

Goffman, E. (1959) *The Presentation of Self in Everyday Life*. New York: Doubleday.

Goldman-Eisler, F. (1950) Breast-feeding and character formation. II: The etiology of the oral character in psychoanalytic theory. *Journal of Personality*, 19, 189–96.

Goldsmith, H.H. (1983) Genetic influences on personality from infancy to adulthood. *Child Development*, 54, 331–55.

Goldstein, M.J. (1973) Exposure to erotic stimuli and sexual deviance. *Journal of Social Issues*, 29, 197–220.

Goodwin, D.W., Schulsinger, F., Moller, N., Mednick, S. and Guze, S. (1977) Psychopathology in adopted and nonadopted daughters of alcoholics. *Archives of General Psychiatry*, 34, 1005–9.

Goodwin, D.W., Schulsinger, F., Moller, N., Hermansen, L., Winokur, G. and Guze, S.B. (1974) Drinking problems in adopted and non-adopted sons of alcoholics. *Archives of General Psychiatry*, 31, 164–9.

Goodwin, J., McCarthy, T. and DiVasto, P. (1981) Prior incest in mothers of abused children. *Child Abuse and Neglect*, 5, 87–95.

Gooren, L. (1986) The neuroendocrine response of luteinizing hormone to estrogen administration in heterosexual, homosexual, and transsexual subjects. *Journal of Clinical Endocrinology and Metabolism*, 63, 583–8.

Gosselin, C. and Wilson, G.D. (1984) Fetishism, sadomasochism, and related behaviours. In Howells, K. (ed.), *Sexual Diversity in Man and Animals*. London: Van Nostrand Reinhold.

Gotz, K.O. and Gotz, K. (1979) Personality characteristics of successful artists. *Perceptual and Motor Skills*, 49, 919–24.

Gough, H.G. (1987) *California Psychological Inventory Administrator's Guide*. Palo Alto, CA: Consulting Psychologists Press.

Grant, I. (1987) Alcohol and the brain: neuropsychological correlates. *Journal of Consulting and Clinical Psychology*, 55, 310–24.

Gray, J.A. (1973) Causal theories of personality and how to test them. In Royce, F.R. (ed.), *Multivariate Analysis and Psychological Theory*. London: Academic Press.

Grinker, R.R. and Spiegel, J.P. (1945) *Men under Stress*. Philadelphia: Blakiston.

Groth, A.N. (1979) Sexual trauma in the lives of rapists and child molestors. *Victimology: an international journal*, 4, 10–16.

Groth, A.N. and Birnbaum, H.J. (1978) Adult sexual orientation and attraction to underage persons. *Archives of Sexual Behavior*, 7, 175–81.

Gundlach, R.W. and Riess, B.F. (1968) Self and sexual identity in the female: a study of female homosexuality. In Riess, A.J. (ed.), *New Directions in Mental Health*. New York: Grune and Stratton.

Guthrie, E.R. (1938) *The Psychology of Human Conflict*. New York: Harper.

Guthrie, E.R. (1944) Personality in terms of associative learning. In Hunt, J. McV. (ed.), *Personality and the Behaviour Disorders*. New York: Ronald Press.

Haberman, M.C., Chapman, L.J., Numbers, J.S. and McFall, R.S. (1979) Relations of social competence to scores on two scales of psychosis proneness. *Journal of Abnormal Psychology*, 88, 675–7.

Hall, C.S. and Lindzey, G. (1957) *Theories of Personality*. New York: Wiley.

Hall, W.B. and MacKinnon, B.W. (1969) Personality inventory correlates of creativity among architects. *Journal of Applied Psychology*, 53, 322–6.

Hammer, R.F. and Glueck, B.C. (1957) Psychodynamic patterns in sex offenders. *Psychiatric Quarterly*, 31, 325–45.

Hampson, S.E., John, O.P. and Goldberg, L.R. (1986) Category breadth and hierarchical structure in personality: studies of asymmetries in judgements of trait implications. *Journal of Personality and Social Psychology*, 53, 235–46.

Harburg, E., Blakelock, E.H. and Roeper, P.J. (1979) Resentful and reflective coping with arbitrary authority and blood pressure. *Psychosomatic Medicine*, 41, 189–202.

Hartshorne, H. and May, M.A. (1928) *Studies in the Nature of Character*. *Vol 1. Studies in deceit*. New York: Macmillan.

Havighurst, R.J., Robinson, M.Z. and Dorr, M. (1946) The development of the ideal self in childhood and adolescence. *Journal of Educational Research*, **40**, 241–57.

Heath, A.C., Jardine, R., Eaves, L.J. and Martin, N.G. (1988) The genetic structure of personality I. Phenotypic factor structure of the EPQ in an Australian sample. *Personality and Individual Differences*, 9, 59–67.

Hegedus, A.M., Tarter, R.E., Hill, S.Y., Jacob, T. and Winsten, N.E. (1984) Static ataxia: a possible marker for alcoholism. *Alcoholism: clinical and experimental research*, 8, 580–2.

Helson, R. and Moane, G. (1987) Personality change in women from college to midlife. *Journal of Personality and Social Psychology*, 53, 176–86.

Helzer, J.E. (1987) Epidemiology of alcoholism. *Journal of Consulting and Clinical Psychology*, 55, 284–92.

Hennigan, K.M., Del Rosario, M.L., Heath, L., Cook, T.D., Wharton, J.D. and Calder, B.J. (1982) Impact of the introduction of television on crime in the United States; emprical findings and theoretical implications. *Journal of Personality and Social Psychology*, 42, 461–77.

Hepworth, J.T. and West, S.G. (1988) Lynchings and the economy; a time series reanalysis of Hovland and Sears (1940). *Journal of Personality and Social Psychology*, 55, 239–47.

Hernstein, H.I. (1963) Behavioural correlates of breast–bottle regimes under varying parent–infant relationships. *Monographs of the Society for Research on Child Development*, 34, no. 4.

Herrnstein, R.J. (1966) Superstition: a corollary of the principles of operant conditioning. In Honig, W.K. (ed.), *Operant Behavior: areas of research and application*. New York: Appleton-Century-Crofts.

Heston, L.L. and Denney, D. (1968) Interactions between early life experience and biological factors in schizophrenia. In Rosenthal, D. and Kety, S.S. (eds), *The Transmission of Schizophrenia*. Oxford: Pergamon.

Heston, L.L. and Shields, J. (1968) Homosexuality in twins; a family study and a registry study. *Archives of General Psychiatry*, 18, 149–60.

Hetherington, E.M. and Brackbill, Y. (1963) Etiology and covariation of obstinacy, orderliness and parsimony in young children. *Child Development*, 34, 919–43.

Hill, S.Y. (1980) Introduction: the biological consequences. In *Alcoholism and Alcohol Abuse among Women: research issues*. Rockville, MD: National Institute on Alcohol Abuse and Alcoholism.

Hinde, R. A. (1966) *Animal Behaviour*. London: McGraw-Hill.

Hollender, M. H. (1956) Observations on nasal symptoms: relationship of anatomical structure of the nose to psychological symptoms. *Psychiatric Quarterly*, 30, 1–12.

Holmes, T. and Rahe, R. H. (1967) The social readjustment rating scale. *Journal of Psychosomatic Research*, 11, 213–18.

Hough, L. (1988) Personality assessment for selection and placement decisions. Paper presented at third annual conference of the Society for Industrial and Organisational Psychology, Dallas, TX, 21 April.

Hough, L. M., Eaton, N. K., Dunnette, M. D. and Kamp, J. D. (1990) Criterion-related validities of personal constructs and the effect of response distortion on those validities. *Journal of Applied Psychology*, 75, 581–95.

Howells, K. (1979) Some meanings of children for pedophiles. In Cook, M. and Wilson, G. (eds), *Love and Attraction: proceedings of an international conference*. Oxford: Pergamon.

Howells, K. (1981) Adult sexual interest in children: considerations relevant to theories of aetiology. In Cook, M. and Howells, K. (eds), *Adult Sexual Interest in Children*. London: Academic Press.

Hrubec, Z. and Omenn, G. S. (1981) Evidence of genetic predisposition to alcoholic cirrhosis and psychosis: twin concordances for alcoholism and its biological end points by zygosity among male veterans. *Alcoholism: clinical and experimenal research*, 5, 207–15.

Huesmann, I. R. (1982) Television violence and aggressive behavior. In Pearl, D., Bouthilet, L. and Lazar, J. (eds), *Television and Behaviour: ten years of scientific progress and implications for the eighties, Vol. 2. Technical reviews*. Washington, DC: National Institute of Mental Health.

Huesmann, L. R., Eron, L. D. and Yarmel, P. W. (1987) Intellectual functioning and aggression. *Journal of Personality and Social Psychology*, 52, 232–40.

Huesmann, L. R., Eron, L. D., Lefkowitz, M. M. and Walder, L. O. (1984) Stability of aggression over time and generations. *Developmental Psychology*, 20, 1120–34.

Hull, C. L. (1951) *Essentials of Behavior*. New Haven: Yale University Press.

Hull, J. G., van Treuren R. R., and Virnelli, S. (1987) Hardiness and health: a critique and alternative approach. *Journal of Personality and Social Psychology*, 53, 518–30.

Hunt, J. McV. (1965) Traditional personality theory in the light of recent evidence. *American Scientist*, 53, 80–96.

Hutchings, B. (1974) Genetic factors in criminality. In De Wit, J. and Hartup, W.W. (eds), *Determinants and Origins of Aggressive Behavior*. The Hague: Mouton.

Isaacs, W., Thomas, J. and Goldiamond, I. (1960) Application of operant conditioning to reinstate verbal behaviour in psychotics. *Journal of Speech and Hearing Disorders*, 25, 8–12.

Janis, I.L. (1951) *Air War and Emotional Stress*. New York: McGraw-Hill.

Jellinek, E.M. (1952) Phases of alcohol addiction. *Quarterly Journal of Studies on Alcohol*, 13, 673–84.

Jenkins, S.R. (1987) Need for achievement and women's careers over 14 years; evidence for occupational structural effects. *Journal of Personality and Social Psychology*, 53, 922–32.

Jensen, A.R. (1962) Extraversion, neuroticism and serial learning. *Acta Psychologica*, 20, 69–77.

John, O.P., Angleitner, A. and Ostendorf, F. (1988) The lexical approach to personality; a historical review of trait taxonomic research. *European Journal of Social Psychology*, 2, 171–203.

Johnson, G.B. (1966) Penis envy or pencil needing? *Psychological Reports*, 19, 758.

Jones, E.E. (1923) Anal erotic character traits. In *Papers on Psychoanalysis*. London: Baillière, Tindall and Cox.

Jones, M.C. (1924) A laboratory study of fear: the case of Peter. *Pedegogical Seminary*, 31, 308–15.

Jones, M.C. (1968) Personality correlates and antecedents of drinking patterns in males. *Journal of Consulting and Clinical Psychology*, 32, 2–12.

Jourard, S.M. and Secord, P.F. (1955) Body cathexis and the ideal female figure. *Journal of Abnormal Social Psychology*, 50, 243–6.

Kagan, J. and Moss, H.A. (1962) *Birth to Maturity; a study on psychological development*. New York: Wiley.

Kallmann, F.J. (1952) Comparative twin study of the genetic aspects of male homosexuality. *Journal of Nervous and Mental Diseases*, 115, 283–98.

Kammeier, M.L., Hoffman, H. and Loper, R.G. (1973) Personality characteristics of alcoholics as college freshmen and at time of treatment. *Quarterly Journal of Studies on Alcohol*, 34, 390–9.

Keller, M. (1972) On the loss-of-control phenomenon in alcoholism. *British Journal of Addictions*, 63, 153–66.

Kelly, E.L. (1955) Consistency of adult personality. *American Psychologist*, **10**, 659–81.

Kelly, G.A. (1955) *The Psychology of Personal Constructs*, vols 1 and 2. New York: Norton.

Kenny, D.A. and Zaccaro, S.J. (1983) An estimate of variance due to traits in leadership. *Journal of Applied Psychology*, **68**, 678–85.

Kenyon, F.E. (1968) Studies in female homosexuality. IV. Social and psychiatric aspects. V. Sexual development, attitudes and experience. *British Journal of Psychiatry*, **114**, 1343–50.

Kierkegaard-Sorenson, L. and Mednick, S.A. (1975) Registered criminality in families with children at high risk for schizophrenia. *Journal of Abnormal Psychology*, **84**, 197–204.

Kinsey, A.C., Pomeroy, W.B. and Martin, C.E. (1948) *Sexual Behavior in the Human Male*. Philadelphia: Saunders.

Kinsey, A.C., Pomeroy, W.B., Martin, C.E. and Gebhard, P.H. (1953) *Sexual Behavior in the Human Female*. Philadelphia: Saunders.

Kirchner, P. and Vondraek, S. (1975) Perceived sources of esteem in early childhood. *Journal of Genetic Psychology*, **126**, 169–76.

Kline, P. (1969) The anal character; a cross cultural study in Ghana. *British Journal of Social and Clinical Psychology*, **8**, 201–10.

Kline, P. (1972) *Fact and Fantasy in Freudian Theory*. London: Methuen.

Kline, P. (1982) *Fact and Fantasy in Freudian Theory*. (2nd edn) London: Methuen.

Kline, P. (1983) *Personality; measurement and theory*. London: Batsford.

Kline, P. (1991) *Intelligence; the psychometric view*. London: Routledge.

Kline, P. and Cooper, C. (1977) A percept-genetic study of some defence mechanisms in the test PN. *Scandinavian Journal of Psychology*, **18**, 148–52.

Kline, P. and Grindley, J. (1974) A 28 day case-study with the MAT. *Journal of Multivariate Experimental Personality and Clinical Psychology*, **1**, 13–22.

Kline, P. and Storey, R. (1980) The aetiology of the oral character. *Journal of Genetic Psychology*, **136**, 85–94.

Klineberg, O. (1940) *Social Psychology*. New York: Holt.

Knapp, R.H. (1958) Achievement and aesthetic preference. In Atkinson, J.W. (ed.), *Motives in Fantasy, Action, and Society*. Princeton, NJ: Van Nostrand.

Knapp, R.R., Shostrom, E.L. and Knapp, L. (1978) Assessment of the actualising person. In McReynolds, P. (ed.), *Advances in Psychological Assessment*, vol. 4. San Francisco: Jossey Bass.

Kobasa, S.C. (1979) Stressful life events, personality and health: an inquiry into hardiness. *Journal of Personality and Social Psychology*, 37, 1–11.

Kobasa, S.C., Maddi, S.R. and Courington, S. (1981) Personality and constitution as mediators in the stress–illness relationship. *Journal of Health and Social Behavior*, 22, 3368–78.

Kobasa, S.C., Maddi, S.R. and Kahn, S. (1982) Hardiness and health: a prospective study. *Journal of Personality and Social Psychology*, 42, 168–77.

Kogan, N. and Wallach, M.A. (1964) *Risk Taking: a study in cognition and personality*. New York: Holt, Rinehart and Winston.

Kohler, W. (1925) *The Mentality of Apes*. London: Routledge and Kegan Paul.

Kragh, U. and Smith, G. (1970) *Percept-Genetic Analysis*. Lund: Gleerup.

Krafft-Ebing, R. von (1886/1965) *Psychopathia Sexualis*. New York; Stein and Day.

Krantz, D.S. and Hedges, S.M. (1987) Some cautions for research on personality and health. *Journal of Personality*, 55, 351–7.

Krug, R.S. (1989) Adult male report of childhood sexual abuse by mothers; case descriptions, motivations and long term consequences. *Child Abuse and Neglect*, 13, 111–19.

Krujit, J.P. (1964) Ontogeny of social behaviour in Burmese red jungle fowl (Gallus gallus spadecius) Bonaterre. *Behaviour Supplement*, 12, 2–201.

Lagerspetz, K.M.J., Bjorkquist, K., and Peltonen, T. (1988) Is indirect aggression typical of females? Gender differences in aggressiveness in 11–12 year old children. *Aggressive Behavior*, 14, 403–14.

Lang, A.R., Goeckner, D.J., Adesso, V.J. and Marlatt, G.A. (1975) Effects of alcohol on aggression in male social drinkers. *Journal of Abnormal Psychology*, 84, 508–18.

Lanning, K. (1988) Individual differences in scalability: an alternative conception of consistency for personality theory and measurement. *Journal of Personality and Social Psychology*, 55, 142–8.

LaPiere, R.T. (1934) Attitudes vs. actions. *Social Forces*, 13, 230–7.

LaTorre, R.A. (1980) Devaluation of the human love object: heterosexual rejection as a possible antecedant to fetishism. *Journal of Abnormal Psychology*, 89, 295–8.

Lay, C.H. and Jackson, D.N. (1969) Analysis of the generality of trait-inferential relationships. *Journal of Personality and Social Psychology*, 12, 12–21.

Leon, G.R., Butcher, J.N., Kleinman, M., Goldberg, A. and Almagor, M. (1981) Survivors of the Holocaust and their children: current status and adjustment. *Journal of Personality and Social Psychology*, 41, 503–16.

Lepley, W. (1947) *Psychological Research in the Theaters of War*. USAAF Aviation Research Report, No. 17. Washington, DC: Government Printing Office.

Lesser, G.S. (1957) The relationship between overt and fantasy aggression as a function of maternal response to aggression. *Journal of Abnormal and Social Psychology*, 55, 218–21.

Levenson, R.W., Sher, K.J., Grossman, L.M., Newman, J. and Newlin, D.B. (1980) Alcohol and stress response damping: pharmacological effects, expectancy and tension reduction. *Journal of Abnormal Psychology*, 89, 528–38.

Lewin, K. (1935) *A Dynamic Theory of Personality*. New York: McGraw-Hill.

Lewis, A. (1942) Incidence of neurosis in England under war conditions. *Lancet*, 2, 175–83.

Lindzey, G. and Tejessy, C. (1957) Thematic Apperception Test: indices of aggression in relation to measures of overt and covert behavior. *American Journal of Psychiatry*, 26, 567–76.

Linsky, A.S., Straus, M. and Colby, J.P. (1985) Stressful events, stressful conditions and alcohol problems in the United States: a partial test of Bales's theory. *Journal of Studies on Alcohol*, 46, 72–80.

Lord, R.G., De Vader, C.L. and Alliger, G.M. (1986) A meta-analysis of the relation between personality traits and leadership perceptions: an application of validity generalisation procedure. *Journal of Applied Psychology*, 71, 402–10.

Lorenz, K. (1966) *On Aggression*. London: Methuen.

Lovaas, O.I. and Simmons, J.Q. (1969) Manipulation of self-destruction in three retarded children. *Journal of Applied Behavior Analysis*, 2, 143–57.

Lovaas, O.I., Shaeffer, B. and Simmons, J.Q. (1965) Building social behaviour in autistic children by the use of electric shock. *Journal of Experimental Research in Personality*, 1, 99–109.

Loehlin, J.C. and Nichols, R.C. (1976) *Heredity, Environment and Personality*. Austin: University of Texas Press.

Lykken, D.T. (1971) Multiple factor analysis and personality research. *Journal of Experimental Research in Personality*, 5, 161–70.

McClelland, D.C. (1961) *The Achieving Society*. Princeton, NJ: Van Nostrand.

McClelland, D.C. (1965) Achievement and entrepreneurship: a longitudinal study. *Journal of Personality and Social Psychology*, 1, 389–92.

McClelland, D.C. (1979) Inhibited power motivation and high blood pressure in men. *Journal of Abnormal Psychology*, 88, 182–90.

McClelland, D.C. (1980) Inhibited power motivation and high blood pressure in men. *Journal of Abnormal Psychology*, 88, 182–90.

McClelland, D.C. (1987) *Human Motivation*. Cambridge: Cambridge University Press.

McClelland, D.C. and Boyatzis, R.E. (1982) The leadership motive pattern and long term success in management. *Journal of Applied Psychology*, 67, 737–43.

McClelland, D.C. and Pilon, D.A (1983) Sources of adult motives in patterns of parent behavior in early childhood. *Journal of Personality and Social Psychology*, 44, 564–74.

McClelland, D.C. and Winter, D.G. (1969) *Motivating Economic Achievement*. New York: Free Press.

McClelland, D.C., Atkinson, J.W., Clark, R.A. and Lowell, E.L. (1953) *The Achievement Motive*. New York: Appleton.

McClelland, D.C., Davis, W.N., Kalin, R. and Wanner, E. (1972) *The Drinking Man*. New York: Free Press.

McConaghy, N. (1987) Heterosexuality, homosexuality: dichotomy or continuum. *Archives of Sexual Behavior*, 16, 411–24.

McCord, J. (1979) Some child-rearing antecedents of criminal behavior in adult men. *Journal of Personality and Social Psychology*, 37, 1477–86.

McCord, W. and McCord, J. (1960) *Origins of Alcoholism*. Stanford: Stanford University Press.

McCord W., McCord, J. and Howard, A. (1961) Familial correlates of aggression in nondelinquent male children. *Journal of Abnormal and Social Psychology*, 62, 79–93.

McCord, W., McCord, J. and Verden, P. (1962) Family relationships and sexual deviance in lower class adolescents. *International Journal of Social Psychiatry*, 8, 165–79.

McDougall, W. (1908) *An Introduction to Social Psychology*. London: Methuen.

McGuire, R.J., Carlisle, J.M. and Young, B.G. (1965) Sexual deviations as conditioned behaviour: a hypothesis. *Behaviour Research and Therapy*, 3, 185–90.

McKennell, A.C. and Bynner, J.M. (1969) Self image and smoking behaviour among school boys. *British Journal of Educational Psychology*, 39, 27–39.

McPherson, F.M. (1965) Comment on Eysenck's account of some Aberdeen studies of introversion–extraversion and eyeblink conditioning. *British Journal of Psychology*, 56, 483–84.

Maccoby, E.E. and Feldman, S.S. (1972) Mother attachment and stranger reactions in the third year of life. *Monographs of the Society for Research in Child Development*, 37.

Maccoby, E.E. and Jacklin, C.N. (1980) Sex differences in aggression: a rejoinder and reprise. *Child Development*, 51, 964–80.

Mahklouf-Norris, F., Jones, H.G., and Norris, H. (1970) Articulation of the conceptual structure in obsessional neurosis. *British Journal of Social and Clinical Psychology*, 9, 264–74.

Manesovitz, M. (1970) Early sexual behaviour in adult homosexual and heterosexual males. *Journal of Abnormal Psychology*, 76, 396–402.

Mangan, G.L. (1982) *The Biology of Human Conduct*. Oxford: Pergamon.

Mann, R.D. (1959) A review of the relationships between personality and performance in small groups. *Psychological Bulletin*, 56, 241–70.

Mannello, T.O. and Seaman, F.J. (1979) *Prevalence, Costs and Handling of Drinking on Seven Railroads*. Washington, DC: University Research Corporation.

Marlatt, G.A. and Gordon, J.R. (1980) Determinants of relapse: implications for the maintenance of behavior change. In Davidson, P. and Davidson, S. (eds), *Behavioral Medicine: changing health lifestyles*. New York: Brunner Mazel.

Marlatt, G.A., Demmings, B. and Read, J.B. (1973) Loss of control drinking in alcoholics: an experimental analogue. *Journal of Abnormal Psychology*, 81, 233–41.

Markus, H. and Kunda, Z. (1986) Stability and malleability of the self-concept. *Journal of Personality and Social Psychology*, 51, 858–66.

Markus, H. and Nurius, P. (1986) Possible selves. *American Psychologist*, 41, 954–69.

Marsh, H.W. and Richards, G.E. (1988) Tennessee self-concept scale: reliability, internal structure, and construct validity. *Journal of Personality and Social Psychology*, 55, 612–24.

Martin, S. (1975) Parent–child relations. In Horowitz, F.D. (ed.), *Review of Child Development Research*, vol. 4. Chicago: University of Chicago Press.

Maslow, A.H. (1954) *Motivation and Personality*. New York: Harper and Row.

Matthews, G. (1989) The factor structure of the 16PF: twelve primary and three secondary factors. *Personality and Individual Differences*, 10, 931–40.

Matthews, K.A. (1982) Psychological perspectives on the Type A behavior pattern. *Psychological Bulletin*, 91, 293–323.

Mayo, C. and Crockett, W.H. (1964) Cognitive complexity and primacy–recency effects in impression formation. *Journal of Abnormal and Social Psychology*, 68, 335–8.

Mead, G.H. (1934) *Mind, Self, and Society*. Chicago: University of Chicago Press.

Mednick, S.A. (1958) A learning theory approach to research in schizophrenia. *Psychological Bulletin*, 55, 316–27.

Mednick, S.A., Gabrielli, W.F. and Hutchings, B. (1984) Genetic influences in criminal convictions: evidence from an adoption cohort. *Science*, 224, 891–4.

Meehl, P.E. (1954) *Clinical versus Statistical Prediction*. Minneapolis: University of Minnesota Press.

Meehl, P.E. (1975) Hedonic capacity: some conjectures. *Bulletin of the Menninger Clinic*, 39, 295–307.

Meehl, P.E. (1978) Theoretical risks and tabular asterisks: Sir Karl, Sir Ronald, and the slow progress of soft psychology. *Journal of Consulting and Clinical Psychology*, 46, 806–34.

Megargee, E.I. (1966) Undercontrolled and overcontrolled personality types in extreme antisocial aggression. *Psychological Monographs*, 80, no. 3 (whole no. 611).

Megargee, E.I. (1972) *The California Psychological Inventory Handbook*. San Francisco: Jossey Bass.

Mello, N.K. and Mendelson, J.H. (1978) Alcohol and human behavior. In Iverson, L.L., Iverson, S.D. and Snyder, S.H. (eds), *Handbook of Psychopharmacology*, vol. 12. New York: Plenum.

Mershon, B. and Gorsuch, R.L. (1988) Number of factors in the personality sphere: does increase in factors increase predictability of real-life criteria? *Journal of Personality and Social Psychology*, 55, 675–80.

Meyer-Bahlburg, H.F.L. (1977) Sex hormones and male homosexuality in comparative perspective. *Archives of Sexual Behavior*, 6, 297–325.

Meyer-Bahlburg, H.F.L. (1979) Sex hormones and female homosexuality: a critical examination. *Archives of Sexual Behavior*, 8, 101–19.

Milgram, S. (1965) Some conditions of obedience and disobedience to authority. *Human Relations*, 18, 57–76.

Miller, N.E. and Dollard, J. (1941) *Social Learning and Imitation*. New Haven: Yale University Press.

Mischel, W. (1968) *Personality and Assessment*. New York: Wiley.

Mischel, W. (1973) Toward a cognitive social learning reconceptualisation of personality. *Psychological Review*, 80, 252–83.

Mischel, W. (1981) *Introduction to Personality*. (3rd edn) New York: Holt, Rinehart and Winston.

Mohr, J.W., Turner, R.E. and Jerry, M.B. (1964) *Pedophilia and Exhibitionism*. Toronto: University of Toronto Press.

Money, J. (1987) Sin, sickness, or status? Homosexual gender identity and psychoneuroendocrinology. *American Psychologist*, 42, 385–99.

Moos, R.H. (1969) Sources of variance in responses to questionnaires and in behavior. *Journal of Abnormal Psychology*, 74, 405–12.

Mowrer, O.H. (1950) *Learning Theory and Personality Dynamics*. New York: Arnold Press.

Mulaik, S.A. (1964) Are personality factors raters' conceptual factors? *Journal of Consulting Psychology*, 28, 506–11.

Mullaney, J.A. and Trippet, C.J. (1987) Alcohol dependence and phobias: clinical description and relevance. *British Journal of Psychiatry*, 135, 565–73.

Murray, H.A. (1938) *Explorations in Personality*. New York: Oxford University Press.

Napalkov, A.V. (1963) Information process of the Brain. In Wiener, N. and Sefade, J. (eds), *Progress in Experimental Brain Reseach. Vol. 1: Nerve, Brain, and Memory Models*. Amsterdam: Elsevier.

Nebylitsyn, V.D. (1972) The problem of general and partial properties of the nervous system. In Nebylitsyn, V.D. and Gray, J.A. (eds), *Biological Bases of Individual Behaviour*. London: Academic Press.

Newcomb, T.M. (1929) *The Consistency of Certain Extrovert–Introvert Behavior Patterns in 51 Problem Boys*. New York: Columbia University Teachers College. Contribution to Education No. 382.

Nidorf, L.J. and Crockett, W.H. (1965) Cognitive complexity and the integration of conflicting impressions. *Journal of Social Psychology*, 66, 165–9.

Norman, W.T. and Goldberg, L.R. (1966) Raters, rates and randomness in personality structure. *Journal of Personality and Social Psychology*, 4, 681–91.

Notcutt, B. (1953) *The Psychology of Personality*. London: Methuen.

Ogilvie, D.M. (1987) The undesired self: a neglected variable in personality research. *Journal of Personality and Social Psychology*, 52, 379–85.

Olds, J. (1958) Self-stimulation of the brain. *Science*, 127, 315–27.

Olweus, D. (1974) Personality factors and aggression: with special reference to violence within the peer group. In De Wit, J. and Hartup, W.W. (eds), *Determinants and Origins of Aggressive Behavior*. The Hague: Mouton.

Olweus, D. (1979) Stability of aggressive reaction patterns in males: a review. *Psychological Bulletin*, 86, 852–75.

Olweus, D. (1980) Familial and temperamental determinants of aggressive behavior in adolescent boys: a causal analysis. *Developmental Psychology*, 16, 644–60.

Orlansky, H. (1949) Infant care and personality. *Psychological Bulletin*, 46, 1–48.

Orwell, G. (1949) *Nineteen Eighty-Four*. London: Secker and Warburg.

Ozer, D.J. and Gjerde, P.F. (1989) Patterns of personality consistency and change from childhood through adolescence. *Journal of Personality*, 57, 484–507.

Parke, R.D., Berkowitz, L., Leyens, J.P., West, S.G. and Sebastian, R.J. (1977) Some effects of violent and nonviolent movies on the behaviour of juvenile delinquents. *Advances in Experimental Social Psychology*, 10, 135–72.

Parker, P.Y. and Cook, M. (1991) Influence of sex and physical attractiveness on self-esteem and body image across the life span. British Psychological Society Annual Conference, Bournemouth.

Parry, M.H. (1968) *Aggression on the Road*. London: Tavistock.

Passingham, R.E. (1972) Crime and personality: a review of Eysenck's theory. In Nebylitsyn, V.D. and Gray, J.A. (eds), *Biological Bases of Individual Behaviour*. London: Academic Press.

Pastore, N. (1952) The role of arbitrariness in the frustration–aggression hypothesis. *Journal of Abnormal and Social Psychology*, 47, 728–31.

Paulhus, D.L. and Martin, C.L. (1988) Functional flexibility: a new conception of interpersonal flexibility. *Journal of Personality and Social Psychology*, 55, 88–101.

Pavlov, I.P. (1927) *Conditioned Reflexes: an investigation of the physiological activity of the cerebral cortex*. London: Oxford University Press.

Pedersen, N.L., Plomin, R., McClearn, GE. and Friberg, L. (1988) Neuroticism, extraversion, and related traits in adults twins reared apart and reared together. *Journal of Personality and Social Psychology*, 55, 950–7.

Peterson, C. and Seligman, M.E.P. (1987) Explanatory style and illness. *Journal of Personality*, 55, 237–65.

Peterson, C., Seligman, M.E.P. and Vaillant, G.E. (1988) Pessimistic explanatory style is a risk factor for physical illness: a thirty-five-year longitudinal study. *Journal of Personality and Social Psychology*, 55, 23–7.

Phillips, D.P. (1983) The impact of mass media violence on U.S. homicides. *American Sociological Review*, 48, 560–8.

Pillard, R.C. and Weinreich, J.D. (1986) Evidence of familial nature of male homosexuality. *Archives of General Psychiatry*, 43, 808–12.

Plomin, R. and Daniels, D. (1987) Why are children in the same family so different from one another? *Behavioral and Brain Sciences*, 10, 1–60.

Plummer, K. (1981) Pedophilia: constructing a sociological baseline. In Cook, M. and Howells, K. (eds), *Adult Sexual Interest in Children*. London: Academic Press.

Pollock, V.E., Volavka, J. and Goodwin, D.W. (1983) The EEG after alcohol administration in men at risk for alcoholism. *Archives of General Psychiatry*, 40, 857–61.

Popper, K. (1963) *The Logic of Scientific Discovery*. New York: Basic Books.

Propping, P., Kruger, J. and Mark, N. (1981) Genetic disposition to alcoholism: an EEG study in alcoholics and their relatives. *Human Genetics*, 59, 51–9.

Quinsey, V.L. (1986) Men who have sex with children. In Weisstuub, D.L. (ed.), *Law and Mental Health: international perspectives*, vol. 2. New York: Pergamon.

Rabin, A.I. (1958) The Israeli kibbutz (collective settlement) as a 'laboratory' for testing psychodynamic hypotheses. *Psychological Record*, 7, 111–15.

Rachman, S. (1978) *Fear and Courage*. San Francisco: Freeman.

Rachman, S. and Hodgson, R.J. (1968) Experimentally induced sexual fetishism: replication and development. *Psychological Record*, 18, 25–7.

Rapaport, D. and Gill, M.M. (1959) The points of view and assumptions of metapsychology. *International Journal of Psychoanalysis*, 40, 153–62.

Read, S.J. (1984) Analogical reasoning in social judgement: the importance of causal theories. *Journal of Personality and Social Psychology*, 46, 14–25.

Reid, R.L. (1960) Inhibition – Pavlov, Hull, Eysenck. *British Journal of Psychology*, 51, 226–36.

Revelle, W., Amaral, P. and Turriff, S. (1976) Introversion/extraversion, time stress, and caffeine: the effect on verbal performance. *Science*, 192, 149–50.

Richardson, S.A., Hastorf, A.H. and Dornbusch, S.M. (1964) The effect of physical disability on a child's description of himself. *Child Development*, 35, 893–907.

Robbins, L.C. (1963) The accuracy of parental recall of aspects of child development and of child-rearing practices. *Journal of Abnormal and Social Psychology*, 66, 261–70.

Robins, L.N. (1966) *Deviant Children Growing Up*. Baltimore: Williams & Wilkins.

Robins, L.N., Helzer, J.E., Weissman, M., Orvschel, H., Gruenberg, E., Burke, J.D. and Regier, D. (1984) Lifetime prevalence of specific psychiatric disorders at three sites. *Archives of General Psychiatry*, 41, 949–58.

Roe, A. (1944) The adult adjustment of children of alcoholic parents raised in foster homes. *Quarterly Journal of Studies on Alcohol*, 5, 378–93.

Roff, M. (1963) Childhood social interactions and young adult psychosis. *Journal of Clinical Psychology*, 19, 152–7.

Roger, D. and Najarian, B. (1989) The construction and validation of a new scale for measuring emotion control. *Personality and Individual Differences*, 10, 845–53.

Rogers, C.R. (1951) *Client Centred Therapy: its current practice, implications, and theory*. Boston: Houghton Mifflin.

Rogers, C.R. (1959) A theory of therapy, personality, and interpersonal relationships, as developed in the client centred framework. In Koch, S. (ed.), *Psychology: a study of a science*, vol. 3. New York: McGraw-Hill.

Rogers, C.R. and Dymond, R.F. (1954) *Psychotherapy and Personality Change: co-ordinated studies in the client-centred approach*. Chicago: University of Chicago Press.

Rose, R.J., Koskenvuo M., Kaprio J., Sarna S. and Langinvainio, H. (1988) Shared genes, shared experiences, and similarity of personality: data from 14,288 adult Finnish co-twins. *Journal of Personality and Social Psychology*, 54, 161–71.

Rosen, B.C. and D'Andrade, R.G. (1959) The psychosocial origin of achievement motivation. *Sociometry*, 22, 185–218.

Rosenberg, M. (1965) *Society and the Adolescent Self-Image*. Princeton, NJ: Princeton University Press.

Rosenman, R.H., Brand, R.J., Jenkins, C.D., Friedman, M., Strauss, R. and Warm, M. (1975) Coronary heart disease in the Western Collaborative Group Study: final follow up experience of 8.5 years. *Journal of the American Medical Association*, 233, 872-7.

Rosenzweig, S. (1945) The picture-association method and its application in a study of reactions to frustration. *Journal of Personality*, 14, 3-23.

Rotter, J.B., Chance, J.E. and Phares, E.J. (1972) *Applications of a Social Learning Theory of Personality*. New York: Holt, Rinehart and Winston.

Rozin, P. and Kalat, J.W. (1971) Specific hungers and poison avoidance as adaptive specialisations of learning. *Psychological Review*, 78, 459-86.

Rusalov, V.M. (1989) Object-related and communicative aspects of human temperament: a new questionnaire of the structure of temperament. *Personality and Individual Differences*, 10, 817-27.

Rushton, J.P., Fulker, D.W., Neale, M.C., Nias, D.K.B. and Eysenck, H.J. (1986) Altruism and aggression: the heritability of individual differences. *Journal of Personality and Social Psychology*, 50, 1192-8.

Russell, D. (1986) *The Secret Trauma: incest in the lives of girls and women*. New York: Basic Books.

Ryle, A. and Breen, D. (1972) Some differences in the personal constructs of neurotic and normal subjects. *British Journal of Psychiatry*, 120, 483-9.

Saghir, M.T. and Robins, E. (1973) *Male and Female Homosexuality*. Baltimore: Williams & Wilkins.

Sales, S.M., Guydosh, R.M. and Iacono, W. (1974) Relationship between strength of the nervous system and the need for stimulation. *Journal of Personality and Social Psychology*, 29, 16-22.

Sandfort, T.G.M. (1984) Sex in paedophiliac relationships: an empirical investigation among a non-representative group of boys. *Journal of Sex Research*, 20, 123-42.

Sanford, R.N. (1937) The effects of abstinence from food upon imaginal processes. *Journal of Psychology*, 3, 145-59.

Sarason, I.G., Smith, R.E. and Diener, E. (1975) Personality research: components of variance attributable to the person and the situation. *Journal of Personality and Social Psychology*, 32, 199-204.

Schein, E.H. (1956) The Chinese indoctrination program for prisoners of war. *Psychiatry*, 19, 149-72.

Schein, E.H., Hill, W.F., Williams, H.L. and Lubin, A. (1957) Distinguishing characteristics of collaborators and resisters among American prisoners of war. *Journal of Abnormal and Social Psychology*, 55, 197–201.

Schmidt, F.L. and Hunter, J.E. (1977) Development of a general solution to the problem of validity generalisation. *Journal of Applied Psychology*, 62, 529–40.

Schmidt, F.L., Hunter, J.E., Pearlman, K. and Hirsh, H.R. (1985) Forty questions about validity generalization and meta-analysis. *Personnel Psychology*, 38, 697–798.

Schmidt, F.L., Ocasio, B.P., Hillery, J.M. and Hunter, J.E. (1988) Further within-setting empirical tests of the situational specificity hypothesis in personnel selection. *Personnel Psychology*, 38, 509–24.

Schofield, M. (1965) *The Sexual Behaviour of Young People*. London: Longman.

Schooler, C. (1972) Birth order effects: not here, not now! *Psychological Bulletin*, 78, 161–75.

Schuerger, J.M., Zarrella, K.L. and Hotz, A.S. (1989) Factors that influence the temporal stability of personality by questionnaire. *Journal of Personality and Social Psychology*, 56, 777–83.

Schuckit, M.A. (1987) Biological vulnerability to alcoholism. *Journal of Consulting and Clinical Psychology*, 55, 301–9.

Schuckit, M.A. and Rayses, V. (1979) Ethanol ingestion: differences in blood acetaldehyde concentration in relatives of alcoholics and controls. *Science*, 203, 54–5.

Schuckit, M.A., Goodwin, D.A. and Winokur, G. (1972) A study of alcoholism in half siblings. *American Journal of Psychiatry*, 128, 122–6.

Schulsinger, F. (1972) Psychopathy: heredity and environment. *International Journal of Mental Health*, 1, 190–206.

Schulsinger, F., Knop, J., Goodwin, D.W., Teasdale, T.W. and Mikkelsen, U. (1986) A prospective study of young men at high risk for alcoholism. *Archives of General Psychiatry*, 43, 755–60.

Searles, J.S. (1988) The role of genetics in the pathogenesis of alcoholism. *Journal of Consulting and Clinical Psychology*, 97, 153–67.

Sears, R.R. (1936) Experimental studies of projection: I. Attribution of traits. *Journal of Social Psychology*, 7, 151–63.

Sears, R.R. (1940) *Survey of Objective Studies of Psychoanalytic Concepts*. New York: Social Science Research Council.

Sears, R. R. (1961) Relation of early socialisation experiences to aggression in middle childhood. *Journal of Abnormal and Social Psychology*, 63, 466–92.

Sears, R. R., Maccoby, E. E. and Levin, H. (1957) *Patterns of Child Rearing.* New York: Harper and Row.

Segal, J. (1956) Factors related to the collaboration and resistance behavior among US Army POWs in Korea. HumRRO Technical Report No. 33.

Seligman, M. E. P. (1971) Phobias and preparedness. *Behavior Therapy*, 2, 307–20.

Seligman, M. E. P. (1975) *Helplessness.* San Francisco: Freeman.

Sells, S. B. (1959) Structured measurement of personality and motivation: a review of contributions of Raymond B. Cattell. *Journal of Clinical Psychology*, 15, 3–21.

Sewell, W. H. (1952) Infant training and the personality of the child. *American Journal of Sociology*, 58, 150–9.

Shaw, M. L. (1980) *On Becoming a Personal Scientist: interactive computer elicitation of personal models of the world.* London: Academic Press.

Sheerer, E. T. (1949) An analysis of the relationship between acceptance of the respect for self and acceptance of and respect for others. *Journal of Consulting Psychology*, 13, 176–80.

Sheldon, W. H. (1942) *The Varieties of Temperament.* New York: Harper.

Shields, J. (1962) *Monozygotic Twins Brought up Apart and Brought up Together.* London: Oxford University Press.

Shostrom, E. (1965) An inventory for the measurement of self-actualisation. *Educational and Psychological Measurement*, 24, 207–18.

Shweder, R. A. and D'Andrade, R. G. (1979) Accurate reflection or systematic distortion? A reply to Block, Weiss, and Thorne. *Journal of Personality and Social Psychology*, 37, 1075–84.

Siddle, D. A. T., Morrish, R. B., White, K. D. and Mangan, G. L. (1969) A further study of the relation of strength-sensitivity of the nervous system to extraversion. *Journal of Experimental Research in Personality*, 3, 264–7.

Siegel, J. (1986) The Multidimensional Anger Inventory. *Journal of Personality and Social Psychology*, 51, 191–200.

Siegelman, E., Block, J., Block, J. H. and von der Lippe, A. (1970) Antecedents of optimal psychological adjustment. *Journal of Consulting and Clinical Psychology*, 35, 283–9.

Skinner, B. F. (1951) How to teach animals. *Scientific American*, 185, 26–9.

Skinner, B.F. (1953) *Science and Human Behaviour*. New York: Macmillan.

Skinner, B.F. and Ferster, C. (1953) *Schedules of Reinforcement*. New York: Appleton-Century-Crofts.

Skinner, H.A. (1981) Primary syndromes of alcohol abuse: their measurement and correlates. *British Journal of Addiction*, 76, 63–76.

Smith, S.L. (1968) Extraversion and sensory threshhold. *Psychophysiology*, 5, 293–9.

Snyder, M. (1987) *Public Appearances, Private Realities: the psychology of self-monitoring*. New York: Freeman.

Snyder, M. and Simpson, J.A. (1984) Self-monitoring and dating relationships. *Journal of Personality and Social Psychology*, 47, 1281–91.

Snyder, M., Simpson, J.A. and Gangestad, S. (1986) Personality and sexual relations. *Journal of Personality and Social Psychology*, 51, 181–90.

Snyder, M. and Gangestad, S. (1986) On the nature of self-monitoring: matters of assessment, matters of validity. *Journal of Personality and Social Psychology*, 51, 125–9.

Snygg, D. and Combs, C.W. (1949) *Individual Behavior*. New York: Harper and Row.

Solomon, R.L. (1964) Punishment. *American Psychologist*, 19, 239–53.

Sommer, R. (1988) The personality of vegetables: botanical metaphors for human characteristics. *Journal of Personality*, 56, 667–83.

Stafford-Clarke, D. (1965) *What Freud Really Said*. Harmondsworth: Penguin.

Stagner, R. (1961) *Psychology of Personality*. (3rd edn) New York: McGraw-Hill.

Starrett, R.H. (1982) Absolute auditory threshold related to trait vs state emotionality. *Personality and Individual Differences*, 3, 17–25.

Stelmack, R.M. and Campbell, K.B. (1974) Extraversion and auditory sensitivity to high and low frequency. *Perceptual and Motor Skills*, 38, 875–9.

Stelmack, R.M. and Wilson, R.G. (1982) Extraversion and the effect of frequency and intensity on the auditory brainstem evoked response. *Personality and Individual Differences*, 3, 272–380.

Stephenson, W. (1953) *The Study of Behavior: Q-technique and its methodology*. Chicago: University of Chicago Press.

Stewart, A.J. and Chester, N.L. (1982) Sex differences in human social motives: achievement, affiliation and power. In Stewart, A.J. (ed.) *Motivation and Society*. San Francisco: Jossey Bass.

Storms, M.D. (1980) Theories of sexual orientation. *Journal of Personality and Social Psychology*, 38, 783–92.

Storms, M.D. (1981) A theory of erotic orientation development. *Psychological Review*, 88, 340–53.

Strang, R. (1957) *The Adolescent Views Himself*. New York: McGraw-Hill.

Suwaki, J. and Ohara, H. (1985) Alcohol-induced facial blushing and drinking behavior in Japanese men. *Journal of Studies on Alcohol*, 46, 196–8.

Swann, W.B. and Hill, C.A. (1982) When our identities are mistaken: reaffirming self-conceptions through social interaction. *Journal of Personality and Social Psychology*, 43, 59–66.

Tartar, R.E., Hegedus, A.M., Goldstein, G., Shelly, C. and Alterman, A.I. (1984) Adolescent sons of alcoholics: neuropsychological and personality characteristics. *Alcoholism: clinical and experimental research*, 8, 216–22.

Tedeschi, J.T., Smith, R.B. and Brown, R.C. (1974) A reinterpretation of research on aggression. *Psychological Bulletin*, 81, 540–62.

Tellegen, A., Lykken, D.T., Bouchard, T.J., Wilcox, K.J., Segal, N.L. and Rich, S. (1988) Personality similarity in twins reared apart and together. *Journal of Personality and Social Psychology*, 54, 1031–9.

Terman, L.M. (1962) *Genetic Studies of Genius. Vol. 1: Mental and Physical Traits of a Thousand Gifted Children*. Stanford: Stanford University Press.

Terman, L.M. and Oden, M.H. (1947) *Genetic Studies of Genius. Vol. 4: The Gifted Child Grows Up*. Stanford: Stanford University Press.

Terman, L.M. and Oden, M.H. (1959) *Genetic Studies of Genius. Vol. 5: The Gifted Group at Mid-life*. Stanford: Stanford University Press.

Thigpen, C.H. and Cleckley, H. (1954) *The Three Faces of Eve*. Kingsport: Kingsport Press.

Thorndike, E.L. (1898) Animal intelligence: an experimental study of the associative processes in animals. *Psychological Review Monograph Supplement*, 2, no. 8.

Towbes, L.C., Cohen, L.H., and Glyshaw, K. (1989) Instrumentality as a life-stress moderator for early versus middle adolescents. *Journal of Personality and Social Psychology*, 57, 109–19.

Trouton, D.S. and Maxwell, A.E. (1956) The relation between neurosis and psychosis. *Journal of Mental Science*, 102, 1–21

Vaillant, G.E. (1977) *Adaptation to Life*. Boston: Little, Brown.

Vaillant, G.E. (1983) *The Natural History of Alcoholism*. Cambridge, MA: Harvard University Press.

Velicer, W.F., Govia, J.M., Cherico, N.P. and Corriveau, D.P. (1985) Item format and structure of the Buss-Durkee Hostility Inventory. *Aggressive Behavior*, 11, 65–82.

Vernon, P.E. (1941) Psychological effects of air raids. *Journal of Abnormal and Social Psychology*, 35, 457–76.

Vernon, P.E. (1964) *Personality Assessment*. London: Methuen.

Veroff, J. (1982) Assertive motivations: achievement versus power. In Winter, D.G. and Stewart, A.J. (eds), *Motivation and Society*. San Francisco: Jossey Bass.

Virkkunen, M. (1976) The pedophilic offender with antisocial character. *Acta Psychiatrica Scandanavica*, 53, 401–5.

Volpicelli, J.R., Tiven, J. and Kimmel, S.C. (1982) The relationship between tension reduction and ethanol consumption. *Physiological Psychology*, 10, 114–16.

Walters, R.H. and Thomas, E.L. (1963) Enhancement of punitiveness by visual and audiovisual displays. *Canadian Journal of Psychology*, 17, 244–55.

Wanberg, K.W. and Horn, J.L. (1983) Assessment of alcohol use with multidimensional concepts and measures. *American Psychologist*, 38, 1055–69.

Warheit, G.J. and Auth, J.B. (1985) Epidemiology of alcohol abuse in adulthood. In Cavenar, J.O. (ed.), *Psychiatry*, vol. 3. Philadelphia: Lippincott.

Watson, J.B. (1925) *Behaviorism*. New York: Norton.

Watson, J.B. and Rayner, R. (1921) Conditioned emotional reactions. *Journal of Experimental Psychology*, 3, 1–14.

Watson, P. (1978) *War on the Mind*. London: Hutchinson.

West, D.J. (1969) *Present Conduct and Future Delinquency*. London: Heinemann.

Whitam, F.L. (1980) The prehomosexual male child in three societies: the United States, Guatemala, Brazil. *Archives of Sexual Behavior*, 9, 87–99.

Whitam, F.L. and Zent, M. (1984) A cross-cultural assessment of early cross-gender behavior and familial factors in male homosexuality. *Archives of Sexual Behavior*, 13, 427–39.

Whiting, J.W.M. and Child, I.L. (1953) *Child Training and Personality*. New Haven: Yale University Press.

Whorf, B.L. (1952) *Language, Thought, and Reality.* New York: Wiley.

Wickert, F. (1947) *Psychological Research on Problems of Redistribution.* Report No. 14. USAAF Aviation Psychology Research Reports. Washington, DC: Government Printing Office.

Wiggins, J.S., Renner, K.E., Clove, G.L. and Rose, R.J. (1971) *The Psychology of Personality.* Reading, MA: Addison-Wesley.

Williams, C. (1959) The elimination of tantrum behavior by extinction procedures. *Journal of Abnormal and Social Psychology,* 59, 269.

Wilson, E.O. (1975) *Sociobiology: the new synthesis.* Cambridge, MA: Harvard University Press.

Wilson, G.D. and Cox, D.N. (1983) *The Child Lovers: a study of paedophiles in society.* London: Peter Owen.

Wilson, G.T. (1987) Cognitive studies in alcoholism. *Journal of Consulting and Clinical Psychology,* 55, 325–31.

Wilson, G.T. and Lawson, D.M. (1976) Expectancies, alcohol, and sexual arousal in male social drinkers. *Journal of Abnormal Psychology,* 85, 587–94.

Wilson, G.T., Perold, E. and Abrams, D.B. (1981) The effects of expectations of self-intoxication and partner's drinking on anxiety in dyadic social interaction. *Cognitive Therapy and Research,* 5, 251–64.

Winder, C.L. and Wiggins, J.S. (1964) Social reputation and social behavior: a further validation of the Peer Nomination Inventory. *Journal of Abnormal and Social Psychology,* 68, 681–4.

Winter, L., Uleman, J.S. and Cunniff, C. (1985) How automatic are social judgements? *Journal of Personality and Social Psychology,* 49, 904–14.

Witkin, H.A., Dyk, R.B., Faterson, H.F., Goodenough, D.R. and Karp, S.A. (1954) *Psychological Differentiation.* New York: Wiley.

Witkin, H.A., Mednick, S.A., Schulsinger, F., Bakkestrom, E., Christiansen, K.O., Goodenough D.R., Hirschhorn, K., Lundsteen, C., Owen, D.R., Philip, J., Rubin, D.B. and Stocking, M. (1976) Criminality in XYY and XXY men: the elevated crime rate of XYY males is not related to aggression. *Science,* 193, 547–55.

Wittenborn, J.R. (1956) A study of adoptive children. III. Relationships between some aspects of development and some aspects of environment for adoptive children. *Psychological Monographs,* 70, no. 410.

Wooster, A. and Harris, G. (1973) Concepts of self in highly mobile service boys. *Educational Research,* 14, 195–9.

Wright, J.C. and Mischel, W. (1988) Conditional hedges and the intuitive psychology of traits. *Journal of Personality and Social Psychology*, 55, 454–69.

Yarrow, M.R., Campbell, J.D. and Burton, R.V. (1970) Recollections of childhood: a study of the retrospective method. *Monographs of the Society for Research in Child Development*, 35, no. 5.

Zaks, M.S. (1960) 'Draw-a-Man-with-a-Club': a technique for study of aggression and relations to authority figures. *Perceptual and Motor Skills*, 10, 46.

Zucker, R.A. and Lisansky Gomberg, E.S. (1986) Etiology of alcoholism. *American Psychologist*, 41, 783–93.

Zuckerman, M. (1989) Personality in the third dimension: a psychobiological approach. *Personality and Individual Differences*, 10, 391–418.

Zuckerman, M., Koestner, R., DeBoy, T., Garcia, T., Maresca, B.C. and Sartoris, J.M. (1989) To predict some of the people some of the time: a reexamination of the moderator variable approach in personality. *Journal of Personality and Social Psychology*, 54, 1006–19.

Author Index

Subject Index